THE MANA OF TRANSLATION

THE MANA OF TRANSLATION

Translational Flow in Hawaiian History
from the Baibala to the Mauna

Bryan Kamaoli Kuwada

University of Hawaiʻi Press
Honolulu

© 2025 University of Hawaiʻi Press
All rights reserved
Printed in the United States of America
First printed, 2025

Library of Congress Cataloging-in-Publication Data
Name: Kuwada, Bryan Kamaoli, author.
Title: The mana of translation : translational flow in Hawaiian history from the Baibala to the mauna / Bryan Kamaoli Kuwada.
Other titles: Translational flow in Hawaiian history from the Baibala to the mauna
Description: Honolulu : University of Hawaiʻi Press, [2024] | Includes bibliographical references and index.
Identifiers: LCCN 2024017639 (print) | LCCN 2024017640 (ebook) | ISBN 9780824897673 (hardback) | ISBN 9780824899950 (trade paperback) | ISBN 9780824899974 (epub) | ISBN 9780824899981 (kindle edition) | ISBN 9780824899967 (pdf)
Subjects: LCSH: Hawaiian language—Translating. | Translating and interpreting—Hawaii. | Hawaii—Historiography.
Classification: LCC PL6449 .K893 2024 (print) | LCC PL6449 (ebook) | DDC 499/.42802—dc23/eng/20240828
LC record available at https://lccn.loc.gov/2024017639
LC ebook record available at https://lccn.loc.gov/2024017640

Cover art: "Mana ʻEleʻele" by Ryan "Gonzo" Gonzales, created in pilina with both the manuscript and the author.

University of Hawaiʻi Press books are printed on acid-free paper and meet the guidelines for permanence and durability of the Council on Library Resources.

To the big love and the little potato

Contents

Acknowledgments   ix
Prologue: Notes on Language   xix

Introduction
    Wahi āna, "Hīkapalalē, Hīkapalalē…"   1
1. In the Beginning Was Translation
    "Publishing Salvation" in the Baibala Hemolele   14
2. Mai ke Kānāwai a i ka Law
    Translation and the Legal System in the Hawaiian Kingdom   56
3. Translation in the Wild
    Mana Unuhi as a Tool for Ea in the Hawaiian-Language Nūpepa   91
4. Entombed in Translation
    Extractive Translation's Golden Era   143
5. "I Don't Want to Translate"
    The Mana of Refusal   173
Epilogue
    He Mau Hua ma ka Umauma: Words for the Future   217

Notes   227
References   233
Index   255

Acknowledgments

He lau, he mano, he kini, he lehu hoʻi. There are multitudes to whom I am grateful, from all of my ancestors, to those who laid the foundation for me in this lifetime, to those who will come after. There have been so many pilina that have carried me through this process, old seeds and new growth, that I can only hope to name some of them.

I never liked school very much until I got to college and truly began to connect with my kumu, so for this genealogy of ʻike, I would like to start with them. The generosity with which they made space for haumāna like me has been breathtaking. I have learned so much from my kumu ʻōlelo Hawaiʻi, my kumu ʻike Hawaiʻi, and my kumu ma ke keʻena ʻo English. Each of them has fought for me in different ways and showed me different ways to move through the world, sometimes in more Hawaiian ways, but also just in more engaged and thoughtful ways. Even when I have stepped out of their malu, e laʻa me kahi pua ʻaʻala e mohala mau ana ma ka haka ʻolu o uka, I am grateful for the foundations that they laid for me.

I am grateful for the support of my kumu and mentors. They are all academic meʻe whom I have looked up to ever since I knew what was what, and to have them engage so closely with my work was a humbling and exhilarating experience. Jon, you have been my role model in so many ways since I first took your classes as an undergrad. I blame you for teaching me how to think critically and question everything. I think that some of my subsequent teachers are upset with you for that as well. I also thank you for putting me in place on an essay I turned in for your class twenty-something years ago. I don't know if you remember that, but I needed that check.

Noenoe, for the span of years that we have known each other, you have always been generous with me, but also never shied away from holding me accountable and letting me know if you thought I was messing up. I am so grateful for the ʻike and manaʻo that you share with me and others through your powerful academic work, but also for the in-person paʻi when I need them. Yours is also so inspirational an example of how caring and supportive you are of your students, always the first to respond with feedback so they don't have to sit and worry, and I have a very fond memory of you taking me to eat at Jimbo's before they closed, just to talk story and offer support.

kuʻualoha, you've been there since the early days of my academic journey, and it has always been a comfort to me that someone like you has already trod this path, paving the way and making room for those of us who come after. Even with all the work that you have done, it is exciting to think of where you might take things in the future. It is so cool to have joined you in the ranks of professors and getting to teach your work to my students.

Shankar, I still remember dying in your South Asian Novel class because I was so out of my depth (and how I asked if I could not write about a South Asian novel for my final), but also how much your translation class brought life to my work and came to inform my scholarship at a cellular level. Your insistence on precision of thought and syntax continues to challenge me to hone my writing and my thinking. The rigor you demanded gave me the confidence I needed in my own work.

And Cristina, my school mom, how I love you so! You were involved in almost all of my academic publications, from gentle prodding to outright badgering, not to mention the actual and deep influence your scholarship has had on my work. I would not be here without you. I have such fond memories of us going to your house for dinner and you quizzing us to guess what ingredients you'd used in the dishes. I also try to emulate your superpower of making babies fall asleep.

Craig, I once wrote a mele for you that referred to you as a kumu kukui, and that is still an image that I hold of you. You have been a beacon for me, in terms of your archival research ma nā ʻōlelo ʻelua, but also just in the generosity that you give your students. I always tell people about the time you sat with me for eight hours straight one evening going over the translation that I did with Beau Bassett and ʻEmalani Case of *Ka Moʻolelo o Kamehameha I*. I also tell people about how you made us walk for two hours to get to the National Portrait Gallery in Canberra because you thought the map that had the directions on it was to scale (it wasn't). But those two examples really are emblematic of the lengths and literal distances you will go with your haumāna to ensure that they get what they need. Lihi holds her hand on the side of her head when she is being fed, just like you do when you are thinking of things, and I can't help but see the connections. I can never thank you enough for what you have done for me, and I know you will just shrug it off, but mahalo. He aloha nui koʻu nou.

Another pilina that has gotten me through so much of this process is the one between me and my ʻohana. Though it is an oft-repeated cliché, they are a strength that is always there when I need it. I would often miss family events because I was writing, and they were always understanding because they felt that what I was doing was important. They never made me feel like I wasn't putting enough into our pilina; I just always knew that they were there if I needed them.

My fierce surfing mother, Gaylien (who will snake your wave but yell at you if you try to take hers), taught me to read at home before she sent me off to school, and if she wasn't taking me bowling, she was taking me to the library, where according to her the librarians let me take out way more than the allowed number of books each time. I don't know if that is true, but I do know that I was always able to check out stacks of books that were up to my waist, and I know that my mother fostered my lifelong love of reading, which has been the engine for all of my academic development. Also I am sorry that I was a more-than-ten-pound-baby when I was born.

My dad, Ken, wasn't much of a reader, but his humble and quietly confident demeanor really set the example for how I would approach not just my work, but my life in general. When I was taking a million years to finish my undergraduate degree, he pulled me to the side one day and said, "Eh, boy, no listen to the people telling you to give up and get a real job. You know what you're doing, so just do it." He also told me not to join the military like he had because I don't like to have to listen to people if I don't think they know what they are talking about. I already wasn't planning on joining the military, but I didn't realize how well that quality would serve me in academia. He also used to leave a cooler of drinks and snacks at the beach when my friends and I were surfing, and when the entire surf crew ended up at our house for dinner, he somehow managed to always have more than enough food for all of us. Being willing and able to feed everyone is one of my favorite things I learned from him.

I probably shouldn't mention my brother, Garrett, because if he's reading this, he'll have fallen asleep with the book on his face by this point. But even though he and I often joke about how different we are in our relationship to school, he has always been someone whose strength, intelligence, and perseverance I have looked up to, since I was young and he would beat up the people who picked on me. Whether it's attaching your wheelchair to an electric scooter that goes 60 mph with zip ties and cargo straps or deciding that you know how to weld after watching someone else do it, I always love seeing what you are up to next, even though I do expect everything you build to turn into a giant fireball. We've been so lucky to spend so much time together with you and Joey and the boys (I don't have a favorite nephew... okay, I might), and those are the kinds of times that helped me get through this process.

And the last of my ʻohana that I want to mention are my kūpuna. I never got to meet my grandfather on my mom's side, but my grandma Lillian Wainani Ortega is a strong presence in my self-identity, as a mānaleo and as someone whose sense of justice involved spanking each and every child who was in the area of a wrongdoing, because if they weren't the ones doing it, they should have been stopping it. I didn't get to spend as much time with her as I would have wanted, but I hold my memories of her dear.

My grandma and grandpa on my father's side were the ones whom I got to spend the most time with, and they shaped this book in unexpected ways. Stories fell from my grandpa Takeo Kuwada's lips almost as if he had a nervous tic that expressed itself as narrative. He would tap at the lid of a jar that he would use as a cover for his water glass (though I never knew what he thought would fall inside) and tell hilarious stories about being punished for not bowing to the emperor's picture or about how he got into a car accident with the only other car on the island when he was on Kiritimati. He taught me that stories are a family trait, and so much of my life has come to be about moʻolelo, so for that, among so many other things, I am grateful. My grandma Jeannette, who worked at our family's restaurant Ocean View Inn in Kona from the time she was eleven, reads everything that I write, whether academic or creative. She gets out her dictionary, and kneels over the work, and reads. And then she often points out typos. But it is because of readers like her that I have written this book the way I have, and hopefully made it so grandmas can read it.

Acknowledgments

Another family that has helped me through the process of writing this book is that ʻohana I made through the work I did with Kanaeokana. The storytelling work that we did has helped me hone my thinking and analysis on so many issues affecting our lāhui. This work has been a fertile ground for imagination and creativity and debate, and it is truly from the efforts of Kēhau and Gonzo that it is that way. Kēhau, your history of working for the lāhui and the powerful way that you live your values have always been an inspiration to me, and I would not have been able to finish my doctorate if you weren't so clearly convinced that it was something important. Gonzo, working for you has been one of the best experiences of my life. I would go to work every day looking forward to what we were going to do next, even though I knew I was going to end up shaking my head at something you said. Sitting in your office and dreaming all day really broadened my understandings of how narratives shape the future for our lāhui. Mahalo nui iā ʻoe, e kēlā mea hana keko. I am still meeting random people who have told me that you made them read my dissertation, and I am assuming you are going to do the same thing with this book, though I suspect you won't even tell them that you did the cover art. "Mana ʻEleʻele" is so fitting and such an honor. I still cry when I look at it because of how much it represents the layers of our pilina. I know you leave the interpretation of it up to those who see it, but when I look at it, I will always see how much aloha you have for our people, our ʻāina, and for me. Aiko thinks that the pilina you and I have would have classed us as aikāne in older times, and I think that she is right.

Another book family has been the people at UH Press, who have so deftly and lovingly brought this book to physical form. Emma, I am honored to be a part of your vision for the press, and Malia, your enthusiasm and careful shepherding of the book through production has been wonderful. Adriana, I have a few copy editor friends, so I can't call you my favorite copy editor without making some people angry, but I absolutely loved what you brought to the manuscript with your care and insight. Wendy, thank you so much for your sharp eyes and warm openness. And to the rest of the UH Press family who grew this book, mahalo nui loa iā ʻoukou pākahi a pau.

The ʻohana that I am closest to in many ways, however, have been my friends. I feel like I have been reborn in many ways, maybe around a decade and a half ago, and in that way, I have been raised by women.

I have learned from mana wahine in ways that I never knew I was missing until I realized how much that learning had fed me. They have taught me how to love ʻāina, how to love the connections between us, how to love myself, how to love as liberation. The constant tree/bird/edna in my life has been Aiko. Always pushing me to grow my branches, my breath, my breadth, and my aloha. My last reader, my first cheerer, the one who reminds me of how tall I am. There is not enough space to write about her, and our stories have been written in bark and stone for thousands of years, so I will put my ea into my words and create more stories with her in person. You sure got us into some scrapes! I am looking forward to what the little fruit bat grows into. Thanks, you.

Cheryl, I know we're sometimes the same person, wearing the same clothes, but I still wish you were here. Your strength, and intelligence, and fierce loyalty always made me feel sheltered, especially because I am pretty sure that I get to go to the Good Party. Chicken rice at Millipede Mansion and hours-long discussions of colonialism or translation or cooking are among my favorite memories. So come back, and bring my friends Naomi and Steven. I can't wait to give Naomi surfing lessons.

Noe, we've been hoa in so many ways. Hoa kākau, hoa haʻi ʻōlelo/moʻolelo, hoa kamaʻilio, hoa paio (at swimming, though I know I was never actually able to compete), and most importantly, hoa aloha. You always show me what a commitment to community should look like in my scholarship and the way I live my life. I am proud to be someone you call friend, and someone you share your aloha with. I see that aloha on display in everything you do, and it is capacious, incisive, inspirational, and inseparable from our ʻāina and our people. He koa maoli ʻoe.

Jean, it's been so long, but the effects you have had on my thinking and the way I carry myself persist. The way that you insist on joy as part of your everyday praxis reminds me of the beauty all around us and has made me marginally less of a curmudgeon! I hope that we get to see you and Ray and Denzel soon. I get to hear a lot less laughter when you are not around.

Friend Lyz! I have your two dollars around here somewhere! Your vortex of strength, love, and sci-fi nerdery kept me going through the months of being sequestered away in my cave. You helping me be a fledgling poet has truly changed my life, in surprising and sometimes distressing ways, and I thank you for that. It is always so much fun to

Acknowledgments

discuss our sci-fi visions of the future, though we both know the truth is that we mostly just want our futures to include baking bread and reading spec fic. Let's have bread soon.

Anjoli, sender of videos of bears being attacked by cats, you have been such a goofy and beloved presence in my life since before this book was even a twinkle in my eye. Your support through the writing process—which includes the aforementioned bear videos, coming up with weird nicknames for me, accidentally taking videos of yourself with the GoPro, sending me perfect songs for my writing/driving soundtrack, and being an all-around great friend—has really been crucial and something that I deeply appreciate. As you know, I show it by being mean to you, so you can expect more of that to come because I really appreciate everything you do. And now an Alakananda has appeared. What a life this is, and what a future we all have in store for us.

CJ, you are one of my best friends. Such a fierce and funny dragon that knows TV trivia but grew up in a cornfield with no TV. It really is a deep and profound honor to be in your life. To be in each other's lives the way we are, to be a part of each other the way we are, there is no other way to describe it than an honor, a privilege, a kuleana. Even though we are fellow murderbots, so much of our connection is of salt, through the ocean that we both love, but also through the savor that salt brings. You are such a surfboard addict. You are literally waxing your brand new 9'4" Euphoric outside my room as I write this. I once read that a dragon ascended to the heavens from Ulleungdo. I wouldn't presume to know anything about what that moʻolelo means, but I will never forget the picture of you touching that ocean, and, somehow, that story does seem fitting. Your heart came from the sea. I love you, swell singer.

Noʻu, I never expected what our pilina has become. I never knew how deep down I had been asking, "I wai noʻu." You have given me so much wai over the years. Wai, waiwai, and even waimaka. We have shared so much, especially this last handful of years, when we have become iwi for each other. You were a kuamoʻo all the times when I was down and broken, and even the lighter times when I was just frustrated at what I was writing. "Shut up, I'm coming over" saved me more than you know. Sharing vulnerability and opening ourselves to each other has really helped me become more rooted in aloha. The way you love has been a sunrise for me. I feel like we have grown together during this time, leaning on each other, but also pushing each other in new directions, and I have absolutely nothing to do with this, but seeing you develop as a poet and performer to where you are now has been utterly life-changing. You have shown me your heart, e kuʻu hoa, and it is stunning. And now let's get in the water.

Last but not least, even though I have known you for the shortest amount of time, you are one of the people I love the most, Kalihi-lihiaʻiaʻipuahoʻomohala Jeong Yamashiro. What a funny little family you have joined. Thank you for all your gummy little smiles and our (long) walks together.

For as long as this section has become, I still do not feel that I have been able to truly acknowledge what these mana wahine mean to me. I am going to include a poem that I wrote for them to end this section. It is still insufficient, but at least some of these images point in the direction of how much I love them and want to acknowledge their mana. And maybe it has something to do with translation as well.

> I have never written a love poem in English.
> This tongue's words far too revealing, rusted consonants
> and hissing sibilants issue forth, opening my mouth
> too wide. In English, meaning rushes out, breathing
> an imbalance of air, and I sound diphthongs for
> protection. In Hawaiian, we appreciate dissembling,
> vowels giving our fears armor of bird's wings or
> flower's petals, rain coming at sunrise and
> leaving at noon. We talk of love to everyone
> we meet, but whisper secret hearts into
> rock hollows and calabashes, life given our words
> by unplain speech
>
> So perhaps these are not my words, not my breath
> speaking love in the night sky of your name, licking
> salt from our friendship. Yet here are tentative
> steps toward ocean, warm salt reaching, offering
> ceremony and connection, saying more plainly what I
> would rather hide. This is seawater in my lungs,
> painful and cleansing, keeping me short of breath, yet

Acknowledgments

your words are sweet and whole as fruit, seeds falling
into furrowed ground. Unfamiliar stones in my mouth
watered by sea. I know only that each will grow
into a star

But I have never written a love poem in English, so
now I fear I have mispronounced our word for star, calling
forth fertility instead, and a sky too crowded for navigation.
My words have misread a flight of birds into a
constellation, and set my course by these stars whose
names I have not yet learned. If I say I love you, which
words have brought me here? Whose words have fallen
from my lips? Carried not on wind but by my fearful
breath. I push the stones from my mouth hoping they
fall into the creases of your palms. Hoping that
you are not burned by their heat, nor frightened by their
weight. You who have always offered me the embrace
of your friendship. The shelter of your arms. The warmth
of your words

So perhaps these are not my words, not my breath,
because they have come so much from you. I have patterned
them on barkcloth for you, alternating triangles becoming a
net, not to entangle, but to feed. And here they are, gentle
words you have grown in my mouth, stalks supple and
slender, roots reaching into my chest. Harvest them when
you wish, and plant them against famine. You who are
land and sea to me. I wish only to be a valley wall, my spine
curving along your length, buffeted by the wind. Only to
be star, fruit, stone, breath, only to speak plainly when
I tell you...

Prologue
Notes on Language

"It's a skirt made out of pala'ā ferns," said the first translator.
"No, it's a skirt with pala'ā ferns printed on it," said the second.
"No, it can't be."
"No, but it is."
"But in this line here, it says 'O ka pala'ā nō ho'i āu i hana ai a pūnohunohu,' which has to mean actual ferns, otherwise why would the skirt pūnohunohu?"
"Because they used actual pala'ā to adorn the printed skirt."
The two translators were furiously digging through lines of the text and checking references. They were even starting to get a little loud. Pages ruffled and keyboard keys clacked.
"Is pala'ā even a traditional kapa pattern? I know they used pala'ā to dye the kapa sometimes."
Clack, clack, clack.
"We've been at this for hours. Let's just fudge it a bit in the wording then."
Clack, clack, clack.
"We can't, because this is one of the scenes that the artist is going to illustrate for the book, and every time she appears, she is going to be wearing her pā'ū."
The third translator, the youngest, who had been pretty quiet, mainly lying on the floor looking at the ceiling and throwing in a "good point" or "that makes sense" here and there and maybe falling asleep a couple of times, piped up at that point and said, "What if we do that whole 'you got chocolate in my peanut butter, you got peanut butter in my chocolate' thing and make the skirt be both? It starts off printed and then transitions into actual pala'ā?"

That story is fiction. The actual process of deciding whether or not Hiʻiaka's pāʻū was made from palaʻā or printed with palaʻā took several days and actually involved some pretty far-ranging research both in the manuscript and in other sources, though the parts about me falling asleep a few times and the chocolate-and-peanut-butter thing are pretty close to how I remember it. The point of the retelling, though, is that translation is all about negotiation and compromise regarding language, whether you are negotiating with co-translators or just figuring things out yourself.

There are no one-to-one correspondences across languages even in regard to what we consider basic things, like how, as Noenoe Silva pointed out to me, the words "kāne" and "wahine" do not equate to "man" and "woman" in English, even though we take it for granted that they do. They do not encompass the same premises and possibilities, and sometimes to truly get across the meaning of a single word in one language, you need fifty words from another language. With that in mind, I would like to present a few terms and concepts that I am going to be using throughout the book. In certain ways this is akin to a glossary, but it is also a concrete demonstration of the incommensurability of language. I will sometimes still give a little bit of explanation for these words in the text, but sometimes I am going to use them as if the reader had the same understanding some Hawaiian readers might. This is a book about translation, but I am not always going to translate. The terms are arranged in the order I felt was most appropriate.

Ea: "Ea" is a powerful word whose meanings overlap with the English-language terms "life," "breath," "rising," "sovereignty," "independence." It means sovereignty and independence because it means breath and life. The concept of ea predates the concept of sovereignty, and the power in ea does not come from a sovereign or from authority. It is the life and breath that come from the people and the ʻāina. Ea is one of the animating forces of so much of the work that Hawaiians do as a community.

Mana: Mana is the main thread of this book, and I will be discussing it several times, but I wanted to have a definition here that could be easily referred to if necessary. Mana is a power that everything can have. Words have it, people have it, places have it, stones have it. Sometimes the power can come from your genealogy, which does not apply only to people because our cosmogonic genealogies include everything (like some of the aforementioned stones), but mana can also increase and decrease through our actions and how they are perceived. The word that most often gets (mis)translated as "religion" is "hoʻomana," which means to give mana to something. Mana, then, is not an individual power that a single person owns. It is contingent on pilina (connection/relationship/closeness), in that you have that mana because of your connection to people or ʻāina or genealogy. You only gain or lose mana through connection.

A related meaning of "mana" that is the foundation of its importance in this book is that "mana" is also the word for when there is another version of something. So a version of a story is a mana of that story. Mana also refers to when branches split off from trunks or when rivers diverge. What these meanings recognize is the power in that divergence. The more versions or mana a moʻolelo has, the more power or mana it has. The "religious" connotation of mana mentioned above has led to mana often being characterized as "supernatural," something akin to magic powers or superstitious beliefs, but mana is actually the opposite of supernatural, as nothing could be more natural than mana. It is in everything, it recognizes the connections between everything, and it has tangible effects in the real world, as we will see throughout this book.

ʻĀina and aloha ʻāina: " ʻĀina" always gets translated as "land," and it is that, but it is also so much more. ʻĀina is the elder sibling of Kānaka Maoli, which puts us in a reciprocal relationship of care with it. An ʻōlelo noʻeau (saying/proverb/wise expression/poetic expression) that describes this relationship is "He aliʻi ka ʻāina, he kauwā ke kanaka," something along the lines of "The land is the aliʻi/ruler/leader, and the kanaka/person is its servant." Another place where "land" becomes insufficient as a translation for ʻāina is water. We often understand ʻāina to be that which feeds, and among other things, that means that the water and the ocean are at times considered ʻāina as well.

Aloha ʻāina then is a deeply rooted devotion to the physical and spiritual health of the ʻāina and those of us (kanaka, plant, bird, stone) who live upon it. It is a commitment to protect our language and cultural practices that are embraced and inspired by the ʻāina, and it is a familial relationship that inspires deep love, ferocity, and sacrifice. Just as with mana, this aloha is all about pilina. We cannot have aloha alone, and without ʻāina, we are not kānaka. Aloha ʻāina is related to ea (described above), as our aloha ʻāina drives us to fight for ea. People who take up this fight are also referred to as "aloha ʻāina" because of how central that is to the struggle.

Lāhui: If you are around Hawaiians a lot, you will often hear us referring to ourselves as the "lāhui Hawaiʻi," or just the "lāhui." It is a word whose meaning has shifted over the years depending on things like our sociopolitical status and allegiances. The earliest usages of "lāhui" in the Hawaiian-language newspapers tended to refer to what we would call "nations," so France, Britain, Spain, etc., were all "lāhui," as were Indigenous nations like the Blackfoot. This meaning remained pretty stable throughout the nineteenth century, and the "lāhui Hawaiʻi" referred to all the people who were a part of the Hawaiian nation. Particularly toward the turbulent end of the nineteenth century, calling together the lāhui Hawaiʻi meant calling together all the Hawaiians, but also all others who were citizens of the kingdom and devoted to it, including Greek hotel owners, Chinese poi factory owners, Japanese plantation workers, Tahitian teachers, and more. When the overthrow of the Hawaiian Kingdom and the subsequent sham annexation took place, it was not just Kānaka Maoli who mourned the loss of their nation.

There was an allegiance among these people that made them the lāhui Hawaiʻi, so when the lāhui was called upon to fight for the kingdom, all these people of different ethnicities would gather. But as time went on, thousands of Americans flooded Hawaiʻi, and more plantation workers were brought in who no longer had this shared history of standing up for the kingdom, and the idea of the kingdom got further and further away. Soon "lāhui Hawaiʻi" came to refer mainly to Hawaiians themselves, and the meaning of "lāhui" itself shifted away from a broader meaning that encompassed the multiethnic kingdom to one that was more akin to American understandings of race. This usage is reflected in the nūpepa, especially during the Massie affair in the early 1930s when "lāhui" was used to refer to the races of the boys who had been arrested. Now, however, with the recovery of the history of who actually made up the Hawaiian Kingdom and talk of Hawaiian as a nationality, there has been a shift back toward the more expansive meaning of lāhui. It is still used to refer to Hawaiians as a group though, and I think that both work.

Aikāne: Missionaries and their intellectual descendants have long tried to curtail the mana of the word "aikāne" through translation, insisting that "aikāne" merely meant "friend." But what it really is is a pilina (relationship/connection/closeness) of intimacy between two kāne or two wāhine. Much has been made of the kāne-kāne and wahine-wahine sexual relations that come out of aikāne connections, but that to me misses the point. In traditional Hawaiian understandings, it is not a big deal for wāhine to have sex with wāhine or kāne with kāne. Everyone pretty much had sex with everyone, so sexual relations between kāne or wāhine were not even worth commenting on, much less having a specialized exalted name for. Sex was for procreation, but to the everlasting horror of the missionaries, it was also for pleasure. A lot of pleasure.

So what is different about aikāne relationships then? Sexually, nothing. Some aikāne had sex with each other, some did not. What made aikāne venerated as a connection was the intimacy and closeness that they engendered in each other. Aikāne were in relationships of trust, devotion, and deep care, almost like aloha ʻāina but for people. In one mana of the moʻolelo of Hiʻiakaikapoliopele, when Hiʻiaka was in a heedless rage and destroying the crater of her elder sister Pele, the only one who could calm her down and help heal the rift was her aikāne Wahineʻōmaʻo.

Kaona: Kaona is a beloved feature of our language, ʻōlelo Hawaiʻi. It is wordplay and metaphor whose meanings are directed to particular listening or reading audiences or even specific members of those audiences. Kaona is commonly described as "hidden meaning," but the meanings are not hidden if you are the intended audience. They are right there in the open, but even more appreciated because of the skill it took to transmit them via kaona. Like many of the terms in this list, kaona comes back to pilina. Your relationship to our ʻōlelo and to the speaker/writer of the kaona is what allows you to understand it. Some kaona are broadly accessible to anyone paying attention—good examples being the sexual innuendo in popular hula songs—while other kaona are much more circumspect. But the truth is that if kaona has no pilina to someone who is reading or listening to your words, and no one can figure out what you are saying, then it is not kaona.

Moʻolelo: Moʻolelo is one of the basic building blocks of this book. It is our word for story/account/history, and it does not make the same generic distinctions that Western literature does. A science fiction story is a moʻolelo, as is a biography, as is a history book.

Hawaiians also did not draw the same kinds of distinctions between fiction and nonfiction that Western understandings tended to do. As mentioned above, when mana are retold, they get more mana.

Note on ʻōlelo Hawaiʻi

By this point, it can probably go without saying that I will not be italicizing Hawaiian words as if they were foreign—though I still sometimes wish they were a little more kamaʻāina to me. Unless otherwise indicated, all translations are my own. I will not, however, apologize for any mistakes or mistranslations, because given the subject of this book, their very presence for those who can recognize them will reinforce how much unchecked power translators have in their hands.

An interesting and innovative approach for dealing with translation has been advanced by Jamaica Heolimeleikalani Osorio. She describes it as "rigorous paraphrase," and her reasoning is as follows: "Recognizing these problems and dangers as a necessary consequence of translation, I will therefore practice a politics of refusal, invoking and articulating instances of aloha ʻāina in the moʻolelo and moʻokūʻauhau without succumbing to the pressure to reduce them, or their informing concept, to a supposed English equivalent. If successful, my method should not only allow aloha ʻāina to suffice, but to resonate accurately and fully because it escapes translation" (J. H. Osorio 2018, 14). The result is that Osorio leaves longer quotations in Hawaiian untranslated but interacts with them in the body of her analysis in ways that indicate to the reader who cannot read ʻōlelo Hawaiʻi what the passage is talking about, thereby granting access while reminding readers that the ʻōlelo Hawaiʻi, rather than a provided translation, is the text at issue.

While this is a strategy that I have used in my previous work and hope scholars will take up as well, I will be providing full translations for the vast majority of the substantial passages I cite in ʻōlelo Hawaiʻi. Many of the insights that inform my analysis have been shaped by my time as a Hawaiian-language translator, and this book's focus requires that I display the workings of translation under discussion, and foreground the visibility of the translator, by actually doing translations. But as this prologue insists, and the body of the text will constantly reinforce, translation is necessarily an interpretation, and I invite you to read each translation as such.

Introduction
Wahi āna, "Hīkapalalē, Hīkapalalē…"

A crowd had gathered. Light from the torches twinkled in the eyes of the men and women as they gazed ahead expectantly. Ka'uiki lay off to the east, a quiet shadow on the horizon.

Captain Cook strode purposefully to the head of the crowd. His confident swagger put a slight swing to the malo tied around his bare waist as he entered the circle of firelight.

Cook looked out intently over the faces of those gathered before him and drew back his strong brown shoulders proudly. The crowd gasped at his baggy skin, pocket of riches, and triangle-shaped head.

He produced a length of pohue vine and set the end on fire, taking a long drag before exhaling the smoke out over the crowd with a cough. He then shoved the vine into his malo, and pulled it back out, before drawing a deep breath.

With a grave countenance, he looked upon the assembled crowd and proclaimed in a loud voice, "A hīkapalalē, hīkapalalē, hīnolue, 'oalaki, walawalakī, waiki poha."

His words echoed out across the bay. The semicircle of people around him continued to stare in wonder for a few seconds at the powerful explorer before them.

And then they collapsed in giggling and fits of laughter.

As it turns out, it wasn't actually Captain Cook standing before them, but a man from Hawai'i Island named Moho, who had been living on O'ahu. He heard from the people of Kaua'i about their experiences with Captain Cook and rushed off to regale the ali'i of his home island, Kalani'ōpu'u and his court, with tales of this new visitor. And as those of you who speak 'ōlelo Hawai'i know, his proclamation makes absolutely no sense—a string of nonsensical syllables that came to mean "gibberish" in later times. Well over two hundred years later, we still have no idea what the "real" Captain Cook actually said.

"Unuhi," our word that gets used as an equivalent for "translation," has marked Hawaiian history since our earliest recorded interactions with outsiders,[1] and for many people, daily life in the kingdom was punctuated with instances of translation. Kanaka traders interacting with sailors from across the sea. American missionaries preaching to gathered crowds. Kuaʻāina from the countryside haggling with Chinese poi factory owners. Though ʻōlelo Hawaiʻi was the primary language for the majority of the populace during the kingdom and into the territorial era, English, French, Russian, Greek, Tahitian, Chinese, Korean, Japanese, and many more languages were heard here, especially in the ports. While English became the main foreign language competing for power in the kingdom, through a treaty in 1853, the French also tried to bring their language into parity with ʻōlelo Hawaiʻi and English (Kuykendall 1953, 48–50). Colonial languages vied with ʻōlelo Hawaiʻi in the same way that colonial values vied with those of Hawaiians, each trying to gain mana for their interests in Hawaiʻi.

In her analysis of the role of language in the formation of the nation-state of Malaysia, Rachel Leow says: "The plurality of languages within a single bounded territorial polity (itself a relatively modern way of organizing space) often appears as a curse to unity: something monstrous to be tamed by the hegemony of a national language, or a standardized vernacular, or carefully wrought policies regulating how, when, and who speaks, in how many languages" (2018, 2). For foreigners, the choice of which language had primacy in Hawaiʻi was almost always related to determining what would give them the most political and economic influence and advantage. Hawaiians were themselves political beings, fully capable of making decisions in their own best interests. But during the kingdom era, choices about unuhi and which language or languages to employ under specific circumstances were shaped by Hawaiians' sense of what would best help bring into being the world they envisioned for the lāhui. Missionaries and others insisted that English was the key to a progressive and modern society. But Hawaiians were highly aware that ʻōlelo Hawaiʻi is what connected them to the ʻāina and made them who they were; it was something of great capacity and mana.

It is part of that mana, specifically mana unuhi, that we are going to track in this book. Mana is a sort of power that inheres in everyone and everything. It is related to "aesthetics, ethics, and power and authority" (Tomlinson and Tengan 2016, 1), but it is much more than that. So much more that it is often characterized as supernatural in scholarship (Tomlinson and Tengan 2016, 2–3, 7, 56, 57; Sahlins 1996, 127; Fornander 1878, 128), with "supernatural" even appearing in the first meaning listed in the Pukui dictionary (Pukui and Elbert 1986, 235), but mana is anything but that. It is not super—meaning above/outside/beyond—natural; it is by its very nature part of nature, in the same way that our four thousand, and forty thousand, and four hundred thousand akua (what some too easily translate as gods) are very much of nature, part of this world, populating the ʻāina and living on it.

Even our word that gets mistranslated and mischaracterized as "religion," hoʻomana, just means to give or imbue something or someone or some place with mana. Mana, however, is "not to signify individuals amassing and exercising power" (N. Silva 2016, 52). When we turn our attention to something, give our time and thought to it, it gains mana from us, because rather than having a supernatural origin based in gods that are separate from us and the ʻāina, mana is about pilina (connection/relationship/closeness) and interaction. As Noenoe Silva says, akua "do not have mana unless some being(s) interact with them in some way" (2016, 40). By forging and reinforcing our connections with people, places, ideas, stones, akua, stories, we hoʻomana them.

A way to help understand mana comes from an unlikely source: a magnet. In 1895, the rhetorically powerful Joseph Nāwahī wrote several editorials about aloha ʻāina, a deeply profound connection and love Hawaiians feel for their ʻāina that animates so much of historical and contemporary struggles for sovereignty, and one of them was entitled "Ka Mana o ka Mageneti" ("The Mana of the Magnet"). In "Ka Mana o ka Mageneti," Nāwahī speaks of how when nails or sewing needles are ʻānai, or rubbed, on a magnet, "lele mai no ka mana ume o ka mageneti iloko o laua" (the drawing/attracting/pulling mana of the magnet leaps into them), and continues on to say:

Pela no na kanaka i piha i ke aloha no ko lakou Aina hanau ponoi. Ua hiki ia lakou ke hoolauna mai i na kanaka a me na keiki, a me na ohana o lakou; a ume mai ia lakou iloko o ka ume Mageneti o ke Aloha Aina. Ua hiki i na makua i piha i ke aloha i ka aina e anai aku i ka ume o ke aloha i ka aina iloko o ka lakou mau keiki... O ka anai mau ana i na naau palupalu o na opio Hawaii, maluna o ka makua i noho ia e ka mana o ke aloha aina, ua like loa ia me ka anai ana i ke Kuikele maluna o ka Hao Mageneti. Hookahi no mea e hoea mai ana, oia ka loaa ana o ka Mana Ume Mageneti iaia.

[It is the same as with people who are filled with aloha for the 'āina upon which they were born. They can meet with other people and children and their families, and they are all drawn into the magnetic pull of aloha 'āina. The parents who are filled with aloha 'āina can 'ānai/rub/transfer the drawing force of aloha 'āina into their keiki.... The constant 'ānai of the tender hearts of the Hawaiian youth upon their parents who are held by the mana of aloha 'āina is just like the 'ānai/rubbing of a needle upon a magnet. There is only one possible result, and that is the transfer of the magnetic mana to them.] (Nāwahī 1895, 7)

While Nāwahī's point is to describe how and why we should ensure that our children learn the magnetic draw of aloha 'āina, he also illustrates how mana works. The 'ume mageneti is unseen but no more supernatural because of its invisibility, and it is the pilina/connection/relationship between the nails and needles and the magnet that allows the mana of the magnet to be passed on. The draw of the magnet is both the mana and the connection between us. A single magnet on its own is nothing but a rock, and the 'ume mageneti, the mana of the magnet, only comes into play when the magnet is in pilina with something or someone else.

With this understanding of mana in mind, let us turn to what makes mana important here in regard to mana unuhi. "Mana" is also the word for another version of a story; it is the word for when a river forks off from another waterway or a tree branches off from its trunk. Thus the more mana/trunks/branches/forks a story has, the more mana, in the sense of power and connection, it has. The story that gets told the most, even through unuhi/translation, gets the most mana. The Māori translation theorist Jillian Tipene poses the following as important ethical questions that translators working in Indigenous contexts should ask themselves: "Who is doing the translation? Who owns the text being translated? Why translate? Whose interests will be served by the translation? and Who will benefit from the translation?...Will the translation process result in a significant loss in relation to the integrity of the source text?" (2014, 32–33). Though Tipene is using these questions to guide contemporary translators in regard to ethically choosing translation projects, these are also the kinds of questions that examining mana unuhi in historical contexts enables us to ask and answer. There are important and sometimes surprising insights to be gained from following the flow of mana unuhi, and that is why it is so important to turn away from merely presenting translation as a violent and lossy transfer that takes place in colonial situations; mana unuhi allows us to pay attention to what is getting hoʻomana ʻia in different situations, who or what is being given mana, which version of the story is becoming ascendant, whose voice carries the most mana, and even which characterization of a culture is given the most weight. Are Hawaiians an amiable but inept and degraded disappearing people with a language characterized by lack? Or are they a confident lāhui using their supple language to bring everything they want into a Hawaiian worldview?

The answer I lean toward is probably obvious, but there is much at stake in these questions. One of our most important and oft-quoted proverbs is "I ka ʻōlelo nō ke ola, i ka ʻōlelo nō ka make," usually translated as "In language there is life and in language there is death." The entirety of our lives and our deaths, and how we see the world, is contained in our ʻōlelo. When we look carefully at how language entwines with culture, we see that the loss of language leads to cultural death, but also that within the language is the capacity for cultural life. That is the crux of why translation and tracing mana unuhi are so important in Hawaiʻi. Hawaiians put such a strong cultural value on our language (as most cultures do, but also in ways unlike how most cultures do), and also because life and death are the stakes of translation here. kuʻualoha hoʻomanawanui shows how much is riding on unuhi when she says, "Moʻolelo reflect how Kānaka Maoli imagined themselves as a lāhui" (2014, 198); even our own self-image is at stake. Translation has affected and continues to affect the life and death of the spirit, the life and death of the ʻāina, the life and death of the lāhui, even the life and death of how we are remembered.

And yet, going even beyond Lawrence Venuti's famous assertion of the translator's invisibility (1995), translation itself has often been all but invisible in our understandings of Hawaiian history. Unuhi has always been assumed to be successful and transparent. From the narrative that Cook was able to understand Hawaiians because of his familiarity with Tahitian to the scriptural discussions between missionaries and their native "helpers" necessary to translate the Bible, the story is always told as if communication flowed freely between both parties, without analysis of the strategies, power dynamics, material practices, and consequences both unintended and intentional that went into these processes. Translation and postcolonial theory scholar S. Shankar points out the need and the potential for making translation more apparent: "When critics who do not themselves translate at least acknowledge the plurality and diversity of translation practice and retune their critical attitudes in the light of such an acknowledgment, the many instances of translation begin to emerge as opportunities for a wide variety of critical intervention rather than simply as 'problems' to be bemoaned" (2012, 107). Though a powerfully illuminating return to the primacy of Hawaiian-language sources has refuted and recast understandings of our history and culture long derived mainly from English-language sources, apart from pointing out that translations of Hawaiian have often been insufficient and had profoundly damaging effects, little academic attention has been paid to the interplay *between* these languages. This sort of examination seems to be lacking but is also possibly fruitful for other Indigenous situations as well. There are certainly good reasons for focusing on the passage from Hawaiian to English, or from Indigenous language to colonial language, and noting that the results have often been bad. But as we will see in chapter 4, if we do not expand upon that notion, the results will continue to be damaging.

Tracing mana unuhi is a highly effective means for examining the power dynamics of languages, and especially how these differential forces engage with each other on ideological and political battlefields, particularly in colonial situations.[2] Because unuhi/translation is itself a process of uneven transfer, with messages picked up or lost or modified along the way, this process lays bare many of the conflicts of colonial interaction. But all too often we give translation a pass, letting it remain the invisible conduit between languages. Whether for reasons of linguistic incapacity or simple convenience, treating unuhi as merely a mechanical process by which words from one language are substituted for their equivalents in another has been, and still is, seductive, because it allows us to proceed as if cultural values and understandings of people and concepts rooted in ʻōlelo Hawaiʻi can be transmitted without complication through the medium of a completely foreign language.

But much of the work of this book is to act as a reminder not to accept easy translation. The seduction of easy equivalency, of creating shorthands, leads to claims that two very different things are essentially the same. It lets us make comparisons too blithely. It lets us ignore mana. It even lets me write "unuhi" where I should sometimes be writing "translation." And because such assumptions about equivalency are already woven into the warp and weft of so many of our historical sources about Hawaiʻi, reproducing such naïve understandings about translation will make our own contestations of these sources less incisive and nuanced. Nor can we treat translation as solely about inadequacy and loss, because this allows many of the consequences of how it has operated and continues to operate in Hawaiʻi (along with the power and possibilities it offered to Hawaiians) to remain hidden. Within postcolonial studies, untroubled assumptions that translation is always bad have led to the term becoming a rather lazy metaphor for any process that results in transformation, or for colonization itself. Through land theft, forced adoption, oppressive education, military force, and so forth, colonizers *translated* Indigenous people into colonized people. It can be argued, perhaps, that translation is an effective metaphor for getting people to recognize that at one point Indigenous people were one way, but then at another point, through whatever forces were inflicted upon them, they became another. But the analogy here does little more than suggest that something changed a people, and if translation as a trope can encompass everything, and apply to every situation, such universal applicability means the analogy brings little of value to analyses. If translation can stand in for everything, it represents nothing.

The ubiquity of this understanding of unuhi should not be surprising, having grown for the most part out of non-translators' reliance on popular conceptions of translation as an exchange of equivalences rather than a fundamental reauthoring. This is not to condemn such scholars or the general public for making such assumptions. Only in the late 1980s and early 1990s did translation scholars themselves, greatly influenced by cultural studies, postcolonial theory, and the work of feminist translators (Tymoczko 2010a, 7), move away from long-held preoccupations with ideas of faithfulness and literalness and toward an engagement with matters of ideology and power. But the enduring presence of notions of equivalence and direct transfer in translation studies and in the popular understanding suggests to what degree such assumptions have generally gone unchallenged.

By studying specific examples of how unuhi has mediated and determined the nature of the back-and-forth between English and Hawaiian from the early kingdom until today, this book demonstrates that paying close attention to the material practices of unuhi, and making these operations visible, can bring into much starker relief the forces at play when these crucial moments of translation occurred. Among other contributions, such a study can give the lie to easy assumptions that the victory of colonialism in the Hawaiian Kingdom was always a foregone conclusion—or even a victory. Translation has never been a one-way process, but always marked by contestation, with settler and Hawaiian mana and ea frequently teetering on translation's razor edge. Taking a closer look at these contestations also gives lie to the idea that translation is exclusively a tool of imperialism and colonial conquest. Mana is never one-way. As Anna Brickhouse states, "the concept of translation as an imperial instrument was as commonplace in Columbus's day—when the fifteenth-century Castilian grammarian Antonio de Nebrija famously observed that 'Language has always been the companion of empire'—as it is in our own" (2015, 3). Yet in Hawaiian hands it was a force to hoʻomana and empower Hawaiian cultural and political sovereignty and later a weapon of opposition and unsettlement, which is perhaps truly a rarity in other colonial situations, but more likely a consequence of translation's invisibility and one-sided assumptions of translation's imperiality.

Chapter 1 focuses on the first major act of unuhi in the kingdom era: bringing the Bible into ʻōlelo Hawaiʻi. Just as the first encounters with "Kapena Kuke" were shot through with translation, the introduction of alphabetic literacy in Hawaiʻi, though inseparable from Christianity by design, somewhat unexpectedly also proved to be inseparable from translation. In this case, reinforced by a nineteenth-century colonial mindset, long-held convictions about the true nature of translation and its actual practice as necessarily a process of interpretation and reauthoring are crucial for understanding how the translation of the Bible and the production of the kingdom's bilingual system of laws actually happened, and what the major ramifications rippling out from these initiatives proved to be. Missionary accounts of the time describe the Hawaiian language as lacking; it simply does not have the vocabulary necessary to encompass Christianity and its doctrines. A close examination, however, reveals that what was really lacking was the missionaries' own skill in 'ōlelo Hawai'i. But their drive to "publish salvation," and thereby figure Hawaiians as a salvable people, led not only to the relatively swift translation of the Bible, but also to the necessary erasure, based in part on their understanding of scriptural translation, of the extensive assistance they required in the process from Hawaiians expert in their own language, many of whom remain unnamed to this day, their names given no mana.

Both the spiritual needs of Christianity and the practical needs of the mission required that this translation would do the impossible: perfectly transfer the Bible from its original languages to Hawaiian. The resulting Hawaiian Bible had to be "hemolele," the Hawaiian word for "holy," but also the word for "perfect," and this "perfect" transfer was the massive set piece upon which the missionaries hung all of their "civilizing" efforts. Repeatedly enacting these efforts through translation, they devoted themselves to "imposing a framework for gender and sexuality with particular consequences for anything deemed outside of a civilized form of heterosexually monogamous male dominance" (Kauanui 2018, 158), to severely hindering the transmission of traditional Hawaiian cultural knowledge and practices, and ultimately to contributing to the displacement of Kānaka from the land. But this inseparability of literacy, translation, and religion also meant that while Christian values were spreading through the lāhui, more begrudgingly in some areas than others, so too were powerful tools that Hawaiians took up immediately to increase the ea and mana of the lāhui.

Chapter 2 tracks the contested flow of mana unuhi as integral to the transition from traditional kānāwai and kapu to a system of law that relied on many forms of British common law even as it modified for its own purposes the relatively new American constitutional model. Because the setting and enforcement of law is where language most affects people's daily lives, given the kingdom's bilingual legal and governmental system, translation was immensely important. Initially determined and authored by Hawaiians, the written ʻōlelo Hawaiʻi versions of the laws had primacy. But the model of unuhi employed for the Bible, with its faith in a perfect transfer into ʻōlelo Hawaiʻi, began to shift as the dictates of "civilizing" efforts increasingly demanded that English, the language of the monied and landed hyperminority, become the controlling language of law. The Hawaiian legal system's heavy reliance on common law led to mana being concentrated in the foreign-dominated judicial branch rather than in the Hawaiian-dominated legislature. Although the translators of the Bible—one of whom actually became a translator of the law—were certain that the Bible could be translated into other languages and still be a perfect representation of the word of God, the idea that law could be relied upon only in its "original" language (despite the fact that many of the laws had been initially written in Hawaiian) came to dominate the legal system within the few decades after the publication of the Baibala Hemolele in its entirety. Legal scholar Rubén Asensio calls this willful misunderstanding of translation "the genealogical axiom," and it not only wreaked havoc on Hawaiian connections to ʻāina, but fundamentally altered how Kānaka Maoli were figured through language.

Whereas the first two chapters are about the institutionalizing of translation, chapter 3 focuses on what happens when unuhi is set loose, becoming a force that increased Hawaiian mana and ea. By the 1860s, literacy in Hawaiian was widespread, and Hawaiian-language newspapers had been around for three decades already. But all of these nūpepa had come from the mission or government press, and while the lāhui read and greatly valued these nūpepa, many kānaka wanted content that wasn't as overtly religious and didactic, wanted more mana for mele and traditional moʻolelo, and a wider variety of foreign moʻolelo. Clearly, the solution was newspapers for Hawaiians written and edited by Hawaiians. But when a coalition of Hawaiians and a few haole produced the first independent Hawaiian-language newspaper, *Ka Hoku o ka Pakipika,* containing much of the content that Hawaiians had been calling for, a massive backlash followed from the missionary establishment and many of the Hawaiian churches. Translation figured prominently in the initial uproar over a mele published in *Ka Hoku,* and the practice was vital to the nūpepa throughout its run. And in the following years, as Hawaiian language newspapers proliferated and flourished, translation was one of the marks of a vibrant, intelligent, and confident people, who freely brought foreign texts into ʻōlelo Hawaiʻi to satisfy the ravenous curiosity of the Hawaiian reading public. Translated foreign moʻolelo appeared right next to traditional Hawaiian moʻolelo, and Hawaiians keenly read the translated news about far-off places. Tracing mana unuhi here therefore means also tracing the emergence and development of a thriving Hawaiian-language literary print culture.

Though some of the nūpepa translators were foreigners, most were totally bilingual Hawaiians, and these translators were frequently political leaders and aloha ʻāina as well. Certainly a tool for entertaining and delighting readers, unuhi also served national political purposes. In chapter 3, I examine the ʻōlelo Hawaiʻi version of Jules Verne's *20,000 Leagues under the Sea,* paying attention to how a new mana/branch/version of the moʻolelo is created in which the descriptions of Captain Nemo are translated to embody certain values of aloha ʻāina crucial to the ongoing debate over the reciprocity treaty with the United States. While the missionary descendants and their associates were doing their best to limit Hawaiian autonomy and mana in the realms of religion, law, and politics through acts like the Bayonet Constitution, or the legal maneuverings related to translation described in chapter 2, the nūpepa remained untamable. Theirs was the voice with the mana. Despite libel suits and a lack of major advertisers—in contrast to the establishment newspapers—the nūpepa run by aloha ʻāina used everything at their disposal, including translation, to increase the mana and ea of the lāhui in the face of constant foreign depredation.

Chapter 4 deals with the aftermath of the overthrow of the Hawaiian Kingdom and the illegal annexation of Hawaiʻi to the United States. The institutional power of ʻōlelo Hawaiʻi had been eroding throughout the last decades of the nineteenth century, and the rapidly increasing numbers of American immigrants, and the often-rabid monolingualism they brought with them, seriously threatened the survival of ʻōlelo Hawaiʻi. The previously vibrant enterprise of translation into Hawaiian became a practice serving a niche market, and the mana unuhi flowed away from the lāhui: translation out of Hawaiian into English took off. The territorial period (1900–1959) was the golden era for extractive misrepresentative translations. Samuel Mānaiakalani

Kamakau, Davida Malo, John Papa ʻĪʻī, and Kepelino were all translated during this time, as part of a shared project devoted to saving "disappearing" Hawaiian ʻike—*not* for Hawaiians but for haole scholars. In the nūpepa, unuhi had given ea and mana to the lāhui. These later translation projects were all about establishing the reputation of Hawaiian knowledge as an academic field of study and giving mana to outside scholars and understandings. For this reason, these scholars and translators were often heavily invested in emphasizing the antiquity of the knowledge entombed within these translations. They were invested in being definitive. Multiple translations would have shown how much mana and how many mana these moʻolelo had, but instead mana was given to a singular narrative, a singular voice. Through text selection, inherent and pervasive bias, and editorial fiat, these translations created a picture in English of a moribund Hawaiian culture and history whose value was as an academically interesting addition to universal human history. The organizations responsible for producing these translations also had vested interests in Hawaiians disappearing. Many were published through the auspices of the Anthropology Department of the Bishop Museum, and many of that museum's trustees had played major roles in the overthrow and subsequent push for annexation in the face of intense opposition from the vast majority of Hawaiians, who most certainly *did not* disappear. But the fact that our moʻolelo through translation were represented as anthropological artifacts, similar in nature to fishhooks or feathered cloaks, contributed greatly to creating the false impression of our disappearance as a living people.

Chapter 5 describes what happens when, rather than disappearing through translation, Hawaiians decide to refuse translation in ways that make us more legible. Three recent and very public refusals to unuhi from ʻōlelo Hawaiʻi to English expose the workings of settler state institutions predicated on eliminating Hawaiians. Representative Faye Hanohano declined to translate in the state legislature, as did activists and educators Kahoʻokahi Kanuha and Kaleikoa Kāʻeo in the state courts, and the generative power of refusal these three Kānaka Maoli wielded through embodied performance within these very powerful arms of settler state power paradoxically opened up rather than closed down avenues of communication regarding the ea and mana of the lāhui Hawaiʻi. In the face of public and official perceptions of ʻōlelo

Hawai'i as something that only exists to be translated, Hanohano, Kanuha, and Kā'eo made legible the ea of the lāhui by questioning the very mana, the authority and legitimacy, of the settler state to dictate who they are and what language they will speak. These refusals hinge on the idea of unsettlement, a way that translation contributes to "the thwarting or destroying of settlement along with the active attempt to discourage future European colonization" (Brickhouse 2015, 2), which in the Hawaiian context means questioning the power of federal and state governments to recognize Kānaka as Kānaka, while at the same time realizing that those same governments will seek to enclose Hawaiians within settler colonial structures of elimination, in this case in the guise of mandating court interpreters for all those who wish to speak Hawaiian in court. Though this is indisputably an important step in renormalizing 'ōlelo Hawai'i, we must also be aware that it serves the purpose of disappearing the potent critique of the state's power itself whenever a Hawaiian refuses to unuhi in court. This chapter ends with a discussion of the relation between the revitalization and renormalization of 'ōlelo Hawai'i and the struggle over 'āina, grounded in an understanding of how Hawaiians are forced to live in translation understood not as a trope, but in a very real linguistic sense. Many of our fundamental understandings of 'āina, and how we relate to each other and the world, come from 'ōlelo Hawai'i, but often require translation for us to practice them today, or fight for our 'āina.

A brief epilogue provides a personal reflection on how translation could play a more liberatory role for our lāhui, as it did in the nineteenth-century nūpepa, if we decide—based on an informed and detailed understanding of the practice—that it is a suitable vehicle for the mo'olelo we are trying to tell.

Chapter 1

In the Beginning Was Translation

"Publishing Salvation" in the Baibala Hemolele

The icy cold gnawed at his bare fingers. Brintnall had made sure to give him gloves, but he was not used to wearing them, and had forgotten them in his sea chest aboard the Triumph. *This was not his first time in the cold, but they had mostly been sealing in Mexico and trading in China, so he couldn't help but compare the numbing bite of New Haven to the warmth and humidity of Kealakekua.*

He had come to Yale because it was a center of learning, and it was where his tutor Hubbard had come from. He had seen the power of this unfamiliar ʻike during his travels and wanted the other kānaka back home to share in it as well.

Hubbard had taught him some English on the ship during the long passages from sealing grounds to trading ports, but he wanted more, knew he could do more. He had spent many shifts in his hammock on the berth deck dreaming of what Hawaiʻi might be like once learning like this was more widespread.

He wasn't familiar with New Haven, though, and it had taken him so long to get here from the harbor. He probably shouldn't have spent so much time wandering on the green first, but it was good to connect with ʻāina, any ʻāina, after so long on the ship.

The grounds of Yale were mostly empty. He shuddered, willing himself to remain calm. His hands were so cold.

He had come so far from home, and he missed the connections of family. His parents and brother were dead, but his desire for the comfort *and pilina of his other relatives remained. For them he would bring back salvation.*

He had been standing before the steps of the imposing red-brick building for the last fifteen minutes, and finally fell to his knees. The shuttered windows looked down impassively. Snow continued to fall, new flakes melting where they mingled with the tears sliding down his cheeks.

"Nobody gives me learning," he cried out.

Publishing Salvation

A widespread—though likely apocryphal—tale relates how a dusky lad from the Sandwich Islands was found weeping upon the steps of Yale College on a crisp and wintry New Haven evening in 1809 (Schiff 2004). When asked why he cried, he replied that it was because no one had given him learning. Though he had already begun to learn the rudiments of English and Christianity from Captain Brintnall while serving on a trading journey to America (Dwight 1819, 13), this moment would come to mark the true beginning of his formal education in Christianity and the literacy that came with it. Though this narrative of the "lost man-child far from home with inarticulate urges toward Christian enlightenment" (Chang 2016, 83) does a great disservice to the real person it portrayed, it was what would garner much of the moral and financial support needed for the Christian mission to Hawaiʻi. No one could have known that the story of this earnest young Hawaiian would be the catalyst for monumental change in the culture and future of his home.[1]

His name was Heneri ʻŌpūkahaʻia, though much of America[2] came to know him as Henry Obookiah. He had been trained as a kahuna (priest/expert) from a young age, and after making the decision to leave Hawaiʻi, he became a dedicated professor of the Christian religion, a skilled amateur linguist, a translator, and the direct impetus for the first company of Calvinist missionaries to travel to Hawaiʻi. ʻŌpūkahaʻia lived with and learned from various pious families in the New England area, and by all accounts, he was driven by a desire to spread the gospel, particularly to his own people in Hawaiʻi. Though no copies are thought to exist, ʻŌpūkahaʻia is said to have been close to completing a grammar, a dictionary, and a spelling book for the Hawaiian language (Dwight 1819, 43–44, 100). He also taught himself

Hebrew and translated portions of the Bible into Hawaiian (ABCFM 1816, 11), including the entire Book of Genesis (Schütz 1994, 36). He reportedly found translating from Hebrew easier than from English, because of similarities in structure between Hebrew and 'ōlelo Hawai'i (Dwight 1819, 101).

Though these translations never reached the people he was preparing them for, 'Ōpūkaha'ia's serious nature, deeply rooted Christianity, dedication to learning, and good humor served as an example to would-be missionaries and their American supporters around the country that the heathen was indeed redeemable, salvable through education in literacy and the gospel. Before he died, 'Ōpūkaha'ia and a handful of other Hawaiians—Thomas Hopu, George Kaumuali'i, William Kanui, and John Honoli'i—made many speaking appearances in various states and were instrumental in securing funding and support for a Hawai'i mission and for the Foreign Mission School in Cornwall, Connecticut, where they were among the first students (Kamakau 1996, 244).[3]

At the mission school, pupils from places such as Hawai'i, the Society Islands, Aotearoa, Timor, Portugal, Greece, China, and Native American nations (Seneca, Iroquois, Delaware, Cherokee, Choctaw, Stockbridge, Oneida, Tuscarora, Narragansett, and Mohawk) (ABCFM 1824, 133) were trained as "a cadre of elite Natives to shape and embody Christianity and civilization in their own nations" (Wyss 2012, 158), and also to help "prepare the American missionaries by teaching them about the different languages and cultures they would encounter in their future missions to foreign parts" (Schütz 1994, 87). An exemplary description of the mixing of Indigenous voices and cultures at Cornwall comes from the American Board of Commissioners for Foreign Missions (ABCFM) 1818 annual report, which describes an exhibition at the school: "M'Kee Folsom delivered a short declamation in Choctaw; Elias Boudinot in Cherokee; Poo-po-hee [a Tahitian who would later come to Hawai'i] in Otaheitan [Tahitian]; Honoree [Honoli'i] in Owhyhean [Hawaiian]; one of the American youth in Chinese, as he had learned it from Botang, Gibbs, Hopoo [Hopu] and others in English" (1819a, 205). In a sort of situational affinity between Hawaiians and Cherokees in relation to literacy/education and the ABCFM that would continue over the next handful of decades, the Cherokee students David Brown and John Ridge, along with Elias

Boudinot, would later become the faces of the school, replacing 'Ōpūkaha'ia and the other Hawaiians (Wyss 2012, 161–162).

In February of 1817, eight years to the month from his fateful arrival in Connecticut, 'Ōpūkaha'ia died of typhus at the age of almost thirty (Chang 2016, 84). The ABCFM had had high hopes for him as part of the mission to Hawai'i. As the living embodiment of salvation through God and literacy, he was proof that the savage could find redemption. In its annual report, the ABCFM wrote of 'Ōpūkaha'ia that "he died as the Christian would wish to die. His divine master knew well, whether to send him back to Owhyhee, to publish salvation to his perishing countrymen, or to call him to higher scenes, in another world" (1819a, 200). And though 'Ōpūkaha'ia ended up being called to "another world," the ABCFM was inspired by his example and decided to pursue the other option: "publish[ing] salvation to his perishing countrymen."

A reference to Isaiah 52:7, this goal was taken quite literally by the ABCFM as part of its mission to bring the gospel to the people of Hawai'i. In 1817, members of the ABCFM had this to say about publishing salvation: "The translation and dispersion of the Scriptures, and schools for the instruction of the young, are parts, and necessary parts, of the great design. But it must never be forgotten, or overlooked, that the command is, to *'preach the Gospel to every creature,'* and that the *preaching* of the word, however foolish it may seem to men, is the grand mean appointed by the wisdom of God for the saving conversion of the nations" (1818, 163; emphasis in original). Preaching the gospel to the far reaches of the world was "the grand mean," but translation and education were "necessary parts," and with these came publication—what Hawaiians would come to call "palapala," because of the way words were pala, or daubed/smeared/designed/printed, on paper. "Palapala" is also related to the word "kāpala," which refers to how designs were stamped on kapa, or barkcloth ("No ka Olelo" 1834, 2). The ABCFM's own bylaws linked salvation, literacy, and the press: "The object of the Board is, to propagate the gospel among unevangelized nations and communities, by means of preachers, catechists, schoolmasters, and the press" (ABCFM 1819b, 8). By this time, the press already had a long history of connecting Indigenous peoples with Christianity, as the first Bible printed in North America had been printed in 1663 in the Wampanoag language (Round 2010, 5). Unsurprisingly, publishing salvation meant publishing the Bible, "the very voice of God," for without the scriptures to guide Hawaiians (or the other Indigenous communities the ABCFM worked in), "their manifestation of Christianity was sure to go astray" (Lyon 2017, 115). The Hawai'i missionary Artemas Bishop asserted that "not only is the Bible the ultimate authority of Protestant belief, but the religion of Protestants cannot flourish where the Scriptures are not dispersed and read in the vulgar tongue" (1844, 74). But as the ABCFM missionaries soon found out in Hawai'i and other Indigenous contexts, bestowing the Bible could not be accomplished without translation. Religion, literacy, and education would become the drivers of enormous changes, both beneficial and detrimental, in the culture, education, and politics of Hawai'i and Hawaiians over the next two centuries, and translation was the engine that drove everything forward.

Translating Salvation

At first, the ABCFM did not know how much of a role translation would have to play in its Hawai'i mission. The ABCFM was the United States' first organization dedicated to foreign missions, and quite a young one at that. Founded in 1810, only nine years before the Sandwich Islands mission was launched, the ABCFM was barely older than its home church, Park Street Church in Boston. Chartered in 1809, the church would become a strong abolitionist center.

Despite its youth, the ABCFM soon became one of the largest benevolent societies in the United States. By 1825, it ranked second only to the American Education Society, and by 1831, critics were warning that the amount of money that the ABCFM was spending abroad on its foreign missions would destabilize the American economy (Shenk 2004, 2). Made up of Presbyterian, Reformed Dutch, and Congregational churches (ABCFM 1826, 21), the ABCFM owed its formation and foundational theology to the eighteenth-century revival known as the Great Awakening (J. K. Osorio 2002, 21). The national westward expansion that justified occupation and colonialism by appeals to manifest destiny and American exceptionalism meant that the mission always had its eyes on the horizon, looking for new lands and peoples to save. The ABCFM would come to have a wide reach, sending missionaries to India, Ceylon (Sri Lanka), Palestine, Choctaw country, Cherokee country, China, Thailand, Singapore, western and southern Africa, Hawai'i, and other sites. But thanks in part to 'Ōpūkaha'ia,

Hawai'i was among the first "unevangelized nations and communities" that the ABCFM's desire to bring the gospel settled upon. As one of the few remaining major island groups in the Pacific that had not yet been missionized by other denominations or countries, it was a fertile field for planting and publishing salvation.

Encouraged and justified by 'Ōpūkaha'ia's fervent desire that the Bible be brought to his people, the ABCFM also saw the Sandwich Islands mission as a means to stake a spiritual claim for itself as a missionary organization, and to a certain extent, for American interests.[4] Hawai'i was an important port, both strategically and commercially, and between 1786 and 1820, more than a hundred ships had called there (Schütz 1994, 10). This influx of what the missionaries saw as dubious characters of loose morals preying on the ignorant and godless Hawaiians also spurred the ABCFM to establish a foothold in the islands quickly.

After a handful of years of fundraising and preparation aided by 'Ōpūkaha'ia and the other Hawaiian youths, the first mission to Hawai'i—made up of "ordained ministers of the Gospel, physicians, teachers, secular agents, printers, a bookbinder, and a farmer" (Hawaiian Mission Children's Society 1969, 3), and the four Hawaiian youths[5]—set out from Boston on October 23, 1819, aboard the brig *Thaddeus*. After a 160-day voyage to Hawai'i, they anchored in Kawaihae on March 30, 1820 (Kamakau 1996, 244). The missionaries arrived immediately after the Hawaiian traditional "religion" had suffered a tremendous blow following the death of Kamehameha I. The 'ai kapu system that organized much of Hawaiian life had been struck down when Liholiho, his father's successor, performed the pale lau'ī after defeating the pro-kapu forces of his cousin Kekuaokalani (Kamakau 1996, 216). As historian Noelani Arista asserts, this was not just a religious move, but one that was religiopolitical (2018, 107). Kamehameha, following the traditional example of the chief Līloa, had given care of the governance of the kingdom to his son Liholiho, but given the care of the war god Kūkā'ilimoku to Liholiho's cousin Kekuaokalani. This was a traditional model that hinged on the idea of pono, which in this case can be understood as everything being in a proper state of balance that ensures the prosperity of both the ali'i and the people. If Liholiho turned out to not be pono and thus an unfit ruler, Kekuaokalani would use the war god to depose him.

When the ʻai kapu was overthrown, which meant the destruction of heiau (temples, places for offerings, ceremonial areas) and kiʻi akua (carved images of akua), as Arista asserts, "the chiefs supporting Liholiho eliminated the ceremonial path to regime change and rule that Kekuaokalani had been granted by Kamehameha when he was given the god, Kūkāʻilimoku. Kekuaokalani was dependent upon the sanction of gods and ceremony in the heiau to legitimate his attempt to rule. What Kaʻahumanu, Kālaimoku, and the other ruling chiefs removed with the casting down of the ʻai kapu was the religious and political path toward legitimate usurpation available to any rivals of Liholiho" (2018, 107). The missionaries thus arrived in the midst of a highly complex Hawaiian political struggle. Predictably, however, when they learned about the destruction of the ʻai kapu, all they concluded was that the hand of Providence had paved the way for Christianity in Hawaiʻi.

Yet what they actually found upon their arrival in Hawaiʻi was a lukewarm reception. The chiefs were not so quickly convinced that the missionaries should be welcomed, much less allowed to stay. But at the urging of John Young, a foreign-born aikāne and advisor of Kamehameha I, the council of chiefs allowed the missionaries a one-year probationary period (Kamakau 1996, 245). Though the aliʻi let them settle, Hawaiian suspicions lingered. The mōʻī Liholiho himself, also known as Kamehameha II, was skeptical from the first. When he asked that his name be written, after the missionary wrote it "Li-ho-li-ho," the mōʻī gave the writing a good long look and declared, "This does not look like me, nor any other man" (A. F. Judd 1889, 53). He also famously shrugged off missionary attempts to convert him:

> A i kona noho ana ma Puuloa i Oahu, hele aku kekahi misionari, o Binamu ka inoa, e hoohuli ia ia ma ka pono, e malama i ke Akua i pomaikai ai oia ma kona aupuni a i ola hoi kona uhane. Olelo mai oia me ka hoohiki pono ole, i mai la: "Elima oʻu makahiki i koe, alaila, huli au i kanaka maikai."
>
> [And when he was staying at Puʻuloa, on Oʻahu, a missionary named Bingham approached him, to try to turn him to the side of righteousness, to worship God in order that Liholiho's government be blessed and his soul be saved. Liholiho responded with a faithless promise, saying: "Five more years, then I will become a good man."]
> (Dibble 2005, 93–94)

Though Bingham and the other missionaries did not end up giving Liholiho the break that he asked for, the mōʻī relented regarding the issue of literacy, sending John Papa ʻĪʻī and Kahuhu to learn from Asa Thurston, and saying that if it did them no harm, he too would learn the palapala[6] (A. F. Judd 1889, 53).

Two observations are worth noting here. The first is that historical accounts, even those written in ʻōlelo Hawaiʻi a mere few decades after the fact, completely elide the effect that unuhi had on all these interactions between the missionaries and chiefs. There were few bilingual people on either side, and it is unclear how effectively any of them were able to communicate, which means that mistranslations (willful or otherwise), misunderstandings, and mischaracterizations abounded. Albert Schütz too casts doubt on the efficacy of earlier interactions of this type when he suggests that even the highly educated and erudite Tupaia, the Tahitian who served as Captain Cook's translator with the Māori, may have exaggerated his ability to communicate with them. Schütz quotes the Māori doctor and anthropologist Te Rangi Hīroa (also known as Sir Peter Buck), the first Pacific Islander to head the Bishop Museum: "The person who says that he can immediately understand all that is said in one Polynesian group because he knows the language of another group lays claim to extraordinary insight. Maori is my mother tongue but I freely admit that I could never understand all that I heard in the Polynesian islands which I visited for the first time" (1994, 50). Thus, while translation is a constant throughout the kingdom era in Hawaiʻi, it is rarely taken into account in our understandings of the time period. In fact, unuhi is hardly considered in most understandings of Indigenous histories in general. Rather than Venuti's formulation of the translator's invisibility (1995), it is *translation*'s invisibility that is at play.

The second observation comes from historian David Chang, who astutely notes that while the missionaries indisputably brought widespread alphabetic literacy, some Hawaiians were already aware from their interactions with other foreigners of the potential value of the written word, displaying an "appreciation of the uses of textuality [that] preceded missionization" (2018, 238). In that way, Christianity was not necessarily something the aliʻi could see the utility of at first glance—Hiram Bingham was disgusted when those learning literacy from the missionaries "demanded what temporal advantage could be derived from listening to preaching" (1847, 209). As John Charlot suggests, the palapala and alphabetic literacy could "easily be appreciated as an aid in memorizing, a recognized and prestigious activity in classical Hawaiian education" (2005, 43). Noelani Arista further says that "the 'new education' of the missionaries would take root in soil already well nurtured for its reception; it would grow out of an already established Hawaiian education" (2018, 142). kuʻualoha hoʻomanawanui recognizes the future-facing nature of Hawaiian learning when she characterizes the palapala as "another site of cultural memory, a vehicle to record and transport Kanaka Maoli values to future generations of the lāhui" (2014, 201).

For very different reasons, other foreigners were suspicious about the mission, and the teaching of literacy. The British sea captain who brought the news of Liholiho's death in England during his diplomatic trip also gave the aliʻi a dire warning about the missionaries and the learning they offered:

> One of the chiefs went on board to receive the letters, but the captain would not deliver them, lest they should fall into the hands of the missionaries. The chief inquired, what would be the harm, if they should. The captain replied: "The missionaries are bad man. They have come here to deceive you. They have come here to get your land away. If you learn the *palapala,* (i.e. if you attend to instruction) you will die." On being asked why learning did not kill Englishmen, the captain answered, that it was very good for white men, but it killed black men. (ABCFM 1827, 77–78)

Though it is unlikely that kānaka maoli or aliʻi thought the palapala would literally kill them, such warnings about the colonial desires undergirding the missionary arm of the church could only fuel aliʻi skepticism of the missionaries as gateways to literacy.

Recognizing that the Hawaiian wish for literacy was accompanied by ambivalence about the new religion, the missionaries ensured that the palapala could not be gotten without the pule, or prayer. In 1824, even before the Hawaiian alphabet was formalized, Levi Chamberlain gave an account of a young Hawaiian man who was castigated by another Hawaiian for being a "kanaka palapala"—something along the lines of "document man" or "literacy man" (1826, 39). It is telling that the man was being insulted for his connection to the palapala (writing/literacy/Western education) that the missionaries brought, rather than the pule (religion/prayers). As longtime scholar of Hawaiian religion John Charlot explains, "*palapala*—rather than some other word, such as *pule* 'prayer' or *lāʻau* 'medicine,' both emphasized by the missionaries—was used as a pars-pro-toto term for the missionary effort argues for its being the most impressive offering of the missionaries in the Hawaiians' view" (2005, 45). For the Calvinist ABCFM, literacy and their model of Christianity were inseparable, because the way to heaven was through reading and interpreting the scriptures as an individual, free from the corruption that festers in a bureaucratic clergy and a corporatic church. In his influential *Institutes of the Christian Religion,* John Calvin himself wrote what was translated as "herein God deigns to confer a singular privilege on his elect, whom he distinguishes from the rest of mankind. For what is the beginning of true learning but a prompt alacrity to hear the voice of God?" (1816, 86). With similar beliefs in mind, the ABCFM spent nearly as much for the printing press and apparatus for the first mission as for furniture, clothing, and mechanical and agricultural implements combined (ABCFM 1821, 308). Sending the press was also a practical decision, as the publishing houses on the East Coast of the continental United States were thousands of miles away, and there was a growing chorus of Indigenous groups in areas proselytized by the ABCFM calling for presses of their own (Round 2010, 81).

Calvin's insistence on "prompt alacrity" also answered the question of who would learn whose language. Because the missionaries clearly felt that they had the most to teach the heathens in Hawaiʻi and other savage places, they initially assumed that teaching these Native peoples English first would be the fastest way of granting them access to the word of God as presented in the Bible. Although the Bible itself had been translated from Hebrew and Greek to English, teaching English would also allow the heathens to benefit from the wealth of existing printed texts on Christianity and other "enlightening" topics. Such logic informed the 1816 mission report, which sets out the goal in regard to Native American education as "the instruction of the rising generation in common school learning, in the useful arts of life, and in Christianity, so as gradually, with the divine blessing to make the whole tribe English in their language, civilized in their habits, and Christian in their religion.... Assimilated in language, they will more readily become assimilated in habits and manners to their white neighbors; intercourse will be easy and the advantages to them incalculable" (ABCFM 1817, 135). These ideas—and particularly the connections between Christianity, civilization, and literacy—were echoed a few years later when the first mission gathered at the Park Street Church in Boston the week before setting out for the Sandwich Islands. But the perspective on language and translation already seemed to be shifting somewhat, likely due to the slow progress the missionaries were making in Choctaw country and Cherokee country in their efforts at spreading English (ABCFM 1827, 63).

The "preachers, catechists, schoolmasters, and the press" were the ABCFM's blueprint for salvation, all represented in the Sandwich Islands mission. The preacher would work with the catechist and the schoolmaster to spread the gospel, with the press as their principal avenue for spreading the cause of Christianity, and the ABCFM, in Hawai'i. A simple, even elegant plan. But no one had thought to include translators on that list—as essential allies for the preachers, and catechists, and schoolmasters—and this lack soon came to be a huge issue for these young missionaries. Though the Hawaiian students from the Foreign Mission School would assist in some ways with translating, with Thomas Hopu in particular acting as an intermediary (Lyon 2017, 131), had the missionaries known how important a role translation would necessarily play in the coming years, they would have anticipated how woefully meager their own linguistic resources would prove to be.

Incorporated as a mission church, the first company received their instructions from Rev. Samuel Worcester and Jeremiah Evarts, which included the following:

> You are to aim at nothing short of covering those islands with fruitful fields and pleasant dwellings, and schools and churches; of raising up the whole people to an elevated state of Christian civilization; of bringing, or preparing the means of bringing, thousands and millions of the present and succeeding generations to the mansions of eternal blessedness. [...]
>
> But it is an arduous enterprise, a great and difficult work. To obtain an adequate knowledge of the language of the people; to make them acquainted with letters; to give them the Bible with skill to read

it; to turn them from their barbarous courses and habits; to introduce, and get into extended operation and influence among them, the arts and institutions and usages of civilized life and society; above all, to convert them from their idolatries and superstitions and vices, to the living and redeeming God. (ABCFM 1819b)

Hiram Bingham later recalled also being directed "to give [the Hawaiians] the Bible in their own tongue, with the ability to read it for themselves" (1847, 60). Even though literacy was only beginning to become widespread in the twenty-two United States of the time, the ABCFM were convinced that reading was the surest way to reach Hawaiians, and thought that the "preachers, catechists, schoolmasters, and the press" they were sending would be enough to promptly accomplish this goal.

Yet the ABCFM's zeal for expediency and alacrity in spreading the gospel forced them to teach literacy in Hawaiian, making the translators missing from that equation the only viable gateway to both publishing and salvation. Though they were largely unprepared for the tasks of translation that lay ahead of them, the philosophy informing the ABCFM's attempts to educate and enlighten Hawaiians, conditioned by the board's religious principles and their experiences with missions to other Indigenous nations, made a reliance on translation inevitable. As Jonathan Kay Kamakawiwo'ole Osorio argues, "the mediator for Calvinists was the Bible. The ability to read, understand, and interpret scripture and gospel was the key" (2002, 21). But English was not widespread in most of the "heathen" nations that the ABCFM targeted for conversion, and in many cases, neither was alphabetic literacy. In practice, then, "the preaching of the gospel, the establishment of schools, and all the means of imparting religious knowledge" (ABCFM 1819b, 37) could take place only through translation.

Along with teaching Hawaiians about the words of the apostles, the missionaries also pushed them to build American-style frame homes with glass windows and to wear Mother Hubbard dresses and wool suits. The people did not quickly accept these exhortations—Princess Ruth Ke'elikōlani famously lived in a grass-thatched hut that was situated on the lawn next to Hulihe'e Palace. Hawaiians came to value alphabetic literacy very quickly, though it took time for the Hawaiian alphabet to be formalized and a writing system developed for the language. Even before the alphabet was finalized, however, the mission began its efforts to educate Hawaiians. Furthermore, the ABCFM focus on expediency meant that the missionaries immediately began their attempts to learn the language, so that they could carry out their primary obligation: teaching Hawaiians the gospel.

This language learning was a necessary departure from what the ABCFM had initially anticipated, and in fact discouraged. Though they would not use this term, English was the language that had all the mana in their estimations, and alphabetic literacy in English was seen as the greatest gift that could be offered: "Were the Bible now translated into all the languages of the Indian tribes, it would be of no more use to them than our English Bible; for they could read it no better. They might be taught to read the Bible in the English language with as much ease, as they could be taught to read it in their own; and having learned to read the English language, the sources of knowledge and means of general improvement to them will be incomparably greater and more various than their own language could ever procure for them" (1817, 135–136). Since many communities and Indigenous nations had no written language recognized by the missionaries—or the missionaries found the native-derived writing systems threatening, as in the case of Sequoyah's Cherokee syllabary—the ABCFM thought it most expedient to skip any efforts to achieve literacy in the language of the people. But problems arose quickly. Even before the arrival of the ABCFM missionaries in Hawai'i, a Frenchman named Jean Rives had attempted to start a small school to teach English to the ali'i, but by most accounts it failed miserably, lasting only a few weeks ('Ī'ī 1869). As for the ABCFM's early efforts in Hawai'i and in Indian Country, the missionaries on the ground realized pretty quickly that while English could still be the goal, it could not be the starting point. According to an 1826 ABCFM report, "from what is now taking place in the Cherokee and Choctaw nations, it is evident that the readiest way to teach an Indian child the English language is to make him able to read and write his own" (1827, 63).

Although 'Ōpūkaha'ia and the foreign mission school students such as Hopu and Kaumuali'i did what they could to teach Hawaiian to the missionaries before setting out for the islands, teaching your own language through a language not your own is a difficult proposition at best, and George Kaumuali'i had been away from Hawai'i so long that he himself had difficulty speaking his own language. The missionaries therefore arrived with nothing more than a rudimentary knowledge of Hawaiian, making their first educational priority educating *themselves* in the language of the people they wished to save.

Later accounts of the mission's work paint a rather rosy picture of the missionaries' language aptitude and eventual "reduction" of the language to writing. The historian William Drake Westervelt's assessment is typical: "all the members of the mission studied as diligently as they taught, and with surprising rapidity learned the pronunciation and the meaning of Hawaiian words and reduced the language to writing" (1911, 18). The truth, however, is that foreigners had been in Hawai'i for at least four decades by that point, and no proven, regularized system of language learning for foreigners was in place, and the missionaries struggled. Missionary journals and other accounts of the day narrate the progress and challenges of missionary language learning, and it was slow. More than three years after arriving, Levi Chamberlain, the secular agent of the first mission, wrote in his journal that "the members of the mission present at this time at this station, are attending to the language of the country with a good degree of application. By the request of Mr. Bingham they are making attempts at composition. I presented this evening my first assay at writing the language" (1826). If it took this long for them to even attempt writing, it can be imagined that language acquisition was a struggle. Granted, as the agent and quartermaster for the mission, Chamberlain was perhaps not out among the people as much. But even Hiram Bingham, the mission's leader and minister on O'ahu, had after two years advanced only far enough to preach brief petitions and statements of praise and adoration, and in May 1824, Stephen Reynolds, an American trader living in Hawai'i, recorded in his journal that a native woman Pualanui, or Puolanui, told him that "Mr Ellis & Mr Bingham spoke so that she could not understand more than half they said" (1989, 31).

This difficulty in learning Hawaiian did not lessen appreciably as the years passed. In 1831, five years into the translation of the Bible, the ABCFM missionaries reported that even after many years among the people, most of them still lacked the skills of a translator (1832, 164–165). A few years later, Lorrin Andrews, generally regarded as one of the most adept missionary speakers and translators of 'ōlelo Hawai'i, argued that the mission needed people who would focus on language and translation (Charlot 2005, 614–615). Amos Starr Cooke, who arrived with the eighth company in 1837 and eventually was responsible for educating aliʻi children at the Hawaiian Chiefs' Children's School, often wrote about his difficulties in learning the language. A journal entry for June 25, 1837, a little over two months after his arrival, records that he went to visit the Sabbath school, but "did not comprehend a single sentence," taking this "for a token that I ought to have staid [sic] at home or that I ought to return" (Cooke 1836–1838). His frustration is palpable, and as anyone who has tried to learn a new language can attest, highly understandable. But on July 17, 1837, Cooke provides a far less sympathetic explanation for his inability: "Have just read a letter from bro. Bailey. He appears to have his soul interested in this people. O that mine were! O Lord why am I so indifferent to the welfare of souls of these dying heathen. It may be that I do not get this language any faster because I care nothing about them.[7] God knows."

Cooke's lack of sympathy for "these dying heathen" and their language speaks to the powerful connection between language and culture. As one of the deep structures that gives a culture its shape and meaning, language is an important repository of values and mores. As already mentioned, one of our most repeated proverbs is "I ka ʻōlelo nō ke ola, i ka ʻōlelo nō ka make," often translated as "In language there is life, in language there is death." This ʻōlelo noʻeau refers not only to the fact that Hawaiians have language-based healing arts like lāʻau kāhea and more lethal arts like pule ʻanāʻanā, but also to the fact that everything in the realms of life and death, that is to say everything, is rooted in our ʻōlelo. Cooke's comments certainly suggest that one of the barriers to the missionaries' language acquisition was their distaste for, or even fear of, Hawaiian culture. They were, in short, facing what Indigenous and/or colonized peoples have confronted for generations. To learn Hawaiian was to open themselves up to our world, our life and death. And this they did not wish to do. Though linguistic difficulties undoubtedly slowed the unuhi process, and the promotion of literacy generally, this reluctance to open themselves up to the "heathenism" embedded in the language of those they were trying to save came into play as well.

And yet, while struggling to find their way in the language at the same time as trying to avoid its cultural content, the missionaries were also constructing a working model for education and translation. At first, they followed the linguistic examples of earlier explorers and visitors, who tried to represent the Hawaiian language in writing through "imitation and invention" (Walch 1967, 356). This changed in January of 1822, however, when the mission received copies of the *New Zealand Grammar and Vocabulary* by Thomas Kendall ("Woahoo Journal" 1822, 42). The shared traits between Māori and Hawaiian observable in the grammar confirmed some of what the ABCFM missionaries had already done and would inform some of the later decisions made for the sake of uniformity. They would also come to have access to grammars on other related languages such as Malay, Tongan, and Tahitian (Schütz 1994, 248). A week after the influential Māori grammar was received, the first Hawaiian-language imprint came off the missionary press. The printing was a bit of an occasion, as the chief Keʻeaumoku, whom the foreigners called "Governor Cox," was taught the rudiments of operating the press and struck off the first pages (Westervelt 1911, 18). Entitled *The Alphabet*, the imprint was used to teach Hawaiians reading and spelling (Schütz 1994, 162).[8]

Though ostensibly produced to teach Hawaiians how to read their own language, most of the explanations for pronunciation and spelling in *The Alphabet* were written in English, which would have been gibberish to them. In contrast, *Te Aebi no Taheiti* (The Tahitian alphabet), the first printing in Tahitian a decade earlier, only included English in the colophon (Schütz 1994, 164). (The London Missionary Society [LMS] rather than the ABCFM published this text.) In addition, despite the title, *The Alphabet* was published four years before the Hawaiian alphabet was formalized. So consonants such as *b, d, r, t,* and *y,* which soon disappeared from the Hawaiian alphabet, appeared in *The Alphabet,* and "Hawaiʻi" was spelled "Owhy."

While Hawaiians were ostensibly being taught the rudiments of literacy in their own language, Christianity was also a building block of that education. "First exercise in reading," table IV in *The Alphabet,* featured the following sentences:

E hele mai oe.
E noho marie oe i loko o ka hale.
E hana pono, a ore hana heva iti.
E hoo lohe i ka mea a ko kumu i i mai la.

[You go.
You stay peacefully in the house.
Act righteously; do not sin even slightly.
Listen to what your teacher has said.] (*The Alphabet* 1822, 3)

Along with exercises such as these, where Hawaiians were instructed to listen to missionary directions and accept castigation for sin, other tables presented Jesus's stature as hiapo, or firstborn—an important indicator of his stature for the genealogy-conscious aliʻi—and directed readers to proselytize on all of the islands (1822, 16). In 1825, the book was expanded and reprinted as *Ka Be-a-ba,* so named for the exercise of pronouncing *b* and then *a* aloud before joining them to pronounce the syllable "ba." The new volume had a print run of ten thousand copies, and the missionaries justified the expansion by observing that "the last one was found to be far too limited and we desired to add as much evangelical matter as possible to the little that has been before printed and in the hands of some thousands of people" (*Mission Journal,* April 8, 1825).

Like this speller, nearly everything that came from the early mission press reflected a strong religious character. First came a small hymn book with forty-seven translated hymns; then *Pooolelo,* a four-page scriptural tract; followed by the *Ui,* an eight-page catechism; then "Thoughts of the Chiefs"; and in 1825, the Ten Commandments (Andrews 1837, 156).[9] Important publications in their own right, they were also preparing the way for the missionaries' defining translation and publication: the Bible.

"Perfect" Salvation

Producing the Bible ma ka ʻōlelo Hawaiʻi was a colossal undertaking. The largest single volume ever printed in ʻōlelo Hawaiʻi, its first edition came in at a door-stopping 2,300 pages (Lyon 2017, 113). Beginning in 1823,[10] the same year that Kauikeaouli decreed the kingdom would observe the Christian sabbath (Judd 1889, 54), the entire translation took sixteen years. Because of its central role in Protestant belief, this volume also had to be what translation scholars of today know is impossible, but missionaries trying to establish a foothold in Hawaiʻi in the early decades of the nineteenth century had to assert: a translation that was "perfect."

From a practical standpoint, perfection proved difficult. Due to the massive source text they were working from, many members of the mission were enlisted to try their hand at unuhi, but only a few proved skilled enough to create translations that could even be considered merely usable. And even then, the overall translation ultimately had to be collaborative and created by committee, for, as Bible scholar Jeffrey Kapali Lyon points out, though missionaries such as William Richards might sit for hours each day with the kākāʻōlelo—the advisors, counselors, and learned ones—of the court, working on their language abilities, "none, even after years in Hawaiʻi, was in a position to translate 2,300 pages of ancient Hebrew and Greek into a Hawaiian that was lucid, forceful, and appealing to *Kānaka*" (2017, 116). Looking back upon that time, Hiram Bingham recalls that "no foreigner or native, at the islands, could illustrate or explain the peculiarities and intricacies of the language" (1847, 153), and while I suspect that more than a few Hawaiians were highly familiar with the "intricacies" of their own language, it is true that the haole had limited access and very few reference tools for making sense of ʻōlelo Hawaiʻi. Indeed, nine years into the translation of the Bible, Lorrin Andrews, a missionary rightly celebrated for his language ability, wrote that "even after a residence of above four years among the people and writing and preaching a great many sermons, I am puzzled every day for want of words and terms to communicate ideas to my scholars" (1832, 50f).

Binamu, Tatina, Rikeke, and Bihopa (or Bingham, Thurston, Richards, and Bishop) were the first four missionaries chosen by the board to unuhi and to serve as facilitators for the collaborative production process ("No ka unuhi" 1857, 57). Sheldon Dibble, Johnathan Green, Ephraim Clark, and Lorrin Andrews later joined the effort. Years later, an 1857 account in the Hawaiian-language newspaper *Ka Hae Hawaii* described the procedure this way. The four missionaries, along with Kuakini and Kēlou Kamakau, had an initial meeting in Kailua, Kona, to discuss the translation strategies and framing. Each returned to his separate charge:

> I ka wa e hana ana lakou, ua koho ka mea unuhi i kanaka akamai ma ka olelo Hawaii, e kokua mai, i pololei ka olelo. Haawi no ke kumu i ka manao, e like me ke ano o ka olelo a ke Akua, me ka pahemahema nae o na hua Hawaii, a loaa pono i ke kokua, ke ano o ka

manao, alaila, lawe kela i keia manao, a hoonohonoho i na hua me ka pololei iloko o ka olelo maoli. A paaia i ke kakauia ma ka pepa, alaila, komo aku ma ka pauku hou, a pela no ka hana ana ia pauku ae, ia pauku ae.

[When they would work, the translator would choose an expert in ʻōlelo Hawaiʻi to assist so that the language would be correct. The kumu would give the idea, pertaining to the meaning of the word of God, in halting Hawaiian, and would then get clarification, an interpretation of the idea, then they would take this and arrange the words accurately with correct language. When it was set, it would be written down, and then they would move on to the next section and continue on in that fashion for each and every paragraph.] ("No ka unuhi" 1857, 57)

Once the assigned book was finished, it was sent to the rest of the translation committee for comparison and critique (ABCFM 1828, 93), and then returned to the missionary translator, who would incorporate the feedback, and transcribe the new version. It was then supposedly ready for printing, though some sections had to be translated multiple times (Lyon 2017, 120).[11]

Each missionary developed his own working methods, relying on as many helpful texts as possible. Bingham began his work on the Gospel of Matthew in 1824 by comparing the Latin, English, and Tahitian versions with the original Greek to shape his Hawaiian translation (Ballou and Carter 1908, 16). Richards also labored to glean more meaning from the Scripture: "In the morning he took Knapp's Testament, Schleusner's Lexicon, and a few other helps, and strictly examined the passage which he designed to translate" (ABCFM 1827, 77). Bishop consulted many texts as well to elucidate the meaning of the sacred text, commenting that "the labors of Rosenmuller, Kenoel, Michaels, Gesenius, Knapp, Griesback, Bloomfield, Doddrigo, Stuart, Robinson, MacKnight, Campbell and others have all contributed to aid us" (1844, 74). At times, they even asked for advice from New England philologists, which took five months or more to reach them (Schütz 2017, 4).

Though very well-heeled in the latest "scientific investigations" (Bishop 1844, 74) of the scriptures, the missionaries found little help there for that crucial phase when they were at their weakest: the actual unuhi. None of those sources they consulted, save the Tahitian translation of the Bible, would give them any real guidance on how to translate into Hawaiian. The aim of this chapter is not to provide a word-by-word or sentence-by-sentence critique of their results, but to show how the eventual existence of this translation effected a "translation" of Hawaiian itself. Through this unuhi, the missionaries gave mana (in the sense of power/authority) to a mana (in the sense of version or retelling or translation) of the Bible that created a mana (in the sense of branch or divergence) in the language, along with the mana that they gave to their particular recounting of the unuhi process itself. But to support this reading, we must first examine how the missionaries and the Hawaiians understood unuhi. For hundreds of years, translation as a process was generally uncontested. According to André Lefevere, since the time of the Roman Republic, translation was generally thought of in such rigid categorical binaries as "faithful" or "free" and "right" or "wrong" (1992, 6), with seventy-two scholars supposedly producing identical translations for the Septuagint as the supreme example of faithful translation. The missionaries were heirs to this long tradition of "inspired" translations of the Bible, which assumed that not only were the original authors of the Bible directed by God, but that the translators who took the words of the Bible from one language to another—Hebrew to Greek, Hebrew to Latin, Greek to English—were also divinely inspired.

With regard to the Septuagint, Philo of Alexandria explains that because each translator was working under such divine inspiration, they therefore arrived at identical phraseology, as if their translations had been dictated to them by God (Metzger 1993, 38). Also speaking of the Septuagint translation, the Greek cleric Irenaeus asserts that because all seventy translators had come up with the "same texts with the same words and the same meanings...even the pagans present acknowledged that the books had been translated by divine inspiration" (quoted in Hengel 2004, 39). Other translations, among them the Vulgate Bible and the King James Version, have been, and sometimes continue to be, considered divinely inspired as well. Though contemporary scholarship on translation (and in some cases on Christianity) has moved away from these notions, at the time of the missionaries in Hawai'i, translation as a complete and unalloyed transfer of meaning was still the overarching understanding. At least in the West, this belief can be partially explained by the fact that most European and American translation audiences were initially multilingual, so that translation was often an exercise or a demonstration to show how capable a language was of expressing "great" things—whether poetry or literature, or, in this case, the word of God.

The ABCFM's 1822 annual report declares that the Bible is uniquely suited for pure and universal transference: "There is no language so difficult that it cannot be learned by the patient and zealous missionary; and none so deficient, but that the simple truths of the Gospel can be ultimately expressed in it. This is indeed a striking trait of the Bible, that when honestly translated by men of competent abilities, it conveys the *same* grand and saving doctrines to persons of all classes and characters, however diverse their external condition or their state of intellectual improvement" (1823, 67; emphasis added). "Same" is the operative word here. This understanding of translation points to the idea that there are universal truths, the "grand and saving doctrines," that can be expressed in all languages. If any issues arise in communicating these truths, it is not because of weaknesses in the translator or in the resulting translation, or because the speakers of the target language have a different worldview and culture, but that their language is "deficient" or that the readers just refuse to accept them.

The deficiency argument will be addressed later in this chapter; here I will examine the claim that the Bible and its translations "convey the *same* grand and saving doctrines." Reading a Bible in English is the same as reading a Bible in Wôpanâak or Tsalagi or ʻŌlelo Hawaiʻi. All are translations, but in content all are equivalent. That the Hawaiʻi missionaries understood scriptural translation this way is confirmed by the Hawaiian-language newspaper *Ke Kumu Hawaii*. In 1834, Binamu (Bingham) wrote:

> O ka unuhi ana i ka Paulo olelo i ko Roma, he mea paakiki ia, aka, ke hooikaika nei makou e hooponopono loa i ka unuhi ana, i like io ka olelo Hawaii nei me ka olelo Helene i ku pono ka manao i ole ai a hiki ia Paulo ke hoole mai, "Aole pela koʻu manao, aole pela ko ke Akua."
>
> [Translating Paul's words to the Romans is very difficult, but we struggle on so that the translation is absolutely correct, that the Hawaiian be truly the same as the Greek and that the meaning be ac-

curate, so that Paul cannot disagree and say, "That is not what I meant, not what God meant."]

Though it is possible that Binamu was not fully aware of the linguistic nuances of every word he used, at this point he had been in Hawai'i for fourteen years and had already translated a large chunk of the Bible, so it is more than likely that he understood what was conveyed by such words as "ho'oponopono" and "like." Furthermore, by not only choosing these words but intensifying them with "loa" and "'i'o," he was clearly trying to indicate that this translation of Paul went beyond being simply correct to being absolutely accurate. "Like" in this sense goes beyond claiming that the Hawaiian and the Greek were similar to insisting that they were truly the same. For the missionaries, then, translation was nothing like the game of telephone, with each successive iteration adding or losing meanings not in the original, but rather, a puzzle to complete by arranging the Hawaiian pieces in precisely the right order to match the picture on the box. This belief was not derived from reading the latest "scientific investigations"; as missionaries, it was in fact the only way they could operate in good faith.

At its heart, translation is actually a highly interpretive act. Translators bring all of their linguistic abilities and cultural knowledge, as well as their ideological and aesthetic biases to a particular text, reinterpreting and re-authoring it for a new audience. But for Christianity to spread in a manner faithful to its tenets, translations of the Bible must occlude the original—not by denying that the original exists, but by insisting that the translation is *exactly* equivalent. A very particular understanding of unuhi is getting ho'omana 'ia here. Christianity, and in particular this brand of Protestant Christianity with its emphasis on the Bible as the true path to God, *cannot* bring the Good News to different nations and peoples if the meaning of God's word depends on the language that expresses it.

Hawaiians sensed the problem as well. As we have seen, the word for translation is "unuhi," which refers to the act of reaching into something and pulling something out. The translator reaches into another language and pulls out meaning. Though it is unclear when "unuhi" came to be equated to "translation," its use suggests that through translation, meaning can be extracted, like "grand and saving doctrines," and placed into Hawaiian. It is also fitting that the Hawaiian Bible translation was entitled *Ka Baibala Hemolele*. Though the title is most commonly translated as *The Holy Bible*, "hemolele" has the added valence of perfection, because it has "hemo" (removed itself) and "lele" (flown) from imperfection and sin. And even when acknowledged by the missionaries as not "perfect," their Bible translation still retained an aura of infallibility. "In looking over the Hawaiian Bible in the several editions, I am far from pronouncing it a perfect work," translator Artemas Bishop concluded. "An approximation to perfect translation is as much as our most sanguine expectations ever aspired to" (1844, 75). The distinction here is crucial. Though not a perfect "work" because there are undeniably typos or misunderstandings, as a *translation,* the Baibala approximates perfection because the missionaries created a text that neither Paul nor ke Akua would dispute. Small quibbles might arise here and there about word choice or an idiom, but both missionaries and Hawaiians believed that translational equivalence was possible, and that for spiritual reasons, the Baibala Hemolele could be nothing other than perfect.

When the missionaries did acknowledge errors or mistakes, they were seen as static in the transmission rather than signs of the impossibility of translation itself. Any shortcomings in translation were chalked up to deficits in ʻōlelo Hawaiʻi or Hawaiians themselves: "the native monitors often mistook the true idea of the sacred writer, as conveyed to him through the medium of his own language" (Bishop 1844, 74). For the missionaries and those who worked on the translation, there had to be a right and a wrong translation, a faithful and a free. Translation was not interpretation, but a massive act of transfer, of unuhi, of extraction. And because of the sacredness of the Bible, its translation had to be hemolele, perfect. Not only is God translated as ke Akua mana loa, the akua with almighty mana, the Bible translation is seen as mana loa as well.

Figures of Salvation

Though the missionaries did not consider themselves agents of colonialism because worldly concerns were supposedly outside their purview, the Christianity they brought, and the translations used to spread it, laid the ideological foundations for many of the most exploitive structures associated with the aims of the United States and all other foreign powers in the Pacific. In colonial encounters, mana unuhi was never one way or only used by one side, but as one of the main "rhetorical technologies that rationalize an ongoing Anglo-American imperialism in the Americas," Eric Cheyfitz observes, "translation was, and still is, the central act of European colonization and imperialism" there (1997, xii). Translation scholar and postcolonial theorist S. Shankar says of Cheyfitz's analysis that "instead of Translation being understood primarily as an instantiation of language, the colonial encounter is understood as an instantiation of Translation" (2012, 105). Shankar moves his own analysis away from the notion of translation as tropic and metaphorical, demanding instead a focus on the actual practice of translation, which we shall do here. But parts of Cheyfitz's analysis remain useful when looking at Hawai'i. In *The Poetics of Imperialism,* he pays close attention to how things get made in language, the "poetics" in his title referring to the figurative aspect of language, derived from the idea of poiesis, of making and bringing things into being. Particular figurations of people are ho'omana 'ia through telling and retelling. Such a poetics is central to imperialism and colonialism, Cheyfitz argues, because how the natives of the Americas appear as figures in the language of the colonizer becomes the justification for treating these natives in various ways.

Through such translations, colonizers "figure" and construct the people, bringing them into a particular kind of being, using language to give the native people particular attributes that would justify their further colonization. Cheyfitz talks about not only how early settlers described the Indigenous peoples of North America but also the effects of such narratives and cultural translations: "What the English and Europeans could not achieve in actuality they achieved textually in these early narratives: the translation of the Indians into proper English. But as the balance of power shifted from Indians to Europeans—and in America this shift was rapid and massive after the Revolution had shattered the Iroquois's power—these narratives became models of actuality" (1997, 10). Since the natives initially outnumbered the settlers, the colonizers could not necessarily force the native peoples to bend to their will. Through translation, however, the colonizers could figure the Native Americans into "proper English." For instance, even though his people did not believe in the individual ownership of land, Paspehay, the *weroance* of the Algonquin-speaking Indians of the Virginia area, supposedly "sold" his people's lands to the English colonizers. One of the tools for making this possible was translation. When describing their dealings with these Indians, the settlers translated *weroance,* an Algonquin-language term referring to tribal leaders, as the English word "king," which "translated Paspehay into English property relations...so that the English can recognize him as having 'sold' 'his' land to the English, who following the 'legal' logic of their language can thus claim 'title' to this land" (Cheyfitz 1997, 60). Through early treaties and encounters, the native leaders became the equivalents of European kings, with the same power to alienate land despite professed communal ownership. (Cheyfitz even argues that articulating the notion of selling land in such Native American languages as those of the Algonquian groups was impossible.)

For Cheyfitz, the history of Anglo-American imperialism arises out of the interplay between the proper and the figurative: "This history begins with, and is still driven by, a theory of metaphor grounded in the desire of what names itself the *domestic* to dominate what it simultaneously distinguishes as the *foreign*—in the desire of what imagines itself as the *literal* or, crucially, the *proper,* to bring what it formulates as the *figurative* under control" (1997, xii). This urge for domination paradoxically arises out of the inability of the domestic, in this case the missionaries, to communicate with the foreign. (In Cheyfitz's analysis, this is why Tarzan must dominate the apes.) Despite their linguistic clumsiness, the colonizers understand themselves and their culture as abiding in the realm of the proper, while the native abides in the realm of the figurative. By attempting to bring the figurative under control of the proper, the colonizer therefore brings the native into the system of European notions of property and identity (1997, xiv).

While initially textual, or at least centered in language, in time this act of translation becomes naturalized, and thus invisible. Each time *weroance,* or mōʻī for that matter, is translated as "king" or "queen" in official contexts makes the next time easier, until the terms seem to become equivalent. At that point, the colonizer no longer realizes—or admits, at any rate—that through language, the native has been actively figured and constructed in this way. A *weroance* simply *is* a king—or at least insofar as this understanding enables the colonizer to get what he wants. These linguistically constructed figures are then reinscribed into literature, laws, and treaties, which bind them "to prescribed paths and which, projected on the Indians proper, are then taken for the proper" (Cheyfitz 1997, 105). As the resulting alienation of land and the replacement of native languages with English accelerate, so too does the claim that native was always understood to be identical to the figure.

Cheyfitz treats "translation" as primarily a metaphorical, cultural, and tropic process. In Hawaiʻi, however, literal linguistic translation enacts these changes through the production of the Bible, and later the law, which will be the subject of the next chapter. Through scriptural translation, the missionaries seek to turn Hawaiians into figures worthy of salvation. When the *Thaddeus* first anchored, the foreign influx into Hawaiʻi was already four decades old. Hawaiians had taken up many of the foreign modes of dress and comportment, and Thomas Hopu, George Kaumualiʻi, William Kanui, and John Honoliʻi from the Foreign Mission School had been with the missionaries aboard the ship for 160 days, to prepare them for what they would encounter. And yet, the missionaries were horrified when they first gazed upon the Hawaiians who greeted their ship and who would later shower them with foodstuffs and hospitality. Mission head and soon-to-be Bible translator Hiram Bingham recalls that "the appearance of destitution, degradation, and barbarism, among the chattering, and almost naked savages...was appalling. Some of our number, with gushing tears, turned away from the spectacle. Others with firmer nerve continued their gaze, but were ready to exclaim, 'Can these be human beings!...Can such beings be civilized? Can they be Christianized?'" (1847, 81). As he looks back over the decades in his recollections *A Residence of Twenty-One Years in the Sandwich Islands,* Bingham answers the last two questions with a smug "Yes."

ʻŌpūkahaʻia had been the first evidence of that "yes"; in fact, the ABCFM had used ʻŌpūkahaʻia's salvation, along with that of Hopu and the others, to justify their fundraising. In a sort of nesting doll of figuration, as living, breathing proof that the heathen could be redeemed, ʻŌpūkahaʻia mā (and later Boudinot and the other Cherokees) confirmed the prevailing belief in Christianity's power, and therefore got donors to loosen their purse strings. Furthermore, ʻŌpūkahaʻia and the others themselves affirmed the script that they not only embodied but performed. During the many fundraising tours the Hawaiian youths made, and in ʻŌpūkahaʻia's 1819 memoir, they spoke of their ascent from "ignorance" and "heathenism." Whether they truly believed it, this was the language and context that those who taught them English and Christianity offered. Or as Cheyfitz would put it, such constructed figures had prescribed paths, and when projected on the Hawaiians, these paths are then taken for the proper. Only these prescribed versions of Hawaiians could have mana in missionary discourse as this was the only versions of Hawaiians that they had any pilina with, the only ones they would give mana to; anything outside of that was literally unthinkable.

Similar to an echo chamber, the figurations continually reinforced themselves with each new encounter. Because of these prescribed paths, Nancy Ruggles, who was also on the *Thaddeus,* describes in her journal the Hawaiian women she first encountered as "monstrous" (1819–1820, 21). Upon arriving three years later, Charles Samuel Stewart, one of the second company of missionaries, echoed his predecessor Bingham, describing these "wretched creatures" as "half-man and half-beast," and asking, "Do they not form a link in creation, connecting man with the brute?" (1830, 88). Even Betsey Stockton, the freed slave and first single American woman to be sent abroad as a missionary, and therefore something of a figure herself, reproduces Stewart's and Bingham's sentiments about Hawaiians: "Their appearance was that of half man and half beast—naked—except a narrow strip of tapa round their loins. When they first came on board, the sight chilled our very hearts. The ladies retired to the cabin and burst into tears; and some of the gentlemen turned pale: my own soul sickened within me, and every nerve trembled" (1825, 36). Because the missionaries had come to save heathens, to do so, the Hawaiians had to be initially figured as beasts, subhuman, chattering, and savage. Otherwise the mission had no mission—if not debased, Hawaiians would not be in need of salvation.

This is not to say that the missionaries' disgust and horror at Hawaiians was feigned or strategic. In fact, there was *no other way* that they could have seen Hawaiians. Even the mission's beloved Obookiah had to be figured in a particular way. Historian David Chang points out several mischaracterizations of ʻŌpūkahaʻia in the English-language account of his life (the one used to raise money for the mission), such as him being older, having himself been a highly trained priest, having a higher genealogical rank, etc., and says that the difference between these openings [in the English- and Hawaiian-language versions of 'Ōpūkahaʻia's life story] suggests that the English-language version was cavalier with the facts and details of 'Ōpūkahaʻia's background because their accuracy was not really relevant to the purposes of the American evangelicals who wrote and read the book. To get that audience to pay for and pray for missionary enterprise to Hawaiʻi it was sufficient that they believe that an ignorant savage was brought to the light of Christian faith, and his tragic death was a call to bring the light of the gospel to his benighted homeland. (2016, 88)

I would go so far as to say, however, that it was not that those who wrote the life of Obookiah in English were playing fast and loose with the facts of his life, but that there was no other way that they could portray his life. As described before, for mana to be given, there had to be pilina, and the missionaries did not have pilina with any other mana of this story. It was not *sufficient* that the audience believe that Obookiah was an ignorant savage who was brought to the light of Christian faith rather than 'Ōpūkahaʻia being "a trained Kanaka spiritual adept whose explorations brought him to study Christianity and to believe that it held power for his people" (Chang 2016, 80); it was *required*. The expense and labor of a mission was only justified if the natives were in dire need of salvation, and salvation was only a true accomplishment if visited upon the wretched. So the missionaries figured Hawaiians as such.

The mission was therefore to raise Hawaiians up from their status as the very basest of creatures by bestowing upon them the gift of humanity through Christ: "Before any great results can be expected, the rudiments of moral truth must be brought to the minds of multitudes; the conscience is to be formed and enlightened; the heart is to be assailed by the simple, yet commanding, motives of the gospel" (ABCFM 1819b, 40). All that was necessary for Hawaiians to become human could therefore be supplied by the missionaries, and whether they accurately understood the people or not, as the missionaries enacted more and more of these figurations and cultural translations, the cumulative result assumed the power of actuality. Or as Tejaswini Niranjana explains, "in forming a certain kind of subject, in presenting particular versions of the colonized, translation brings into being overarching concepts of reality and representation" (1992, 2).

This projected dehumanization of Hawaiians was therefore paradoxically the first stage in the erasure of difference, a process commonly executed by translation in colonial situations. Though it may seem counterintuitive that open disgust is laying the foundation for erasing difference, through their distaste and visceral disregard for Hawaiian humanity, the missionaries enfolded the natives within a teleological model of development that was (and still is) so prevalent in the Western understanding of the world. Hawaiians and other Indigenous peoples were situated within a hierarchy of peoples that defined them as lesser-developed humans who could aspire to the telos of enlightened European and American society. Binamu's smug "Yes" therefore testifies to his certainty that the Bible, and through it Christianity, would move Hawaiians up this developmental ladder. The barbarous and savage Hawaiians and other peoples under the threat of colonization therefore could not possess epistemically different ways of relating to each other and to the world, since a self-sufficient, culturally complete people with their own proud traditions and cultural practices, and different aspirations for their lāhui, would have no need to be saved through the Bible. Even if Christianity managed to gain a foothold, it would be only as a foreign curiosity. If, however, Hawaiians were seen as situated within the Christian teleological model of the world, then the Bible and its attendant civilizing powers would represent the only path available for a savage and benighted people to achieve the telos of Euro-America. Hawaiians were therefore not autonomous or distinctive. They were simply waiting to be translated up into the modern era, and this erasure of essential difference—but insistence on retarded development—became the justification for the missionaries' transformation of Hawaiians from chattering, bestial savages into people worthy of the Christian God's grace. And translating the Bible would be the key to their ascendance, and eventual salvation.

The Language of Salvation

What the missionaries themselves, along with some historians who were their contemporaries, were saying reveals how Hawaiians were being figured into a salvable people. Examples arise throughout the Bible translation process, not in terms of the word- and sentence-level transactions between 'ōlelo Hawai'i and English, but through how the Bible was translated and discussed. In this section, I will focus on who is presented as carrying out the translation, and how 'ōlelo Hawai'i is presented as deficient, which supposedly justified the missionaries' practice of making up new words.

Who actually did the translation? Who had the mana unuhi? Although missionary correspondence and independent sources list who translated which sections of the Bible, given the missionaries' language limitations, Hawaiians undoubtedly played a major role in the translation. And yet, although Richards mentions regularly working with David Malo (ABCFM 1827, 77) and sometimes the "governor" (Kuakini) gets mentioned as assisting (ABCFM 1828, 93), by and large, the Hawaiians who helped with the translation are not named. An 1857 article in *Ka Hae Hawaii* provides a few familiar names:

> Eia kekahi mau kokua i ka unuhi olelo ana, o Keoni Ii ia Binamu, o Davida Malo me Hoapili ia Rikeke, a o Kuakini me Kamakau ia Tatina ma i Kailua.
>
> [Here are some of the helpers in the translation process: John 'Ī'ī with Bingham, David Malo and Hoapili with Richards, and Kuakini and Kamakau with Thurston and the others in Kailua.] ("No ka unuhi" 1857, 57)

But the use of "kekahi mau" (some of the) suggests that there were indeed more, and Richards says that he would read his translations "to a number of people" (ABCFM 1827, 77). Artemas Bishop also reported that the translators would avail themselves of the "best native aid" (1844, 75), but there is little to no indication of who these other natives might be.

It would be easy, and probably justified, to chalk this erasure up to the missionaries' casual disregard for Hawaiians, apparent in the comments they made upon first arriving about the barbarous and savage nature of the people. But while some of this may be at play, that the missionaries acknowledge elsewhere they could not have carried out this translation at all without the cooperation of Hawaiians rules out the possibility of easy dismissal alone. William Richards's account of his cooperative translation process suggests how sober the missionaries actually were about their lack of language proficiency. "My inability has lain in my ignorance of the language," he writes, so "the course I pursue is this. In the morning I take Knapp's Testament, Schleusner's Lexicon, Dodnedge's Exposition and a few other helps and strictly examine the passage I design to translate. In the afternoon, *Maro* [Malo], my teacher comes, and Taua, the Tahitan [*sic*]. I give the passage to Maro according to the best knowledge I have of the language. Then Taua gives it to him from the Tahitan [*sic*] translation, then Maro puts it into pure Hawaiian and I write it down" (ABCFM 1827, 77). Bishop also claimed that "the labor of obtaining the true interpretation of obscure passages was comparatively easy, to that of finding suitable words and phrases by which to express it in the Hawaiian language" (1844, 75), and so, just as the missionaries had consulted Thomas Kendall's Māori grammar to guide their efforts with the speller and other translations, they also relied on translations (and translators) coming out of Tahiti to aid their Bible translation. In fact, they welcomed any assistance at all.

Much is made of the arrival of the LMS missionary William Ellis at the strong urging of the Hawaiian mission because he was well-versed in Tahitian, and quickly able to communicate with Hawaiians, serving as a conduit that granted the ABCFM missionaries greater access to the people. But for the translation of the Bible, the many converted Tahitians who either came with Ellis or at the request of the aliʻi were of greater influence and value. They had a much stronger pilina to Hawaiians than the missionaries and were thus given more respect. Due to their shared culture and linguistic overlap, they could also compare notes with the Hawaiians about the word choices for the Tahitian scriptures.

The Tahitian missionary Auna, who came with a visiting English delegation of missionaries in 1822 (Barrère and Sahlins 1979, 22), was said to have done "more at the time to accelerate the spread of the Gospel than any other person" (Maude 1973, 191). Auna lived with the powerful aliʻi wahine Kaʻahumanu for well over a year, teaching literacy and Christianity to the mōʻī and aliʻi (*Sandwich Island Mission Journal,* May 9, 1822, 19; Barrère and Sahlins 1979, 22), and he is also credited as one of the major reasons that the mōʻī Liholiho began to accept the missionaries (Maude 1973, 189). An earlier Tahitian arrival, Toketa, is said to have learned to read ʻōlelo Hawaiʻi after an hour's instruction; he helped with the Bible translation and was the author of what was possibly the first manuscript in ʻōlelo Hawaiʻi (Barrère and Sahlins 1979, 19–20). Other Tahitians included Tauʻa and Tauʻawahine, Kaʻaumoku, Stephen Pupuhi (who had also attended the Cornwall school, though they wrote his name as Popohee), Tute, who was the tutor and chaplain of the mōʻī Kauikeaouli and other aliʻi for thirty-three years (Barrère and Sahlins 1979, 22–23), and Kahikona, whose influence Dorothy Barrère described as "at least as effective as that of the missionaries" and who had been rewarded by the chiefs with gifts of land (1989, 77). And yet, although it seems like they played an important role in the translation process (and the early history of Christianity in Hawaiʻi), like the Hawaiians involved, these Tahitians are barely mentioned at all. Though the missionaries themselves looked at the Tahitian translations, alongside the Greek, Latin, and English (Ballou and Carter 1908, 16; Loomis 1824–1826, entry for March 8, 1825, 29), without the native translators, their still-limited Hawaiian-language proficiency probably meant that they could only seek out Hawaiian analogues to the Tahitian words they could recognize.

For the most part, the missionaries were quite honest about their language deficiencies, and generally acknowledged that Hawaiians (and Tahitians) were crucial to the translation process. Why then were John Papa ʻĪʻī, David Malo, Kēlou Kamakau, Hoapili, and Kuakini, some of the most respected Hawaiian intellectuals of the time, consigned with the Tahitians to the footnotes in accounts of the translation process? Though this was at least partly the result of missionary chauvinism, the more likely explanation is that for the Bible translation to be successful, they *could not* be mentioned. The mana unuhi had to come from the missionaries and the missionaries alone. The missionaries were the ones bringing salvation to Hawaiʻi, with the Bible translation as the main pillar supporting their efforts. They possessed the religious training, the missionary zeal, the religious imperatives. They were the bearers of the light. If the benighted heathen savages were responsible for the translation, were beings of mana unuhi in their own right and therefore necessary contributors to spreading Christianity's influence across the lāhui, how could this Bible be trusted as truly representing the word of God? If important parts of the translation came from the bestial Hawaiians themselves, wouldn't that also mean that they had provided some of the keys to their salvation? And that some of these were even grounded in their knowledge of heathen traditions and culture? At a time when the missionaries hesitated to even baptize Hawaiians until they were absolutely sure their conversion had fully taken hold, it was unthinkable that Hawaiians could be recognized as prime actors in the production of the main avenue to salvation.

The same thing can be seen happening in Cherokee country, where David Brown (with the assistance of the chief George Lowrey) and John Arch had created very popular manuscript translations of the New Testament into Cherokee. Yet, when the missionary Samuel Austin Worcester—the nephew of the reverend who had given the first company of ABCFM missionaries to Hawaiʻi their instructions upon departure—arrived in 1825, one of his first acts was to begin a new translation of the Bible in collaboration with Elias Boudinot, who had gone to the Cornwall school (Wyss 2012, 200–201). The initial translations by the young Cherokee men were characterized by Pamela Jean Owens as "the New Testament translated by their own kinsmen, into their own language, using a writing system developed, refined, and popularized entirely as their own," and "it struck fear into the hearts of church leaders back in New England" (2006, 8). Hilary Wyss states further that "David Brown and John Arch were guilty of no linguistic or cultural errors other than simply being Cherokee and taking control of Cherokee meaning" (2012, 201). Even though, just as in Hawaiʻi, many Cherokee played a crucial role in Worcester's translation of the Bible, "the missionary society arguably replaced one Indian Bible with another, although Samuel Worcester's presence assured them that the Bible remained in the hands of white missionaries, not Indian ones" (Wyss 2012, 204).

The best way to explain how threatening Indigenous Bible translators were to the missionary establishment is to turn to two Hawaiian concepts that appear throughout this book: ea and mana. Ea means many things, but the important shades here are life, breath, sovereignty, and rising. None of these words are equivalents; ea exists where they overlap. Ea is our connection to the ʻāina of Hawaiʻi, and also what Hawaiians exercise when we control our lāhui. For this reason, the anniversary of the return of Hawaiian control over Hawaiʻi after a brief takeover by a British agent in 1843 is called Lā Hoʻihoʻi Ea—the day when ea was returned. As explained earlier, mana, as we have heard, is a power or presence—a metaphorical weight almost—that inheres in all things. Anything of potential importance or value—places, people, akua, pōhaku, fishing implements—possesses mana. To translate "hoʻomana," to give mana or make something have mana, as "religion" is a misguided but extremely common practice, but it suggests something about the power of the process.

I bring up both mana and ea here because they are what is at stake. By putting their breath, their ea, into the words of the Hawaiian Bible, the aliʻi and knowledgeable kāhuna who helped the missionaries are infusing that work with mana and growing the ea of the lāhui as well. Though the missionaries never would have explained it this way, and were clearly unqualified as translators, they had to focus the attention on themselves, because anything more than mentioning the scant handful of names of such Hawaiian-language experts as ʻĪʻī, Malo, Kamakau, Kuakini, and Hoapili (or David Brown and John Arch, for that matter) would acknowledge that native peoples had their own mana and ea outside of what the Bible was going to bring them.

Denying this possibility led to some interesting logical turns in the missionaries' accounts of the unuhi process. For instance, Artemas Bishop's recollections quoted a few paragraphs ago take a surprising turn. Because the missionaries' command of Hawaiian was shaky, "we constantly availed ourselves of the best native aid we could procure to put each sentence into the true idiom of the language." This did not, however, mean that these experts *understood* these sentences: "As the native monitor often mistook the true idea of the sacred writer, as conveyed to him through the medium of his own language, he was liable to give us a wrong sentence, according to his own conception of the idea. A constant vigilance was therefore necessary on our part, in order to detect his mistakes, and take nothing for granted as correct which the native assistant proposed, and much effort and ingenuity was often required to get him to comprehend the true meaning which we wished him to clothe in suitable phraseology" (Bishop 1844, 75). The native speaker is blamed somehow for mistaking what they were being told the sacred writer was saying. In a footnote to his detailed analysis of the Bible translation, Kapali Lyon remarks that "it is curious that Bishop's mean-spirited account actually censures Hawaiians, rather than missionary ineptitude, and then praises his own and his ABCFM colleagues' 'vigilance' in keeping the Hawaiians on track" (2017, 143). The use of the passive voice when describing how the true idea of the sacred writer was "conveyed" to the Hawaiian expert "through the medium of his own language" presents another example of the transparency of translation in these kinds of colonial accounts. There is an assumption of complete communication between parties, and Bishop's language erases the missionary translator's halting and incomplete understanding of the language as a possible cause for any mistakes, leaving the Hawaiians responsible for any errors in "conveying" what the Bible was saying. But if the primary goal is to erase, or ignore, the role of the lāhui Hawai'i's mana and ea in figuring Hawaiians as salvable people, then the mental gymnastics Bishop performs here make sense. Hawaiians cannot be the agents of their own deliverance. The potential weak points in the translation are their language and they themselves. Only missionary vigilance can ensure accuracy and spiritual progress.

That same leap in logic takes place with regard to 'ōlelo Hawai'i. Especially early on in their language learning, the missionaries frequently comment on the paucity of Hawaiian. Its lack. How there is not enough raw material to craft a translation of the Holy Bible from it. Although they had little to no familiarity with the Hawaiian language, or with the Choctaw, or the Cherokee, or the languages of other heathens they were saving, the ABCFM instructed the second company to expect this: "the progress of divine truth among pagans, speaking a strange tongue, and not even having any language adapted to moral subjects, must be slow at first" (ABCFM 1819b, 40). Apparently, the deficiency of native languages was a matter of general knowledge, and Artemas Bishop found what he was supposed to, describing 'ōlelo Hawai'i as "a language which had never been cultivated, and whose words are limited by the paucity of ideas attained by an untutored people" (1844, 74).[12] As for Sheldon Dibble, who joined the four initial missionaries as a translator of Hawaiian, he remarked that "another obstacle may be imperfectly termed a destitution of ideas, and a consequent destitution of words on the subject of true religion" (1839, 135). Although Hawaiians had been writing highly metaphorical mele across multiple genres and giving mana to their four hundred thousand akua for more than a thousand years, somehow the language could not express religious concepts. Of course, the operative word for Dibble is "true," but ignoring or discounting a trove of "religious" vocabulary and then complaining about not having anything to work with when translating a spiritual text seems a little disingenuous. An observation from Lorrin Andrews further compounds missionary ignorance of the language: "The disposition of the Hawaiians to accommodate themselves to the ignorance of those who consult them, is a difficulty in the way of getting pure expressions. When consulted respecting any word or phrase, their object seems to be to find out how much the person consulting them knows respecting the point himself. And if he appears to know *anything* they will tell him he knows *everything*" (1837, 13; emphasis in original). Perhaps the observed "lack" and "destitution" inherent in ʻōlelo Hawaiʻi can be chalked up merely to Hawaiian politeness and missionary hubris. At any rate, Dibble goes on to explain that "in consequence of the destitution of terms, missionaries are obliged in their conversation, their preaching, and in their translations of the scriptures too, to use words nearest allied to the sense they would express" (1839, 137–138). What Dibble is complaining about here is the essence of translation—what anyone must do when moving from one language to another. No direct equivalence ever exists between words in different languages.

While paternalism runs through these assessments of Hawaiian, the conviction that the people must be tutored ties back into the missionaries' overarching project of figuration. Though the missionaries' poor language skills prevented them from recognizing the depths of ʻōlelo Hawaiʻi, they attributed it to problems with the language itself. The solution they adopted as early as 1824 should therefore not be a surprise: "A considerable number of words must doubtless be introduced from the Greek into the Hawaiian version, as there are many terms, and many ideas, for which there is nothing in this language to answer; even the most common terms, faith, holiness, throne, dominion, angel, demoniac, which so frequently occur in the New Testament, cannot be expressed with precision by any terms in the Hawaiian language" (*Sandwich Island Mission Journal,* October 21, 1824, 50). The Hawaiian term for making up new words is "haku"; it also means "boss" or "lord," and is the word actually chosen to translate *"the Lord"*—more evidence for Eric Cheyfitz's claim that "the imperialist believes that, literally, everything can be translated into his terms; indeed, that everything always already exists in these terms and is only waiting to be liberated" (1997, 195). Though the missionaries probably did not notice that choosing to haku new words gave them this particular status of haku in relation to Hawaiian, the practice reinforces their larger acts of figuration, designed to ensure that they must be the ones to introduce and explain concepts of salvation to the Hawaiians.

Here is how Bishop describes this process of haku:

> As our investigations into the structure of the language advanced, we discovered that by the combination of simple and familiar words descriptive of the thing intended to be expressed, whether a noun or verb, we were able to form new words to an *indefinite* extent, in perfect accordance with the genius of the language, and intelligible to the native reader. The *constant use* of this power enabled us to meet and overcome nearly every difficulty arising from the paucity of Hawaiian words, besides enriching the language with many hundreds of new terms, which are now common in use throughout the archipelago. (1844, 74; emphasis added)

In short, every time the translators encountered a word that was difficult to translate, they just made up a new word and said that that was the correct translation. Though they followed a rubric to guide the adoption of new words, the allure of making up new words and controlling their meaning must have been seductive for those missionary translators floundering in the shallows of ʻōlelo Hawaiʻi. The power to haku also countered the reticence of people like Amos Starr Cooke, who, as mentioned earlier, thought he could better learn the language if he actually cared about Hawaiians. By making up words, the missionaries were able to create safe zones for themselves within the language. To give themselves the mana unuhi. They did not need to bump up against the mana of the Hawaiian cultural values and mores—the life and the death—embedded in ʻōlelo Hawaiʻi because they could dictate exactly what a word meant. Though Bingham downplayed the extent of this process in his memoir, saying that "a few foreign words are introduced, and a few original words retained" in the Bible translation (1847, 531), Bishop puts the number somewhere north of "many hundreds" (1844, 74).

Bishop is confident that the words they have created are "in perfect accordance with the genius of the language, and intelligible to the native reader." Sheldon Dibble, whom J. S. Green called one of the best missionary translators, is less certain—not about the act of haku, but about just how intelligible the resulting words are:

In many instances they succeed, in a measure, by circumlocution; in others they use a sort of patch-work of native words. For instance: manao means thought, and io means true or real;—so the combination manaoio, is used for faith. Again, manao means thought, and lana means buoyant,—so the combination, manaolana, is made by us to express hope. Ala means to rise, hou means again, and ana is a participial termination;—so we make alahouana to signify the rising again, or the resurrection. We are obliged to manufacture many of the most important words expressive of religious subjects. *It is perplexing to the ignorant people, but it is unavoidable.* (1839, 137–138; emphasis added)

In practice, these portmanteau words must have often been as suggestive and bewildering as such contemporary fusions as *bromance, frenemy, froyo, glamping, jeggings,* or *cronut.* With almost two hundred years of usage, manaʻolana and manaʻoʻiʻo have become normalized. But some words—alahouʻana, for instance—can still rankle, much in the way *Belieber* does.

The process of haku allowed the missionaries to believe in the veracity and faithfulness of their translation, because they were the ones dictating that "manaʻolana" means "hope," and that "alahouʻana," as ugly as it is, means "resurrection." Without the certainty that accompanies making up new words, at least for the first couple of decades, the missionaries could not have so easily believed in the accuracy of their Biblical translations. But this was a moot point. Ultimately, neither the beauty nor the accuracy of the translation mattered; only the existence of the Holy Bible in ʻōlelo Hawaiʻi did. Once Hawaiians could read it, ask for it, and take it into their homes, they were a salvable people, worthy of the blessings the mission was promising through publishing.

Once the entire Bible translation was completed and published in 1839, "ua koho ka Aha Misionari ia Binamu laua me Bihopa, e hooponopono hou i ka Baibala okoa, no ke pai hou ia" (the mission council chose Bingham and Bishop to revise the entire Bible for a reprinting) ("No ka unuhi" 1857, 58). When Bingham returned to the United States, Bishop was left in charge of this revision. He eventually reported that around seven thousand changes were made, mostly "corrections of the Hawaiian idiom," which he was still attributing to "the difficulty of finding corresponding words and phrases in the native language to express the ideas of the sacred writers" (1844, 75). Though Hawaiians such as Barenaba were writing in to the missionary-run Hawaiian-language newspapers to correct words being misspelled in the Bible translation (Charlot 2005, 42), no Hawaiian publicly called the translation a failure, or called for a complete overhaul. This should not be surprising. When Binamu and others told Hawaiians that the translation of the Baibala was "maikaʻi" (good, proper, well-done) (1839, 91), and even "hemolele," or perfect, or when they patiently preached and taught Hawaiians what new words like "manaʻolana" and "manaʻoʻiʻo" meant, the Hawaiians literally took their word for it. By translating the Bible and figuring the Hawaiians as a salvable people, the missionaries claimed to be the kumu and mākua of the people—their teachers and parents.

The fidelity of the translation was also taken for granted by those without a direct hand in its production and maintenance. The visitors and haole residents who saw the result assumed it was maikaʻi. Richard Harvey Dana Jr., for instance, claimed admiringly that "I found no hut without a Bible and hymnbook" (1969, 17), these being the only signs he needed to confirm the Hawaiians' progress toward salvation. Still later accounts, such as those by historian John Lydgate and Chief Justice Albert Francis Judd, praised the translation enthusiastically. Considering his importance in shaping Hawaiian law, which we will see in chapter 2, it is not surprising that Judd approved of this translation. On the jubilee of the Baibala Hemolele's first printing, he echoed Dana on its ubiquity in Hawaiian households, and celebrated it: "There can be no more useful thing done than to supply every Hawaiian house with a Bible—from Hawaii to Niihau.... Better let the Hawaiian be without his calabash and his meat dish, his holding of land, his bed, or his right to vote, rather than be without his Bible" (1889, 57). For Judd, neither the aliʻi nor their advisors are the equals of the mana-filled translators who made this possible, for "they who furnish a people with the Bible, which is the bread and water of life, are more to be honored than those who found a kingdom" (1889, 57). For a Supreme Court justice to elevate the Baibala above the ea of the people, or even their need for food, shows how this translated scripture came to override or erase such Hawaiian concerns as ea, ʻāina, lāhui, ʻai, ai, nā mea a pau. This first major act of translation by missionaries in the Hawaiian Kingdom also contributed to the hoʻmana ʻana, the introducing, reinforcing, and institutionalizing of many of the colonial structures—including Western understandings of relationships to land and people, and heteropatriarchy as a foundational structure of society—that would come to damage so profoundly the nohona Hawaiʻi—the way we live as Hawaiians.

Historians such as Lydgate went still further, crediting the missionaries with saving the Hawaiian language through their translation:

> With characteristic wisdom they made use of the best Hawaiian learning available, so that the translation was rendered into idiomatic Hawaiian, not Hawaiianized English. The result has been that the Hawaiian Bible, being the one classic vernacular, has stamped the language and given it permanent form. In a word, it has done for Hawaiian what the King James version has done for English. *If it had not been for this fixative influence of the Bible the language would probably have gone to pieces, or degenerated into a mongrel slang.* As it is, the Hawaiian Bible will pass into History as the classic presentation of the Hawaiian language; which surely reflects no small degree of credit on the Missionaries. (1917, 85; emphasis added)

A particular mana of the moʻolelo of how the Baibala Hemolele claimed the mana of primacy, and the Bible translation has certainly passed "into History as the classic presentation of the Hawaiian language." Over a century and a half later, Jack Keppeler, the project manager of the Bible digitization project Baibala.org, claims that as "the first major document in the conversion of an oral tradition into a standardized written language," the Baibala Hemolele "was *the* primary document in the Hawaiian language." Helen Kaowili, the assistant project manager, agrees, asserting that "this translation gives us the Hawaiian language as it was heard in 1830, as it was first recorded" (quoted in Adamski 2006).

As we have seen, however, the Baibala Hemolele was not a "recording" of ʻōlelo Hawaiʻi in any way, shape, or form. The supposed "fixative influence" that Lydgate describes was actually a force for great change. Though still a cherished document for many Hawaiians, and often the text from which many kūpuna learned Hawaiian (Lyon 2017, 140), a translation—*any* translation—cannot and should not be the standard by which a language is judged. Those truly responsible for preventing 'ōlelo Hawai'i from "going to pieces" or "degenerating into a mongrel slang" were the Kānaka Maoli themselves. Initially skeptical of the missionaries and the literacy they offered, Hawaiians' pursuit of alphabetic literacy nevertheless became a national effort. Largely by means of translated texts, by 1832, nine hundred missionary schools were educating fifty-three thousand students, mainly adults—roughly 40 percent of the total Hawaiian population (Beyer 2014, 8). In telling contrast, as late as 1837, only 1,259 Hawaiians had become members of the church—though that number would soon jump exponentially, thanks to the completion of the Bible translation and accompanying spiritual revival near the end of the decade (Frear 1906, 22). And only then did educating children become the priority, as the nation moved toward universal literacy in Hawaiian.

The first Hawaiian-language newspaper, *Ka Lama Hawaii* (The Hawaiian torch), was published in 1834 at Lahainaluna High School. Only four years later, Laura Fish Judd, wife of the missionary doctor Gerritt P. Judd, wrote that the proportion of Hawaiians who could read and write in their own language was "estimated as greater than any country in the world, except for Scotland and New England" (1880, 79). Twenty years later, the *New York Tribune* reported that Hawai'i had surpassed New England (Day and Loomis 1973, 31). Literacy grew so quickly and became so widespread that by 1841, an understanding of "reading, writing, geography, and arithmetic" was required for the positions of governor, judge, tax officer, land agent, or "any office over any other man." Furthermore, couples could marry only if both could read (Townsend 1897, 49).

Though educational opportunities and publication venues such as the newspapers initially came through the mission, in almost no time at all, Hawaiians grasped literacy and Western education so well that they began to take over the literary means of production themselves. Both the missionaries and the foreign business establishment were soon scrambling to keep up with kānaka 'ōiwi often wielding not only bilingual literacy but the specific translation skills necessary to navigate that literacy, and to forward the interests of the lāhui. These Hawaiians would soon be authoring and publishing their own laws, books, newspapers, and pamphlets, creating original works in 'ōlelo Hawai'i and translating important texts from other languages. Print was also enlisted to mālama, or care for, traditional moʻolelo and mele, and certain cultural practices. Editorials in the newspapers called out corruption, whether kanaka or haole. Poetically worded petitions from around the kingdom advocated limiting the power of the haole. Though a stunning and unqualified success for the mission, alphabetic literacy also gave Hawaiians powerful tools for realizing their own sovereignty. The next several decades would be highly contested ground, with mana unuhi flowing back and forth and foreign influences trying to use translation and literacy to curb Hawaiian ea, while Hawaiians in turn were using the same tools to assert their own powers.

Chapter 2

Mai ke Kānāwai a i ka Law

Translation and the Legal System in the Hawaiian Kingdom

"E Boasa, ua lohe anei 'oe?"
Boaz snapped out of his reverie, quickly dipping his nib into the ink and noting the changes the ali'i had requested, " 'Ae, 'ae, e ke ali'i."
The mō'ī and ali'i were ranged about him. Various kahu moved about unobtrusively in the background, bringing refreshments or attending to the needs of the ali'i, sometimes ducking close to whisper something to one of their charges.
Despite it all, the ali'i all watched him intently. It was unfamiliar but important work.
They had been at it all day for the last three days already, and Boaz was feeling the strain. But this was exactly why he had gone to Lāhainaluna.
Well, maybe not exactly. Everyone who went to school there was trained to serve the lāhui in some way, but he had never expected that he would be the one writing laws for the kingdom.
He glanced at Malo and the others. They had all gone to school together, but the mō'ī felt that he had gotten the best grasp of political economy, which is why he was here now, reading aloud the laws he had written.
He was proud of his grasp of English, and he had sometimes used the haole laws as models where appropriate, but he was glad that the ali'i were here to make sure that the laws fit with what was pono for the lāhui.
After each day's session of getting rewrites from the ali'i, he spent several more hours incorporating them and copying out the revised laws. He wished he could close his eyes, just for a bit.
"E Boasa, ua lohe anei 'oe?"

While translation had a huge ideological impact on how Hawaiians were to be perceived—i.e., as a salvable people—in the first decades of the nineteenth century, translation initially played little role in the day-to-day lives of kānaka living outside of the ports. Those who lived out in the countryside and were known as kuaʻāina (the back of the land/those who carried the land on their back/those who worked the land) had few dealings with foreigners, save for the occasional sightseer or migrant missionary. But mana unuhi soon became an important force affecting everyone, because as the kingdom moved away from the familiar traditional governmental structures to what would become a constitutional monarchy, translation increasingly came to dictate much of what kānaka were allowed to do in their daily lives, specifically through its inextricable role in law. Law was the principal agent in the refigurations of Hawaiians through translation that wrought massive changes, giving mana to very specific mana/versions/narratives of kānaka, redefining how Hawaiians could interact with the ʻāina and even with each other.

Unlike many things foreigners presented as requirements for a civilized life—stuffy clothes, enforced monogamy, last names—Hawaiians were not unfamiliar with the idea of law. Though not as universal and regularized as the kind of law the haole envisioned, the kapu system had governed Hawaiian life for countless generations. It was complex, and often based on time, context, and place—for instance, when kapu were placed that restricted the gathering of particular fish during their spawning season. Kapu often had to do with the maintenance and sanctity of mana, which is, as we know, the power inhering, and sometimes accumulating, in all things. For the aliʻi, kapu mandated or prohibited certain actions depending on context, and these kapu came into play for them at all times. For the makaʻāinana, however, while still governed by the kapu, their distance from aliʻi, both physically and spiritually, likely affected their behaviors and activities less. For instance, preparing and eating food were activities strictly divided between men and women. Men were responsible for all the food preparation, preparing separate imu, or earth ovens, for the men and the women, who then had to eat separately. Yet Mary Kawena Pukui remarks that "though the mashing of cooked taro corms to make poi was normally the work of men every woman knew how to do it and would make poi for herself when left alone" (Handy and Pukui 1950, 176). It would make sense that practicality at times took precedent over kapu, particularly outside of aliʻi oversight.

The word that came to be used for "law" in a Western sense was "kānāwai," a term that had previously referred to particular named edicts that akua and aliʻi could proclaim. The most well-known kānāwai today is ke kānāwai Māmalahoa. It is enshrined in the State of Hawaiʻi's constitution, in translation, and is depicted on the Honolulu Police Department's badge. Though Hawaiʻi's current status as a militarily occupied nation makes such uses gross appropriations of our cultural patrimony by the occupying settler colonial establishment, they suggest just how ubiquitous the Māmalahoa is. Kamehameha I famously came up with this kānāwai after raiding a fishing village as a young aliʻi. When he came ashore, the villagers fled. Kamehameha gave chase to two fishermen, but when his foot became lodged in a lava crevice, one of them struck him on the head with a paddle. Kamehameha's edict arose from his shame about his own unprovoked attack: "E hele ka ʻelemakule a moe i ke ala; e hele ka luahine a moe i ke ala; e hele ke keiki a moe i ke ala, ʻaʻole mea pepehi wale iho" (Let the old man go and lie in the road, let the old woman go and lie in the road, let the child go and lie in the road, none shall hurt them) (Hoʻoulumāhiehie 1905–1906b, April 3, 1906). The haʻi moʻolelo (historian/storyteller) Hoʻoulumāhiehie even claims that wishing to proclaim the kānāwai Māmalahoa across the entire pae ʻāina is what drove Kamehameha to bring all of the islands under his sway (June 12, 1905).

Another well-known kānāwai was the Kaiʻokia. After Kekaihinaliʻi, the great flood, Kāne proclaimed this law separating the land from the sea (Pukui and Elbert 1986, 127). It was also the restriction that Pele placed upon her lover Lohiʻau after coming to him in a dream. When she sent her youngest sister Hiʻiakaikapoliopele[1] from Hawaiʻi Island in the east to fetch Lohiʻau on Kauaʻi in the west, she proclaimed the Kaiʻokia. Everyone was to keep separate from Lohiʻau upon pain of death; none were to sleep with him (Hoʻoulumāhiehie 2007b, 12). Another familiar proclamation, the Mauʻumae kānāwai, kept canoes off the water for three days (Dibble 2005, 20). Though often associated with particular individuals, divine or earthly, and usually contingent on time or context, kānāwai were still similar enough to Western notions of law that Hawaiians could make the connection.

It is tempting to look back at our history and believe that at one point we were governed by our traditional kapu and kānāwai, then at a later point we had a system of Western laws giving primacy to English, and that a gentle curve of gradual but inevitable change joined them, with unuhi the means for the smooth transition from deficient 'ōlelo Hawai'i to the linguistic riches of English. Yet as historian Noelani Arista asserts, "kapu continued to have a life as oral law to which Hawaiian people were subject, even after the 1819 casting down of the 'ai kapu" (2018, 133), reminding us that as with any major cultural transition, what actually occurred was a contested zigzag that could have completely reversed course several times. To this day, Hawaiians continue to push for changes in the laws regarding the status of our language; we shall see a few examples in chapter 5. But by paying attention to mana unuhi and the course of law in the nineteenth-century kingdom, we can trace how translation functioned as the oft-contested engine domesticating Hawaiians and Hawaiian cultural understandings into forms legible to foreigners[2] through a process of figuration, similar to the one described in chapter 1, that literally stripped Hawaiians of their connection to 'āina and severely damaged their legal agency.

While poetry is often identified as the highest use of language because of the art and skill involved, in pragmatic terms, legal language is arguably the most powerful because it directly affects people's lives, dictating our actions and how we interact with the world around us. According to postcolonial language scholar Rachel Leow, "of all the aspects of governance, the negotiation of justice and social conduct is where the most attention to language and its communicative nuances is required, and where the daily business of governing comes most closely into contact with the largest range of society" (2018, 33). As Hawaiian scholar Kēhaulani Kauanui asserts, there was still "some consistency of customary practice outside formal law" (2018, 143), particularly in regard to how Hawaiian women were affected by the legal system, but as Jon Osorio notes, "all of the most significant transformations in nineteenth-century Hawai'i came about as legal changes: in rulership, in land tenure, in immigration, and especially in the meaning of identity and belonging. The Hawaiian saying 'I ka 'ōlelo nō ke ola, i ka 'ōlelo nō ka make' reminds us that language is a creator and a destroyer, and law is nothing if not language" (2002, 251). Though I would add massive population decline due to disease to the list as a significant transformation that did not come about due to legal change, his point is well-taken. "I ka 'ōlelo nō ke ola, i ka 'ōlelo nō ka make" (in language there is life, and in language there is death) really underscores not just the power of language in the law, but in nineteenth-century Hawai'i in particular, the power of unuhi. After all, if life and death are in our 'ōlelo, what happens when you translate into English? Though it was not always seen as such in the nineteenth century, translation is a dependent, interpretive act, which necessitates an uneven transfer of the ola and the make in 'ōlelo.

For Jon Osorio, legal language was the prime force undermining mana and ea:

> Our submission to the language of law and especially to its ubiquity and its fickleness is what, I believe, has so altered our sense of ourselves and our inherent sovereignty. It was law that positioned Natives and haole as subjects and citizens in the kingdom through the promulgation and termination of constitutions, through the election of Native and haole officials, all of which, in the long run, deprived Natives of any meaningful participation in their own governance. In the process the kānaka were continually subjected to the pronouncements of their difference and inferiority, which both enabled and validated their dispossession. (2002, 251)

One important disagreement I would have with Osorio's assertion, however, is that *law* did not position kānaka maoli as subjects and citizens in the kingdom, *translation* did. As they had been for generations, kānaka were still maka'āinana. They still saw and carried themselves in ways that venerated the ali'i and the 'āina. But the mana of those figurations began to be undermined. Trouble arose when translation began to say that "maka'āinana" was the same as "subject" or "citizen." Hawaiians were figured as having the same rights, duties, and motivations as any proper Englishman or American—no more and no less. Not only did translation redefine the word, it redefined our relationships and connections to the land and to the government.

This figuration is the subject of this chapter. During the 1820s and 1830s, when the Bible was being prepared, translation was going in one direction—into Hawaiian—and only a handful of people could participate. In the late 1830s and 1840s, however, as the nation increasingly assumed the forms of written law and a constitutional monarchy, and as more haole assumed powerful positions in government, translation became increasingly necessary for the day-to-day operations of the kingdom. It also became multidirectional—into, but also *from* Hawaiian—as more and more Hawaiians translated texts for Hawaiian purposes, developing a powerful and cosmopolitan practice that we will examine in chapter 3. Such intentions clashed with those of the haole, with the assertions of each group seen as threatening to disempower the other. But I will show, mana unuhi and who had the power to translate became one of the primary sites of contestation, and due to the legal model that prevailed, Hawaiian participation in the process of translation did not translate into Hawaiian empowerment.

Along with traditional kapu, the translated Bible and the laws of God it articulated were the foundations of the eventual legal system, but because Hawaiʻi's circumstances meant that the laws had to be constantly translated, the practice of unuhi itself was as influential as the Bible, if not more so. To trace mana unuhi in this chapter, we will first describe how the early laws were proclaimed, then identify who was writing and/or translating the laws, and in what languages. How the kingdom dealt with the fact that it essentially had two sets of related but different laws will also be addressed, and I will conclude with the kingdom's Supreme Court, and how one justice embodies the fact that with the force of law behind it, translation could easily cause harmful ruptures.

The Troubled Early Development of Law

While I explained earlier that Hawaiians' kapu and kānāwai were similar to the succeeding concept of law, when I use that term from here on, I will be referring only to the development of codes and statutes in a Western style of law. This distinction also serves as a reminder not to accept easy translation. All too often we create easy equivalences in our minds, losing nuance and analytical edge, especially in a place like Hawaiʻi, where so many understandings of how history played out were and are being contested. The easy equivalency that comes from translation is seductive in that way, creating shorthands and allowing you to say that two things that are very different are essentially the same. That two very different worldviews can map neatly and exactly on top of each other. And this damaging equivalency is what would come to happen with the Hawaiian system of law.

As more Hawaiian aliʻi and their followers were brought into the Christian fold, they began to want to reshape Hawaiian society to more closely fit the model of what their missionary teachers told them was civilized. The missionaries claimed to be taking a hands-off approach and not pushing specific laws. But at their 1823 annual meeting, as part of reviewing the previous year's accomplishments, setting the course for the upcoming year, and preparing the mission report for the ABCFM board back in the United States, they both embraced and rejected an obligation to advise the Hawaiian lawmakers:

> In regard to the preparing and establishing a code of laws for the regulation and government of these Islands, the committee are of the opinion that we ought not to be indifferent to the kind and nature of the laws about to be promulgated.... It will *doubtless* be the wish of the rulers of the nation to make their laws accord with and be founded upon the word and laws of God. Such being the case, it will be expected that we shall make known to them the laws of God, as well as the nature of those codes of laws that are adopted by Christian nations.
>
> [...]
>
> At the same time we are to leave entirely to the Rulers to adopt or reject such as they choose, *without our interference* or attempt to procure the adoption of any law or set of laws. (1824, 40–41; emphasis added)

The apparent contradiction here is in fact nothing of the sort. Though vowing not to interfere with the aliʻi's *choice* of laws, as the aliʻi were the final arbiters of what would become law, the missionaries committed themselves to making known "the laws of God" and the Christian-inspired laws of nations, which the aliʻi would then presumably be bound to follow. Of course, had this conversation taken place a decade later, the missionaries might have been less confident about the word "doubtless," but we will get to that.

In 1823, the mōʻī Liholiho and Kamāmalu made their ill-fated trip to London (they both would pass away there). While they were gone, Kaʻahumanu, the indomitable kuhina nui, was in charge—though some might argue that she was always in charge, whether the king was there or not. While individual aliʻi had been issuing laws here and there, and particularly in the ports, where sailors were known to be trouble (Kamakau 2001, 38), the kuhina nui proclaimed the most laws and held the most sway: " ʻO kēia ka wā kānāwai nui, hana kīpapa ua kānāwai, kū koʻa ka hana paila" (This was the time of a great many laws, so many they were tightly packed like paving stones, so many that they were heaped like piles of coral) (49).

As Kamana Beamer points out, there were many practical reasons for proclaiming laws, because

> law allowed a nation to stand as a theoretical equal in diplomatic negotiations with a country of superior military power. Law could set semiautonomous regulations within the defined boundaries of one's nation. Embracing the concept of law could also keep foreign powers from using their military strength to assume control over a "lawless" nation and population. For a nation without infantry, naval vessels, and steel, law was a tool that could be manipulated nonviolently to maintain effective control domestically while decreasing the likelihood of external intervention. (2014, 105)

The first government document printed was in fact a notice that seamen would be locked up in the fort if they disturbed the peace (Forbes 1998a, 388). Then, as now, laws were necessary to protect Hawaiʻi and Hawaiians from visitors who felt that they could do whatever they wanted once they set foot in our islands, and it was "the aliʻi themselves [who] recognized the need to adopt kānāwai, or written and published law, in the islands as the best way to control and discipline foreigners behaving badly on Hawaiian soil" (Arista 2018, 137). As Beamer also suggests, many of the Western trappings of "civilization" adopted by Hawaiians were strategic, and there was a particular mana to law. Knowing that how they presented themselves on the international stage would heavily influence how other nations treated them, aliʻi and other kānaka wielding power chose to garb the lāhui in what other nations recognized as civilized and sovereign.

The more "pious" aliʻi passed laws intended to turn Hawaiʻi into a Christian nation, feeling strongly that some of the population "needed the restraints of law to preserve them from the temptations to which they were exposed" (ABCFM 1828, 78). The first laws were all based on the Judeo-Christian laws of God; there was even talk of granting the Ten Commandments the power of statute. The laws proclaimed by Kaʻahumanu outlawed the following:

- murder;
- robbery;
- theft;
- adultery;
- prostitution;
- polygamy;
- worshipping idols, wood, stone, shark, spirits, ancestors;
- worshipping any god other than Iēhova;
- hula, oli, mele, swearing;
- planting or drinking ʻawa;
- making alcohol. (Kamakau 2001, 64)

Punishments included death for offenses such as murder, and lashings for prostitution. Penal colonies were established on Kahoʻolawe for men and on Lānaʻi for women (Kamakau 2001, 49). According to Kēhaulani Kauanui, "by 1827 and 1829 the major elements of Christian law were set in Hawaiian law" (2018, 135).

Because these laws were proclaimed orally by criers, and applied to all, including foreign sailors and merchants, unuhi was involved from the start. Historians of Hawaiian law such as William Westervelt and former territory governor Walter Frear describe a relatively smooth and uninterrupted transition from kapu and kānāwai to law, recording little or no resistance to this Christianity-based approach. The only speed bumps mentioned were foreign challenges to particular laws, such as whaler riots over the banning of prostitution, or foreigners demanding that they be allowed to determine their guilt or innocence themselves, as in the case of British consul Richard Charlton and the famous Cow Proclamation (Kuykendall 1938, 126). But Hawaiian acceptance of these Christian laws was not universal. In fact, in 1829, the church only had 185 members—and 117 of them had been admitted that same year (Frear 1906, 22). Admittedly, many of these were very influential aliʻi, but the mission was still on rather shaky ground. Kamana Beamer briefly describes some of the aliʻi resistance to these new laws and ideology:

Not all aliʻi were supportive of Christian ethics and many aliʻi openly challenged Kaʻahumanu and her Christian policies. Liholiho himself never converted to Christianity and once rebutted Hiram Bingham's pleas for him to follow the ways of the Christian God by saying, "I am God myself. What the hell! Get out of my house!"

In ways similar to his brother, Kauikeaouli also rebelled against Christian ethics. Following the death of Kaʻahumanu in 1832, the nineteen year-old mōʻī reinstated aspects of Hawaiian traditional culture by taking an aikāne and considering a union with his sister. Even prior to Kaʻahumanu's death, her Christian policies were openly challenged by a faction of traditionalist aliʻi led by Kauikeaouli's kahu, Boki, and Liliha. Some even went as far as to call for the assassination of Kaʻahumanu: "E kaha i ka ʻōpū o Kaʻahumanu, a e ʻoki i ke poʻo"—let us slice her from end to end and remove her head. (2014, 114)

I would also like to draw further attention to Kauikeaouli's actions, because ka wā iā Kaomi, the time of Kaomi, was an important disruption of the burgeoning dominion of Christianity and law, which as Kēhaulani Kauanui points out, "were central to the nineteenth-century Western civilizing process, where the bourgeois family was the model to be emulated" (2018, 136). Refusing to be treated as a salvable people, or be translated, and therefore enfolded and defined by these newly introduced Christian laws, those who participated in ka wā iā Kaomi were rejecting such figurations and models as irrelevant to Hawaiian ea. They were reclaiming the mana unuhi.

Kaomi was the aikāne of Kauikeaouli. While we are still recovering the true depths of what aikāne relationships and connections entailed, to get a sense of what an aikāne is, one can think of someone of the same sex who is an intimate/favorite/friend/lover/partner/confidante/ally, and more—sometimes all at the same time. In contemporary contexts and discussions, much is made of whether or not aikāne had sex with each other, but truthfully such pleasure was not the defining aspect of aikāne or most other traditional relationships because Hawaiians did not draw sharp lines between the intimacy of friends and of lovers. (Indeed, "hoʻāo," one of the words used for the Christian concept of marriage, really only refers to someone who stayed the night.) Not surprisingly, though, the missionaries—who had translated

1 Corinthians 7:2 as "Aka, o moe kolohe auanei, ua pono no i kela kane i keia kane, kana wahine iho, a ua pono no i kela wahine i keia wahine, kana kane iho," mandating that to avoid fornication, each man needed his own woman, and each woman her own man—considered anything that sounded like moe kolohe (something like "mischievous sleeping") as horrifying and sinful.[3] This is to say nothing of the "homosexuality, polyandry, polygyny, and chiefly procreation among those within close degrees of consanguinity"[4] that the missionaries found in Hawaiian society (Kauanui 2018, 171). Aikāne relationships thus crossed that even-sharper line, so whenever they could, the missionaries translated the word as "friend," stripping from it any of its Hawaiian cultural aspects, reserving mana through unuhi only for their Christian ideals. Clearly then, the missionaries would have agreed with Hawaiian scholar Jamaica Osorio, who in her work on recovering Hawaiian pilina and relationships declares that "aikāne offers a first step into a world unmolested by toxic monogamy and heteropatriarchy" (2018, 78). The difference, of course, is that this step appalled and terrified the missionaries.

It should not then be surprising that a powerful early challenge to Western religion and law's figuration of Hawaiians as salvable people would arise from an aikāne relationship. Kauikeaouli, the young mōʻī, and his beloved aikāne Kaomi acted in stark contrast to the mission's teachings and the proclaimed laws against moe kolohe. Because of their aikāne pilina, Kauikeaouli elevated Kaomi to the title of mōʻī kuʻi, something along the lines of joint paramount chief (Kamakau 2001, 117), which made them the two most powerful people in the kingdom. Moe, Kaomi's father from Borabora, was himself an aikāne of Kahekilikeʻeaumoku, the brother of Kaʻahumanu. Kaomi's mother was a Hawaiian named Kahuamoa (Kamakau 2001, 117). A very bright young man, Kaomi was one of Hiram Bingham's first students after the mission arrived; Kaʻahumanu installed him as a teacher of Christianity and literacy for her followers ("No ka Holo" 1868, 1), and he had taken over the school of Auna, one of the Tahitians mentioned in chapter 1 (Barrère and Sahlins 1979, 22–23). But because the missionaries remained suspicious of how authentically Hawaiians had converted to Christianity, Kaomi was refused baptism, and soon grew disillusioned ("Ka Wa ia Kaomi" 1861, 94).

Though Kaomi and Kauikeaouli were in overlapping circles,

Kamakau said that it was Kaomi's healing abilities that brought him to the mōʻī's attention:

> He wahi ʻoihana akamai ma ka lapaʻau kāna wahi ʻoihana i makemake ai ka mōʻī. He wahi ʻike nāna i ke ʻano o ka maʻi, a he wahi ʻike hāhā.[5]
> [His skill at healing is what brought him to the attention of the mōʻī. He had knowledge of the symptoms of disease and some understanding of diagnosing illness through touch.] (Kamakau 2001, 117)

He was also amusing and smart and a good storyteller, and in time, Kaomi and Kauikeaouli became aikāne. When Kauikeaouli then made him mōʻī kuʻi, Kaomi could distribute land, clothing, and money, and even draw upon the kingdom's budget (Kamakau 2001, 117). He was indisputably the kingdom's most powerful aikāne, and his reach and influence show how woefully inadequate the mission's attempt was to refigure Kaomi and other aikāne by translating the term merely as "friend."

Kauikeaouli was nineteen years old at this point, and the very powerful and driven aliʻi Kaʻahumanu had just died, so "early in March [1833] a crier was sent through the streets to proclaim the abrogation of all laws except those relating to theft and murder" (Kuykendall 1938, 134). Ka wā iā Kaomi had begun on Oʻahu. It was not so much a rolling back of Western law as an assertion of the power of tradition not to be abrogated, diminished, or refigured through translation. It was a reclamation of the mana surrounding unuhi. When they learned about the changes in law, many foreigners were ecstatic, but the missionary establishment and Christian aliʻi were horrified. All the laws against "licentiousness" had been repealed. Two male lovers were running the kingdom. Rum, ʻawa, and ʻōkolehao were freely made and distributed. Hula and mele were performed again. Gambling ran rampant. People were again having sex with partners other than their spouses, sometimes in groups, and sometimes in groups with their spouses. Schools were closed. While some islands maintained the laws, hundreds of people were flocking to Oʻahu, which had already been a site of continuing struggle over Calvinist reforms while Boki and Liliha ruled a few years earlier (Kauanui 2018, 168–169), because "a Kalaeokalāʻau a Kaʻieʻiewaho, waiho aku ke kānāwai" (from Kalaeokalāʻau [most southwest point of Molokaʻi] to Kaʻieʻiewaho [the channel between Kauaʻi and Oʻahu], the law ends) (Kamakau 2001, 120).

Histories in English tend to represent ka wā iā Kaomi as an orgiastic explosion of lawlessness; Hawaiian-language accounts refer to it as a "haunaele," something like a riot or tumult or ruckus. But the length of time that it went on, and the thousands of Hawaiians who took part, some from other islands, suggest that it was more accurately a resurgence of previously suppressed activities that followed a freeing return to tradition. Though perhaps some simply wanted to have sex and drink when the opportunity arose, just as many, if not more, were expressing their discontent at their figuration as subjects under a Western law that criminalized Hawaiian values and practices in their lāhui, their aupuni. It is also important to note that the people were abandoning foreign law, not regulation itself. Though official kapu had been abrogated by the ʻai noa, the so-called free eating, and the pale lauʻī after Kamehameha's death, individual practices were still governed by kapu that dictated performance, context, and transmission. So for instance, the return to hula and mele was not a rejection of regulation, but the choice of a preferred kind of regulation. It was an assertion of ea and mana, and not just by the aliʻi who supported Kauikeaouli and Kaomi. The makaʻāinana involved were not Christians bound by these laws; they were not salvable people, nor did they need or want salvation. Instead of letting the Bible and the law, with their refiguring translations, dictate what it meant to be a Hawaiian, they themselves determined what they as makaʻāinana could do.

Though ka wā iā Kaomi was just as much about the desires of Kauikeaouli, those unhappy with the rejection blamed Kaomi, and plotted against his life. Although Kauikeaouli put guards around him, and proclaimed that no one was to enter his compound on pain of death, an aliʻi named Kaikioʻewa captured Kaomi. As Kaikioʻewa prepared to execute the young mōʻī kuʻi, Kaomi's guards fetched Kauikeaouli, who emerged victorious from a fistfight with Kaikioʻewa (Kamakau 2001, 121). In previous times, just to have touched Kauikeaouli's sacred person would have been unthinkable, so a fistfight indicates that some shifts in tradition had already taken place. And even though ka wā iā Kaomi had been going on for months, tensions ratcheted down after this, perhaps because both sides feared the possibility of civil war. The mōʻī and the Christian chiefs largely reconciled, Kaomi fell out of favor, and within a decade, Kauikeaouli would give his people their first Western, American-style constitution. But with an important difference—he would no longer be following the dictates of such law but authoring it.

Authors of the Law

At the age of twelve, Kauikeaouli had ascended the throne with the promise that "he aupuni palapala koʻu" (mine will be a nation of literacy/learning). After ka wā iā Kaomi, and in response to continued problems in the 1830s with France, Britain, and the United States over legal matters, he became more amenable to the advantages of a formal system of law, including staving off the consistent stream of colonial depredations. He decided that the best way to approach implementing such a system would be to have the aliʻi learn more about the options. As early as 1836, following the traditional model of enlisting teachers of religion and other branches of useful knowledge, the mōʻī began looking for an American teacher to teach them the science of government (Frear 1906, 34). When none was forthcoming, in 1839, William Richards at the urging of the aliʻi left the mission to work for the kingdom. According to Richards, "I engaged to act as interpreter and translator in government business of a public nature when called to it, and was to receive for my services 600 dollars a year, to be paid in quarterly enstalments [sic], of 150 dollars each." But he had instructional responsibilities as well, for "as soon as the arrangements were completed, I commenced the compilation and translation of a work on political economy, following the general plan of Wayland, but consulting Lay, Newman and others, and translating considerable portions from the 1st mentioned work" (1943, 66). He then delivered a series of lectures on the topic for the aliʻi (Frear 1906, 34).

While the vast majority of the population spoke ʻōlelo Hawaiʻi, English was already becoming a prestige language spoken by a small but very influential number of people. For this and other reasons, translators played major roles in the inner workings of the kingdom, and by all accounts, in this capacity, Richards had a major impact on how Kauikeaouli and the other aliʻi came to understand law and governance. As Kamakau notes,

I ka heluhelu ʻana o nā aliʻi i ka buke kālaiʻāina, a hoʻomaopopo i ke ʻano o nā aupuni kumukānāwai a me nā aupuni kumukānāwai ʻole, a laila, maopopo ihola. ʻO ke aupuni kumukānāwai, ʻo ia ke aupuni kaulana ma ka honua, a ʻo ia nō hoʻi ke aupuni poʻokela o nā mōʻī, nā aliʻi a me nā makaʻāinana. ʻO ia nā aupuni ʻoi kelakela ma ka naʻauao a me ka waiwai, a ʻo ia nā aupuni i kanu ʻia i ka holomua, i ka ʻimi waiwai a me ke kālepa. A laila, ua ao kanaka aʻela ka manaʻo o nā aliʻi, eia kā ka pono, eia kā ka waiwai, eia kā ka hanohano.

[When the aliʻi read the book on political economy and began to understand the aspects of constitutional and non-constitutional governments, it all became clear. The constitutional government was the most celebrated governmental model in the world, and it was also the most outstanding for the mōʻī, the aliʻi, and the makaʻāinana. They are the governments that are superior in enlightenment and wealth, and the governments that are planted in progress, economic growth, and trade. So it came to the aliʻi, that here indeed was good, here indeed was wealth, here indeed was glory.] (2001, 129)

Within a handful of months, Hawaiʻi had a Declaration of Rights and a constitution. Promulgated at Luaʻehu, Lāhaina, it came to be known as the Luaʻehu Constitution. While the legal system drew heavily upon Anglo-American common law, the United States' Constitution was the model for the 1840 Hawaiian Constitution—which took the form of a single document, unlike the amalgam of parliamentary acts, common law, conventions, and treaties that made up the UK "constitution."

As Kamakau suggests, the aliʻi quickly grasped the advantages of becoming a constitutional nation, not just because it would shape how the aupuni governed itself, but also because of the hanohano, or the favorable impression, it would make upon other nations. As Hawaiian historian ʻUmi Perkins notes, it would also show that the kingdom was progressive: "Aside from the Magna Carta forced upon King John in the 13th century, the US Constitution is the first modern constitution. Considering the slowness of a process such as 'constitutionalism,' we should appreciate the fact that the Hawaiian Kingdom had a constitution only 50 years after the US—this is a very quick response to the trend of devolving power from monarchs to people, ideas and rules" (2015). Perkins further asserts, albeit provisionally, that Hawaiʻi's 1840

Constitution was only the fifth single-document constitution in the world (2016), and the "very quick response" set the pattern for how the lāhui Hawai'i would pick what it considered to be progressive, modern ideas and ways to run the government. In the constitution of 1852, for instance, Article 12 outlawed slavery, further declaring, eleven years before Lincoln's Emancipation Proclamation, that any slave who made it to Hawai'i would be considered free. Since the kingdom did not have a history of slavery, abolishing it was not difficult in practical terms, but Article 12 shows that the mōʻī and aliʻi were not afraid to declare what kind of nation we were.

The drafting of the 1840 Constitution also set the model for how later laws would be enacted. A brilliant young Lāhainaluna student named Boaz Mahune was given the initial responsibility of writing the laws, but without much guidance (Frear 1906, 36). Kauikeaouli merely directed him to make them conform to the principles of political economy that they had learned (Richards 1943, 67–68). Then the mōʻī and aliʻi discussed "what had been written for several hours a day for five days and then ordered particular rewrites; then they discussed them again, ordered more rewrites, and so on until they passed unanimously" (Frear 1906, 36). When published in 1842, the compiled laws were credited to David Malo, John Papa ʻĪʻī, Boaz Mahune, Timothy Keaweiwi, Daniel ʻĪʻī, and others (Thurston 1904, vii). But as with the constitution, the mōʻī, the kuhina nui, the House of Nobles, and the House of Representatives modified these laws. Many accounts of the development of law in Hawai'i give mana to the same old story, crediting the missionaries with bringing law to Hawai'i, showing them to be "the bringers of law and order, the champions of enlightened civilization and salvation—both physical and spiritual," leading to "a missionary-driven move to a Western system of land use, laws, and constitutional monarchy in the 1830s and 1840s" (Arista 2018, 5). But, as is made clear here, Hawaiians were the ones who took the lead in the creation and choosing of the laws and governmental system.

Most significantly for our purposes of discussing translation and agency here, the English translation of the constitution came with the following Translator's Note: "The translation is not designed to be a perfectly literal one, but wherever there is a variation from the letter of the original it is always made with the design of giving the sense more clearly.... The original [Hawaiian] will *of course* be the basis of all judicial proceedings" (emphasis added). The translator[6] is making it clear here that while liberties have been taken for the sake of clarity for those who cannot read the original, the translator can only exercise this freedom because "*of course*" the Hawaiian original, in the language spoken and written by the aliʻi and legislators, is the deciding version. The mana unuhi rests with kānaka. What this chapter hinges on is that this understanding would come to change.

Who is writing these laws is crucially important. Though different from kapu and traditional kānāwai, this foreign legal system is not a foreign imposition. Hawaiians are setting down the laws in the Hawaiian language for Hawaiian purposes. Although specifically Christian laws were rejected during ka wā iā Kaomi, Kauikeaouli did not resist the Western mode of proclaiming laws that would benefit the lāhui. Things got complicated as time went on, however, and Hawaiians seemingly started to lose control over setting the laws. One contributing factor was that, like the United States, the kingdom relied heavily on the British common law system, with its juries, separate jurisdictions of equity, and strong reliance on judicial precedent (Asensio 2010, 18). One judge's decisions could therefore ripple through the entire system of Hawaiian law, and some of the most consequential precedents rested upon which version of the law was the translation and which was "the original." This uncertainty arose because while the model for drafting the laws still generally held—someone composed the text, then the mōʻī and legislature gave feedback—very soon Hawaiians were not doing the initial writing.

In 1844, a young American lawyer named John Ricord arrived in Hawaiʻi. As the only trained lawyer in the kingdom, he was persuaded to take up the post of attorney general. He dove in and reorganized the government, setting out to make more comprehensive statutes while following procedures established earlier:

> The compiler in obeying that resolution, has submitted at intervals portions of the succeeding code to His Majesty in cabinet council of his ministers, where they have first undergone discussion and careful amendment; they have next been transferred to the Rev. William Richards, for faithful translation into the native language, after which, as from a judiciary committee, they have been reported to the

legislative council for criticism, discussion, amendment, adoption or rejection. The two houses have put them upon three several readings—debated them section by section with patience and critical care, altering and amending them in numerous essential respects, until finally passed in the form in which they now appear. (Kingdom of Hawaii 1845–1846, 7)

Ricord left the kingdom in 1847, but not before setting an important precedent—this "compiler" did his work in English, which was then translated into Hawaiian. Ricord also helped to recruit the twenty-six-year-old William Little Lee, the second trained lawyer in the kingdom. Lee came with his fellow "adventurer" Charles R. Bishop to Hawai'i from America, in search of a better climate for the tuberculosis he had contracted the previous year (Dunn 2004, 60–61). Lee's ascent was swift. In addition to becoming a judge and then chief justice of the Supreme Court, he was appointed to the privy council, became president of the Board of Commissioners to Quiet Land Titles, and was later elected to the legislature, where he became Speaker of the House of Representatives (61).

William Little Lee authored the 1847 Act to Organize the Judiciary Department, which mandated that the framers of kingdom law rely upon both common and civil law (McKean Jr. 1929, 199), even though in practice, like its American and British models, Hawaiian law relied heavily on common law. He went on to write civil and criminal codes, and to serve as the primary author of the 1852 constitution, which was reviewed by R. C. Wyllie for the cabinet and John Papa 'Ī'ī for the nobles (J. K. Osorio 2002, 86). A Scotsman opposed to universal suffrage, Wyllie complained that this constitution was too republican, and felt strongly that the British constitution would make a better model for Hawai'i (Kuykendall 1938, 115–116). Lee himself wrote in his preface to the penal code of 1850 that he believed that common law, rather than "the ancient laws and usages of the kingdom," could provide "the foundation of a code best adapted to the present and approaching wants and condition of the nation" (Kingdom of Hawai'i 1850, iv). Had Lee relied more on civil law, more power would have stayed in the hands of the mainly Hawaiian legislature, because in civil law–dominated contexts, judges are generally constrained to apply only the statutes enacted by the legislative branch, whereas in common law, judicial decisions and precedent play a much stronger part. This placed far more power over the law in the hands of the judiciary, which, as we will see, was largely made up of foreigners.

Uneven Transference in the Shift to English

Once the constitution was ready, the House of Representatives offered a joint resolution to print two thousand copies in Hawaiian and five hundred in English (Kingdom of Hawai'i 1851–1853, 287). The numbers speak to the proportions of language speakers. Hawaiian is by far the language in most common usage across the pae 'āina, and, despite the presence of thirteen haole among the forty-six legislators, in government as well (Lydecker 1918, 35). But the fact remains that the number of haole legislators is far out of proportion to their actual percentage of the population, and that the laws must be printed in English at all suggests that the kingdom is at a transition point in terms of translation of the law. From the time the first laws were proclaimed, and especially after the first printed laws appeared, legal translation became increasingly necessary, and therefore more and more institutionalized. In places more directly under colonial sway, such as South Africa, Canada, and parts of India, different sets of laws governed you if you were European or one of the local subjects under foreign rule (Merry 2004, 132; Massoud 2013, 47). Geographical proximity of the islands and the unified state of the kingdom allowed Hawai'i to enact one set of laws holding jurisdiction over everyone. But once the kingdom had laws, it needed translated laws, and unuhi became the hinge upon which the entire legal system swung. Every law had to be in Hawaiian and English—Hawaiian because it was the language of the people and the legislature, English because foreigners needed to be able to read the laws they were subject to, and because other nations could then see what kinds of laws Hawai'i was passing, and therefore gauge the "progress" it was making. It is not coincidental that after Keauikeaouli voluntarily gave his people a constitution, international recognition through treaties soon followed.

The problems arose from the actual application of the laws. The government understandably rejected the colonial practice of establishing two different legal systems—one for the people, another for the occupying foreigners—as something no enlightened nation would do. But the inherently interpretive nature of unuhi meant there were still two related but nonetheless different sets of laws. The result was a lot of baggy logic, dedicated to the progressive cause of insisting that the Hawaiian and English versions of the laws were equal because one was the original and one was the translation. For this reason, those who held mana unuhi—translators, interpreters, and bilingual speakers—became extremely important to the kingdom. Up until the overthrow of the kingdom, every session of the legislature dealt with the hiring and replacing of good interpreters and translators, and in 1890, the salary of the Supreme Court's interpreter was second only to those of the justices themselves (Asensio 2010, 16). One good example of the intellectual gymnastics and equivocation necessary to make laws in different languages seem equivalent is the tripartite treaties the kingdom would sign, such as the one between Great Britain, France, and Hawai'i in 1846 (Kuykendall 1938, 369). By definition, it is difficult to impossible for any translation to duplicate the original text, but in this case, a single translation into Hawaiian had to represent documents in two different languages.

The definitive example of the difficulties involved in insisting on the equivalence of the two sets of laws could well be Albert F. Judd's ruling in 1892. As Hawaiian lawyer and legal scholar Nāhoa Lucas notes: "In a later decision, Chief Justice Albert F. Judd, writing for the Supreme Court, attempted to reconcile any discrepancies in the translation and interpretation of the dual laws holding that 'the two versions constitute but one act. There is no dual legislation. As a rule, one version is the translation of the other. The effort is always made to have them exactly coincide, and the legal presumption is that they do'" (2000, 4). Though one language remains the "original," and thus binding, they are therefore somehow also exactly equivalent. This claim might seem to simplify matters legally, but a look at a few key terms immediately reveals the problems. Take for example the practice of having the word "kanaka" mean "man" in the Lua'ehu Constitution and subsequent statutes. A foreigner, and particularly a speaker of English, would understand "man" as something like a male human and beneficiary of the heteropatriarchal rights, privileges, and dominance laid out in the Bible and woven throughout the fabric of Western society. For a Hawaiian, however "kanaka" refers to someone always junior to the land, and in relationships that require service. The Pukui and Elbert dictionary entry offers "subject, as of a chief; laborer, servant, helper; attendant or retainer in a family (often a term of affection or pride)," and while the English word "service" may conjure up images of drudgery and servitude, in Hawaiian, "kanaka" contains within it the conviction that no one can avoid the rights, responsibilities, duties, and kuleana of service—not even the aliʻi, some of whom were said to be akua who walked the earth. Though generally seen as of higher status than kānaka, they too had to provide service to the land, and to the people as well. When the aliʻi referred to someone who might be called a "servant" or a "retainer" in English, they would most commonly call that person "koʻu kanaka" (my kanaka), and without going into linguistics too far, the o-class possessive in that construction ("koʻu" instead of "kaʻu") puts the kanaka on a relatively concomitant level with the aliʻi, implying a relationship of respect and trust, and a parity of sorts.

Furthermore, when kānaka referred to themselves when speaking to the aliʻi—at the end of a piece of correspondence, for instance—they would often say something along the lines of "ka hunahuna lepo ma lalo o kou wāwae" (the speck of dirt below your feet). In English, this sounds like abject debasement. In Hawaiian, it acknowledges the reciprocal relationship between kanaka and kanaka, aliʻi and kanaka, and kanaka, aliʻi, and ʻāina. When kānaka equate themselves with dirt, they are undeniably humbling themselves. But they are also drawing parallels between themselves and the land. With the dirt, they are the ground upon which the aliʻi stand. They are what feeds the aliʻi; and in the role of kanaka to the land, the aliʻi must care for them, nurture them, and protect them. To be "kanaka" in a Hawaiian context does not give you much in the way of individual rights; it puts you in a web of reciprocal care and duty.

Those are just some of the differences that can come from a single term. Similar gaps in cultural understandings about rights and responsibility exist between many of the key legal and constitutional terms. Translating "mōʻī" as "king," for instance, dangerously parallels some classic colonial moves. As mentioned in chapter 1, translation made possible the claim that Paspehay, the *weroance* of the Algonquin-speaking peoples of the Virginia area, "sold" the lands of his people, even though his people did not believe in the individual ownership of land. Translating *weroance,* a term for tribal leaders, as "king" also "translated Paspehay into English property relations... so that the English can recognize him as having 'sold' 'his' land to the English, who following the 'legal' logic of their language can thus claim 'title' to this land" (Cheyfitz 1997, 60). A single word turned communal land into personal property, which Paspehay could, and—however unwittingly—then did, alienate to the English.

Setting Shaky Precedent

Hawaiians knew that life and death are contained in one language; if anything, however, there is even more potential for life and death when shifting from one language to another. In the case of Hawai'i, at first the linguistic gap between the two versions of the law was not too damaging. When the 1840 Constitution was promulgated, the translator wrote that "the original [Hawaiian] will *of course* be the basis of all judicial proceedings," and that is indeed how things proceeded for several years. Because even if foreigners mistakenly thought Hawaiians or they themselves were "men," the binding version of the law spoke of "kanaka," and therefore "maka'āinana," in familiar/familial relationships with the 'āina and the ali'i, backed by generation upon generation of mo'olelo and tradition and practice. However, when the Hawaiian legislature declared in 1846 that all enacted laws needed to be published both in English and Hawaiian (Lucas 2000, 3), conflicts regularly arose between the two languages. At first the legislature tackled them on a case-by-case basis, enacting amendments as necessary (Asensio 2010, 22). But in the mid 1850s the courts began to weigh in, and the kingdom's heavy reliance on common rather than civil law meant that precedents set by largely foreign judges had huge ramifications.

In 1856 came *Metcalf v. Kahai*. The owner of a tract of kula land brought suit against his neighbor for wrongful detention and impounding of his cattle, which had wandered onto the adjoining land tract. There was, however, a clear disagreement between the English and the Hawaiian in the pertinent statute. The English states that the owner of the stray animals must pay "four times the amount of damage done, or of value destroyed." The Hawaiian, however, would translate along the lines of the owner having to pay "a fair and reasonable amount of compensation for the loss and damage sustained" (Hawaii Supreme Court 1857, 404). The plaintiff's attorney argued successfully that the court should be "guided by the provisions of the Hawaiian version," and Associate Justice George Robertson agreed, writing that "such, we believe, has been the practice of this Court hitherto, in such cases, and we conform to it in this instance" (Hawaii Supreme Court 1857, 404).

A handful of months later, in *Hardy v. Ruggles,* a very protracted case about mortgages, Chief Justice Lee also determines that "in case of collision between the Hawaiian and English, the Hawaiian must prevail" (Hawaii Supreme Court 1857, 461). Most discussions of this case generally stop here, because this is the part directly affecting language. I, however, will spend a bit more time on it, because in his decision, Lee discusses unuhi. Lee also contends that the Hawaiian phrase "na palapala hoolilo" translates into "all bills of sale and conveyances of personal property," rather than "absolute sales, transfers, or conveyances" (which would preclude mortgages), because this is the agreed-upon usage, confirmed by the fact that the same translation shows up in five separate places in this statute, and in all subsequent statutes (Hawaii Supreme Court 1857, 461).

Lee's discussion of translation here is interesting because it comes closest to talking about how legal translation actually operates. As mentioned numerous times, there can be no true equivalence in translation, but as with the Bible translation, in order for the system to function, the ʻōlelo Hawaiʻi and English sets of laws must be understood and applied as if they were equivalent, and the way that that is done specifically for legal translation is through precedent and agreement. As Lee points out, "nā palapala hoʻolilo" refers to all bills of sale and conveyances of personal property because it appears on five other occasions where "all bills of sale and conveyances of personal property" would appear in the English. Legal translation is contingent, and particularly in contracts, conveyances, etc., where two parties are involved, each time the English would call for the usage of "appurtenances" and the Hawaiian used "nā mea e pili pono ana," and both parties are happy with at least the way the terms of the contract are understood, the equivalence is strengthened.

This formulaic nature of law and conveyances is why legal document translation is the only kind of translation where I believe that you can actually have a "right" translation and a "wrong" translation. Literary translations can miss certain aspects of the moʻolelo, or focus on themes more tightly than the original, yet still do a decent job of representing a story. If, however, you translate "koʻu ʻāina" as if it read "kaʻu ʻāina," even though both mean "my land," a lawyer would pick up the phone and call you immediately, because one means that you have the right to convey the land, while the other doesn't. For this reason, Hawaiian legal document translation is paradoxically the easiest kind to do, because once familiar with what everyone agrees the main concepts mean, the correct phrases can be substituted in and out. When for example "e ʻike auaneʻi nā kānaka a pau ma kēia, ʻo wau ʻo _____" appears, you can safely paste "know all people by these presents, that I am _____" virtually every single time without worrying that you are losing nuance or cultural references. Due to this contingent nature of legal translation, the Hawaiian versions of laws can convey all the necessary meaning required of them, no matter how complex the law or statute, and while certain issues of precision or scope may still arise, it is no different than English in that sense.

The crux of *Hardy v. Ruggles* was that Justice Lee had to decide if the English word "pledge," when used in a legal sense, included the meaning of "mortgage." So in one of the cases setting initial precedent for the power that ʻōlelo Hawaiʻi had to express law, what Lee was ruminating upon was *English's* capacity to express law, and his understanding of legal translation as contingent is most likely why he is reaffirming the primacy of the Hawaiian version here. The problem came when someone with a very different understanding of translation addressed the issue of the controlling language in law. In Lee's *Hardy v. Ruggles* decision, he quotes Judge Lorrin Andrews, a noted speaker of ʻōlelo Hawaiʻi, as asserting that the words "lilo" and "hoʻolilo" are "very broad and indefinite in their meaning," and therefore "capable of answering to a hundred different words in the English language" (Hawaii Supreme Court 1857, 462). Andrews seems to be saying that since these words do not have exact English equivalents, they are difficult to translate. But of course, *most* Hawaiian words do not have exact equivalents, because as any translator knows, languages *do not* have exact equivalents in other languages. It is the nature of the beast. What began to change the legal realm in Hawaiʻi, however, was the fallacious but powerful expectation that each word in an English law *should* have a one-word equivalent in Hawaiian. And if it doesn't, as the barely competent Bible translators insisted over and over again, ʻōlelo Hawaiʻi, not their own skill, is deficient. Mana unuhi is claimed for one language, but denied to the other.

In this instance, even though Lee seems to agree with Andrews, he still rules that "where there is a radical and irreconcilable difference between the English and Hawaiian, the latter must govern, because it is the language of the legislators of the country. This doctrine was first laid down by the Superior Court in 1848, and has been steadily adhered to ever since. The English and Hawaiian may often be used to help and explain each other where the meaning is obscure, or the contradiction slight" (Hawaii Supreme Court 1857, 463). Though these rulings may have put Hawaiians at ease for a short time, they had long been worried about the growing foreign influence on the government. Ka wā iā Kaomi was among many things an expression of that concern, as were the many petitions and letters that maka'āinana sent to their mō'ī. As Jon Osorio explains:

> In another petition from Lanai, said to have been signed by three hundred people, the Makaainana told the Moi that neither the size nor the wealth of the nation mattered as long as the nation was theirs:
>
> Below is what we desire
> 1. For the independence of the Hawaiian government
> 2. Refuse the foreigners appointed as ministers for the Hawaiian Government
> 3. We do not want foreigners sworn in as citizens for Hawaii...
> 7. Do not be afraid of our petition for you are our father.
> 8. Do not have any fear—because your Government is not very rich, of your own people.
> 9. We do not want you to open doors for the coming in of foreigners. (2002, 31)

This petition is representative in many ways, reaffirming the maka'āinana's aloha 'āina and aloha mō'ī, but clearly not trusting the haole. Certain events sharply increased this mistrust. Over the clamoring of the people, "the legislature authorized haole voting and office holding in an act approved on 30 July 1850, three weeks after it permitted foreigners to purchase lands. Land ownership conferred the suffrage on male citizens and denizens alike" (J. K. Osorio 2002, 63). Denizens were resident foreigners; this act granted them the same rights as Hawaiians without requiring them to renounce their citizenship to their home countries.

Other attempts to push for more legal authority for 'ōlelo Hawai'i failed—for example, in 1852, when the House of Nobles turned down legislation preventing people without at least a passive command of Hawaiian from being appointed judges in the circuit and district courts (Asensio 2010, 15). The nobles defended this action by claiming that "as persons possessing skill in the law, good character and knowledge of the language, were scarce to be found,—the House preferred a man who had the two former, to him who had the latter qualification alone" (quoted in Asensio 2010, 15). Legal knowledge is supposedly being valued over Hawaiian-language ability, but in fact, few foreigners had the qualification of legal knowledge either. When he arrived in 1846, William Little Lee was only the second lawyer to take up residence in the kingdom, and the first one, John Ricord, left a year later. So even though "he was not trained in law but was a graduate of Princeton Theological Seminary," missionary Lorrin Andrews became a judge (Silverman 1982, 56).

Like Andrews, George Morrison Robertson was another person who had no formal legal training, but he too became a judge, and had a large effect on Hawaiian law and its translation. First coming to Hawai'i as an "okohola," a whaler, he worked as a clerk before leaving for the California Gold Rush. When he returned, he became a member of the Land Commission, and "i ka pau ana o kona noho ana ma ia oihana, ua hooikaika nui oia i ka heluhelu a me ka hoopaa i na Kanawai; a ma ia wa mai, he Loio kana oihana mau" (when he was done acting in that capacity, he put all his efforts toward reading and memorizing the law, and from that time forward, he was a full-time lawyer) ("Ka Make" 1867, 2). Just as the missionaries arrived in Hawai'i with few language skills and proceeded to attempt to translate the Bible, so too did Robertson come with few legal skills and ended up as a Supreme Court justice. Rather than formal legal training, clearly "the ability to read and write English and teach oneself common law would substitute [for] licenses and law degrees," as "haole were assumed to know law without being requested to prove so by actually codifying and translating it in Hawaiian as Justice Lee did" (Asensio 2010, 40). A piece from the Hawaiian-language newspapers lays out this philosophy explicitly:

Eia kona ano nui, "e koho no ke alii i kekahi haole i kakauolelo, a i unuhi olelo hoi, no ke aupuni." No ka pilikia o ke aupuni i na haole keia kanawai. Aole ike na 'lii i ka olelo a na haole; aole hoi ike i ka lakou hana, a nolaila, keia kakauolelo.

[Here is the major reason why "the ali'i should choose a haole to be secretary, and translator, for the government." This law is in regard to problems we are having with haole. The ali'i do not know the words of the haole; they also do not understand their actions, therefore: this secretary.] ("He Olelo" 1842)

Since haole presumably know more about haole things, such as law, than Hawaiians, the obvious solution is to hire a haole—a logic reminiscent of the ridiculous idea that "only a ninja can kill a ninja" so common in the movies I watched as a child.

This belief in the preternatural abilities of haole people to know haole things like the law also contributes to an idea that linguistic scholar Rubén Fernández Asensio calls a "genealogical axiom, i.e., the assumption that concepts, and especially legal ones, cannot be truly expressed and understood but in the language where they were first worded out" (2010, 27–28). Though Robertson is not solely responsible for the shift from the primacy of Hawaiian to the primacy of English in the law, he is a hinge. The large reliance on common law in the kingdom and its reliance on judicial precedent meant that a single foreigner, like Robertson, who held a great amount of mana unuhi, could be instrumental in the formalization of those shifts, not just through his adherence to the common misunderstandings of language and translation captured in Asensio's genealogical axiom, but in his use of linguistic translation as well.

Robertson displayed his prejudices about language well before he became a judge. While a clerk in the Ministry of the Interior, he filed impeachment charges against Gerritt P. Judd, the treasury minister, for sixteen supposed instances of misuse of his position, power, and public funds (Van Dyke 2007, 80). During the proceedings, the charges were read in English by R. C. Wyllie, and in 'ōlelo Hawai'i by Charles Gordon Hopkins. Judd asked which version would guide the commissioners, since there were slight differences (Kingdom of Hawai'i 1848–1849, 11). Robertson replied that he had sworn to the English version before the governor; the other was *"merely a translation"* (Kingdom of Hawai'i 1848–1849, 13; emphasis added). After returning from the Gold Rush, as vice president of the Land Commission in 1853, he was

remembered for his efforts to keep the Kuleana Awards of land to
makaʻāinana as small as he possibly could (Van Dyke 2007, 81). And
while he would briefly uphold the primacy of the Hawaiian statute in
1856 with *Metcalf v. Kahai*, Robertson would go on to sound the death
knell for the primacy of Hawaiian in law during the last half of that
decade.

Deciding on the Genealogical Axiom

Robertson's actions are directly related to his understanding of
unuhi. After Justice Lee died in 1857, Robertson was the justice presiding over *Haalelea v. Montgomery*, a case regarding whether exclusive
fishing rights had been conveyed through the sale of a part of the
ahupuaʻa of Honouliuli. The key phrase of the Hawaiian version of
the deed reads "A me na mea paa a pau e waiho ana maluna iho, a me
na mea e pili pono ana"; the English version, "And all the tenements
and hereditaments situate thereon" (Hawaii Supreme Court 1866, 68).
Arguing that the words "a me na mea e pili pono ana" are "sufficiently
broad in their signification to carry everything appurtenant to the land
embraced in the conveyance," the defendants maintained that the court
should follow the Hawaiian version for two reasons. First, the grantor
was a native, and a person of intelligence, and therefore had to be presumed to have intended to convey whatever would pass under the terms
of the deed "as expressed in her own language." Second, the court had
decided in several previous cases that wherever an irreconcilable difference existed between the two versions, the Hawaiian must govern
(Hawaii Supreme Court 1866, 68). The plaintiffs argued that the
grantee, an Englishman, received the deed in both languages, and accepted the English version as the equivalent of the Hawaiian. He and
those claiming under him should therefore be bound by the English
version because the Hawaiian and English deeds are one instrument;
if the languages are not identical (which the plaintiffs were not conceding), then the deed should be voided for uncertainty (Hawaii Supreme
Court 1866, 68).

In terms of the translation, what is at issue is whether or not the
Hawaiian and English are equivalent. If they were considered to be so,
as Justice Lee previously determined regarding Hawaiian and English
versions of statutes, then the Hawaiian would continue to control
because it has the necessary specificity and the contingent equivalency.

But this is what happened instead. Robertson acknowledged that "it is true this Court has repeatedly ruled, as stated by the defendant, that, in the case of an irreconcilable difference between the Hawaiian and English versions of a statute, the former shall control." However, he then went on to assert that "it seems to us that the same considerations which constrained the Court so to decide in that case, do not exist in the present instance: The deed before us, with the exception of those parts of it which are descriptive, consists of a printed formula, in the two languages, which has been extensively used here, in dealings between natives and foreigners, since the enactment of laws requiring conveyances of real estate to be made in writing. The English version of this formula is, of course, the original, and the Hawaiian *merely a translation*" (Hawaii Supreme Court 1866, 68–69; emphasis added). Whether the Hawaiian or English deed were drafted first is unclear, but it actually doesn't matter. What Robertson is claiming is that the "formula," or the understanding of law itself, is "of course" of English origin, and that Hawaiian is only an imprecise pathway to the meaning—"*merely a translation*," repeating what he had said as a plaintiff years earlier. He is therefore a devotee of Asensio's genealogical axiom: concepts, and especially legal ones, can only truly be expressed and understood in the language where they were first worded out.

Examining the French, Latin, and other non-English roots of English common law as adopted in Hawai'i is outside the scope of this book. Suffice it to say, however, that the genealogical axiom is a chauvinist approach, based on a dismissal of the validity of ʻōlelo Hawaiʻi and a misunderstanding of translation, legal and otherwise. Robertson compounded his errors by going on to assert that the Hawaiian language was not fit to be the controlling language of law. "There do not exist in the Hawaiian language, two words which would exactly represent the two English words *tenements* and *hereditaments*" (Hawaii Supreme Court 1866, 69), he declares, and while he does not explain why a one-to-one correspondence between words is an important criterion for translating one language into another, he is echoing Lorrin Andrews's comments quoted above. He then argues that "the exact legal signification of those terms could not be expressed in Hawaiian without great difficulty, and therefore words, which if used in some other connection, or under other circumstances, would convey a widely different meaning, have, when used in the printed formula of conveyance now before us, been accepted by the general consent of natives and foreigners using such formula, as meaning precisely the same things, and neither more or less than those two legal terms" (Hawaii Supreme Court 1866, 69). The problem here is not the argument. Echoing Justice Lee in *Hardy v. Ruggles,* "the general consent of natives and foreigners using such formula" describes precisely the kind of contingent equivalency that should inform legal translation. But Robertson attributes the need for such equivalency to weaknesses inherent in the Hawaiian language, limiting the mana unuhi of the language itself: "So far then as purely legal phraseology, or words of technical import, are concerned, it would seem to us both unsafe and unreasonable, to hold that the Hawaiian translation, and not the English original, should govern, when a question arises upon the construction of any part of the deed, where such legal or technical language is used. Such a course would unbar the door to endless litigation and fraud, and involve our courts in a maze of uncertainty" (Hawaii Supreme Court 1866, 72). Robertson's highlighting of "purely legal phraseology, or words of technical import" hearkens back to the missionaries' common complaint about the paucity of the Hawaiian language when translating the Bible. *There were just no words that could say what they needed to say.* Never mind that they all had a very shallow understanding of ʻōlelo Hawaiʻi, the problem must be with the language itself. Robertson is simply joining in on the common refrain that Hawaiian could not be specific enough for sophisticated modern usage. Never mind that Hawaiian has a word for the small piles of detritus left outside of an octopus's den after it has eaten, or hundreds of evocative names for specific winds and rains. Because Robertson couldn't find a one-for-one substitution for "hereditament," the language was clearly lacking.

Regardless of the order of composition, Robertson places the English version in the category of undying original. Since Robertson sees law as coming out of the English language, the English versions of laws/deeds/etc., are always the originals, and the Hawaiian versions are always translations. Despite Lee's pages-long foray into English legal dictionaries when trying to determine the meaning of "pledge," or Robertson's own use in this case of the Hawaiian phrase "Aole nae e hookomo ana i ka papa koa mawaho" to clarify the intent of the English (Hawaii Supreme Court 1866, 67), he could only see English as having the necessary specificity to convey law accurately.

While many of Robertson's arguments duplicated the missionaries' (mis)understanding about 'ōlelo Hawai'i, his "theory" of translation was also moving into even greater error, and the powerful precedents he was setting as a judge based on his "understanding" were moving the Hawaiian legal system away from its own translation principles. For all their grumbling, the missionaries believed that translation was capable of equivalent transfer. Because it was an article of faith that a translated Bible could convey the meaning of scripture found in its original languages, 'ōlelo Hawai'i could therefore grant you direct access to Christianity. When Hawaiians said "Aloha ke Akua," they were speaking its language. By enshrining the genealogical axiom into law through his rulings, however, Robertson was declaring that laws in 'ōlelo Hawai'i were merely paths to the English laws, not containers of the laws themselves. This understanding led Robertson to make other significant changes. While up to this point I have characterized his remarks on translation as a misunderstanding, there may be more deliberate dimensions to his institutionalization of the genealogical axiom because of how extensively it affects Hawaiian relations to land legally and culturally. To be blunt, he does this by deciding that *English* words will mean whatever he wants them to as well. For example, under the contingent agreements that govern legal translation, the word "hoa'āina" was usually translated as "tenant." Robertson gets his desired result by redefining the English term: "We understand the word tenant, as used in this connection, to have lost its ancient restricted meaning, and to be almost synonymous, at the present time, with the word occupant, or occupier, and that every person occupying lawfully, any part of 'Honouliuli,' is a tenant within the meaning of the law" (Hawaii Supreme Court 1866, 71). Another consequence of the genealogical axiom is that Hawaiian words can never be used in English versions of the law. Maka'āinana and hoa'āina are never allowed to just be "maka'āinana" and "hoa'āina" in legal contexts. They have to be translated into "citizens," and "tenants," and "occupants." If they had been left in Hawaiian in the English documents, not only would the Hawaiian-language versions have very clearly been the controlling version, but so too would the Hawaiian cultural understanding have been the controlling version. But as I will show in chapter 5, then and now, this is a haole understanding of the world: unless you are Hawaiian, 'ōlelo

Hawai'i exists only to translate from, ignoring the fact that Tahitians, Greeks, Spaniards, Chinese, and other peoples who lived here spoke 'ōlelo Hawai'i themselves.

To return to hoa'āina, although customary practice understood this word as referring to a particular connection to the land, Jon Osorio notes that with regard to the maka'āinana, the Kuleana Act of a few years earlier had "called for the legal dissolution of their traditional status even to the point of changing their identity. Makaainana who applied for kuleana lands were renamed hoa aina (literally, friends of the land), which the law translated as tenants" (2002, 53). Osorio further explores the consequences of the maka'āinana's forced transformation into hoa'āina/tenants in the Kuleana Act: "Its most enduring cost was the ending of an official recognition of the appurtenant rights of Makaainana. On 6 August 1850, a legislative act set out rules defining and 'guaranteeing' the hoa'āina appurtenant rights to gather timber and thatch and secure water and rights of way.... Although it was still theoretically possible for each hoa'āina to reach individual agreements with their landlords (whether they were the familiar konohiki or not), ultimately their rights, and only those rights, were to be secured not by tradition but by statute and judicial decision" (2002, 54).

Robertson's retranslation of "hoa'āina" to "tenants" to "occupants" also set the stage for severely limiting hoa'āina/tenant rights in another high-profile case of that same year: *Oni v. Meek*. Oni was a hoa'āina who pastured his horses on the kula land of Honouliuli as part of his traditional relationship with the konohiki of that area. When John Meek leased this kula land, he seized Oni's grazing horses and sold them under the kingdom's estray laws. Oni wanted to recover the value of his two horses, but he also wanted to confirm that he had the right to pasture his horses by custom or by statute. Robertson's decision was as follows:

> For it is obvious to us that the custom contended for is so unreasonable, so uncertain, and so repugnant to the spirit of the present laws, that it ought not to be sustained by judicial authority. Further, it is perfectly clear that, if the plaintiff is a hoaaina, holding his land by virtue of a fee simple award from the Land Commission, he has no pretense for claiming a right of pasturage by custom, for so far as that right ever was customary, it was annexed to the holding of land by a

far different tenure from that by which he now holds. (Hawaii Supreme Court 1866, 90)

Just as in *Haalelea v. Montgomery,* when he changed hoaʻāina from "tenant" to "occupant" to abrogate any special rights Hawaiians might have to land, here Robertson is once more redefining the hoaʻāina's relationship to the ʻāina as without customary rights other than those specifically established by statute. Robertson contended that any rights that Oni and his fellow hoaʻāina had enjoyed on the konohiki's land were due to the labor that they performed, rather than any customary or traditional relationship that makaʻāinana had with ʻāina and their aliʻi (Hawaii Supreme Court 1866, 91).

Robertson's genealogical axiom eroded the standing of ʻōlelo Hawaiʻi and Hawaiians under the law, and his legal decisions became precedents that accelerated this stripping of legal power. Not content with deciding so many cases against the primacy of Hawaiian language, however, in 1858, Robertson completed the draft of the civil code initiated by the late justice Lee. During the last year of his life, Lee withdrew from two sessions of the court so that he and Robertson could work on this code (Silverman 1982, 61). Unsurprisingly, when section 1493 of the Hawaiian Civil Code was amended on May 17, 1859, the sentiment was entirely Robertson's: "If at any time a radical and irreconcilable difference shall be found to exist between the English and Hawaiian versions of any part of this Code, *the English version shall be held binding*" (emphasis added).

In the aftermath of the Māhele and the Kuleana Act, Hawaiians had been translated again. In the first decades of the century, they were figured through translation as a salvable people. In the middle decades, they came to be figured as "tenants" and "occupants" of land. Even in their own laws, Hawaiians were no longer makaʻāinana, in relationships of mutual aloha with the aliʻi and the ʻāina. They were "citizens" who had "rights" rather than pono. Law was the realm in which this happened, and translation was the instrument. Robertson's wish to make English the controlling language of the law set the stage for the further disenfranchisement of Hawaiians, and for the political upheaval at the century's end. Hawaiians still held a majority in the legislature, and had the kingdom more closely followed the path of Roman civil law rather than British common law, the power would have remained there, with judges mandated to make decisions only in accordance with the statutes coming from the legislature, and judicial precedent carrying much less weight. And even if the kingdom had followed the British constitutional model more closely, the Hawaiian-led legislature would have retained much more power because, in that British model, Parliament held sovereignty over the judiciary. As implemented in Hawaiʻi, however, the American model split power between the mōʻī, the legislature, and the judiciary, with a strong reliance on common law granting greater latitude to the foreign-dominated judiciary to interpret the laws as they saw fit. For this systemic reason, even though Hawaiian lawmakers fought tooth and nail to pass legislation to mitigate or reverse the effects of Robinson's precedents and laws, introducing bills to change the controlling legal language back to ʻōlelo Hawaiʻi right up to the end of the kingdom, English remained the standard.

Though a Hawaiian mōʻī was still in charge, and the number of Hawaiian lawyers was rising, tracing the flow of mana unuhi through legal translation reveals how and why Hawaiian political power was eroding. Hawaiians may not have started off with much knowledge of Western law, but the "very quick response" the kingdom made in adopting a constitution, and the succeeding progressive laws and institutions that it passed, suggest that Hawaiians picked it up very quickly indeed. In fact, something similar had already happened to the missionaries' gift of alphabetic literacy, which took root and spread in Hawaiʻi far faster than they could have dreamed. But in both those arenas, once Hawaiians began to excel, built their own mana, and threatened to take over the reins, the colonial structures represented by the missionaries and foreign judges moved the goalposts again and again, thanks to the genealogical axiom and people like Robertson. And in chapter 3, we will see how the missionary establishment responded predictably when Hawaiians sought to employ the means of literary production for themselves.

Chapters 1 and 2 have tracked the translational flow in Hawaiʻi. Who is doing the translation? For whom? And who controls the narrative? In chapter 1, though Hawaiians were essential to the process, they did not have control over the unuhi of the Bible or the narrative around it, which led to their strategic erasure. In chapter 2, though the control of translation in the legal realm is more contested, a reliance on common law and judicial precedent cuts Hawaiians out of the process once more. Chapter 3 will examine what happens when Hawaiians seek to exercise mana unuhi and control over language through the newspapers, translating for themselves for purposes they deemed appropriate. Though this too is a contested zone, this examination begins to suggest how powerful a tool translation becomes when Hawaiians are the ones wielding it—and how dangerous the foreign residents find them.

Chapter 3
Translation in the Wild
Mana Unuhi as a Tool for Ea in the Hawaiian-Language Nūpepa

"Mai, mai, mai!" Jonah called out to his 'ohana. It was Saturday, and the week's nūpepa was out.

He clapped the road dust off his worn dungarees as he walked up the stairs and sat down on the bench in the center of the lānai. Even though it was January, the weather was hot, and it was muggy in the house. Jonah fanned himself with his hat, enjoying the respite from the sun.

Tūtū Anna came out of the house with a smile, and a gaggle of barefoot kids in an assortment of shorts and trousers and dresses made from old palaka shirts came belting around the side of the house. Tūtū Anna sat next to Jonah on the bench, her hand patting his knee, and nodded as he read aloud the news about the kaua nui ma Europa, and how the kula Bīhopa just had its annual hō'ike. Maile leaned up against a post and idly mended a torn work shirt to the comforting sound of Jonah's voice.

The kids, dotting the stairs with a few outliers fidgeting in the grass, had sat surprisingly still while Jonah continued to read aloud. But when he moved on to the shipping schedule, all the keiki groaned.

Kamalei, his little keko, called out, "E ku'u papa, i hea ana ka Nautilo?"

Jonah's brow creased and his eyebrows pulled down in mock anger. Kamalei's laugh tatted out of her, followed by all the other children.

He knew what everyone was waiting for. Jonah skipped ahead to the last page and began to read: "He 20,000 legue ma lalo o ke kai. Nā mea kupanaha o ka moana..."

As noted in chapter 1 and in numerous other sources, Hawaiian literacy rates skyrocketed with each succeeding decade of the nineteenth century. The eagerness with which the Hawaiians of that time appropriated alphabetic literacy, and to a lesser extent translation, meant that they created a massive body of native-language writing, made up primarily of Hawaiian-language newspapers. Historian Noelani Arista describes it as "arguably...the largest literature base of any native language in the Pacific and perhaps all native North America" (2010, 665). Literary scholar kuʻualoha hoʻomanawanui observes that for Hawaiians then and now, it is "the largest and most accessible body of written material documenting Kanaka ʻŌiwi thought, tradition, and society" (2014, 22). Many people in the Hawaiian community still have the sense that writing and alphabetic literacy are outside impositions, foreign tools that are categorically not Hawaiian, but this enthusiasm with which our ancestors picked up this practice and the prolific archive that has been created by Kānaka Maoli is a clear indicator of a powerful traditional literary practice that Hawaiian literary practitioners continue to this day. And while Indigenous literature and translation in native North America had a long history at the point when alphabetic literacy was introduced to Hawaiʻi, with the 1663 Bible translated into Wôpanâak, the language of the Wampanoag people, and Samson Occom becoming the first Native American to publish his work in 1772 (Round 2010, 7), if we take into account the relatively short amount of time between the introduction of alphabetic literacy in Hawaiʻi and the end of the Hawaiian-language newspapers in 1948, the size of that archive is doubly impressive.

Hawaiians were of course not alone among Indigenous peoples in recognizing the possibilities and mana in print, alphabetic literacy, and unuhi. Circuits of knowledge and knowledgeable people ran through native North America and the Pacific and had profound effects on Indigenous communities. Ideas about philology spread through scholar and missionary alike along these circuits, as did printing materials and people. John Pickering's proposed uniform orthography in 1820 (Schütz 1994, 130) made the rounds. Printing materials also traveled, such as when the Lapwai Mission press in what is now Idaho printed the first book in a syllabic version of the Nez Perce language in 1839 on a Ramage press that came from the Hawaiʻi mission (Round

2010, 92). Even people themselves circulated, as when Elisha Loomis, who had supervised the printing of the first books of the Bible translated into Hawaiian, took his print skills and became a missionary to the Ojibwe (Benedetto 1982, 47).

What goes unwritten into mainstream understandings of this time period is, unsurprisingly, the circuit of Indigenous peoples and knowledge, such as the Tahitians mentioned in chapter 1, or people like John Makani, who was possibly a Nisenan Maidu or Valley Miwok from Sacramento, but educated in Hawai'i and able to speak and write 'ōlelo Hawai'i, English, and at least one California Indian language, and who set up schools of his own in Colfax, California, near Hawaiian settlements for the Indigenous people of the area (Farnham 2021). Even the Hawaiian, Pacific, and other Indigenous artisans who ran the presses as compilers, editors, translators, typesetters, and more were routinely left unmentioned or uncredited, as was the case with the Nipmuc Wawaus, or James Printer, whose role in translating the 1663 Bible was widely effaced (along with Cockenoe and Job Nesuton, and possibly Joel Iacoomes and Caleb Cheeshateaumuck), but so were his efforts in the actual printing of that Bible (Brooks 2018, 87). Yet despite (or because) of this marginalization, Indigenous groups began to demand presses of their own and publications in their own languages, which led to some missionary organizations like the ABCFM shipping presses far into Indian Country and out into the Pacific (Round 2010, 81). As Philip Round would say, "in the hands of these Indigenous craftsmen, polemicists, writers, and readers, the European ideology of the book [and print] was put to the service of Native nation building in ways that far surpassed the expectations of the colonizers" (2010, 23).

Various modes of orthography and communication systems were considered across the Pacific and North America for "reducing" Indigenous languages to writing and creating avenues for translation. In Hawai'i alone, the mission had discussed various possible approaches such as sign language (inspired by the work of Thomas Gallaudet), the Russian alphabet, and a syllabary (inspired by both the Japanese and Cherokee systems), before finally settling on an alphabet somewhat similar to the English alphabet and to the ones that had been used for Māori and Tahitian (because they thought that would mean that the same books could be used for both Hawaiian and Tahitian, which they considered "dialects" at the time) (Schütz 2020, 100–101, 106).

Though philologists like John Pickering thought a widespread universal orthography and alphabetic literacy would contribute to the American nationalist cause and help obtain "the means of communication with the various tribes on our borders, either with a view to the common concerns of life or the diffusion of the principles of our religion among them" (1820, 9), Indigenous peoples took up alphabetic literacy for their own reasons, often having to do with sovereignty, with print acting as a powerful weapon in their battles against "relocation, allotment, and cultural erasure" (Round 2010, 5). Print was burgeoning in many Indigenous contexts during this time, with Hawaiians achieving a near-universal literacy, the Cherokees printing more than fourteen million pages of vernacular texts between 1816 and 1860, and the Choctaws more than eleven million (Round 2010, 22).

This example from the Cherokees shows both how powerfully subversive Indigenous-language publishing can be, but also the lengths that colonial powers will go to quash threats to their own power. The Cherokee people too achieved near total literacy in their own language after 1821, when Sequoyah introduced his syllabary, which was a syllabic written form of the Cherokee spoken language that was not derived from the Roman alphabet (Round 2010, 123). The syllabary itself was threatening to the missionary power structure because it had come from a non-Christian member of the tribe, but it was what the Cherokees began to print with the syllabary that came to be the real threat. They began translating the Bible around the same time as Hawai'i, as mentioned in chapter 1, and established a national press that printed in the syllabary and published the *Cherokee Phoenix,* a Cherokee- and English-language newspaper, in 1828. Initially edited by Elias Boudinot, who like Thomas Hopu and the other Hawaiians went to the Cornwall Foreign Mission School, this paper, appearing six years before the first Hawaiian-language newspaper, often included news about Hawai'i because the ABCFM had an influential Cherokee mission. But while the Cherokee nation was fighting legal battles against the state of Georgia for attempting to settle Cherokee land, the Georgia Guard destroyed the printing press for being subversive ("History of the Cherokee Phoenix" 2015). Philip Round points to the fact that the Cherokee were among the nations able to hold out the longest against removal as "in part a testament to their early decision to harness print literacy to the service of their emerging sense of national identity" (2010, 132). Though this was not the end of Cherokee-language print literature, we see how swiftly colonizers feeling threatened will try to derail or destroy native-language archives.

Although Hawai'i's distance from the continent and its sovereign control of its own borders nourished the development of our large archive of 'ōlelo Hawai'i, efforts to suppress Hawaiian voices in the newspapers continued for several decades. While the structures of power in place, like the church and the judiciary system, made it very difficult for Hawaiians to maintain their ea in these realms, the newspapers proved a different story. In a highly contested arena, once Hawaiians took control of the press, their nūpepa displayed high levels of technical and rhetorical skill. They also deployed translation as part of Hawaiian efforts to strengthen and cultivate their ea, culminating in the political unrest of the nineteenth century's last decade.

The nūpepa carried a lot of weight in terms of the roles they played as sites of contesting discourses, cultural perpetuators, mouthpieces of law, windows to the outside world, and communications channels for the large numbers of Hawaiians who went abroad. Noelani Arista characterizes the newspapers in this way: "The nūpepa knitted together an archipelagic kānaka maoli world, introducing new modes of sociability, a sense of nationalism not necessarily predicated on maoli genealogies, and citizenship, which sat alongside older modes of aloha ali'i (honoring the chiefs, and chiefly regard for people) and the mana of the ali'i" (2020, 41). Speaking of the traditional mele and mo'olelo printed in the newspapers, Mary Kawena Pukui, the premier Kanaka scholar of the twentieth century, says:

> Hawaiians regarded the lore of their ancestors as sacred and guarded it jealously. Such subjects were not talked about lightly nor too freely.... There had to be quiet during story telling period so that the mind would not be distracted. Strict attention had to be paid to every word of the narrative. No unnecessary movement was permitted except to change the sitting position when uncomfortable. The call of nature must be attended to before the story telling began, for it was kapu to attend to such matters in the middle of a tale. Tales learned were not repeated casually without thinking to whom and where one spoke (n.d., 1602).

She goes on to mention her own way she learned moʻolelo, saying that "it didn't matter whether it was told interestingly, but it did matter that it be told correctly" (1603).

But with all due respect to Mrs. Pukui, kā kākou kumu, tracking the Hawaiian-produced newspaper content reveals that for traditional and translated foreign moʻolelo, "interesting" does matter, as aesthetics, reading for pleasure, and presenting simple useful knowledge became primary concerns. These were important things that the lāhui wanted to give mana to. Of course, the tellers/authors of moʻolelo often did have lessons for their audiences, and this chapter will show how important they were. But as early as the first mission papers, Hawaiian literary practitioners were becoming so adept in alphabetic literacy and translation that their moʻolelo and writings were soon collectively representing a powerfully Hawaiian literary aesthetic.

Like other materials from the mission press, such as the spelling primers and catechisms, the early newspapers had a heavily didactic approach. Often, however, they tried to add items of interest as well, much of it coming through translation—an article about a man in Lithuania who was 168 years old ("He Mau Elemakule" 1834, 2), for instance, or descriptions of other Polynesians ("No na kanaka o Polenesia" 1834, 21), letters to the editor, a surprising amount of information about elephants ("No ka Elepani" 1834, 3; "Ke Akamai o na Elepani" 1834, 19), travelogues ("Holo ana mai Maui i Oahu" 1837, 49), and woodcuts of scenes from Hawaiʻi and abroad, such as the girls' school in Wailuku ("Kula Kaikamahine, Wailuku, Maui" 1842). These newspapers piqued Hawaiians' interests, and kānaka Hawaiʻi were involved in the newspapers early on as writers and producers of content. Readers and writers alike soon saw the benefits of presenting ʻike and moʻolelo in published form. The early papers were still under editorial control of the mission, but as with many introduced technologies, Hawaiians paid attention to what they wanted, identifying the aspects of the technology or form that would advance Hawaiian values and interests and leaving the rest. And as we will see, when letters to the mission and government press requesting different content or particular forms of moʻolelo proved unsuccessful, Hawaiians eventually published their own nūpepa that hewed more closely to the literary aesthetic that they had developed.

Of course, these Hawaiian-produced moʻolelo passed down important cultural information. But to view them as mere vessels of the oral tradition (Krug 2016, 102–103) is to underestimate Hawaiian literary practitioners, both authors and translators, who were pushing literary boundaries to form an aesthetic of Hawaiian literature. None of this contradicts Mary Kawena Pukui, but it does suggest that different times and contexts affected how moʻolelo were shared—and especially as Hawaiians lost control of the press during the unfolding of the territorial period. In itself, the noble intent of preserving and passing down cultural knowledge cannot explain the Hawaiian-language newspaper boom of the nineteenth and early twentieth centuries, especially since the undeniable penetration of Christian values into the Hawaiian psyche made a fair number of Kānaka Maoli feel that holding onto Native traditions was backward and ignorant. Hawaiians latched on to alphabetic literacy at an amazing pace not only because it provided a pathway to knowledge and enlightenment, but also because of the aesthetic and entertainment value they found in the moʻolelo they read, whether the latest news (understood also to be moʻolelo), or the history of the Kamehameha lineage, or the most recent adventures of the Lightning Detective.

The Hawaiian-language newspapers started during a fertile time for Native-language newspapers: the abovementioned *Cherokee Phoenix* started in 1828; the first ʻōlelo Hawaiʻi newspaper, *Ka Lama Hawaii,* started in 1834; the *Siwinowe Kesibwi,* or *Shawnee Sun,* started in what is now Kansas in 1835 (Round 2010, 88); the Māori-language *Te Karere o Niu Tireni* started across the Pacific in Aotearoa in 1845 (Frean 1997); the *Choctaw Intelligencer,* which was mainly in English but also ran Choctaw-language articles, started in 1852 (Round 2010, 145); and likely there were more. While it was indisputably the missionaries who ended up providing the broad framework for Hawaiians to pick up alphabetic literacy and a desire for reading, the ABCFM used similar models with other Indigenous groups without it resulting in the same kind of massive Native-language archive. In Hawaiʻi, though, accounts and images of mākua or keiki reading the nūpepa aloud to the entire family, then passing it on to the next house, became so common that the publishers pleaded for each family to buy its own copy so that the papers could stay in business, and in the twentieth century, kūpuna often recalled in interviews being responsible as children for reading aloud (Nogelmeier 2010, 81). In short, Hawaiians' keen appetite for reading was largely due to themselves. Though skeptical at first, the aliʻi, and then the makaʻāinana, quickly saw benefits of alphabetic literacy above and beyond what the missionaries offered. And there's the rub. Hawaiians became like thoroughbreds, needing the open track, but the missionaries and their editor allies wanted them to keep pulling plows.

While these were clearly contested spaces, only a few Hawaiians and missionaries took part in the Bible translation process, and only aliʻi, elected officials, and a handful of Lāhainaluna students wrote and translated the law. Once the newspapers took hold, however, the arena was open to all, as letters and moʻolelo from ʻelemakule and luahine from remote locations like Keʻei appeared next to editorials by the most well-known intellectuals in the kingdom (and some of those ʻelemakule and luahine were the most well-known intellectuals). The nūpepa became a Hawaiian realm for learning, entertainment, grief, debate, and more. Mana unuhi became something available to everyone, and translation played a big role in the newspapers and the spread of literacy, bringing news and moʻolelo into ʻōlelo Hawaiʻi from all over the world—primarily from English sources, but also from French, German, Chinese, and other Pacific language materials ("Poe Haku Manao no ke Kuokoa" 1867, 2; "Halawai ma Kaumakapili" 1862, 1). But Hawaiians had to fight constantly to claim and reclaim this realm, because when the missionaries, and then their descendants and the sugar planters, recognized how much power the nūpepa could potentially grant and how influential widespread mana unuhi made them, they did what they could to undermine Hawaiian agency in print.

As chapters 1 and 2 have argued, translation is never simply an unmarked process that carries something from one language to another, and in Hawaiian hands, mana unuhi became a confident strategy for asserting the power of ʻōlelo Hawaiʻi, and by extension Hawaiian culture, to hold everything that the world had to offer. There is nothing that cannot be brought into Hawaiian. The Bible and legal translations addressed our afterlives and our bodies, but what about the life of the culture, the life of the lāhui? As Bacchilega and Arista put it,

> we will venture to make a generalization at this point: translation in Hawaiʻi's public sphere in the latter part of the nineteenth century served very different sociopolitical purposes depending on whether it

was translation into or from Hawaiian. Hawaiians translated a wide variety of texts from English into Hawaiian for Hawaiian-language newspapers, taking a cosmopolitan approach to different narrative conventions and cultures, just as their King Kalākaua would be doing in the 1880s when upon returning from his world tour he brought novelties such as the telephone, the flush toilet, and electrical lights to ʻIolani Palace.

This open-minded use of translation was a sign of confidence in the Hawaiian language and culture, and as such an inclusive practice; it was also a sign of acculturation into the settlers' worldview and cultural codes. (2007, 165)

I would like to lean on the last line of this quotation a bit. While the desire to translate foreign moʻolelo and news, and thus bring them into the Hawaiian realm, involved some degree of foreign acculturation, I would argue that, especially in what was chosen as "worthy," translation often powerfully served distinctly Hawaiian purposes.

Let us revisit mana unuhi here. Unuhi gives mana to moʻolelo. A version of a story is called a mana; the word refers to the way trees or streams or roads branch out and go in different directions. Mana is also the power that inheres in everything, and can be increased or lost through certain actions, often ritual in nature. What that means is that the more a moʻolelo is told, translations included, the more mana it has. Translation, then, is an act of consecration too. It takes time, effort, and skill, and only certain texts merit that outlay. But when Hawaiians translate foreign texts, ʻōlelo Hawaiʻi gets mana/consecration as well. Translating the news and the latest scientific developments shows how supple and nimble Hawaiian can be; translating what foreigners deem great works of literature shows how profound and nuanced Hawaiian can be. And after taking over the press, when the nūpepa place traditional mele and moʻolelo side by side with these translated texts, Hawaiians are declaring not only that we recognize and celebrate the greatness of *your* moʻolelo, but that *our* moʻolelo can measure up to and often exceed them.

The next section tracks how Hawaiian-language newspapers and translation worked hand in hand to create a powerful and critical site for discourse with a Hawaiian audience in mind. After looking briefly at how newspapers developed, we will examine what happened when

Hawaiians began using the presses for themselves, then identify the roles that the nūpepa and translation played in the nineteenth century's tumultuous final decades.

Early Development of the Nūpepa

As far as printing went, until 1836, the missionaries were the only game in town (Kuykendall 1938, 106), but even though the missionaries decided what was printed on the old Ramage press they carried around Cape Horn, Hawaiians were learning the mechanics of publication from the start. When their first printer, Elisha Loomis, left in 1827 for health reasons, Hiram Bingham took over, running the press with a journeyman printer and three Hawaiians: Richard Karaiaula, John Ii, and Kuaana (Ballou and Carter 1908, 33). By 1834, twelve Hawaiians were "employed most of the time in the Printing office and bindery" (ABCFM 1835, 47), developing a "commendable proficiency" (Kuykendall 1938, 105). When the Honolulu missionaries received a new press in 1831, they shipped the Ramage to Lāhainaluna, on Maui, and the Reverend Lorrin Andrews, who had been a compositor and pressman in Kentucky, began to teach his male students how to gather information, write it up, and print it (Chapin 1996b, 16). Hawaiians grasped how to run a press even more quickly than they acquired literacy. Andrews himself admitted that he could not run the Ramage as well as the Hawaiian printer, who knew the business far better (Ballou and Carter 1908, 39–40).

On February 14, 1834, the fifty-fifth anniversary of the death of Captain Cook, the first Hawaiian-language newspaper, *Ka Lama Hawaii,* was launched. As its masthead declared, "he mea ia e hoolaha ike, a he mea hoi e pono ai ke kulanui" (it was something to disseminate knowledge and also something for the benefit of the high school). *Ka Lama* was meant just for the haumāna, the students, of Lāhainaluna, and according to Lorrin Andrews, it would feature "first Natural History with a plate, one piece & plate per week beginning with the largest animals. The cut to come on the first page as soon as size will admit. The description of the animal not generally to exceed two columns. The last page is for the scholars or for native genius. The remainder to moral & religious essays [and] news from different stations particularly whatever relates to schools on the islands, notes of foreign countries. &c." (Forbes 1998b, 75). Helen Chapin, one of the foremost authorities on Hawai'i newspaper history, describes *Ka Lama* as follows:

> The Reverend Andrews and his students printed 200 copies of each issue of Ka Lama and distributed them free. In half-sheet quartos, approximately nine by eleven inches in size.... *Ka Lama* also introduced the illustrated periodical... by reproducing prints made from wood blocks on a lithograph press. Dr. Alonzo Chapin, a physician posted to the mission, hand carved forty four-footed beasts like the lion, camel, zebra, buffalo, and reindeer, all of which except for the dog and horse were unknown to the Hawaiians. Explanatory text spoke to the "superiority" of American culture, the Christian religion, and the Protestant work ethic.... Accounts relate how, upon receiving their copies, students would immediately sit down and read them through. (1996b, 16)

Though a modern reader paging through the early mission papers might find them heavier on the "instruct" than on the "delight" side, that their Hawaiian audience read them right away suggests that even early on, kānaka were attracted to the form as a means for disseminating 'ike and mo'olelo; and once they realized what they liked and didn't like, they demanded more of what they liked. A quick indicator of *Ka Lama*'s content and style, which set the tone for the missionary-run press for the next three decades, appears in the first article following the text explaining why *Ka Lama* was being printed, and whom it was for. Entitled "Ke Kumu o ka Naaupo" (The source of ignorance), the article begins with "O ka hewa ke kumu o ka naaupo" (Sin is the reason for ignorance) ("Ke Kumu o ka Naaupo" 1834, 1).

Probably the result of a mistranslation, a grammatically ambiguous but interesting statement in *Ka Lama*'s opening article anticipates what the newspapers will become. The editors say that the newspaper and other published materials are *for* "ka poe paahana, a na ka poe kalepa kekahi, na ka poe imi naauao kekahi, na ka poe haipule kekahi, a na ka poe kamalii kekahi" (industrious people, merchants, seekers of knowledge, religious people, and even children). What makes this interesting is that the word used for *for*—"na"—more often means something akin to "by." Though it would take a few decades to happen, the Hawaiian-language newspapers did become something by "industrious people, merchants, seekers of knowledge, religious people, and even children"—in short, the lāhui Hawai'i, and a lot of what it became was the result of mana unuhi.

That newspapers did become the voice of the people in Hawai'i parallels events happening thousands of miles away in Britain, and to a lesser extent in the United States. Though there is little evidence of press suppression in Hawai'i during the earliest years—after all, the missionaries, with the support of the government, were in charge of printing—the fight for a free press was fierce in Britain. The Newspaper and Stamps Duty Act of 1819 put heavy taxes on newspapers, making them so expensive to produce, and therefore to purchase, that the penny sheet *Medusa* referred to the act as "a Bill to Prevent the Poor from Reading" (Wiener 1971, 3). Although print technology made it feasible to disseminate inexpensive newspapers and publications for working-class people, the government was afraid not only of the spread of radical ideals, but also of plain old general education, which could lead people to aspire above their station (Ashton 2008, 4). High duties on newspapers and liberal use of the Blasphemous and Seditious Libel Act of 1819, something that we will see happen in Hawai'i close to the end of the century, kept most radical journalists in check until the early 1830s (Wiener 1971, 3), when printers began publishing cheap, and therefore illegal papers—the often radical "unstamped." A similar history, with a similar rationale, would surface in Hawai'i in the 1860s in response to the perceived threat of the nūpepa aloha 'āina.

Though claiming to be for everyone, *Ka Lama* was printed by and for the haumāna of Lāhainaluna. Only twenty-five issues appeared, featuring primarily religious and devotional materials, often translated from English-language texts, with additional moralizing sometimes added. But its editor, Lorrin Andrews, warned against an overreliance on this translated religious material in *Ka Lama,* and in education more generally: "If the missionaries really wish to lay a broad and deep foundation upon which the future welfare of the islands may rest, we wish to give stability to this kingdom, and the churches we are now planting; to build up and perpetuate those institutions, which are the glory of all [l]ands; if to do this, we are persuaded that literature and religion, *as means,* should go hand in hand; that knowledge should expand the mind and religion purify the heart" (quoted in Charlot 2005, 28). He asks the rhetorical question, "Have we complied in the best manner we were able with the real wants of the nation, by preaching to them so much, and teaching them so little?" (quoted in Charlot 2005, 28), and goes on to argue that a "just proportion" needed to be established between the teaching of religion and of literature. For the most part, though, his pleas fell on deaf ears, and the religion-heavy "preaching" tone of the mission and government-sponsored papers would continue, with little literary or entertaining content providing variety or balance, until Hawaiians were fed up.

A second general circulation mission paper, *Ke Kumu Hawaii*, appeared the same year (Forbes 1998b, 79). Lorrin Andrews, perhaps unsurprisingly, was no longer the editor, having been replaced by Ruben Tinker. At their annual meeting, the ABCFM missionaries reaffirmed their belief in the inseparability of proselytizing and the press: "To promote the cause of Christianity and civilization most advantageously in any country, and to secure to any people the early, ultimate and permanent advantages of moral reform, intellectual improvement and national prosperity, the pulpit and the press and a legitimate exercise of their powers are indispensable" (ABCFM 1835, 82). Besides alliteration, "the pulpit and the press" hearkens back to the goal of publishing salvation, and speaks to the need of taking up more popular publications' approaches: "the periodical press may be advantageously employed... to exhibit truth in an attractive form before the eyes of several thousand readers" (1835, 83).

As it did in Britain and the United States, the "attractive form" caught on with the public, as Hawaiian readers fell in love with the very idea of nūpepa. Just as the Lāhainaluna students' delight in reading their own language caused them to sit down immediately and read *Ka Lama*, the initial excitement of having "news" to read fueled people's interest through the first handful of newspapers. But these nūpepa were hardly responsive to the interests of the ever-growing and voracious Hawaiian reading public. Even the translated offerings meant to be entertaining and literary, such as hymns, information about famous Biblical cities, and children's scripture stories, displayed a pervasive moral tone, and did not appear as regularly as readers desired. In a similar vein to Andrews, because he felt that the ABCFM held too tight a rein on its content, Tinker resigned the editorship of *Ke Kumu* in protest, and left the mission soon after (Chapin 1996b, 17). Chapin identifies these two papers as the first members of "the establishment press—establishment in that even though they spoke for just a handful of people and not for the vast majority of the native population, in just a few years they had come to exert a dominant influence on the Islands" (1996b, 16). With both the Bible translation and the early establishment newspapers, mana unuhi is still firmly in the hands of the mission.

Though a few English-language newspapers began appearing around this time—and the first, the *Sandwich Island Gazette,* was actually very anti-missionary (Forbes 1998b, 142–143)—their readerships were small, and Hawaiians did not take to them. So for the next few decades, Hawaiians read the papers of the mission press, whose content Helen Chapin describes as follows: "Lead articles in *Ka Lama* and *Ke Kumu* discussed the rights and responsibilities of Native Hawaiian leaders in Western terms, along with the desirability of an American-style government, and promoted the Declaration of Rights in 1839 and a Constitution in 1840" (1996b, 17). Kanaka scholar Noenoe Silva continues in the same vein as Chapin, observing that "for forty years missionaries controlled the power of the printed word in Hawai'i. The missionaries used this power not just to save souls but to assist in the progress of plantation/colonial capitalism, to control public education, to mold government into Western forms and to control it, and to domesticate Kanaka women" (2004, 55). It is undeniable that literacy spawned an industry in Hawai'i. Sheldon Dibble reported that at the mission press's height, "four printing-presses and two binderies are in constant operation, except when stopped for want of funds, employing about 40 native young men in both departments, who execute their work well with very little superintendence" (1839, 115). But the content was generally more of the same, and eventually tiring of rewarmed translated fare, in the 1860s, Hawaiians, at least some of them, responded with *Ka Hoku o ka Pakipika.*

A Press of Their Own
Dueling Voices

In 1855, Alexander Liholiho came to the throne. A man of broad tastes, he could speak some French and Spanish (Kuykendall 1953, 34), and it was said that "aohe mea i oi ae me ia ke akamai pau pono i na mea a pau o ka olelo Beretania, a me ka olelo Hawaii" (there is no one who exceeds the completeness of his mastery of English and Hawaiian) ("Na Mea Hou" 1862, 2). As very young men, he and his brother Lot had traveled with Gerrit P. Judd across the United States and Europe. Encountering overt racism in the United States, but a kind and respectful reception in Britain, the brothers understandably came to be pro-British in their leanings (Chapin 1996b, 42). Drawing upon his mastery of English and Hawaiian, Alexander Liholiho translated the Book of Common Prayer ("Na Mea Hou" 1862, 2) and invited the Anglican Church to establish itself in Hawai'i as a check against the growing influence of the ABCFM's missionaries, many of whom had migrated into government positions.

Noenoe Silva describes succinctly the political power dynamics at the time:

> In King Kamehameha III's later years, after two decades of resistance, the missionaries were allowed to become a relatively uncontested moral force that enjoyed influence over the government. They had engineered the māhele and the political structure of the newly formed kingdom, and they had moved into positions of power in the cabinet and privy council. But Kamehameha IV (Alexander Liholiho) and his brother Ke Kamāli'i Lota Kapuāiwa, a member of the House of Nobles and minister of the interior (who would reign later as Kamehameha V), constituted a new force in politics that did not accept or appreciate that the Calvinist missionaries' ideas alone should reign. (2004, 46)

Literacy was high enough by midcentury that when literacy and property qualifications were proposed for voting, delegates to the constitutional convention for what became the Constitution of 1864 fought every proposed property qualification (even as low as $25), yet passed virtually uncontested the literacy qualification (Kuykendall 1953, 132). Many of these highly literate Hawaiians shared their mō'ī's opinion that Calvinist missionary ideas should not reign. The resulting actions started what became Hawai'i's first major print war, and it all hinged on translation.

Ka Hoku o ka Pakipika

As Bacchilega and Arista point out, "settlers and Hawaiians struggled for competing systems of governance, land development, language, and culture" in what would become a "hotly contested public sphere"

(2007, 163). But the contest did not begin in earnest until Hawaiians stepped into the ring in 1861. Before then, Hawaiian-language publications were a rather amiable mix of missionary and government-backed periodicals, although foreigners like Abraham Fornander and Henry Sheldon were stirring things up in the English-language papers (Chapin 1996b, 41). Though the mission and government papers had pushed for individual learning as a way of self-improvement, what they hadn't pushed for was Hawaiians taking over the press as a way of lāhui improvement. As Noenoe Silva says, the pivot came when "in 1861, to the shock and outrage of the missionary establishment, a group of Kānaka Maoli, makaʻāinana, and aliʻi together, transformed themselves into speaking subjects proud of their Kanaka ways of life and traditions and unafraid to rebel. Their medium was a Hawaiian-language newspaper called *Ka Hoku o ka Pakipika* (The star of the Pacific)" (2004, 55).

This impending conflict mirrors what Hilary Wyss describes as happening with Native tribes in the area known as New England (where the ABCFM was also active) due to the missions' desires to create "Readerly Indians" more than "Writerly Indians." Wyss characterizes the mission's ideal Readerly Indian as "a docile, passive Indian figure" better trained for the reception of knowledge, values, and cultural models by "reinforcing a skill set that did not require self-expression" (2012, 6). For our purposes here too, we can see the Readerly Indian as one who does not have mana unuhi to create unuhi, only to receive unuhi. The figure of the Writerly Indian, on the other hand, ensured that missionaries "lost control of the message," and the mana, as the Writerly figure used the cultures and conventions of colonial society that they had learned but were also "fully committed to Native community as an ongoing political and cultural concern" (Wyss 2012, 6). Though Wyss makes it clear that there are liberatory possibilities for Indigenous peoples in both reading and writing, she goes on to characterize Writerly Indians as having "used written discourse to manage their own sovereignty in ways that often challenged, confused or contradicted missionary desire" (2012, 7). As we know, Hawaiians and the Native nations of North America have very different histories, but this figuration of the Readerly and Writerly Indians fits well into what happened in Hawaiʻi, particularly as the ABCFM were the ones feeling threatened by Writerly natives in both places.

The great nineteenth-century newspaper advocate and scholar Joseph Kānepuʻu described the people who started this paper as "he poe no ia i uluhua i kahi manao haiki a laula ole o ka 'Hae Hawaii,' he nupepa Aupuni ma o Limaikaika la, na Mr. J. Fuller ka hooponopono" (people who had been fed up with the narrow-mindedness and lack of breadth of *Ka Hae Hawaii,* a government newspaper established by Richard Armstrong, and edited by Mr. J. Fuller) (Kānepuʻu 1878, 1). Readers had petitioned *Ka Hae* to increase its size and its offerings of foreign and island news, mele, legends, and letters (N. Silva 2004, 56), but nothing came of it, so they formed a hui, a group/organization, to create a newspaper of their own, shifting their mode to the more Writerly side of the spectrum.

Kānepuʻu names Haleʻole, Keolanui, Komoikehuehu, Bila ʻAuwana, Kapahi, J. W. H. Kaoahi, Kahalewai, Pualewa, Kalākaua, Kaunamano, Pinehasa, S. K. Kuapuʻu, Simon K. Kaʻai, and J. Moanauli as members of this hui, though some of them did split off to help Henry Whitney establish *Ka Hoku o ka Pakipika*'s rival *Ka Nupepa Kuokoa,* which we will discuss later (Kānepuʻu 1878, 1). J. W. K. Kauwahi, who authored the first book written and published by a Hawaiian (on how to write legal documents), was named as the overall editor of *Ka Hoku,* though the haole G. W. Mila, who had translated *Robinson Crusoe* into Hawaiian for *Ka Hae Hawaii* the year before (Kānepuʻu 1862, 3), was also an editor, brought on specifically for his translation ability, since a great proportion of desirable material in Hawaiian-language newspapers came from translation (Chapin 1996a, 44). As for David Kalākaua, his contributions to the paper earned him the sobriquet "editor King" when he ascended the throne (Forbes 1998c, 294). In *Hoku*'s first issue, the editors make their position clear:

> No na makahiki he kanaha i hala ae nei, aole o kakou he nupepa nui a kulike hoi me ka makemake o ka lahui Hawaii, kahi i hiki ai ia kakou ke hookomo i ko kakou mau manao ponoi, nolaila, aole i loheia na mea akamai me na na [sic] mea lealea, a ko kakou manao i hookupu ai, ua waiho keia mau mea ma ka papa, me ka manao ole ua loaa ia kakou kekahi wahi naauao iki, a ua nele loa kakou i ka nupepa ole e hoihoi ai, a ua hoka loa ka makemake o ka poe maa i na manao maikai no kahi ole e hiki ai ia lakou ke hoolaha ae i na manao o lakou....a ua hooholo...he pono no e hookumu i kekahi

nupepa hou nui o ke kino, i hooponoponoia e na kanaka Hawaii, a malaila auanei e lawa ko kakou makemake.

[For the past forty years, we have not had a newspaper that answered the desires of the Hawaiian people, a place where we can let our thoughts be known, meaning that none of the learned and joyful things that our minds have come up with have been heard. These things have all been discarded upon the floor, without thinking that we have even the tiniest bit of knowledge to contribute. We are lesser without such a newspaper to hold our interest, and those people who are used to intelligent thought are left frustrated because they have no place to express their ideas. So we decided that it was a must to establish a new large-format newspaper, edited by Hawaiians, and it would be there that our desires would be met.] (1861)

Helen Chapin praises this accomplishment, saying "it was a remarkable achievement that within three short decades of acquiring literacy and newspaper technology Native Hawaiians set up and controlled their own press" (1996b, 59), but a particular segment of the public at that time did not agree.

Even before their first official issue went to press, *Ka Hoku o ka Pakipika* had raised the ire of the missionaries and those who clung most closely to their beliefs. Under any circumstances, these opponents would have been apprehensive about Hawaiians taking the press into their own hands, but a mele published in an unnumbered preview issue had the missionaries frothing at the mouth. The resulting uproar had to do with translation. The piece was titled "He Mele Aloha i ka Naauao" (A mele of love for enlightenment), and a scathing letter to *Ka Hae Hawaii* signed by "Punima'ema'e" (Favoring chastity/cleanliness/purity/order) blasted *Ka Hoku* for publishing it. Punima'ema'e claimed the new newspaper was not only full of "na olelo pelapela, lapuwale, he mea hoohaumia i ka naau o ke kanaka" (indecent language, worthless, something that will desecrate the heart of a person) but had also printed "na mele pelapela, haumia i haku ia e kanaka moekolohe no ko lakou mau wahine hookamakama!" (filthy, degraded mele that had been written by adulterers for their whores!) (Punimaemae 1861, 102). According to Punima'ema'e, even if you try to hide the filth within a mele by calling it a "mele aloha" (mele of love/aloha) for something, "e hoopalahinu wale no oe ia waho o ka hale kupapau, aole nae e nalo ka pilau oloko, a malaila e ike ia ai oia he kupapau" (you are merely polishing the outside of a crypt; the odor from inside shall not be banished, and that is how you will know that it is a corpse) (Punimaemae 1861, 103). With this mele's publication in mind, Punimaʻemaʻe condemned *Ka Hoku* as a "makua nana e hanai i ko Hawaii poe keiki i ka apu awaawa o ka make" (a parent that is feeding Hawaiʻi's keiki the bitter poison of death) (Punimaemae 1861, 102).

What made this attack a translation issue was that the editors and supporters of *Ka Hoku o ka Pakipika* were convinced that Punimaʻemaʻe was haole—a missionary or a descendant, perhaps—and did not have the skills to understand the meaning of the mele. After reprinting Punimaʻemaʻe's letter, the editors looked at the mele involved, searching for any indecent language, and found nothing. Therefore, "ina ua loaa i ka mea nana i kakau ka mea i oleloia maluna (he haole no ia) i kekahi olelo maemae ole, na kona naau kuko no i hookupu mai ai ia mea ana i olelo ai he pelapela" (if the person who wrote the words printed above [they are clearly haole] found an unclean word, it was their own lustful heart that made what was said seem indecent) ("No Loko ae o ka Hae Hawaii" 1861, 2).

In a letter to *Hoku,* someone writing under the name Puni Nūpepa, or Favoring Newspapers, responded. Per Silva's account,

> Puni Nūpepa argued that no newspaper is perfect, and even the Bible is not free of words such as "adultery." He then challenged Puni Maʻamaʻe further: "Ina he haole oe e Punimaemae, e hoohalike kaua i ka hale kupapau, aole nae aʻu i ike he hale kupapau ulaula kekahi, koʻu ike he hale kupapau keokeo" (If you are haole, let us compare our tombs, I have never seen a brown tomb, what I have seen is a white tomb). Puni Nūpepa thus dared Puni Maʻemaʻe to reveal himself as a haole, and implied that if death were resulting from anyone's actions, it was from the haole, not from the Kanaka. (2004, 65)

Even two decades later, when Joseph Kānepuʻu looks back on the creation of *Ka Hoku o ka Pakipika,* he recalls Punimaʻemaʻe and says: "Ma ka manao ia, ke ola nei no ia kanaka, a he haole no nae" (It is thought that this person is still living, and is a haole) (Kānepuʻu 1878, 1).

No extant copies of the *Hoku* preview issue have been found, so we cannot look at the mele, and Punimaʻemaʻe did not quote the specific lines that were supposedly indecent, as the *Hoku* staff duly noted. But the comments from staff and readers alike suggest that they felt Punimaʻemaʻe's mana unuhi and translation abilities were too meager to understand the mele's manaʻo Hawaiʻi fully—itself evidence why a newspaper run by Hawaiians without being filtered through a haole lens was essential.

Punimaʻemaʻe was not the only one objecting, however. Outrage spread through mission churches, and reports began surfacing that those who subscribed to *Ka Hoku o ka Pakipika* would be expelled (Nailiili 1861, 2). *The Polynesian*, then edited by Abraham Fornander, an ally of Hawaiians who puni nūpepa, reported on the public scourging of *Hoku* and the mission's hypocrisy in regards to the Hawaiian turn toward being Writerly:

> To judge from the contents of the *Hoku o ka Pakipika*, the greatest opposition which the editors and managers of that journal experience, comes from the Protestant Missionaries, who, it would seem, use every endeavor to crush the *Hoku* and stop its circulation among their church members and others, whom they hope to influence, alleging that it is a wicked, vulgar and scurrilous sheet.... The sympathy of the natives is gathering strongly on the side of the Hoku in spite of clerical tabus, threats and admonitions, and the spirit of the conflict seems to be one of mental emancipation from a sway that was cheerfully submitted to when discreetly used, but against which even Hawaiians revolt when iterfering [sic] with the liberty of speech or opinion. (*The Polynesian*, November 23, 1861, 2)

Knowing that some Hawaiians are bilingual and will read his writing, Fornander here is not only showing his support for *Ka Hoku*, but also providing a translation of sorts of that newspaper for English-only readers potentially sympathetic to its cause, since many foreigners did not side with the mission. Fornander then cuts to the heart of the issue: "The truth is, that there is a mental revolution going on among the native population, which the Missionaries are equally incompetent to comprehend, to master or to avert, and of which evidently the *Hoku o ka Pakipika* (the people's journal), is more properly the result, rather than the cause." Though many opposed to *Hoku* continued to focus on the paper's "obscenity," its editors and readers, along with a few English-language newspapermen like Fornander, understood that the issue was more about the threatening power of Writerly Hawaiians finding their own voice through mana unuhi and writing than about any sort of obscenity.

Hawaiians were even more explicit about what they were up against, speaking to the opposition they were facing as something located within the missionary establishment but also within what would later come to be understood as plain ol' deep-seated racism. In a letter published in *Hoku* about the opposition they were facing, J. W. H. Kauwahi formally addresses his compatriots:

> Aloha ino kuu mau makamaka; kuu mau hanauna o ke kupuna hookahi; kuu mau hoa o ka hoino like ia, a me ka mahalo like ia, kuu mau hoa ili hoowahawaha hookahi ia e ka poe a oukou e hilinai nui nei.
>
> [Alas, my dear friends, my beloved generations who have come from the same ancestor, my comrades who have been collectively reviled and praised, *my friends whose skin has been reviled by the very people we are supposed to trust the most.*] (J. W. K. Kauwahi 1861, 3; emphasis added)

Language like this suggests that the relational ties connecting Hawaiians to the missionaries were fraying. While many remained under the sway of the mission, Hawaiians like the ones publishing *Hoku* clearly wanted to step out from their teachers' shadows, write their own moʻolelo, and translate material that they themselves found appealing to Hawaiian tastes and purposes.

Hoku's supporters also explicitly decry the hypocrisy of the mission and their descendants—a charge that became a well-worn critique over the next three decades:

> O ka poe nae i keu aku o ka hoino, oia ka poe nana i lawe mai ka naauao ia kakou, a oia naauao ka kakou e hana nei e like me ke akamai a lakou i ao mai ai. Makehewa maoli ka lakou lawe ana mai e haawi mai ia kakou i ka ike a me ke akamai, a oia ike a me ia akamai ka makou i hana iho ai, a e lilo ka ia ike a me ia akamai i mea enemi no lakou.
>
> [Those who are the most abusive, they are the very ones who brought knowledge/enlightenment to us, and it is that enlightenment that we are using now through the skills that they taught us. It's truly

unfair that they would give us this knowledge and these skills, and those same knowledge and skills are what we are using, and yet they have now become anathema to them.] (J. W. K. Kauwahi 1861, 2)

The editors of *Hoku* continue their trenchant analysis of the treatment they are receiving from the missionary establishment, also pointing to the paternalism of those who still believed they knew what is best for Hawaiians:

> He kanaha makahiki i hala mai ka hoomaka ana mai o keia lahui-kanaka e aoia, a e ike i ka palapala a me na mea naauao o keia noho ana, mamuli o ke ao ana a na misionari Amerika; a hiki i keia maka-hiki, ua kanaka makua na keiki, ua kani moopuna, a nolaila ke kukulu nei a ke hoolaha nei i Nupepa no lakou iho, e hoonaauao i ko lakou lahui; ua pau ka noho ana ma lalo o na makua oia na Kumu, a ua oo hoi, ua paa ka manao, e hoonaauao aku i na makamaka. Aka, ke keakea mai nei na makua, me he mea la e olelo ana, aole oukou i hiki i na makahiki e oo ai, na makou no ia hana, a ma ia ano, ke hoohuli ia nei i kekahi mau keiki.
>
> [It has been forty years since our lāhui was first taught to know literacy and the enlightened things of this age through the instruction of the American missionaries; until this year, when the children have reached adulthood, been blessed with grandchildren, and have there-fore decided to establish and distribute a newspaper for themselves, to enlighten their own people. Their living under the sway of their parents, the teachers, has come to an end; they have reached maturity, made up their minds that their friends should receive knowledge. Yet the parents are blocking the way, as if they are saying that you have not yet reached maturity, this work belongs only to us, and in that manner, we have been turned back into children.] (*Ka Hoku o ka Pakipika*, October 3, 1861, 2)

Many of the first generation of missionaries had by this time passed away; others like Hiram Bingham, Artemas Bishop, and Lorrin Andrews were elderly, and had even left the islands. Later company missionaries such as Amos Starr Cooke were still around, and in positions of power, but by the 1860s, their children and grandchildren were taking up the mission torch, which they would grasp for the rest of the century. In short, those missionaries the editors of *Hoku* call mākua did not ultimately step aside for their Hawaiian "children," and missionary descendants such as Sanford B. Dole and Lorrin Thurston established the Reform Party, often called the Missionary Party, which was pivotal in the usurpation of Hawaiian governmental power, and therefore the political power of individual Hawaiians.

Though the editors here are using the images of parents and children metaphorically, the generation of Hawaiians coming of age was also among the first for whom alphabetic literacy, and to a lesser extent unuhi and bilinguality, were simply a part of their lives. In 1861, Joseph Nāwahī and John E. Bush are nineteen years old, and their future mōʻī Liliʻuokalani is twenty-three. Literacy is something that has always been around them, a tool that they have always had at hand, not something that was absent until the missionaries brought it. This was just before the time when the first generation of professional Native writers were entering school on the continent: Zitkala Sa at White's Manual Institute and Carlos Montezuma at Carlisle, a fertile time for Indigenous writers to have their voices heard on their respective national levels (Round 2010, 7). For Liliʻu mā and their generations and those that follow, literacy is a Hawaiian practice, and once the newspapers begin, so is translation. That is why the idea of Hawaiians taking over the press is so threatening to the missionary party. The milk can't be unspilled, even though the Reform Party, the provisional government, and the republic in turn would try their best to bottle up Hawaiian voices and put the cap back on.

Though the critiques from *Hoku* editors and readers are speaking about trying to start a Hawaiian-led newspaper, they invoke the ideological—and sometimes the literal—battle between Hawaiians and the tenets of Western, and specifically American, civilization. Hawaiians made good-faith efforts to learn written language, law, governance, and religion because they could see the value of these things for ensuring the security and prosperity of the lāhui. And thanks to those efforts, they excelled. In unprecedentedly short amounts of time, Hawaiians achieved near-universal literacy, created their own constitution and laws, and set up their own government based on Hawaiian values and modeled on the principles they had learned were the hallmarks of justice and fairness. And yet, whenever the haole/missionary establishment felt that Hawaiians had gained too much mana, everything they had been taught to "civilize" them went out the window.[1] Upon *Hoku*'s publication, Hawaiians were critiqued from the pulpit and decried as evil. As we have also seen, when Hawaiians began gaining a powerful familiarity with the law, the genealogical axiom and a predominantly foreign judiciary put an end to that. And when in the 1890s the government tried to reestablish its powers through legitimate mechanisms and precedents, U.S. troops were landed and the Queen was overthrown. Yet even with these forces in play, the *Hoku* editors stood strong and resilient, reassuring the lāhui:

> Mai hopohopo oukou e na kanaka Hawaii, o ko kakou pepa keia; na na keiki papa o keia paeaina i kukulu ai; no laila e puili mai kakou e like me ka puili ana o ke kowali i ke kano o ka laau, a e hookahua maoli i kona ola mau iwaena o keia lahui.
>
> [Do not fear, O Hawaiian people, this is our paper. The native-born children of this archipelago are the ones who built it; so let us hold fast, just as the kowali vine wraps around the trunk of a tree, and let us set a strong foundation for its life here in our lāhui.] (*Ka Hoku o ka Pakipika*, September 26, 1861, 2)

Despite or because of the early controversy surrounding its birth, *Hoku* only lasted for a little less than two years. For all their cleverness and ideological maneuvering, what made the nūpepa vibrant yet vulnerable was their status as businesses. And that meant attracting not just subscribers, but advertisers. Because the mission/plantation interests were the business elites, *Hoku* not surprisingly had a hard time finding advertisers, even after placing notices in such English-language papers as *The Polynesian* offering the availability of advertising space and free translation into Hawaiian ("Advertise" 1862, 1). And yet, although it would not enjoy a long run of its own, *Ka Hoku o ka Pakipika* laid a firm foundation in the lāhui, planting the seeds and providing the inspiration for future literary practitioners and the vibrant Hawaiian-language newspaper public sphere to come.

Ka Nupepa Kuokoa

Ka Nupepa Kuokoa was essentially started when publisher Henry Whitney was unable to take control of *Ka Hoku o ka Pakipika*. It became *Ka Hoku*'s business and ideological rival. Kānepu'u and the others had arranged for the government press to print *Hoku,* but then Whitney offered to rent them his press. But his prices kept rising, so Kānepu'u mā decided to stay with the government press. Then Whitney offered to take on all the printing expenses if they would dissolve their 'ahahui and give him control (N. Silva 2004, 68). That was hardly acceptable, so the 'ahahui stayed with its plans to print *Ka Hoku* at the government press—although some members joined up with Whitney instead to produce *Ka Nupepa Kuokoa*. A missionary descendant and longtime newspaperman, Whitney established the English-language *Pacific Commercial Advertiser* in 1856 (Hori 2001). By 1858, Whitney was doing all of the mission's printing, and in 1859, he bought the press for $1,300. Though its influence did not wane, the mission press therefore officially ended in that year (Ballou and Carter 1908, 44).

Whitney may have called his new publication *Ka Nupepa Kuokoa* (The independent newspaper), but he placed it firmly in the tradition of the mission-run Hawaiian-language newspapers. The objectives announced in the first issue on October 1, 1861, could have appeared in *Ka Hae* or *Ke Kumu*:

> Alua. E hoolaha ia ana na manao haole o kela aina o keia aina; ke ano o ko lakou noho ana, hana ana, ao ana, ikaika ana, kuonoono ana, ia mea ae, ia mea ae, i hiki ai i kanaka ke ike ia mau mea, a e lilo ai i poe like me na mea naauao.
>
> Akolu. E hoolahaia hoi na oihana mahiai pono, a e hoike i na mea paahana maikai e hiki ai ke mahi e like me na haole naauao. E paipai hoi keia pepa i na hana me ka molowa ole.
>
> [...]
>
> O ka manao nui ma keia pepa, ka hoolaha aku i na mea hoonaauao a pau i ku i ke kanaka pono ke ike maopopo, i hoolikeia'i ko lakou noho ana me ko na haole.
>
> [Second. The haole ideas of each and every land will be spread; how they live, work, teach, grow strong, reach prosperity, and so on, so that Hawaiians can see these things and become like the enlightened peoples.
>
> Third. Proper agricultural techniques will be shared, so that the industrious ones can farm like knowledgeable haole. This paper will also encourage work without laziness.

[…]
The main idea of this paper is to make known all the enlightened things so that the pono Hawaiian can see clearly and so that their lives resemble those of the haole.]

Though it can be argued that *Kuokoa* was less devoted to propagating and celebrating the gospel, many of its early mission-press features were intact. As *Ka Lama Hawaii* had done seventeen years before (February 14, 1834), the first issue featured a block print of a camel with accompanying "entertaining" text.

Predictably, those accusing the Hawaiian-run *Ka Hoku o ka Pakipika* of poisoning the youth of the lāhui saw the Whitney-published *Ka Nupepa Kuokoa* as their champion. A letter from *Hoku* translated in *The Polynesian* quoted Rev. W. P. Alexander as saying "*The Star of the Pacific,* it is on the side of pleasure; it is for the Devil." The recipient of the letter, who had been asked to act as newspaper agent on Maui for *Hoku,* was urged to tell people to take *Kuokoa* instead ("The New Native Newspaper" 1861, 2). Congregations in Kona were told not to subscribe to *Hoku,* "for it was a great sin in a church-member to do so," and one teacher lobbied for a regulation that any member or officer who subscribed to *Hoku* should be declared a bad member, kicked out of church, and refused forgiveness for sins ("Ecclesiastical Thunder" 1862, 2). Even prominent Hawaiians, such as John Papa 'Ī'ī, a keeper of traditional mo'olelo himself, came down on the side of *Kuokoa:* "Some discussion arose, in which the Hon. John Ii took a conspicuous part, and according to him 'the evils which afflicted the country most and stood in greatest need of legislative revision, were the law of the 24th of August to mitigate the evils arising from prostitution,' and who would have thought it! the Hawaiian newspaper, the 'Hoku o ka Pakipika.' The first he stigmatised as a disgrace to the country and the age, the latter was the sum and essence of all iniquity" (*The Polynesian,* November 16, 1861, 2). So deep was the church's hate of *Hoku* that just reading it was apparently enough to send you to everlasting damnation or brand you as "evil," as if you had been engaging in prostitution.

Though Whitney's relationships with the planter and business class went up and down, *Kuokoa* became the longest-running Hawaiian newspaper, going for seven decades. Whitney was a canny businessman and knew that it was not necessarily the creed of a paper that ensured its longevity; rather, it was how many advertisers they could get to buy space (his other paper was actually called the *Pacific Commercial Advertiser*). Pro-American through its entire run, the paper also lobbied for the "advancement" of the lāhui, though what that meant often reinforced its U.S.-friendly stance. Whitney could, however, recognize talent. *Kuokoa* had some fantastic editors throughout its seventy-year run, including Simeon Nawaa, who was actually born on a missionary ship in the Marshalls and acquired a vast knowledge of moʻolelo and language (Hori 2001), and Joseph Kawainui, later editor of *Ko Hawaii Pae Aina,* whom Kānepuʻu called a "kanaka Hawaii kuokoa" (an independent Hawaiian) (1878, 1). Like Joseph Poepoe, some of these editors ended up editing nationalist papers, and despite its own avowed goal of making Hawaiians more like haole, *Kuokoa* printed a good bit of content about traditional practices, moʻolelo, and mele, including huge series by John Papa ʻĪʻī and Samuel Kamakau (Chapin 1996b, 56–57).

But being the longest-running Hawaiian-language newspaper did not mean *Kuokoa* was the most influential or widely read. Helen Chapin notes that during some of the most tumultuous times of the kingdom, including the aftermath of the overthrow, it just barely made it by: "*Kuokoa* once enjoyed a circulation of perhaps 5,000 but had lost readers who no longer were willing to overlook its pro-Americanism, or as John Sheldon [also known as Kahikina Kelekona], editor of the nationalist *Holomua,* expressed it, *Kuokoa* had to be 'given away free' to Islanders who used it to start morning cooking fires" (1996b, 93). Even though *Kuokoa* was avowedly and proudly establishment, as Chapin has called it, there is much to be gained from perusing its pages. Recognizable and relatively inoffensive to the establishment, *Kuokoa* undeniably attracted business.

Evolving Models of Translation in the Nūpepa

Chapters 1 and 2 dealt with institutional translation—by the church and the government. Translation in the nūpepa, however, is essentially literary translation in the wild. It shows the true mana in mana unuhi. I am using "literary" here to distinguish translation of written works from the type used in everyday contexts, such as business transactions. I am therefore calling many works "literary" that might not necessarily be considered "literature" by some—religious tracts and news articles, for instance. Translation was the driving engine for scriptural and legal texts; in the newspapers, translation was one of a number of tools used to speak to other Hawaiians. Though ʻōlelo Hawaiʻi was spoken by people of all ethnicities and national origins in the kingdom, the nūpepa's main audience was Hawaiians. For them, translation was a means for informing themselves about Hawaiian and foreign knowledge, for granting Hawaiians a voice in the print world, and for entertaining themselves. Thus, while translation "was, and still is, the central act of European colonization and imperialism" (Cheyfitz 1997, xii), as mentioned in chapter 1, it was also a means by which Hawaiians reaffirmed their own voices and narratives. Translation into ʻōlelo Hawaiʻi was also a signifier of Hawaiian cultural confidence as all of the moʻolelo and ʻike being brought into the Hawaiian language were seen as additive and there were no great worries about diluting Hawaiian culture and identity, each one another mana of the story being told of a cosmopolitan culture rooted in its history and ready for the future. Mana unuhi in the nūpepa was an expansive, confident, powerful beauty.

As it was for the book trade and the circulation of newsprints across America and the Atlantic (Reichardt 2018, 802), translation was essential to the day-to-day operations of the Hawaiian-language newspapers. Foreign news was translated from foreign newspapers or other trustworthy sources coming through the port. Translations of foreign fiction and nonfiction, ranging from histories and classic literature to bodice rippers and pulpy detective stories, were printed next to Hawaiian moʻolelo. Laws, proclamations, and treaties with other countries were translated, and by law, government notices appeared in Hawaiian and English. Even the advertisements were often translations. The newspapers critiqued each other's translations as well. The editors of *Hoku* called out *Kuokoa* for a shoddy translation of an article from the *Pacific Commercial Advertiser* ("Unuhi Olelo Paewaewa" 1862, 2), and *Kuokoa*'s pages hosted a several-months-long heated debate kicked off by someone named G. M. Koha that involved several challenges back and forth regarding translations of various passages between Hawaiian, Latin, Greek, and Hebrew (Piliole 1862, 3).

As the papers got larger and the type more tightly packed, the challenge of filling the columns only increased. Some pieces no doubt were carefully chosen for translation because of the effect they would have on the reading public. It is just as likely, however, that others were chosen because they supplied those last two column inches needed for an issue to go to press. This is one of many reasons why the nūpepa are so interesting to study. Since translation was practiced by every newspaper, and editors had to develop their own methods of selection and execution, a systematic survey of the translated foreign moʻolelo—involving assessments of themes and possible reasons for publication at particular moments—would yield amazing insights into the Hawaiian editorial mind. Why, for instance, was Robert Hoapili Baker's translation of the life of Stonewall Jackson published on July 13, 1876, in *Ka Lahui Hawaii*? What light do the multiple translations of Tarzan stories in the twentieth century shed on the colonial imagination? Though such a study is outside the scope of this book, here I will focus briefly on two instances that reveal something about how translation was working in the nūpepa.

A Lesson in Translation

As part of Whitney's efforts to help Hawaiians make their lives like those of the haole, he published several translated European fairy tales. Since these tales frequently offered explicit lessons about morality and behavior—women shouldn't be curious, for instance—it should not be surprising that Whitney was drawn to them. Rubellite Kawena Johnson lists fourteen stories published in the first year of *Kuokoa*'s publication (1976, 204–205); the entire run of fairy tales and folktales included "Snow White," "Beauty and the Beast," "The Frog Prince," and more. Charles Perrault's "Bluebeard" is my focus. I have written about this translation at length elsewhere; here the subject will be the powerful effects of moving even a loaded tale meant to "civilize" and "enlighten" Hawaiians into ʻōlelo Hawaiʻi.

Translation is still most often understood as a "lossy" transfer. "Lost in translation" is an oft-repeated aphorism. And in a way it is true; throughout this analysis, we have been talking about how translation is not a process of complete transfer, that it is an interpretation and a reauthoring, and one part of that is meaning that was in the source text but for some reason did not make it into the translation. In Hawaiian academic and community discussions, we often focus on this aspect of loss as well. Larry Kimura, one of the pioneers of the Hawaiian language revitalization movement, lays out this "lost in translation" understanding pretty clearly: "English is a vehicle of its own culture and... English words carry their own connotations and history. Whenever Hawaiian is translated into English, the English words used add cultural connotations to the idea conveyed, while eliminating intended connotations and meanings of the original Hawaiian" (1983, 182). He goes into further detail about why this imperfect correlation between languages is troublesome for all involved: "Descriptions of the indigenous Hawaiian aesthetic culture and base culture through the medium of the imposed English language cannot absolutely transmit a full picture of Hawaiian culture. English inevitably implies Anglo-American culture in direct proportion to the part of Hawaiian culture that is lost in the description. This has a negative impact on Hawaiians, not only in the impression gained by outsiders, but also in the self-impression gained by English-speaking Hawaiians using such descriptions" (1983, 184). But there are also a multitude of other planes that come into play besides loss: among them gain, shifting, reemphasizing, reframing, obscuring, reinvigorating.

This focus on loss alone is why many contemporary Hawaiians are so leery of translation. It undergirds the familiar history of the practice, which we will examine more closely in chapter 4. But as articulated by Larry Kimura, this paradigm refers solely to those extractive translation practices moving from Hawaiian to English, carried out largely for the benefit of mainly non-Hawaiian scholars. The same is likely true about many other Indigenous contexts across the Pacific and Native North America, which bears further investigation, but a somewhat different legacy and understanding of translation emerges when we consider translation of the Bible into Hawaiian, or the back-and-forth between Hawaiian and English in legal translation, or, most pertinent for our discussions here, the results when Hawaiians chose to translate moʻolelo for other Hawaiians. For when you invert Kimura's model, translating into Hawaiian represents a cultural *gain*. This is what makes paying attention to mana unuhi so important; as we mentioned earlier, mana is never one way and it is all about pilina. To recast Kimura's remarks: because the medium of the *Hawaiian* language cannot absolutely transmit a full picture of *Anglo-American* culture, it follows that *ʻŌlelo Hawaiʻi* inevitably implies *Hawaiian* culture in direct proportion to what of *Anglo-American* culture is lost. As a result, these foreign moʻolelo are drawn into a Hawaiian understanding and worldview, as the added connotations from the chosen Hawaiian words shift the foreign mores and values closer to the mana of ʻāina, ea, lāhui, kanaka, ʻohana—all things we hold dear. Bringing something into the Hawaiian language does not of course automatically make it culturally Hawaiian, but it does—and sometimes deliberately—bring it into our sphere of influence and give mana to our epistemologies. So when a nūpepa like *Kuokoa*, committed to pushing Hawaiians toward making their lives more like those of the haole, publishes a fairy tale like "Bluebeard" within a year of its first issue, the editors may intend the story to entertain and delight, to teach women to restrain their curiosity (Tatar 2004, 3), and to communicate valuable lessons about "civilized" behavior. But through the act of translating into Hawaiian this account of a brutal male serial killer, complete with its misogynistic moral, some of its supposed "enlightening" content shifts.

On June 14, 1862, *Ka Nupepa Kuokoa* published "Umiumi Uliuli," a version of Charles Perrault's "Bluebeard." Known only as JW, the translator was responsible for versions of a handful of other fairy tales.[2] Because it does not follow the French original, it was likely translated from an English-language chapbook—probably a version printed through 1889 and republished in *Amusing Prose Chap-Books, Chiefly of the Last Century*, edited by Robert Hays Cunningham, since the translation follows this version closely. For those unfamiliar with the story, here is a summary. A woman falls in love with a rich man with a blue beard. When they are married, he gives her the keys to every room in his house, saying that she may go into any room except one. He then goes off on a business trip. Left to her own devices, she gets bored and looks around the house, finally ending up in the forbidden room, where she finds the remains of all his murdered previous wives. Understandably freaking out, she drops the key in their blood, which will not come off. The man of course returns soon after, sees the blood on the key, knows she has gone into the room, becomes enraged, and prepares to kill her. She asks for time to pray, and he agrees. She then calls out to her sister to keep an eye out for her brothers, who are supposed to arrive that day. The man gets angrier and angrier. He calls out to his wife, but she delays until her brothers arrive in the nick of time and kill him.

In the original French, Perrault simply identifies the key as "fée" or "enchanted." In the English chapbook, the key is "a Fairy, who was Blue Beard's friend." In the Hawaiian version, however, the key has "mana" and is an "aikane" of 'Umi'umi Uliuli's. As mentioned earlier, mana refers to a branch or version of a moʻolelo, but it is also a power that inheres in people, places, and objects. JW could have used a few other words for magic/enchanted, but "mana" probably would have come to mind first. But mana is not magic. No uncanny supernatural/unnatural force, it is very much *of* the world. Everyone has mana, though in varying degrees. Neither separate or outside, it is something that we feel and witness every day. Describing the key as having "mana" also ties it to ʻāina, kānaka, and even the kini akua, the pantheon of Hawaiian deities/elements. In the Bible, mana's connection to the kini akua is reinforced because the Christian God must be referred to as the "Akua mana loa"—often translated as "Almighty God," but also meaning the god with the most mana. Though Christianity clearly has a powerful foothold at this time, many Hawaiians have not given up the kini akua, and almost a hundred years later, in a 1951 interview with Flora and Homer Hayes for the Bishop Museum, my own kupuna Lui Pānui talks about reading the Bible and then going outside to find the akua Pele at his house. Though he refers to her as an aliʻi rather than an akua, he still observes certain kapu when approaching her. The key's mana therefore brings it into the realm of a traditional Hawaiian understanding. This does not mean that readers thought the key was an akua or a Hawaiian cultural object; rather, the associations readers would make upon reading about the mana of the key would be with the kini akua and non-Christian understandings of mana.

The English word "friend" in the chapbook version is probably what JW was trying to get across with "aikāne," since, as mentioned in chapter 2, the mission and polite society had for some time been trying to equate the two terms. Why? Because missionaries and their descendants raised on a steady diet of heteropatriarchy and Eve-coming-from-the-iwiʻaoʻao-of-Adam ("iwiʻaoʻao" even became a colloquialism for wife during the nineteenth century) were horrified by what an aikāne actually was. As Hawaiian scholar Jamaica Osorio describes them, aikāne are "intimate pilina" (2018, 79). Aikāne relationships appear most often in moʻolelo, though aliʻi had very public aikāne relationships well into the nineteenth century. Kamehameha had many, including the former sailor John Young, who was at his deathbed, and we saw Kauikeaouli's aikāne relationship in chapter 2. Aikāne are in a very intimate relationship/friendship with someone of the same sex—often a sexual relationship, but based first and foremost on the 'upena of intimacies that Osorio discusses, with the sex arising out of that closeness, rather than being required. Although I have never encountered a Hawaiian story in which a human, or a demigod, took an object as an aikāne, by using that word for the key, the translator unavoidably brings to the Hawaiian reader's mind the "intimate pilina" of aikāne relationships, rather than the bowdlerized "friend" that the mission was pushing for. Through translation, then, the magical aspects of the story that make it a "fairy" tale end up invoking a traditional Hawaiian worldview.

Even the wife's much-critiqued (at least at that time) curiosity is transformed in the translation. In *The Hard Facts of the Grimms' Fairy Tales*, Maria Tatar writes that "nearly every nineteenth-century printed version of 'Bluebeard' singles out the heroine's curiosity as an especially undesirable trait" (2019, 158). But in those places where the wife's reckless and insatiable curiosity is often condemned, the Hawaiian version uses such phrases and words as "e kaunui ana kona manao e ike i na mea oloko o ka lumi" (her thoughts were greatly set upon seeing what was in the room) and "makemake loa" (greatly desired or wanted). In this version, the woman makes up her mind to look in the room not because of some innate curiosity that will prove her downfall, but because she decided she would.

When this decision undeniably gets her into trouble, she calls out to her sister Anne (or 'Ane in the Hawaiian), who also appears somewhat differently due to the shift into a Hawaiian cultural context. As 'Umi'umi Uliuli prepares to kill his wife, she cries out, "E kuu kaikuaana, e Ane!" "Kaikua'ana" is not what is interesting here; as a Hawaiian kinship term referring specifically to an elder sibling of the same sex, it is the only appropriate choice. Just as the wife calls her older sister "kaikua'ana," a younger brother would call his older brother "kaikua'ana." Our 'ōlelo offers no other option. What *is* interesting, however, is what a Hawaiian reader would make of the sisters' relationship because of that kinship term.

The relationship between elder and younger siblings is foundational to Hawaiian understandings of the world. Our most cherished elder/younger sibling relationship is the one between the kanaka, the person, and the 'āina, the land. It is embodied in the story of Hāloa, the first kalo. Hāloa was the child of Wākea, the Sky Father, and his daughter, Hoʻohokukalani.[3] That first Hāloa was stillborn, and buried near the house, where the first kalo plant then grew. Another Hāloa was born of Wākea and Hoʻohokukalani, and he became the progenitor of the Hawaiian people. The reciprocal relationship between elder and younger brothers here actually made life possible. Kalo became the staple of the lāhui Hawaiʻi, feeding the people for generations upon generations, and in turn, feeding and providing for those younger became the elder's responsibility. As for the younger, they cared for the elder—the kalo, but also the ʻāina from which it grew. The younger must therefore create the conditions of abundance that make it possible for the elder to grow. As the kaikuaʻana, then, ʻAne's watching for their brothers, instead of being the passive act of the Western versions, is part of a reciprocal assertion of care for her younger sibling.

Translation does not change "Umiumi Uliuli" into a powerful moʻolelo about mana wahine of the kind celebrated in Hiʻiakaikapoliopele, or Haumea, or even the history of Kaʻahumanu. But it does shift the mana from a story blaming men's violence on a woman's curiosity to the tale of two sisters relying on their elder/younger sister reciprocal pilina to protect themselves against the enraged ʻUmiʻumi Uliuli until their brothers can dispatch him. Though Whitney may have wanted to foist more of his precious haole manaʻo on the Hawaiian reading public, these tales went through massive transformations merely by entering the world of ʻōlelo Hawaiʻi through the process of translation.

Introducing Captain Nemo, Staunch Aloha ʻĀina

The example of "Umiumi Uliuli" suggests how powerful unuhi could be as a tool for reshaping Western knowledge into forms more understandable and relevant to the lāhui Hawaiʻi. Unlike the concerted effort of Bible translation to maintain an equivalence with the original, even if it meant creating new words, many of the nūpepa translations are tailored to enlighten, but also to entertain—and to sell papers. Traditional, translated, or newly authored, good moʻolelo were the blockbusters of the day, drawing in readers and advertisers. Less explicitly didactic than tales like "Bluebeard," translations of stories like *Tarzan*, *Ivanhoe*, and *The Count of Monte Cristo* might have expanded Hawaiian intellectual ethical horizons somewhat, though their principal purpose was entertainment. But narratives, and especially Hawaiian moʻolelo, also had mana, and were deployed by Hawaiian literary practitioners to shape public opinion about certain issues. *He Moʻolelo Kaʻao o Kamapuaʻa,* for instance, the story of the sexually voracious pig akua, was published at the height of Kalākaua's push for Hawaiians to hoʻoulu lāhui, or increase the nation, which in one sense meant having more children. Similarly, the 1893 moʻolelo of Kaluaikoʻolau, about a Hawaiian family resisting the aggression of an outside authority, was republished in the nūpepa during the Massie case in the 1930s, when U.S. newspapers were attacking Hawaiʻi and its residents. And Hawaiian translators were also canny enough to bring foreign moʻolelo into the Hawaiian toolbox for pushing values important to the lāhui.

A good example of this is G. W. Kanuha's translation of *20,000 Leagues under the Sea.* Jules Verne's hugely popular novel was first published in its entirety in the original French in 1870. Kanuha's translation began to appear in *Ka Nupepa Kuokoa* in 1875. The translation was announced thusly:

> E unuhiia ana keia kaao mai ka olelo Farani mai, e ka unuhi moolelo kaulana o Hawaii nei, a e kakauia ana ma na ano olelo a ko Hawaii nei e hialaai ai, i maopopo ai i na kanaka ui a me na hapauea.
>
> [This tale will be translated from French by the famous translator of Hawaiʻi, and it shall be written in an idiom that will delight those of us from Hawaiʻi, and it shall be understood by young and old alike.] ("He Kaao Hou" 1875, 2)

Besides Kanuha's status as the "unuhi moʻolelo kaulana o Hawaiʻi nei," the announcement is playing up the very aspect we are discussing here, that the story will be brought into the terms familiar to the people of Hawaiʻi. It is also worth noting that Kanuha is described as kaulana (renowned/famous/celebrated) for his work as a translator, showing the mana and perceived importance of translation and literary practitioners for the lāhui Hawaiʻi at the time. Though Kanuha is said to have translated the moʻolelo from the original French ("He Kaao Hou" 1875, 2),[4] he was renowned for his knowledge of English:

> He kupa Hawaii o Mr Kanuha ma ka ili a ma ka hanau ana, aka, kona waha he waha o ke kanaka Pelekane ma ka olelo Beretania, a e hiki ia ke unuhi laelae mai ka olelo Enelani a i ka olelo Hawaii.

[Mr. Kanuha is a native of Hawai'i in his skin and in his birth, but his mouth is that of a British person when he speaks English, and he can translate with great facility from English to Hawaiian.] ("He Eehia" 1876, 2)

Kanuha was a prolific and respected translator, with a number of stories published in *Kuokoa*. He also helped Sunday schools by translating texts ("He Eehia" 1876, 2). Though he translated *20,000 Leagues under the Sea* in its entirety, he died in 1876 at the age of thirty-one, before seeing all of it published.

Especially in the English-speaking world, Captain Nemo is often seen as a cynic, disgusted with society. Steampunk scholar Diana Pho describes him as "short-tempered, tyrannical, and driven by an arrogant misanthropy that leads him to attack civilian and military warships and fund revolutions" (2009). Once translated into the moana and the kai, rather than the *mer*, however, he became something different, something altogether more aloha 'āina.

A powerful concept, aloha 'āina is the foundation for much of Hawaiian belief and culture. Deserving of a description that would fill a series of books, rather than a few scant paragraphs, it is so important to the argument here that I will nevertheless offer a brief overview. Jamaica Osorio writes that "aloha 'āina is central to any mo'olelo of Hawai'i because our specific connection and relationship to land informs all of Kanaka Maoli ontology and epistemology" (2018, 11). This reciprocal dynamic between land, or 'āina, and kanaka, or person, ensures that everything in the realm of the kanaka is tied to 'āina: where they are from, where they are at, how they interact with those around them, what they eat, what they wear, what they hear and see and smell. All of these states and actions are related to 'āina because of our genealogical connections to the land, because our bones return to it, because everything we need comes from it. Some even make the case that we indeed *are* 'āina: "expressions such as 'āina, one hānau, kulāiwi, kua 'āina, pua, and kupa, all words that seal the intrinsic notion of people = land in a Hawaiian context" (Arista 2020, 34). Aloha 'āina also drives Hawaiians to work for the lāhui, the people or the nation, which is bounded by the 'āina. Made explicit on innumerable occasions in print and in speeches, whenever any Hawaiian is working to benefit the people or protect/increase the mana and ea of the lāhui, they are driven by aloha 'āina.

This might be a weird trait to associate with a man who almost never wishes to set foot upon dry land, preferring the company of the sea. Yet that too is merely a translation problem. "'Āina" does not mean "land," but that is the closest understandable shorthand. For us to say "elder sibling who feeds" in places where a reader would expect "land" would draw too much attention to itself and cause confusion. 'Āina to a Hawaiian is that which feeds and must be cared for and has a genealogical connection to all of us, and what English-speakers understand as "sea" falls into that category of 'āina as well.

Shoddy early translations of Verne's original French into English diluted much of what made Captain Nemo a staunch anti-colonialist. While most popular versions of Nemo present him as a white European, he was actually Prince Dakkar, an Indian man whose family was killed in the 1857 uprising against the East India Company (Perschon 2009). Jordan Stump's modern translation of Verne's sequel *The Mysterious Island* renders the author's description of Dakkar/Nemo as "Indian in his heart, Indian in his longing for revenge, Indian in his dreams of reclaiming his native land, driving out the invaders, and inaugurating a new era of independence" (Verne 2004, 672). Though Nemo's background is not revealed in *20,000 Leagues under the Sea*, it is hinted at in a scene involving an Indian pearl diver. It is not known, but it is highly possible that Kanuha read *The Mysterious Island* before translating *20,000 Leagues*, since the former story was published in 1874, and Kanuha's obituary describes him as a voracious reader. No matter how he sat, "aia no ka buke imua o kona maka" (he always had a book in front of his face) ("He Eehia" 1876, 2).

But whether Kanuha knew Nemo's Indian identity or not, his anti-colonial leanings—what some read as his misanthropy—were clear from *20,000 Leagues* and from the Hawaiian translation. Kanuha also seems to be portraying the *Nautilo* (*Nautilus*) as Nemo's 'āina, inviting readers to see the submarine as Hawai'i and Kāpena Nimo as an aloha 'āina. Kanuha's version was published in the midst of the fierce debates over the Reciprocity Treaty, a free trade agreement that would allow sugar to enter the United States duty-free, making Hawaiian sugar competitive with American domestic sugar. What made the debate so fraught, among other things, was the United States' desire to take control of Pu'uloa, now known as Pearl Harbor, and build a deep draft harbor. Many Hawaiians, such as Joseph Nāwahī, the representative from Puna, were staunchly opposed to any loss of 'āina to foreign nations. In Kanuha's translation, when Kāpena Nimo first meets Aronaxa, Nede Lana, and Kosila, he tells them that "ua hiki mai oukou e hoopilikia wale i ko'u aupuni a me ko'u noho ana" (you have come to trouble my aupuni and my lifestyle) ("He Iwakalua" March 4, 1876). Because the *Nautilo* is Nimo's aupuni, he won't countenance threats to it. And because "aupuni" is the word used for "government" or "nation," the valence in this scene differs substantially from the original.

Later in the same chapter, Aronaxa observes regarding Nimo, whose name he has not yet learned, that

> aole o na kanawai pili lahui wale no kana i kaupale aku ai: ua hoolilo maoli no iaia iho, he haku kuokoa no kona mau manao, i kaa loa aku mawaho o na palena a ko ke ao i apono ai, a mawaho hoi o na palena o ko lakou mana!
>
> [it was not merely the laws relating to lāhui that he refuted: he had truly turned himself into a haku with kū'oko'a based on his own desires; he is beyond what the world at large deems appropriate, and he is free from the boundaries of their mana!] ("He Iwakalua" March 4, 1876)

With a rogue British captain's six-month takeover of Hawai'i in 1843 still in living memory, and at a moment when the United States was encroaching on the Hawaiian Kingdom's ea in exchange for economic concessions through the Reciprocity Treaty, Kanuha's Nimo embodies the weary but resolute aloha 'āina whose fight for his aupuni and the 'āina (kai/moana/*mer*) constitutes the core of his being. Nimo is explicitly pushing for kū'oko'a, a word Hawaiians use when they speak of independence, both on a national and a local scale. Though it is possible modern 'ōlelo Hawai'i readers could read "aole o na kanawai pili lahui wale no kana i kaupale aku ai" (what I have translated as "it was not merely the laws relating to lāhui that he refuted") to mean that Nimo is beyond the idea of lāhui/nation itself, meaning he would not be thinking of kū'oko'a on a national scale, I think that that is too modern of a reading for the context of political discussions of the time and undercut by Nimo referring to the *Nautilo* as his aupuni earlier.

Nimo later addresses his friend Aronaxa passionately:

A! e noho—e noho iloko o ka poli o na wai! Malaila wale no e loaa ai ia oe ke kuokoa! Malaila i ike ai au, aohe mau haku maluna iho oʻu! Malaila ua lanakila au!

[Indeed! Live—you must live within the bosom of the waters! It is only there where you will find kūʻokoʻa! It is there that I found there to be no lord over me! There I was victorious!] ("He Iwakalua" March 25, 1876)

Again, kūʻokoʻa is the subject, and for Hawaiian readers, the sea would echo ʻāina, leading to a likely reading of this passage that would affirm their kūʻokoʻa in the ʻāina, and remind them to hold fast to aloha ʻāina and the connections that make them Hawaiian. It is not certain whether Kalākaua, the new mōʻī of the Hawaiian Kingdom, read Verne's original, an English translation, or Kanuha's translation. But the character of Kāpena Nimo, and no doubt his call to return to the ʻāina/kai/moana/*mer* in the search for kūʻokoʻa, must have resonated, because Kalākaua built a model of the *Nautilo* that he kept in ʻIolani Palace.

Kalākaua later founded the Papa Kūʻauhau, or Genealogy Board, an entity responsible for checking and collecting aliʻi genealogies. But as Hawaiian historian Kealani Cook states, because of a far-ranging understanding of genealogy and its connection to knowledge, the charter actually proved much more expansive: "Though restricted by law to research only kūʻauhau and mele, the broad definition of kūʻauhau included a vast number of sub-disciplines, including: 'Physiology, Psychology, Philology, Paleontology, Zoology, Botany, Ornithology, and Choncology [the study of mollusks], and other scientific subjects pertaining to the Hawaiian Islands, without which the work of the board would be incomplete'" (2018, 179–180). The board and its successor, the Hale Nauā, were founded as means for insisting on the validity, importance, and mana of Hawaiian knowledge. The goal was to create and live as modern Hawaiian peoples standing on the foundations of their culture, rather than always having to react to and refute incorrect assertions by haole. In fact, the board stated that it would not "hooponopono i keia mau buke a me na moolelo i kakau ia e ka haole" (correct these books and moʻolelo written by the haole) because it had more than enough to do fulfilling its own mission (N. Silva 2004, 95). As for the Hale Nauā, it was essentially a private outgrowth of the government-sponsored Papa Kūʻauahu. A secret organization, its "object" was "the revival of Ancient Science of Hawaii in combination with the promotion and advancement of Modern Sciences, Art, Literature, and Philanthropy" (Hale Nauā 1890, 6). The Hale Nauā also ignored the haole moʻolelo about Hawaiians, devoting itself to publishing its own books: "the Genealogy Book of Hawaii, Diametral, Physiography, the practices of high-diving and surfing" and more (*Hale Naua Society* 1999, 123).

Kāpena Nimo's strategy of stepping away from the rest of the world to care for his own aupuni (the *Nautilo*), while constantly educating himself, echoes the philosophy of these two organizations. The Hale Nauā and the Papa Kūʻauhau refused to define themselves in haole terms, or set legibly haole goals. So of course, the predictable critics demonized them, with the Hale Nauā in particular denounced as "an agency for the revival of heathenism, partly to pander to vice, and indirectly to serve as a political machine. Enough leaked out to intensify the general disgust that was felt at the debasing influence of the palace" (Alexander 1894, 32). So threatening was the idea of Hawaiians adopting their own approaches to science and modernity, and so intimately linked to the kūʻokoʻa that Nimo (and Kanuha) said would be found in the ʻāina/kai/moana/*mer,* that in 1895, the newspaper *Ka Makaainana* concluded that "a o kekahi ka hoi o na kumu i kahulihia ai o ke Aupuni Moi, no ka Ahahui Hale Naua" (indeed, one of the reasons that the kingdom was overthrown was the Hale Nauā) ("Maloo na Iwi i ka La" 1895, 5). Kalākaua's model *Nautilus* and his understanding of Nemo have their correlatives in the mōʻī's enlistment of technology and knowledge of the ʻāina/kai/moana/*mer* in the cause of staving off foreign depredations.

In the final sessions before the passage of the Reciprocity Treaty, Joseph Nāwahī plays a powerful Kāpena Nimo himself, crying out that

> he wahi aupuni ko kākou i makaleho ʻia e nā Haole e lilo no lākou, akā, ua hoka wale nō ia mau hoʻāʻo ʻana a pau. He nui wale nō nā hoʻāʻo ʻana a lākou i loko o nā makahiki i hala aku nei, a ʻo ka hāʻawi ʻana iā Puʻuloa kā lākou hana hope loa i hoʻāʻo ai, a nele ihola. Akā, ʻānō, ke kāpili nei lākou i kiʻi lio lāʻau me ka hoʻokomo ʻia o ka ʻenemi i loko.
>
> [we are a small nation that the foreigners have cast a greedy eye upon like an octopus coveting a cowry, desiring that it pass into their

possession, yet their efforts have met with only frustration. They have tried over and over again during these past years, and the attempted cession of Puʻuloa was their latest gambit, and nothing came of it. But here and now they have given us a wooden horse in which our enemies lay in wait.] (Kelekona 1996, 92)

I am not suggesting that Nāwahī had been reading *20,000 Legue malalo o ke Kai,* though he probably had, or that he took his inspiration from Nimo. But I am pointing to affinities between aloha ʻāina like Joseph Nāwahī and the character of Kāpena Nimo as G. W. Kanuha portrayed him and gave mana to through his translation. Especially when its founder Whitney was the editor, *Kuokoa* was explicitly dedicated to assimilating Hawaiians to haole ways of thinking, and he also probably saw Verne's phenomenally popular novel as a way to sell more papers and advertising space. But in *20,000 Legue malalo o ke Kai,* G. W. Kanuha used mana unuhi to produce a thrilling and entertaining moʻolelo that could also inspire Hawaiians to stand for their ʻāina and their ea, and to fight against the forces of colonialism, as Nimo and his *Nautilo* did.

"Umiumi Uliuli" and *20,000 Legue malalo o ke Kai* are two examples from one not especially sympathetic newspaper of the power that translation could potentially offer Hawaiians to push for their ea and their mana. When we consider that hundreds and thousands of translation moments occur in each issue, and sometimes on every page, of the nūpepa, and that they continued on well into the territorial period, the sheer amount of contextual and thematic contestation/mitigation/attenuation involved in the shifting of material into a Hawaiian worldview is awe-inspiring. And Hawaiian translators were negotiating this every day with ease, using the tools for their own purposes and ends, all the while developing a more sophisticated and pragmatic understanding of what unuhi can do.

Descendants of *Ka Hoku*

Though at certain moments, and with certain editors, *Kuokoa* can be a nūpepa that acknowledges the ea and mana of the lāhui Hawaiʻi, *Ka Hoku o ka Pakipika* is the true progenitor of nationalist Hawaiian newspapers, and its keiki and moʻopuna were legion. Kānepuʻu traces the genealogy from the just over eighty weeks of life before *Ka Hoku* hiamoe (slept), through *Ke Au Okoa* in 1865, *Ko Hawaii Ponoi* in 1873, *Ka Lahui Hawaii* right after, and then *Ko Hawaii Pae Aina* in 1878, when he is writing (Kānepuʻu 1878, 1). If Kānepuʻu had been around to continue the list decades later, he would have included *Ka Leo o ka Lahui* in 1889, *Hawaii Holomua* in 1893, *Ka Makaainana* in 1894, and *Ke Aloha Aina* in 1895. Especially when edited by John E. Bush, *Ka Leo o ka Lahui* had a circulation of four thousand; *Hawaii Holomua*, with the Hawaiian side edited by Kahikina Kelekona and Joseph Poepoe, had a circulation of five thousand (Chapin 1996b, 94).

The editors of these papers—Bush, Kelekona, Robert Wilcox, Joseph Poepoe, and F. J. Testa—were impressively bilingual, writing and translating in English or Hawaiian ("F. J. Testa, (Hoke)" 1895). These nūpepa provided a forum for arguments regarding everything from elections, to the Reciprocity Treaty, to people's opinions about translations of textbooks, and supplying such a forum was an especially important service at the time of the Bayonet Constitution, when a cabal of businessmen and missionary descendants forced Kalākaua to sign a constitution they had drafted. It severely limited his powers; disenfranchised Asians, who had been largely supportive of the monarchy; and used property and income qualifications to ensure that the electorate was disproportionately made up of wealthy whites. Or as Kanaka historian Jon Osorio explains, it was with the 1887 constitution that "haole businessmen would finally succeed in taming, once and for all, the power of the monarch and the Native electors" (2002, 129). The Missionary Party had undoubtedly grabbed a great deal of power, and the law no longer provided much recourse for Hawaiians. But the nūpepa were in full force and even getting stronger, becoming one of the last battlefields where Hawaiians held the upper hand. As Hawaiian scholar Tiffany Ing points out, "*Ka Leo* featured some of the most explosive and exhilarating nationalist writers and editors—John Bush, J. W. Mikasobe, F. Meka, J. K. Kaunamano, S. P. Kanoe, and Thomas Spencer. They publicly declared their deep-seated Hawaiian nationalism, were often fearless in their language and accusations, and expressed anger against Kalākaua's opponents. They could be meticulous in their investigations, and undeniably steadfast in their devotion to the mōʻī and Kānaka ʻŌiwi. Printing their allegations in English as well, *Ka Leo* boldly sought the attention of the Hawaiian League" (2015,

308). Though *Ka Leo* boasted a deep bench of such highly bilingual people as John Bush and Thomas Spencer, who could challenge opponents of the lāhui in Hawaiian and in translation, it was not alone in its attacks. Because establishment papers formerly critical of Kalākaua's government were now trying to prop up the Bayonet Constitution, the nūpepa aloha 'āina knew they were in the sights of the Hawaiian League and its supporters: "In an editorial on 'Christian Civilization,' [*The Hawaiian Gazette*] accused *Ka Nupepa Elele* (The newspaper messenger) (1885–1892) and *Ka Oiaio* (The truth) (1889–1896) of 'falsehoods and irritating statements' about the new government leaders and added a veiled threat: 'We have simply this to say to the conductors of these journals that there is a point beyond which it is not safe to proceed, and it will be wise to heed this advice'" (Chapin 1996b, 84). As it had in Britain through the stamp duties and the resulting War of the Unstamped, a minority establishment using all the means at its disposal to prevent the oppressed from having a voice would lead to violence, suppression, and arrests. The threats were real, but the nūpepa editors kept on. Even though the nūpepa were not always of the same opinion—some were critical of Kalākaua[5] and later Lili'uokalani—they continued to resist, because they knew that supporting those backed by the establishment papers would ultimately lead to the loss of Hawaiian sovereignty. So they kept urging the lāhui to stand up and agitate, and Lili'uokalani, hearing the voice of her people in the nūpepa and petitions, decided to promulgate a new constitution that would undo the injustices of the Bayonet Constitution. Spoiling for rhetorical fights, the nationalist papers supported her, but once again, when Hawaiians had mastered the rules of the game and started using them for their own benefit, just as the missionaries had demonized *Ka Hoku*, and the haole judges had undermined the authority of Hawaiian law, the Missionary Party and the sugar planting cabal, no longer able to win at their own game, upset the board. In 1893, with the help of U.S. minister John L. Stevens and American troops, a conspiracy of white businessmen, sugar planters, and missionary descendants overthrew the lawful government of the Hawaiian Kingdom. To avoid loss of life, Lili'uokalani yielded her authority under protest to the United States, placing her hopes in the negotiated diplomacy that Hawaiians had been taught ensured justice and fairness in the interactions between civilized nations. It had worked five decades earlier, when Great Britain restored

Hawaiian sovereignty after a six-month takeover by the rogue Lord George Paulet, and it was a fundamental principle of the legal system that the mōʻī had been trying to preserve with her new constitution. But in the aftermath of the overthrow of the kingdom, diplomacy seemed only to work for the haole.

At this point, translation and mana unuhi became an even more important tool for the nūpepa aloha ʻāina, allowing them to disseminate important documents that the lāhui would not have access to otherwise. It was, for example *Hawaii Holomua,* edited on the Hawaiian side by Kahikina Kelekona, that printed Liliʻuokalani's protest and her appeal to President Grover Cleveland in both Hawaiian and English (*Hawaii Holomua,* January 18, 1893, 2). After the formation of the Hui Aloha ʻĀina, or Hawaiian Patriotic League, many of its resolutions and memorials were printed in Hawaiian and English, again deploying translation for Hawaiian purposes. On the eve of the formation of the so-called Republic of Hawaii in 1894, for instance, *Ka Leo o ka Lahui* printed the Hui Aloha ʻĀina's resolution against it, while *Hawaii Holomua* printed a translation:

> *E hooholoia,* ke kue kupaa loa nei ka Hui Hawaii Aloha Aina a me na Hui Aloha Aina e ae, a me na kupa aloha aina o ke Aupuni Hawaii, i akoakoa ma kekahi Halawai Makaainana Nui, e hoike ana me ka oiaio maoli o lakou ka hapanui loa o ka poe i kuleana kupono i ke koho balota, a ma keia ke kue loa aku nei i ke kuahaua ia ana o kekahi Kumukanawai Hou i hana ia me ka ae ole ia me ka lawelawe pu ole hoi o ka Lehulehu; a ke kue pu aku nei no hoi makou i ka hooloi ana aku i ke ano o ke aupuni mai kona ano a makou i noho ai me ka maluhia a me ka pomaikai no na makahiki he lehulehu.
>
> A ke olelo paa nei makou o ka makemake o ka hapanui o ka poe i kuleana kupono i ke koho balota ma Hawaii nei o lakou no ka mana maloko o ka aina, e like me ia i ike a i ae ia o ua mana la ma na aina malamalama a me na aupuni naauao a pau o ke ao nei. ("Haehae ka Manu" 1894, 2)
>
> Be it resolved. That the Hui Aloha Aina and other patriotic leagues, together with the loyal subjects of the Hawaiian Kingdom, in mass meeting assembled, representing by far the greater majority of the legitimate voters of this country, do hereby most solemnly protest against the promulgation of a new Constitution, formed without the consent and participation of the people, and we also

> protest against changing the form of government from the one under which we have lived peacefully and prosperously for many years. And that we maintain that the will of the majority of the legitimate voters of Hawaii should be the supreme power of the land, as such power is so recognized and accepted in all civilized countries, and by all the enlightened governments of the world. (*Hawaii Holomua,* July 3, 1894, 2)

Publishing the Hawaiian version ensured that the lāhui would know what was going on. But why the English, since the provisional government and most foreigners would hardly be swayed? I would suggest the English audience lived elsewhere. At a time of widespread distortion and misrepresentation, the constant flow of newspapers between the United States and Hawai'i meant that those in power in America could know what the people of Hawai'i actually believed.

The nūpepa aloha 'āina were such a thorn in the oligarchy's side after the overthrow that in its imposed constitution, the republic essentially eliminated freedom of the press, and made it easier to prosecute newspaper editors for libel.[6] The proposed Article 3 of the 1895 constitution was breathtakingly hypocritical:

> Except as herein provided, all men may freely speak, write and publish their sentiments on all subjects; and no law shall be enacted to restrain the liberty of speech or the press; but all persons shall be responsible for the abuse of such right; and no person shall advocate, by writing printing or speaking, the restoration or establishment of a monarchical form of government in the Hawaiian islands; nor advocate the use of force for the accomplishment of any change in the system or form of government hereby established; nor seek or advocate the action of any foreign power for such purpose, except by treaty duly made in accordance with the provisions of this Constitution. (1–3)

The intentions here are obvious. People who oppose the new government do not have freedom of speech; nor may anyone advocate for carrying out a change of government *using exactly the same mechanism that the republic supporters had to gain power.* Then, in the last clause, the supposed political leaders exempt themselves from their "nation's" own law by allowing for the possibility of negotiating an annexation treaty. What is really motivating this article, however, is fear. Threatened by the very existence of a nationalist press, the republic's constitution wanted to make suppression of the native voice the law of the land.

When examining this time period, people trot out the old standby argument that colonialism always wins out, that America was a juggernaut that was always going to be victorious, or that we are lucky we are not speaking Japanese, the implication being that if the United States had not illegally occupied Hawaiʻi, another nation would have. Anna Brickhouse refers to this kind of thinking as "the anachronistic but deeply structuring assumption of conquest's inevitability" (2015, 147). It is too easy to look back at history and see it as a linear trajectory leading inevitably to colonial (or, in the case of Hawaiʻi, the occupying force's) victory, so Brickhouse argues for the kind of "reparative practices of reading the historical past that emerge once we achieve critical distance on the assumed inevitability of European settlement" (2015, 4). Though she is speaking of the colonial history of Don Luis de Velasco and La Florida, these insights are particularly fitting for Hawaiʻi. How different does our history look when we refuse this inevitability the same way that our ancestors did? What kind of reparative practices can grow from this refusal? What lessons have we missed by reading our history for the inevitability of the outcome not for the possibilities that arose from the struggle?

Here is a moment when Hawaiians can demonstrate that no one, least of all the oligarchy, was sure of the outcome. It truly was a moment of possibility. Chapin estimates that the "opposition papers" then represented roughly 85 percent of the population (1996b, 93–94). Mana unuhi was in full effect, the nūpepa aloha ʻāina were the voice of the people, and also had their ear, stirring them to action. Supported neither by the public, nor any coherent rule of law, the oligarchy had no real option other than to arrest anyone who reminded people of these facts. The result was a farcical series of newspaper editor arrests. Kelekona was charged and fined for libel (*Holomua,* February 15, 1893). G. Carson Kenyon was charged with criminal libel. Edmund Norrie was fined $100 for seditious libel. The most extreme response came six months after the declaration of the republic:

> Aia hoʻi i ka mahina ʻo Kekemapa, 1894, ua hopu ʻia ihola ʻo Hon. J. Nāwahī me J. Ailuene Buki no ka ʻōhumu a hoʻāla kipi, a hoʻopaʻa ʻia i loko o ka hale paʻahao. A i loko mai o Ianuali, 1895, ua hoʻokuʻu

'ia lāua. Akā, 'a'ole nō na'e i li'uli'u ma hope iho, ua ulu hou a'ela he mau kumu ho'ouIukū i nā no'ono'o o nā mana ho'okele i ke Aupuni Kūikawā no ka ho'ā'o 'ia e ho'iho'i hou mai i ke kūlana a me ka mana Aupuni Mō'ī. No laila, ua ho'opa'a loa 'ia ihola 'o ia me J. Ailuene Buki me ke kia'i pa'a 'ia a me ka ho'omalu loa 'ia a hiki i ka manawa i pau ai i ka hopuhopu 'ia a ho'opa'a 'ia he mau haneli o nā Hawai'i Pono'ī a me kekahi po'e Haole o ko nā 'āina 'ē i ho'ohuoi 'ia.

[In December of 1894, the Hon. J. Nāwahī and J. Ailuene Buki (Bush) were arrested and jailed on charges of sedition and fomenting rebellion. In January 1895, they were released. But in almost no time, more reasons that perturbed the driving powers of the provisional government arose with the attempt to restore the status and power of the monarchy. So Nāwahī and Bush were detained again under severe restriction with guards posted until the arrests of hundreds of Hawaiian suspects and their haole allies were finished.] (Kelekona 1996, 135)

The counter-revolt of 1895 was an armed attempt to promulgate a new constitution, written by Charles Gulick (Alexander 1896, 216), that would undo much of the Bayonet Constitution and restore Lili'uokalani to the throne. The multiethnic revolutionaries, coming from all the different Hawaiian, Indigenous, and immigrant communities that made up the Hawaiian Kingdom, were known as koa aloha 'āina, or those who fought on behalf of aloha 'āina. The plot was uncovered, and leaders Sam Nowlein and Robert Wilcox had to set everything in motion too early. After a firefight that included cannons, the rebels were defeated, and over three hundred people were arrested. The day after the failed counter-revolt of 1895, along with Bush and Nāwahī, nūpepa editors and contributors E. C. Crick, Daniel Logan, Edmund Norrie, Thomas Tamaki Spencer, W. J. Kapi, J. K. Kaunamano, G. C. Kenyon, and F. J. Testa were arrested for seditious libel (Chapin 1996b, 103), and the fact that these journalists were jailed alongside the armed revolutionaries shows just how much the republic feared the power of the papers. (Editors Bush and Norrie tied for the most arrests, with five each between 1893 and 1895.)

If writing and translating were what led to the prosecution of these nūpepa aloha 'āina, mana unuhi was one of the tools used to keep them out of jail as well. As mentioned above, in 1895, George Carson

Kenyon, a haole editor, was arrested for seditious libel, and some of the correspondence about his trial sheds light on the surprising ways the nūpepa aloha ʻāina were using translation. Both Kenyon and Kelekona were editors at *Hawaii Holomua,* one of the most radical papers of the time. Referring to the 1895 counter-revolt, E. G. Hitchcock, marshal of the republic, states that "to the *Holomua,* as conducted by Kenyon, and later by Norrie, must be assigned the chief part in my opinion in promoting and stirring up the uprising that took place in January last" (*Correspondence* 1899, 133). Though he chauvinistically refuses to mention the agency of Kahikina Kelekona, Hitchcock clearly acknowledges the power of the nūpepa aloha ʻāina, concluding that "revolutions are not started these days without the aid of newspapers" (*Correspondence* 1899, 133).

In his deposition, Kahikina Kelekona testified that while Kenyon himself wrote many of the radical articles appearing in Hawaiian, he also exhorted Kelekona to use his considerable literary talents in the same cause: "Following his instructions, I wrote as violently as I dared against the Government, yet Kenyon said I was not writing hot enough, and kept stirring me up to write hotter still" (*Correspondence* 1899, 138). But since Kenyon and Kelekona knew that the understanding of ʻōlelo Hawaiʻi among those serving in provisional government and the republic was often weak, "the English portion of the paper [...] was not so strong as the native. Kenyon would sit down and write a very violent article in English for me to translate into Hawaiian, then he would tone down his English copy a great deal and then put it into the paper" (*Correspondence* 1899, 138), thereby often eluding the government monitors.

According to Kelekona, "the whole plan and policy of the Hawaiian portion of the paper as run by Kenyon and myself was to fire the native to an extent that there could be no reconciliation between them and the new government. The one object being the restoration of the Queen. Kenyon and I were working for nothing else" (*Correspondence* 1899, 138). With no small measure of pride, Kelekona went on to declare that

> our paper was the most radical paper published in the Hawaiian language, at the time and it fired the natives so that they were prepared to revolt against the Government if it was necessary to get the Queen

back. The honest truth was that it was a revolutionary paper and nothing else. Its policy was to make the native irreconcilable, and it succeeded. It had subscribers among the natives all over the Islands. To this day you will hear natives say that no paper published since the overthrow has exceeded in the violence or has been stronger or more effective than that paper published by Kenyon and myself. It has had a great effect on the native people. (*Correspondence* 1899, 139)

Of course, this is *exactly* what the republic's constitution had outlawed. How then did the *Holomua* get away with this to such an extent that Hitchcock called it the chief cause of the 1895 counter-revolt?

The answer was translation, in fact—a kind of translation that Anna Brickhouse refers to as "motivated mistranslation," an understanding that seeks to make visible and call into question the invisibility and "success" of translation that is often assumed in reading colonial interactions (2015, 5, 26). One of the main purposes of motivated mistranslation is what Brickhouse terms "unsettlement," rather than resistance, which she says "broadly encompasses any kind of action against an imperial or colonizing agent, undertaken by anyone in almost any context, and for a host of reasons, ranging from struggle on behalf of a collection to the leveraging of personal power or advantage within a structure of dominance" and is "so broad and ubiquitous that it almost implies a certain futility" (2015, 2)—the inevitability of conquest that we mentioned earlier. In the place of resistance, she offers "unsettlement," which is "undertaken by an indigenous subject and involves the concrete attempt to annihilate or otherwise put an end to a European colony, or to forestall or eliminate a future colonial project. As a term, unsettlement signals not merely the contingency and noninevitability but the glaring incompleteness of the history of the New World as we currently know and write it" (2015, 2).

In Hawai'i's case then, the nūpepa aloha 'āina editors used translation to "unsettle" by attempting to forestall or eliminate the future project of overthrowing and annexing Hawai'i to the United States, and as can be seen, the oligarchy was indeed unsettled, both in the sense of having their efforts blocked but also in the sense of unsettling their minds. Since the law "allowing" for freedom of speech itemizes what *cannot* be said, the intelligent multilingual editors of the nūpepa knew exactly what to avoid saying—or to say they avoided saying. Missionary descendant William Luther Wilcox, the official government interpreter and translator since 1867, was also deposed, and offered a highly informed explanation of how the editors of *Hawaii Holomua* and other nūpepa aloha ʻāina managed for the most part to avoid arrest: "The Hawaiian language is one peculiarly adapted to convey intelligence by innuendo or suggestion merely, and the natives are a very secretive people and peculiarly fitted to convey intelligence to each other in the same way. These facts could not fail to be known to anyone reasonably well acquainted with them. Language in the mouth of a Hawaiian often means something serious when the same in the English language would mean nothing" (*Correspondence* 1899, 140). Wilcox is describing kaona, a foundational feature of ʻōlelo Hawaiʻi by which different audiences receive different messages from the same words and sentences depending on whether they are meant to know. Such metaphorical and/or contextually based references were present in all manner of speech, from elevated pule directed to the akua to the more pedestrian interactions in everyday life. Common conventions include referring to lovers as embodying ʻāina (J. H. Osorio 2018, 124), or particular kinds of flowers or birds. Similarly, speaking of drinking water from a particular kind of leaf might actually be referring to sex or intimate relationships. What distinguishes kaona from metaphorical speech, however, is that the meaning is always directed. The same reference may have completely different connotations depending on whether you are the intended audience or not, and there can be comprehension levels within that audience as well. At the fiftieth birthday party for my Hawaiian-language mentor, for instance, I gave a very metaphor-filled speech in Hawaiian honoring the knowledge he had given me, and his effect upon my life. But the imagery I used to craft the metaphors honoring him also contained metaphorical references acknowledging my love for friends of mine in the audience. If you were not one of those friends, you heard a speech honoring an important figure in our community. If, however, you were part of my circle, you certainly heard how much I cared for my mentor, but knew that my friends deserved honor as well.

This feature of ʻōlelo Hawaiʻi is much appreciated and enjoyed when we can decipher kaona and/or the kaona is directed toward us; however, its prevalence in so many aspects of our language makes kaona a nightmare for translators today. But it proved a blessing for those seeking to evade, outwit, and unsettle the provisional government's and the republic's clumsy legal system. Though the authors were almost always saying something politically pointed, the surface meaning of the Hawaiian words and sentences was presenting something that could be translated as totally innocuous. Wilcox confirms this strategy: "Many of these editors were arrested now and then, but nothing came of the prosecutions. They always had a plausible and harmless interpretation to give to their utterances and it was next to impossible to convict them before juries" (*Correspondence* 1899, 140). So even though they were pouring it in hot, most editors avoided conviction by "accurately" translating their words in the hair-pullingly blandest way possible.

Though the brilliant, fiery, and beloved Joseph Nāwahī was jailed for several months, contracting the tuberculosis that soon cost him his life, translation kept many other nūpepa aloha ʻāina from serving significant jail time. The lāhui, however, had suffered a tremendous blow with the overthrow. Compounded by the failed counter-revolt, and the mandated change of the language of instruction in schools to English in 1896, these blows would contribute heavily to separating future generations of aloha ʻāina from their language and culture. But at the time, the nūpepa aloha ʻāina pressed on with their project of unsettlement, fighting in the face of persecution for the ea and mana of the lāhui, and getting the word out about such anti-annexation efforts as the Hui Aloha ʻĀina's and Hui Kālaiʻāina's huge petition drives and mass meetings. And when Liliʻuokalani wrote *Hawaii's Story by Hawaii's Queen* in English (1898), though addressed as "a plea to Americans in general, and to members of the U.S. Congress in particular, to consider the retention of Hawaiian sovereignty, rather than proceeding with the annexation of the Islands" (Forbes 1998d, xv), soon after its release, the nūpepa began to translate it into ʻōlelo Hawaiʻi, assuring Hawaiian readers that their Queen supported them and was speaking on behalf of the lāhui. Though the whole work was never completely translated, the installments that were translated appeared, fittingly, in *Ke Aloha Aina,* the newspaper founded by the late Joseph Nāwahī and his wife Emma, for according to the editors at that time, the Queen's moʻolelo was filled with "na olelo walania a ku i ke aloha no Kona hookahuli ia ana. Aloha no Oia" (anguished words full of aloha in regards to her overthrow. Aloha to her!) (*Ke Aloha Aina,* March 19, 1898, 5).

But even as the nūpepa stood firm in their aloha for the mōʻī and the lāhui, their audience grew smaller and less powerful. Hawaiian literary practitioners kept the nūpepa going until after World War II, with translations remaining a fundamental component until the end. As the overthrow and annexation receded further into the past, however, the stakes became less urgent. Mana unuhi was no longer the one thing that might stand between you and jail time. The translated foreign moʻolelo were no longer offering insight into treaties being negotiated with the United States. Moʻolelo like *Tarzan* were still being translated, but they were appearing alongside editorials with titles like "Pehea e Mau ai ke Ola ana o ka Olelo Hawaii?" (How will ʻōlelo Hawaiʻi keep living?) (*Ka Naʼi Aupuni,* January 5, 1906); "Mai Haalele i ka Olelo Makuahine" (Don't abandon your mother tongue) (*Kuokoa Home Rula,* March 22, 1907); "E Ae Anei Kakou e Make ka Olelo Hawaii?" (Are we truly going to allow ʻōlelo Hawaiʻi to die?) (*Ka Nupepa Kuokoa,* January 6, 1922).

Our language did not die, but it was a close call. Nearly nine decades passed before we could teach schoolchildren in Hawaiian again. During those years, as the number of speakers dwindled and the fortunes of ʻōlelo Hawaiʻi waned, so too did the power of translation into Hawaiian. No longer a tool of ea and mana that the lāhui could use to make something their own, translation became something wielded primarily by those who wanted to talk *about* Hawaiians, not *to* them. Translation no longer gave mana, becoming instead a means for extracting ʻike and moʻolelo out of ʻōlelo Hawaiʻi.

Chapter 4

Entombed in Translation
Extractive Translation's Golden Era

She couldn't help but smile when she saw the Royal portable typewriter waiting for her as she approached her new desk. The keys gleamed and the duotone crinoline blue was so modern! She knew the museum had money, but this was state-of-the-art, and she was just a volunteer.

She had been directed to a creaky metal chair and a thick wooden desk next to rank upon rank of filing cabinets. The newness of the typewriter was incongruous with the smell of old paper that seemed to permeate every surface in the office. Everything was so imposing and stern, even the two smiling kūpuna in front of her, though she tried not to let it show.

She fidgeted with her newly permed hair as she sat down. She felt a little overdressed in her dark blouse and long skirt next to the two grayhaired women. Both wore understated muʻumuʻu with muted floral patterns, but if they made anything of her outfit, they gave no sign.

The one with glasses on, Lahilahi, patted her hand and told her to make herself comfortable. The other, wearing a kukui lei, had introduced herself as Mary, though that was unnecessary. Mary Kawena Pukui and her work were the reasons that she was there.

All these translation projects were so exciting. Her parents still spoke Hawaiian, though she didn't, so she was thrilled to help preserve Hawaiian knowledge in any way that she could.

Mary handed her a heavy file folder, and asked if she could standardize the papers into the same format, something that would make it easier to work with. She paged through them quickly just to assess the contents and saw a mishmash of handwritten and typed documents. One had even been typed in all capital letters!

It looked like a big job, but that was what she had signed up for. And it looked important. Mary and Lahilahi told her to feel free to go see them if she had any questions and left her to her work.

Lahilahi looked back over her shoulder and gave her a surprisingly mischievous grin. She also heard Mary mutter in an undertone that some of the translations didn't even deserve to be typed up.

When they left, she shrugged and got to work, arranging the documents for transcription. She smiled to herself. She was just happy to be doing work that mattered here in the Anthropology Department at the museum.

As recounted in chapter 3, though Hawaiian-language publications continued to appear, the provisional government and then the republic kept trying to silence aloha ʻāina newspaper firebrands such as John E. Bush, Joseph Nāwahī, and Kahikina Kelekona through libel laws, accusations of sedition, and press confiscations. Under the watchful eye of sharpshooters, the republic deported Hawaiians whom they felt threatened their unjust rule or sent them to work on road crews with other "criminals" (Palmer 1895, 8–9). ʻŌlelo Hawaiʻi was in the paradoxical position of simultaneously being at the peak of its expressive power but also quite far along in its decline in popular usage. And predictably, the wielding of mana unuhi by Hawaiians for Hawaiian purposes shared the fortunes of ʻōlelo Hawaiʻi. Besides the overtly material clashes between Hawaiians and the ruling oligarchy, the end of the nineteenth century also brought about the culmination of many of these less obvious forces vying for control in the kingdom. When the language was strong and vibrant, Hawaiians had used translation confidently, as a sign of mana and a certain cosmopolitanism, and even during the troubled times at the end of the century, Hawaiians employed it strategically to serve national ends. With the decline of ʻōlelo Hawaiʻi, however, translations shifted from being primarily *by* Hawaiians to being primarily *about* Hawaiians. This chapter deals with the changing mana around translation and how this shift of purpose, the assumed audience for translations, and the actions of the people involved in producing them have affected how Hawaiian history has come to be understood, and in many cases misunderstood.

As Hawaiian literary scholar kuʻualoha hoʻomanawanui points

out, translation in this time period resulted in "translation practices of language and culture that disparage Native people and substantiate colonialism" (2014, 27). The undermining of ʻōlelo Hawaiʻi as the foundation upon which Hawaiian culture rests, and the declining status of the language—and Hawaiians themselves—in the educational system, severely affected Hawaiian exercises of ea and mana over the first decades of the twentieth century. And translation into Hawaiian can be thought of as the canary in the coal mine, signaling the danger facing the lāhui. The erosion of translational activity in Hawaiian pointed to declining sovereignty over how Hawaiians interacted with the outside world. Rather than being translated, considered, and valued through the lens of a Hawaiian worldview, information and knowledge from Western sources now arrived in English and stayed that way. In addition, the growing practice of translation out of, rather than into, Hawaiian paralleled the steady rise in the number of exclusively English-speakers, mostly non-Hawaiian, whose access to Hawaiian history and culture was therefore restricted to such translations. Even more chilling, ʻōlelo Hawaiʻi use declined so swiftly that within a few decades, English translations were often the only sources of Hawaiian-originated information that Hawaiians could access about themselves.

In 1898, eleven Hawaiian-language nūpepa were appearing simultaneously—the largest number ever—and literary practitioners such as Kahikina Kelekona were writing experimental moʻolelo and fiction using highly elevated and sophisticated ʻōlelo Hawaiʻi in genres that had never been attempted before. Yet at the same moment, the education system was salting the ground from which Hawaiian-language translators had grown. By 1895 only three schools in Hawaiʻi out of 187 (Board of Education 1895, 11) were using ʻōlelo Hawaiʻi as their medium of instruction, reaching 59 students out of a total of 12,616 (11, 21). None of the schools were in an urban center. Two were on Hawaiʻi Island, and one on Niʻihau (Board of Education 1895, 14), and petitions were already circulating to convert them into English-language schools as well (21). This process had started during the kingdom. Fifteen years earlier, when the number of Hawaiian-language schools had already dropped from a previous high of 226 to fewer than 80 (Board of Education 1895, 22), Charles Reed Bishop, the president of the Board of Education, had reported that "the continuance and increase of public day schools for teaching Hawaiians the English language has been construed to imply the gradual supplanting of the Hawaiian by the English, and the final extinction of the Hawaiian language" (Board of Education 1880, 9), a "policy" that the Educational Committee of the Legislature had grave doubts about. At that time, however, the Board of Education denied that this was the desired end of its push for English-language education. Hawaiian could never be so easily extinguished.

With the downward trend in Hawaiian-medium schools well under way, these 1880 Board of Education protestations seem particularly disingenuous, and by 1895, linguist, historian, fervent supporter of the overthrow, and then-president of the Board of Education W. D. Alexander approvingly announced that "schools taught in the Hawaiian language have virtually ceased to exist and will probably never appear again in a Government report." He wrote that "Hawaiian parents without exception prefer that their children should be educated in the English language. The gradual extinction of a Polynesian dialect may be regretted for sentimental reasons, but it is certainly for the interest of the Hawaiians themselves" (Board of Education 1895, 6–7). This is the death knell for institutional Hawaiian-language translation. There is no longer a need for textbooks and learning materials in Hawaiian, and in the view of some of the board, like Alexander, no longer a need for speakers in Hawaiian. Though he wrote a book on Hawaiian grammar, Alexander's response to the loss of this "Polynesian dialect" speaks for itself.

In his report, Alexander continued on to call for the revision of school laws because they were based on a system of Hawaiian-language schools that had all but disappeared. So rather than Hawaiian, his calls that school instruction be in English actually come only in response to a different language:

> Another thing that should receive attention is the establishment of certain private schools conducted solely in the Chinese language.
>
> An amendment to the school law should require that all children shall be instructed in the English language, which would compel the closing of such schools. There are only 74 children attending these schools at present, but they will undoubtedly increase unless something is done. (Board of Education 1895, 24)

The Republic of Hawai'i granted Alexander's Yellow Peril–inflected wish in 1896, with the passage of Section 30 of Act 57: "The English language shall be the medium and basis of instruction in all public and private schools, provided that where it is desired that another language shall be taught in addition to the English language, such instruction may be authorized by the Department, either by its rules, the curriculum of the school, or by direct order in any particular instance. Any schools that shall not conform to the provisions of this Section shall not be recognized by the Department." Though some scholars mistakenly point to Act 57 as the beginning of the decline of the Hawaiian language (K. Silva 1997, 92; Oliveira 2014, 79–80) or inaccurately refer to it as the banning of 'ōlelo Hawai'i, the Board of Education reports quoted above reveal that the Hawaiian language's place in education was precarious well before Act 57, as shown by the declining number of schools teaching in 'ōlelo Hawai'i. While motivated mainly by the Chinese-language schools, this amendment would hinder Hawaiian-language revitalization efforts for ninety years. The Organic Act of 1900 further entrenched the primacy of English, mandating that all legislative proceedings be held in English, and that while voters could be fluent in Hawaiian or English, court jurors had to be able to speak English (Nogelmeier 2010, 15).

At this point, over 99 percent of Hawaiian students were taught in English, and social stigma and sometimes physical punishment awaited those who spoke Hawaiian at school. Kūpuna who grew up in the wake of Act 57 interviewed by Larry Kimura on his radio show *Ka Leo Hawai'i* in the 1970s recalled how they were punished for speaking 'ōlelo Hawai'i. Helen Wahineokai remembered that it was forbidden at Mauna'olu Seminary on Maui, and that her letters were censored if written in Hawaiian even after she began attending Kamehameha. When other students heard Dan Hanakahi speaking Hawaiian and reported him to the teacher, he was beaten with a stick. Small wonder, then, that Sarah Nākoa's kupuna told her "aia ke ola o ka noho 'ana ma kēia mua aku i ka 'ike pono i ka 'ōlelo a ka po'e Haole" (the way to survive from now on is to know thoroughly the language of the haole) (1993, 19).

The proper language of instruction, whether English or Hawaiian, had been debated publicly at least since 1860, when *Ka Hae Hawaii* described the arguments in the English-language newspapers about this issue. *The Polynesian* came down on the side of English, the *Pacific Commercial Advertiser* on the Hawaiian side ("Hoopaapaa Nupepa" 1860). Editorials decrying the decline in quality/usage and even the possible disappearance of ʻōlelo Hawaiʻi began appearing around this time as well, but they took on a new urgency decades later, after Act 57.

In 1906, the newspaper *Ka Naʼi Aupuni*, edited by Joseph Poepoe, ran an editorial entitled "Mai Haalele i Kau Olelo Makuahine" (Do not forsake your mother tongue). In it, the author states that the people of the nation have not been well-served by putting their efforts only toward learning English:

> Oiai makou e kakoo aku ana i ua iini holomua o na poe ike olelo Beritania, ma ke ano, he mea pono i ko Hawaii nei lahui opio ke hoomaamaaia ma ka ike olelo Beritania, oia hoi ka olelo Enelani, i mea e loaa ai i ka opio na keehina holo mama ma ke au awiwi o ka holomua e nee nei maluna o ka hapanui o ka ilihonua, mamuli o na hoonee ana a ka olelo Beritania, eia nae, aole no he mea hewa no ka opio hanau o Hawaii, o ka oi aku nae, ke ike maopopo i ka olelo a kona mau kupuna.
>
> [While we support the idea that those knowledgeable in English hold, namely that it is necessary for the youth of the lāhui Hawaiʻi to get familiar with English, so that they are able to move nimbly through the swiftly flowing currents of progress driven by English and running across the majority of the earth's surface, we must nevertheless say that there is nothing wrong, and indeed it would serve them even better, if they were well-versed in the language of their kūpuna.]

The author blames the fact that the government schools are no longer taught in Hawaiian for a lot of issues facing the lāhui, and mentions the ever-shrinking pool of places where young people can gain knowledge of Hawaiian: the churches and Sunday schools, books and newspapers ma ka ʻōlelo Hawaiʻi, and places where "na Hawaii maoli" (true/real Hawaiians) gather. As this pool shrinks, so too does the pool from which both Hawaiian-language translators and the audience for Hawaiian-language translations are drawn.

In "Ka Olelo Makuahine a ka Lahui Hawaii," a 1912 article from *Hawaii Holomua,* the author argues that English is hardly the easy path to progress that Hawaiians have been promised, and particularly when racism gets involved. The author notes how Black Americans speak English perfectly well, and yet

> he poe Amelika lakou, aka, ua lohe anei kakou e kapaia ana lakou ma ia inoa? Aole, he Nekelo no lakou.... I keia la, ua ikeia ka lahui Hawaii, aka, ke namu mai na keiki Hawaii, aole lakou e kapaia aku ana he poe Amelika, a i ole ia, he poe Pelekane paha, aole loa. He poe Nekelo.
>
> [they are Americans, but have we ever heard them referred to as such? No, they are called Negroes.... These days, people are familiar with the lāhui Hawai'i, but should Hawaiian children speak English, they too are not thought to be Americans or British, not at all. They too are called Negroes.] (25)

This author goes astray in their later analysis of the racism faced by Black people in the United States, blaming much of their suffering on being cut off from their ancestral languages, rather than colonialism, the global slave trade, or the specific American legacy of slavery. But the writer entreats Hawaiians to stand together and demand a return to Hawaiian-language schools, or at least a few hours a day of Hawaiian-language schooling, because if 'ōlelo Hawai'i disappears, so will Hawaiians.

A decade later, even *Ka Nupepa Kuokoa,* historically very pro-American and pro-establishment, ran an article entitled "E Ae Anei Kakou e Make ka Olelo Hawaii?" (Are we truly going to just let the Hawaiian language die?). The ramifications of Act 57 are still being felt almost three decades later:

> Ua kamaaina kakou, o ka olelo Beritania ka olelo lahui i keia la, no ke kumu, o ia ka olelo a ke kanawai e kauoha mai nei. A aole e hiki i ka ahaolelo e komo mai, a kauoha e a'oia ka olelo Hawaii maloko o na kula aupuni, elike me ko kakou makemake. He oiaio e hiki ana no e a'oia ma kekahi mau papa, elike me ka olelo Palani ame Italia, e a'oia mai nei; aka, aole o ia ano a'o ka kakou i makemake ai, no ke kumu, aole e loaa ana ka ike i makemakeia e kakou.
>
> [We are all well aware that English is the language of our people today, because it is the language that the law has demanded. And the

legislature cannot step forward and order that Hawaiian be taught in the schools as we wish it to be. It is true that it can be taught as a subject, just like French and Italian are, but that is not what we want because they will not attain the level of knowledge that we want them to.]

For this author, the answer is to build schools for Hawaiians to learn 'ōlelo Hawai'i, and since the government will likely not support them, the lāhui Hawai'i itself must pay for the buildings and teachers.

Along with the legal obstacles, and the pressures to give Hawaiian keiki the tools to "succeed," according to U.S. census reports, between 1900 and 1950, 293,000 Americans immigrated to Hawai'i, exacerbating the linguistic, political, and cultural challenges facing the lāhui. The sham annexation and illegal acquisition of Hawai'i aroused a great deal of curiosity about the islands. Periodicals such as *Paradise of the Pacific* helped whet American appetites for human-interest stories about Hawai'i, and more scholarly treatments were brought to bear on the multiracial population as well. And while translation was still a major feature of the nūpepa, bringing into 'ōlelo Hawai'i pulpy adventures like Tarzan or lesser-known tales like *Geoffrey's Victory; Or, the Double Deception,* the papers themselves were declining in numbers and circulation. The forces of "Americanism," essentially a movement to whitewash difference out of any non-white person (meaning nearly all of Hawai'i), really came into play in the 1940s as well (Kam 2006, 137). Its "Talk American" campaign led to attacks on Japanese- and Chinese-language schools, and 'ōlelo Hawai'i continued to be denigrated as an obstacle to progress and Americanization. Consequently, the direction of the vast majority of translation shifted, moving from 'ōlelo Hawai'i into English, often explicitly justified as an effort to save Hawaiian knowledge and other intellectual curiosities as the people themselves disappeared. The disappearing Hawaiian was the only story these translators had a pilina to, so that is the story that got the most mana, told and retold, translated and retranslated.

Outward Bound

As the political sovereignty of the lāhui Hawai'i waned and the kingdom seemed increasingly a thing of the past, literary sovereignty declined as well. Hawaiians had little control over what stories were told about them, or how these stories were circulated—whether in advertisements offering willing brown hula maidens to tourists, or in the sensationalistic news coverage of the Massie case, warning America about lurking bestial savages. Mana unuhi was equally out of Hawaiian hands, as for nearly a century, extractive models would become the norm. No longer for other Hawaiians or even citizens of the kingdom, these translations were almost exclusively directed at foreign scholars, social scientists, and researchers. Though many of these Hawaiian-to-English products were eventually made available to the general public, and therefore to Hawaiians themselves, these audiences did not ask for nor shape these translations.

Seldom directed at a living, vibrant language, extractive translation responds to the felt needs of academics in various branches of study. As historian Noelani Arista posits, Hawaiian-language sources "have been devalued by scholarly praxis, while colonial processes over time significantly decreased the population that could speak and write Hawaiian, resulting in the deskilling of an organic knowledge and scholarly labor force that might have continued to perform and produce scholarly discourse on Hawaiian history in the native language" (2020, 32). Thus the translation of select sources provided a certain kind of access to these sources that had been devalued. The demand for such translations confirms that these readers are by definition not Hawaiian intellectuals, and are instead foreign "experts" who cannot understand Hawaiian, but see this as no obstacle to studying Hawai'i. One reason that Lili'uokalani herself gave for translating the Kumulipo while she was imprisoned in 'Iolani Palace was that "it may also be of value to genealogists and scientific men of a few societies to which a copy will be forwarded. The folk-lore or traditions of an aboriginal people have of late years been considered of inestimable value" (1897, vii). According to its editor and translator Thomas Thrum, Abraham Fornander's collection of folklore was published with the Hawaiian source material because it would "add to its scientific value" (Fornander 1916–1917, 2), but the greatest value, given the readership, came from the translations. Accompanying "He Mele no Kuali'i," for instance, was the observation that "Polynesian scholars are under great obligations to Mr. C. J. Lyons for the translation of it" (C. J. Lyons 1893, 161), and although this could conceivably be referring to scholars who were Polynesian, the far more likely audience is white scholars studying Polynesia.

As for the most massive translation project prepared during this time, the writings of Samuel Mānaiakalani Kamakau, which eventually filled four separate volumes, Martha Beckwith explicitly described it as "not for popular consumption, but in order to put into the hands of ethnologists who do not read Hawaiian or who have no access to the original text, a version as nearly literal as possible of Kamakau's text" (quoted in Nogelmeier 2010, 126). The most well-known and influential historian of his time, Kamakau had himself written in 1865 for the nūpepa *Ke Au Okoa* that "he makemake ko'u e pololei ka moolelo o ko'u one hanau, aole na ka malihini e ao ia'u i ka mooolelo o ko'u lahui, na'u e ao aku i ka moolelo i ka malihini" (I want the mo'olelo of the sands of my birth to be correct; it is not the foreigner who shall teach me the mo'olelo of my people, I shall be the one to teach it to the foreigner). Unfortunately, though his reputation as the go-to historian continued on after his work transitioned into English via translation, that same process of translation ensured that he would likely no longer consider his mo'olelo pololei, as the malihini, those American scholars and folklorists for whom he was translated, then took control over disseminating and teaching "his" mo'olelo.

Here we will examine briefly a few of the translations produced primarily, but not exclusively, during the first half of the twentieth century to see how this extractive model of translation produces a version of Hawaiian history vetted by Kamakau's "foreigners," how the translators effaced their interpretive presence by claiming to practice "literal" translation, and how through their framing, these translations unavoidably gave mana to the only mo'olelo they had pilina with, one that portrayed Hawaiians, our language, and our culture as dead or dying. Puakea Nogelmeier's *Mai Pa'a i ka Leo* (2010) and other works go into detail about the contexts in which the originals and the translations were created. I will focus on how the supposedly well-intentioned process of translation proved to be so detrimental to the ea and mana of Hawaiians.

A major justification offered for many of these translations is that because the numbers of Hawaiians, and especially knowledgeable ones, are declining, soon no one will be left who can understand the meaning of these texts. For foreign specialists on Hawai'i, while the loss of 'ōlelo Hawai'i might be regrettable, and the disappearance of kānaka Hawai'i might be sad, the loss of the embedded knowledge, the real material for their research, would be absolutely unconscionable. Not surprisingly, then, rather than trying to push for the renormalization of ʻōlelo Hawaiʻi, as Hawaiians were calling for in the nūpepa and legislature, or deciding that they should learn Hawaiian, and therefore pushing for the republication of the ʻōlelo Hawaiʻi versions of the moʻolelo, the scholarly community exhorted translators to go into salvage mode. This rationale and its underlying assumptions were already flourishing during the kingdom. Referring to the original of his translation of "He Mele no Kualiʻi," C. J. Lyons remarks that the mele "is so antique in language, construction and imagery, that very few of the natives at the present day can understand much of it" (1893, 161). Similarly, Thomas Thrum stresses the value of Fornander's text by explaining that "these tales [cannot] be secured from original sources today. The bards, or haku mele, and chanters have passed away, and even those capable of interpreting the mele and antiquarian subjects are few" (Fornander 1916–1917, 2). And many years later, anthropologist Katherine Luomala describes Kamakau producing his own text at a time "when the customs and beliefs of 'the people of old' were still remembered" (1966, 501), even though many of these traditions were still being practiced, and much of the history he offers was in the living memory of his contemporaries, and especially his own.

They participate in the colonial dream of the disappearing native, which rests firmly upon the foundations of a teleological understanding of culture, where the more "enlightened" the natives, the closer they have progressed toward the telos of Euro-American society. That natives will disappear is therefore only proper, because *as natives* they have no place in the modern world. As a result, the value of their knowledge has nothing to do with the survival of their culture or themselves. Rather, it contributes to the project of constructing a universal history of modern—read Western—societies that accounts for how they have successfully risen out of such "primitive" ones (Medicine 2001; Deloria 2004; Tuck and Yang 2012; TallBear 2013).

In Hawaiʻi, this extractive model of translation with the mana unuhi firmly on the side of the extractors has led to what Nogelmeier has called a translated canon of literature, made up of David Malo's work translated as *Hawaiian Antiquities,* John Papa ʻĪʻī's columns from the Hawaiian-language newspapers translated as *Fragments of Hawaiian History,* Kepelino's manuscript translated as *Kepelino's Traditions of Hawaiʻi,* and Samuel Kamakau's voluminous newspaper contributions translated as *Ruling Chiefs of Hawaiʻi, The People of Old, The Works of the People of Old,* and *Tales and Traditions of the People of Old.* (Abraham Fornander's work is sometimes considered part of this canon, though his status as a haole scholar complicates matters.) Before the relatively recent resurgence of scholars who insist on using Hawaiian-language sources to research Hawaiian topics, these translations were all you needed to consult if you felt it necessary to include "the native voice": "Within the setting of English primacy, certain contextual factors helped to generate and foster the cumulative power of the Hawaiian canon. These factors include the relative vacuum of Hawaiian resources into which the English texts emerged, the imprimatur of the presenting institution, an absence of contradiction or disagreement between the texts, and the apparent authority of the individual authors and texts themselves. Each of these four factors became and remained applicable as translations were published and the canon developed over a period of 80 years" (Nogelmeier 2010, 45). Nogelmeier discusses at length how the systematic translation of these texts eliminated explicit and sometimes fundamental disagreements between their authors. This idea goes against the express wishes of one of the authors themselves, as Kamakau explicitly states that he published his materials so that they could be criticized and corrected, worrying that after he died people would take his writings to be their "guiding source or teacher, *i kumu alakai no* lakou," despite particular errors that Kamakau noted (Charlot 2005, 543; emphasis in original). He even felt that "all knowledgeable people should join together to compose several books of Hawaiian history and tales; in this way, *ua loaa ka Buke Hawaii oiaio* 'would be obtained the true Book of Hawaiʻi' " (Charlot 2005, 543). But with the cohesive and relatively narrow picture of Hawaiian culture that these translations put at hand, scholars capable of working only in English were hardly motivated to look outside.

If we count only the Indigenous authors, the translated canon consists of 1,542 pages of content, including paratextual materials such as tables of contents, introductions, indexes, and so forth. From the kingdom era to the mid-twentieth century, roughly one hundred thousand pages were published in Hawaiian-language newspapers, with each page representing between eight and twelve 8.5 × 11 manuscript pages. The translated canon is therefore a minuscule fraction of this output, but its supposed synecdochic relationship to the 'ōlelo Hawai'i written archive has predictably resulted in numerous, significant, and repeated misrepresentations and misunderstandings of Hawaiian history, worldview, and culture. And as was the case with both the Bible and the legal system, misguided understandings of the process and product of translation have had very detrimental effects on Hawaiians. As I hope has become clear by now, translation is necessarily a highly interpretive act. Its practitioners bring all their linguistic capabilities and cultural knowledge, giving mana to all their inevitable ideological and aesthetic biases in their chosen texts, which they reinterpret and reauthor for a new audience. As the poet and translator Brian Swann says of translating Indigenous works, "the translator needs to draw on many resources to present such a universe convincingly, a world so different from the one most of us are familiar with, a world where transformation and metamorphosis are the norm, where forms are fluid and being is polysemous and ambiguous, where everything possesses some sort of life in a 'participatory universe' " (2011, 4). But this is not what happened in most cases, because in the popular understanding, translation is a mechanical process, which translation theorist Gayatri Spivak has aptly and dismissively described as "the stringing together of the most accurate synonyms by the most proximate syntax" (2005, 93).

By their very nature, mechanical/technical operations of this sort supposedly cannot be ideological or political—perhaps one reason why at least some people uncritically trust machine translation such as Google Translate or the Large Language Models coming out now. Chapter 3 described how translation into Hawaiian could act as a kind of consecration, a ho'omana 'ana—a process through which Hawaiians bestowed further value on what they thought worthy. Something similar occurs when 'ōlelo Hawai'i is translated, but the results are also reversed. In *The World Republic of Letters,* Pascale Casanova describes how translation consecrates or canonizes literary works from the "periphery" status within the colonial centers: "Translation is the foremost example of a particular type of consecration in the literary world. Its true nature as a form of literary recognition (rather than a mere exchange of one language for another or a purely horizontal transfer that provides a useful measure of the volume of publishing transactions in the world) goes unrecognized on account of its apparent neutrality" (2010, 133). For Casanova, the colonial "center" is Paris, but similar power imbalances between Hawaiian-language texts and mainstream English-language sources mirror this center/periphery model.

In her account of the creation of what she calls a "legendary Hawai'i" through the deployment of folklore, Cristina Bacchilega also refers to the consecratory nature of translation: "Often perceived as faithful or innocent documentation paradoxically *because* they are translations, these texts go unquestioned in the Western context and become the dominant representations of colonized peoples" (2007, 14; emphasis in original). In the case of the Hawaiian-language canon, such translation has helped to construct what Houston Wood has called "monorhetoric"—a singular, linear, empirical understanding of the past, with no room for varying explanations of the world (1999, 129). Wood argues that Hawaiians viewed, and continue to view, their cultural productions as a "polyrhetoric," with "multiple, shifting, and context-specific meanings" (1999, 129–130). Eric Cheyfitz also understands this widespread colonial process of creating the history of an Indigenous people through translation as a struggle between the univocal and the equivocal (1997, 155). Taking Native American cultures as his subject, Cheyfitz describes the Anglo-European system of belief as dedicated to the domination of a single voice. The kinship-ordered societies that this domination clashed with in America, however, were "equivocal." Though often hierarchical in terms of rank or status, numerous voices were taken into account.

Univocality and monorhetoricity stand in stark opposition to the Hawaiian understanding of mo'olelo getting more mana, in the sense of power, through having more mana, in the sense of multiple branching versions. This fundamental distinction is often lost in translation through the process of consecration. During the over-a-century-long history of the Hawaiian-language newspapers, at least thirteen different versions of the story of Hi'iakaikapoliopele were published (ho'omanawanui 2014, 25), and none were presented as more authoritative than the others. In fact, author and translator Joseph Poepoe gave this explanation as to why his version of Hi'iaka being published in *Kuokoa Home Rula* in 1908 was a little different from the version that was published in *Ka Na'i Aupuni* in 1906:

> O keia mau aui hou e ikeia ia ana mai keia puka ana mamuli o ka loaa hou ana mai i ko makou mea kakau moolelo, he Hiiaka i kapaia

o ko Maui Hiiaka ia. O ka mahele Hiiaka mua i puka ai ma KA NAI AUPUNI, a i hoomaka ai nohoi ma keia pepa ma ia manawa no, ua olelo o ko Hawaii Hiiaka ia.

[These new variations that will be seen in this publication are because the author has just come into the possession of a Hi'iaka called Maui's Hi'iaka. The first version of Hi'iaka that appeared in *Ka Na'i Aupuni*, and which actually began in this paper at that time, is said to be Hawaii's version of Hi'iaka.] (1908)

No attempt is made to declare which one is better or "right"; Poepoe seems more excited about presenting the new version than determining which is the "real" one.

The monorhetorical and univocal representations created by the canonical/extractive translations of Hawaiian texts became so dominant, however, that they almost obscured the originals themselves from even the translators. When Bacil Kirtley and Esther Mookini critiqued an earlier translation of Kepelino's "Hoiliili Havaii" that they had just retranslated, they argued that "to translate certain portions of his text into their mere literal English equivalents would be an evasion, for the Hawaiian language remains basically a spoken tongue" (1977, 40–41). In 1977, when they were writing this critique, the written Hawaiian alphabet had been formalized for *150 years,* at least 100 Hawaiian-language newspapers had come and gone, and Hawaiians had achieved a higher literacy rate in their own language than virtually any other people on earth. Even more confusing is that only three years prior, Esther Mookini herself had published a slim volume entitled *The Hawaiian Newspapers,* which contained a statistical record of those nūpepa, several indexes, and a brief history of newspaper publishing in Hawai'i. Perhaps the quoted statement can be attributed to Kirtley, which may shed light on the power dynamics of their writing relationship. But the Western cultural assumption that 'ōlelo Hawai'i had to be primitive, with no real written form, is apparently so strong that it can cause even scholars who know better to discount or ignore Hawaiians' highly developed literary traditions.

Though the translated canon texts were not the only texts to be translated into English from Hawaiian during that time, they were influential enough to set the mode in which the vast majority of other translations would be performed. Correctness was a major component.

Any understanding of translation as a mechanical and therefore "innocent" process leads translators and readers to think in terms of right and wrong. And while there can certainly be a wrong translation because of simple misinterpretation, the range of meaning, history, and cultural context that inheres in words and phrases means that there can never be just one "right" translation. As the philosopher and translator José Ortega y Gasset explains, "since languages are formed in different landscapes, through different experiences, their incongruity is natural" (2000, 51), and even when translation theorists claim that only "proper names, geographic, scientific and technical terms, days of the week, months, and numerals have full lexical correspondence in several languages" (Visson 2005, 57), they are still on shaky ground. Hawaiians, for instance, have different systems for keeping track of days and weeks, and even different ways of counting, based on groupings of four, forty, four hundred, four thousand, forty thousand, and four hundred thousand.

Yet this kind of "full lexical correspondence" is the very thing that is implied when translators claim to have carried out a "literal" translation. It gives mana to a very specific story of translation. They are claiming that they are on the straight and narrow; they are not interpreting, merely "carrying across." But translators who use the term "literal" often have completely different practices in mind. It could be keeping the syntactic order of a sentence. It could mean using very unadorned language. It could be using short words for short words and long for long. When readers see the word "literal," however, they understand it to mean that the translation is a "good" one, which gives only the "actual" meanings of the words. When translators claim that their work is "literal," they therefore appear to such readers as technicians, switching out words accurately and objectively, rather than as arbiters of interpretation, whose assumptions, methods, choices, and values create very particular kinds of translations.

It is therefore no surprise that the extractive model of translating Hawaiian claimed to be literal, and went unquestioned for so long. All the translators believed they were creating "good" and "right" translations. When introducing her version of Kaluaikoʻolau's moʻolelo, for instance, Frances Frazier claims that she has tried to "follow as literally as possible the language of the original with all its richness of poetry and pathos" (2001, x). Sometimes the assertion comes from others:

Kenneth Emory called Mary Kawena Pukui's translation of John Papa 'Ī'ī's work "literal" (1959, xii). As for Kamakau's text, much of the translation produced by a committee of scholars including Mary Kawena Pukui, Thomas G. Thrum, Lahilahi Webb, Emma Davidson Taylor, John Wise, and others (Kamakau 1992, v) was deemed "incoherent" by Martha Beckwith and Mary Kawena Pukui, who then had to edit it (Nogelmeier 2010, 126). Yet Dorothy Barrère and Katherine Luomala both called the result "*completely* literal" (Barrère 1964, vii; Luomala 1966, 501; emphasis mine).

Though all these translations would at some point become available for public consumption, scholars and scientists were still the primary audience for them, so the idea of transparency—the attempt to erase the presence of the translator—contributed to the sense of authenticity surrounding these translations. The less the translator was present, the more easily the translation would be seen as giving direct access to the original source material. A good number of the problematic effects of these translations did not even come from the translators themselves, but from the way that editors and publishers presented the translation. The more mechanical or literal that editors and publishers claimed a translation to be, the more authority it therefore had. Brian Swann points out the root of what is at issue here: "The art of translation [is] a discipline that is as much a matter of translating the spaces and silence between and around words as it is of translating the words themselves, of snagging the emotional and cultural associations words trail and of breathing the atmosphere they both make and live on" (2011, 6). The translators are so focused on asserting how correctly/literally they translated the words themselves that everything else (spaces and silences, emotional and cultural associations, the atmosphere the words made and lived on) was up for grabs.

For this reason, readers were often unaware of many silent changes or unmarked additions made to the texts. For example, *Hawaiian Antiquities*, the translation of historian David Malo's work, provides a great deal of valuable information and commentary about traditional Hawaiian society and practices. But while Malo is certainly critical of some traditional practices, many of the derisive "insights" are actually Nathaniel B. Emerson's. And because they are not attributed to Emerson, or distinguished from Malo's text, these additions become part of the atmosphere of the translation. Take for example

David Malo's descriptions of the akua worshiped by women. The Hawaiian text reads: "Eia no na 'kua i hoomana maopoopoia e na wahine, o Lauhuki, ke akua o na wahine, a o Papa o Hoohoku ko kakou kupuna, ke akua o kekahi poe, o kapo, o pua, ko kekahi, a o ka nui o na wahine, aole o lakou akua, he noho wale iho no" (1987, 62).

Now, paraphrasing Emerson's own words, here is how the passage could read: "The following deities were objects of definite special worship by women: Lau-huki, [the goddess of women]. Papa and Hoohoku, our ancestors, were worshiped by some. Kapo and Pua had their worshippers. The majority of women, however, had no deity and just worshiped nothing." Though I have added a few words to ensure that everything in the Hawaiian text is accounted for, this translation largely reflects the original. But, here is what actually appears in Emerson's "translation" of Malo: "The following deities were objects of definite special worship by women: Lau-huki *was the patron deity of the women who printed tapa cloth. Pele and Hiiaka were the deities of certain women.* Papa and Hoohoku, our ancestors, were worshiped by some *as deities.* Kapo and Pua had their worshippers. The majority of women, however, had no deity and just worshiped nothing" (Malo 1951, 82; emphasis mine). Emerson has added the italicized portions, and though they may seem relatively minor changes, there are still several of them. Imagine this practice employed across the entire manuscript—because it is. The first addition, an explanatory note regarding Lauhuki, could be considered helpful. The second bit is entirely new to the passage, however, and wrong: Pele and Hi'iaka were not worshiped only by women. But since Emerson's factual mistake is masquerading as the words of the historian David Malo, whose in-depth knowledge of and training in Hawaiian traditions were legendary, this "fact" about Pele and Hi'iaka worship is likely to go unquestioned, and especially by readers who cannot read the Hawaiian-language originals. The translation's textual apparatus actually makes the situation worse. Since the edition includes clearly marked notes and commentary by Emerson and W. D. Alexander, the reader naturally assumes that everything in the translation itself comes straight from Malo. Which it does not.

Another silent change affects the ordering of material in the translation in Kamakau. Cristina Bacchilega, folklore and translation scholar, describes one of the main tenets of colonial translation as follows: "With translation from colonized languages, it is instead common for the target language—English in the cases I discuss—to dictate its cultural logic. The rewriting that all translation involves is best driven in colonial translation by a discursive strategy of containment or domestication that requires re-writing the other in the dominant language's terms. This violation is 'epistemic' in that the colonized or Native world is recoded in terms of the colonizers'" (2007, 14–15). For the most part, Kamakau's newspaper columns produced a continuous narrative, following the lives and genealogies of different ali'i or delving into particular practices in ways that made sense to him and his readers, while steadily filling out the mo'olelo he was trying to tell. Translation shattered and reassembled that narrative. "Recoding" it into a more palatable and comprehensible form for Western audiences, the editorial committee divided up the narrative. Those parts considered history went into one book, called *Ruling Chiefs;* parts considered cultural practice went into another, *Na Hana a ka Po'e Kahiko: The Works of the People of Old*. Material considered to be about cultural belief went into *Ka Po'e Kahiko: The People of Old,* with the leftovers deposited in *Tales and Traditions of the People of Old*. To make this happen, individual sentences were moved and reordered, resulting in content from completely different issues of the newspaper now sitting next to each other, as if placed there by the author himself.

Again, these changes are not indicated in the text. The foreword of *Ka Po'e Kahiko* somewhat vaguely and dishonestly remarks that "the material has been rearranged to provide a continuity of thought, with the original newspaper sources footnoted" (Kamakau 1964, viii). It is true that the general newspaper source is noted, but the reordered individual sentences are not noted. Even if a sentence comes from an issue two weeks later, it is still noted as being a part of the issue into which it was moved. In a review, Katherine Luomala mentions this, but as an improvement: "Kamakau jumped about at times from subject to subject and the new arrangement gives continuity" (Luomala 1966, 502). Such recoding is commonplace in translations produced in colonial situations, and serves to erase differences between the colonizer and the colonized. This may sound like a benevolent act, striving for equivalence between the two, but it is in fact one of the most pervasive, damaging, and continuing aspects of translation. Here all the spaces and silences around the words were stripped away, and they were then replaced by colonial implications in a completely different atmosphere. Indigenous and other peoples under the threat of colonization were and are not understood as having *fundamentally different* ways of relating to each other and the world at large. So Kamakau's work did not, for example, have its own internal logic and continuity based on Hawaiian epistemologies and ontologies, but "jumped around." Once again, such erasure reframes Indigenous peoples into linear models of historical and cultural development for which European and American societies are at the telos—the glorious end of the line. Rather than functioning as a completely different society, or following a different line, or maybe even inscribing a circle, Indigenous communities become absorbed into the grand and very linear history of "human culture" (Kirch 2011).

Sandra Bermann, in her introduction to *Nation, Language, and the Ethics of Translation,* points to the issue at the heart of this erasure of difference: "If we must translate in order to emancipate and preserve cultural pasts and to build linguistic bridges for present understandings and future thought, we must do so while attempting to respond ethically to each language's contexts, intertexts, and intrinsic alterity" (2005, 7). Extractive translations from ʻōlelo Hawaiʻi were explicitly about emancipation, preservation, and communication; what was missing was the ethical response and the acknowledgment of intrinsic alterity. We saw these lacks at work in chapter 2, when judges and other administrators translated something like " ʻāina" into "real estate" and "property," stripping away all familial connection to the land, and turning it into a commodity, which outsiders then had no qualms about swooping in to purchase when the makaʻāinana left it unclaimed, further seeing this lack of self-interest or "initiative" as proof that Hawaiians were less developed and ignorant (Kuykendall 1938, 289–290). Claiming Indigenous beliefs are the same as Western beliefs has even more global results. When "aloha" is translated as "love," a truly poor substitute, Hawaiians are then expected to act and react *exactly* as the colonizers would, as if the way they love something is the way that we aloha something.

Entombed in Translation

Forcibly translating Hawaiians into a teleological model of development demands their relegation to the past. If our culture was dissimilar from Euro-American culture, it was either because we had not yet reached their stage of cultural development, or perversely retained those practices that made us inferior. Either way, we were still culturally embryonic, an immature culture who had no real place in the present. The editors of Kamakau's translations betrayed this belief through another silent global change. If reordering the sequence of events supposedly strengthened "continuity," this second change, at least for Hawaiian tradition, denied it entirely. Especially when describing cultural practices, Kamakau is very careful about tense in his writing. Many sections are in present tense because people are still performing the activity (Nogelmeier 2010, 193–194). Hawaiians were farming kalo when Kamakau wrote about it, when his account was translated, and when we read it today. And yet, in translation, his description of growing kalo and creating 'ai is entirely in the past tense (Kamakau 1976, 31–36). In her foreword to *Na Hana a ka Poʻe Kahiko: The Works of the People of Old*, Dorothy Barrère, who edited the translation of Kamakau for publication, acknowledges that "some aspects of the older Hawaiian culture were already abandoned or were fast disappearing by Kamakau's day," but that "some were still very much alive" (Kamakau 1976, v). She even notes that "Kamakau often differentiated in his text by the use of past and present tenses" (v). But with the sweep of an editorial pen, she confesses that "we have *for the sake of conformity* used the past tense almost exclusively" (v–vi; emphasis added), relegating all Hawaiian cultural practices to the past. Again, this moʻolelo of the disappearing Hawaiians only gets mana if those translating have pilina to it, so through this meticulous practice, virtually every sentence of the translation reinforces a belief that Hawaiians, our language, and our culture, are dead.

How translations of Hawaiian appeared on the page could also sustain the myth of the dead or disappearing native, with no place in the modern world. The Loeb Classical Library is a renowned series that publishes facing-page translations—original on one side, English translation on the other—of Greek and Latin texts. Initiated in 1912 under the patronage of banker and philanthropist Amos Loeb, and dedicated to "making the Classical world, its literature and its *realia*, accessible to more than the specialist" (Horsley 2011, 37), according to its U.S. publisher, Harvard University Press, the Loeb Classical Library "is the only existing series of books which, through original text and English translation, gives access to all that is important in Greek and Latin literature" ("Loeb Classical Library, 2021" 2021). Jacketed in the appropriate colors—red for Latin, green for Greek—the affordable volumes became highly influential, setting the model for what a series of antiquarian texts should look like. Annotations and critical texts guided and enlightened readers, and the facing-page translations were a major innovation—at least in English: "The significance of the parallel text format needs to be underscored, since it is so characteristic of the LCL series that it can be taken for granted today. To translate Greek texts into Latin had long-established precedent; and translations alone were also common well before the Loeb series began. But to provide the original text and a translation into the vernacular had hitherto only been done in a concerted manner by the French" (Horsley 2011, 39). As fewer and fewer modern scholars were able to read Greek and Latin, they too began to turn to the Loeb Classical Library, though they had not been its initial audience.

And that's what the canonical translated texts were meant to be. With the Loeb Classical Library model in hand, the predominantly haole scholars of Hawaiʻi began to recreate through translation "all that is important" in Hawaiian literature. Some, such as Beckwith's translation of Kepelino or the collected works of Abraham Fornander, actually reproduced the facing-page presentation and the annotations. Others restricted themselves to the critical apparatus and annotations, leaving the ʻōlelo Hawaiʻi behind. But together, the translated texts adhered to the Loeb stated goal: a series in which "our entire classical heritage is represented...in convenient and well-printed pocket volumes" ("Loeb Classical Library, 2021" 2021). Though perhaps not designed for the pocket, the result was a handy selection of moʻolelo, chosen by foreign scholars as fully representative of our knowledge and existence, entombed within facing-page antiquarian caskets, offered as *memoria* of a people who have faded away into the anonymity of the universal "human culture" (Kirch 2011).

At the time, like classical Greek and Latin, Hawaiian writing of the nineteenth century was seen as the substantial residue of a dead language. Publishing the Hawaiian translation canon was therefore erecting the tombstone for a nearly dead people. Much of their ʻike would now survive—not as a living and growing knowledge, but as terminal objects of study. Encasing the Hawaiian translations in Loeb-like apparatus also raised their status as texts. Since Greek and Latin were widely considered as the progenitors of well over two thousand years of human culture, placing the translated Hawaiian texts in similar garb would implicitly argue that they too represented a lineage of knowledge—some "1,400 years of human culture" (Kirch 2011). What was actually elevated and given mana, however, was neither Hawaiian knowledge/language, nor Hawaiians themselves, but the study of Hawai'i as a branch of academic inquiry. En-Loeb-ing the Hawaiian translations foregrounded the antiquity of the knowledge found in the original texts, justifying a continued relegation of Hawaiians to the past.

As I have suggested, in some cases, it was the editors who, as part of their efforts to impose order and improve readability, "fixed" Hawaiian culture in the past. But the translators had their own biases, and the common belief that Hawaiians were of the past, not the present, informs many of their word choices. For a clear illustration of such "primitivizing," let's return to Nathaniel B. Emerson's translation of David Malo. The third chapter of his manuscript is entitled "Ke Kumu Mua o ko Hawaii Nei Kanaka" (Malo 1987, 4), which means roughly "The Origins of the People of Hawai'i." Emerson offers "The Origin of the Primitive Inhabitants of Hawaii Nei" (Malo 1951, 4), placing his assessment of Hawaiian culture fully on display.

Robert Morris offers another example of how damaging colonial ideologies drove translations. In a letter published in *Ka Hoku o ka Pakipika,* Kapihenui, the author of the 1861–1862 "He Mooolelo no Hiiakaikapoliopele," took issue with a different serial about Pele and Hi'iaka written by P. W. Kaawa, which attributed a cluster of three mele to Pele. Kapihenui insists they were actually composed by Kahuakaiapaoa (also known as Kauakahiapaoa in other versions), a male, for his male lover Lohiau. But when Thomas Thrum translates Kapihenui's letter, despite its explicit reference to the couple as aikāne, Kahuakaiapaoa somehow becomes a woman, so that the relationship is no longer between members of the same sex (Morris 2008, 234). Though I disagree with many of Morris's other conclusions, I entirely agree that Thrum mistranslated the letter, and most likely on purpose. The Hawaiian is simple enough, and Thrum's command of the language was formidable. He was not confused. Though discussing a different set of circumstances, in his groundbreaking *Translating Literature: Practice and Theory in a Comparative Literature Context,* André

Lefevere offers some handy advice for evaluating these kinds of translation "choices": "Here is a possible rule of thumb: Isolated deviations are mistakes; deviations that can be shown to follow certain patterns indicate a strategy the translator has developed to deal with the text as a whole" (1992, 109).

Another strategy often found in extractive translations is consigning Hawaiians and other native peoples, whether considered as the authors or the subjects of the text, to the realm of the natural. No matter how highly developed, complex, and sustainable our societies might have been, when Westerners did not see what they understood as signs of development—fences, wooden-framed houses, acceptable clothes, a codified set of laws, individual rights, and so on—as people we are portrayed as artless or primal. However intricate the kinship systems and cultural values were that distributed resources and regulated behavior, native people were just "naturally" friendly or giving. Hawaiian congeniality was stamped on our faces, for as Captain King reported in his journal, "many of both sexes had fine open countenances, and the women in particular had good eyes and teeth, and a sweetness and sensibility of look, which rendered them very engaging" (Cook 1906, 434). Visitors also noted an innate articulateness. No matter how much time, work, tradition, and expertise went into creating a strong rhetorician, Hawaiians were just "naturally" eloquent—a fortunate accident of language and character, rather than any training or effort. In an obituary of George Pilipo, the famed legislator and orator known as "the Lion of Kona 'Ākau," his white eulogizers noted that "among a nation of born orators he excelled" ("The Late Hon. G. W. Pilipo" 1887). Though a highly educated man who had honed his speaking skills through years as a teacher and decades as a legislator, he was really just one of the better examples of a people who were born that way.

Indigenous people were also assumed to be passive carriers of culture. For example, oftentimes the closest thing native people had to what outsiders regarded as literature was the oral tradition, which was seen as consisting only of things like legends, folktales, and songs, but nothing that took any artistry or authorship. Though individual tellers and performers heavily edit, alter, and compose their narratives, they are treated as receptacles and informants for scholars, rather than actors who create and continuously reinvent their traditions. Eighty years after Hawaiians took up alphabetic literacy, the translators approached their chosen texts as data, rather than as the product of native authors. In the foreword to the 1959 translation of John Papa 'Ī'ī's work published as *Fragments of Hawaiian History*, the pioneering anthropologist Kenneth Emory stated that 'Ī'ī's writings "provide a sound basis for reconstructing *early Hawaiian life*" and "supply considerable information" (Emory 1959). This static understanding of culture presumes that someone hundreds of generations from its beginnings still has direct access to its character. What is especially striking here, however, is that one of the most prominent Hawaiian intellectuals, historians, and public figures of the nineteenth century was not an author, but an informant—a source of unfiltered information that the Western translator will analyze, organize, and evaluate. And indeed, the title page of the first few published editions of the translation announced that these were *Fragments of Hawaiian History* "as recorded by John Papa Ii."

Thomas Thrum describes Abraham Fornander creating his collection "with a corps of native helpers of known ability (notably S. M. Kamakau, the historian; J. Kepilino [*sic*], and S. N. Haleole)" (Fornander 1916–1917, 2). At least Kamakau is listed as a historian here, although this might be merely to distinguish him from Kēlou Kamakau, another Hawaiian scholar often described as an artless informant as well. In any case, these far more experienced and knowledgeable Hawaiian peers are presented almost as if they were Fornander's graduate students. As for Kamakau's own work, in a cover blurb for a more recent printing of the translation *Ruling Chiefs of Hawai'i*, anthropologist Patrick Kirch presents him as a scribe: "Samuel M. Kamakau painstakingly recorded the oral traditions and histories of the Hawaiian people prior to the sweeping cultural changes of the later 19th century" (1992). In O'ahu Cemetery, Samuel Mānaiakalani Kamakau's gravestone reads "S. M. Kamakau 1815–1876 He Kuauhau—Historian." "Kuauhau" is connected to mo'okū'auhau—genealogy and lineage. But it is also how we identify a historian—someone who knows the genealogies that inform so many of our mo'olelo. His gravestone therefore reminds us not only who he was, but that he was himself part of the lineage of people who knew our mo'olelo and mele, who held our genealogies and told our stories. Historians in short, but actually much more. Yet these translations would not have you remember him as such.

Finally, as Puakea Nogelmeier has noted at length, as a group, the most substantial twentieth-century translations of Hawaiian create the impression that they have preserved the only texts that matter. Speaking as a former translator, I recognize that publishing any substantial Hawaiian text was a huge undertaking, requiring the combined efforts of the translator or translators; the editors, copy editors, reviewers, and layout and design staff; and the printers, marketers, and distributors as well. So I can understand why such a narrow range of translations were produced, and, as major Hawaiian literary figures, Kamakau, Malo, Kepelino, and ʻĪʻī were certainly legitimate choices, although Kahikina Kelekona, Joseph Poepoe, Kalokuokamaile, Solomon Peleioholani, Haleʻole, Moses Manu, and still others[1] would have been as well. But a closer look at who was selecting these texts for translation, and mandating their Loeb-inspired, dead-language presentations, reveals the settler colonial underpinnings of this era of extractive translations.

All of the canon of Hawaiian translations were published by the Bishop Museum, founded by Charles Reed Bishop in 1889 in honor of the late Bernice Pauahi Bishop (Creutz 1978, 15), who through her will founded the Kamehameha Schools. By 1898, the year William Brigham transitioned from curator to director, membership on the museum's Board of Trustees seemed to require previous service on the Committee of Safety that overthrew the Hawaiian monarchy. Sanford B. Dole was president, William O. Smith was his vice president, and Samuel Damon was a trustee. In the subsequent provisional government and republic, Dole was president, Smith was attorney general, and Damon was minister of finance (Siddal 1921, 121, 133, 367). W. D. Alexander, the Department of Education head who felt that the extinction of ʻōlelo Hawaiʻi would benefit Hawaiians, was serving as a museum trustee when the translation of David Malo was published (Malo 1951, 18). Albert F. Judd Jr., son of the Supreme Court justice who had participated in the overthrow, was also a trustee, and served several terms as president of the board (Siddal 1921, 225). These were the administrators of the institution largely responsible for creating the textual picture of Hawaiian history that persists today. The very people who overthrew the kingdom and jailed Hawaiians for speaking out against them were presiding over the institution that decided which Hawaiian-language texts would be translated to represent Hawaiians as a people. Not surprisingly, none of the texts chosen were Hawaiian-language accounts of any of the political turmoil that the trustees themselves had helped foment, meaning that the so-called native accounts of Hawaiian history that they were having translated all stopped short before the final decades of the nineteenth century, which would have painted these treasonous administrators in a pretty poor light indeed.

The specific arm of the museum that chose and translated the actual texts came to be known as the Department of Anthropology, whose mandate, as former museum director Edward C. Creutz explains, stems from the original deed of trust, which stated that the museum should be developed "as a scientific institution for collecting, preserving, storing and exhibiting specimens of Polynesian and kindred antiquities, ethnology and natural history...and the publication...of the results of such investigation and study" (Creutz 1978, 14–15). The language here makes the understood status of the translations clear. They are artifacts—specimens and antiquities for study and exhibition. For this reason, while Fornander's work on Hawaiian folklore appeared as volumes 4, 5, and 6 of the *Memoirs of the Bernice Pauahi Bishop Museum of Polynesian Ethnology and Natural History*, volume 1 was devoted to traditional featherwork, a key to native birds, and a discussion of traditional stonework. Volume 2 focused on mat and basket weaving, home construction, and carving. Volume 3 was about making kapa. After the three volumes of Fornander's collection and writings, volume 7 published more notes on featherwork and then a monograph on Hawaiian lobelia. Moʻolelo are therefore bracketed by discussions of pieces in the museum's collections—or its gardens. All are treated as remnants of a bygone Hawaiian era. Small wonder, then, that Dorothy Barrère would feel comfortable casting an entire book on cultural practices in the past tense. Since the people themselves were not long for this world, this verb shift would soon be accurate. Similarly, though a great number of the moʻolelo by such authors as ʻĪʻī and Kamakau were eyewitness accounts of contemporary events, the translation titles emphasized their antiquity. ʻĪʻī's moʻolelo became *Fragments of Hawaiian History*, and three of the four Kamakau translations feature the phrase "the people of old" in their titles.

Translating Tūtū: Mary Kawena Pukui

The mana unuhi was so concentrated in the hands of people who had actively worked against Hawaiian political, cultural, and rhetorical sovereignty that even someone who would become one of our greatest kūʻauhau had her own mana unuhi constrained. For several of the early years, the only person with a Hawaiian last name listed as museum staff was Thomas Keolanui, a janitor. Soon, however, two Hawaiian women appeared. However, despite the breadth and depth of their knowledge, Lahilahi Webb was a "Guide to Exhibits" (Gregory 1923, 4), and while Mary Kawena Pukui later became an associate in Hawaiian culture, and despite her scholarly preeminence, she never held a position of leadership—though her aversion to the spotlight may have come into play as well. Often referred to as Tūtū Pukui, she became the greatest Hawaiian scholar of the twentieth century, and was the equal or perhaps even the better of many of the most prominent authorities of the kingdom as well. And translation occupied a great deal of her time. She was the acknowledged translator of John Papa ʻĪʻī and a major contributor to the project of translating Kamakau, and her many shorter translations on topics ranging from place-names to sharks to moʻolelo to cloud lore make up the museum's Hawaiian Ethnological Notes (HEN) collection.

Her largest contribution to translation, however, was undoubtedly the Hawaiian-English, English-Hawaiian dictionary (Pukui and Elbert 1986). Regarding her role, her co-author Samuel Elbert wrote that "the new dictionary is Mary Kawena Pukui's book.... She is the expert in Hawaiian. This is her dictionary, a monument to her. My task has been the humble one of technician" (Elbert 1953, 14). It is a humble and honorific statement, but one wonders then, if it is true, why his name is right next to hers in terms of authorship. At any rate, this dictionary is indisputably the most important tool in the ongoing movement to revitalize and renormalize ʻōlelo Hawaiʻi, and before the advent of the online dictionary, few of us seeking to learn our language could be found without our dictionary at almost all times. It is also a stellar translation dictionary. Entries for Hawaiian words supply much more than a one- or two-word gloss, regularly providing context and examples of usage. To take one example, the entry for "kū," a particularly versatile and supple word in ʻōlelo Hawaiʻi, is 863 words long. Besides drawing on her own vast knowledge, Mary Kawena Pukui was so diligent in seeking out further examples that almost anyone trying to translate a particularly obscure word in a passage will at some point discover that her dictionary entry offers that exact passage as an example.

While the achievements and legacy of Mary Kawena Pukui deserve several volumes of coverage and even praise, the reason she is being brought up here in such a limited capacity is because many of her amazing contributions as a translator were constrained by the institutional confines of the fields of academic study that dealt with ʻike Hawaiʻi, and by the Bishop Museum administrators and trustees, some of whom had been partly responsible for the language decline and loss of Hawaiian national identity that Mary Kawena Pukui's work has ultimately helped so much to reverse. Though some of her projects, such as the collecting of ʻōlelo noʻeau, or Hawaiian sayings, she initiated herself, the translations she produced or worked on were chosen and overseen by anthropologists. The Kamakau project, for instance, was initiated in 1923 by the Historical Commission of the Territory of Hawaii, with John Wise supplying the first translations (Nogelmeier 2010, 123), and much of the HEN collection resulted from individual requests from museum-affiliated scholars looking for more information about their chosen fields of study, whether heiau, or mele, or fish.

I am not denying the significance of her contributions as a translator, which surpass all others. What I am pointing out are the institutional restrictions and biases she had to navigate in order to exercise any sort of mana unuhi, many of which remain hidden. For this reason, we should not exempt her translations from scrutiny and critique, just because she produced them. Some years ago, I worked on a book entitled *Ka ʻOihana Lawaiʻa: Hawaiian Fishing Traditions,* a Mary Kawena Pukui translation of an early twentieth-century moʻolelo about Hawaiian fishing techniques written by a Lahaina judge named Daniel Kahaulelio. I was assigned to check the accuracy of her translation, editing it as appropriate—which at the time felt like a blasphemous act. We enlisted Gabby Kawelo, whose family had fished Kāneʻohe Bay for generations, to help us understand the described techniques. We soon realized that Pukui had misunderstood some of what Kahaulelio had written, and we fixed the translation. I offer this experience not as proof that Mary Kawena Pukui made mistakes, but as a reminder that no one, no matter how smart and knowledgeable, or how traditionally they were raised, knows everything about our culture, and furthermore, that the canonical and many other texts translated in the territorial era involved a limited number of Hawaiians with limited decision-making abilities, who unavoidably helped produce reductive pictures of Hawaiian culture intended for a limited audience of mostly non-Hawaiians.

The knowledge and tools Mary Kawena Pukui left for us are the foundations for erecting sound representations of our culture. Her legacy, and those of her forebears and contemporaries, have nurtured the beautiful resurgence of our culture, language, and historical understanding, and made it possible to take ʻōlelo Hawaiʻi and our moʻolelo to places we never imagined, and especially back to our young, whom we are educating in immersion and culture-, language-, and ʻāina-based schools. But today, a handful of decades on from the Hawaiian Renaissance, what role does and should translation play, and who is it giving mana to? Prior to the surge in Hawaiian-language learning in the 1970s, the lāhui itself relied on the limited picture of Hawaiian history/culture supplied by the extractive translations of the early twentieth century, often without understanding how much translation and editing had misrepresented or altered the Hawaiian texts. But now, when thanks to our own forebears more of us can read the originals, and up-and-coming generations of kānaka once more claim ʻōlelo Hawaiʻi as their first language, what role should translation play in shaping the future of our lāhui? During the twenty years I have worked as a translator, I have certainly seen the need for translation from English to Hawaiian decline. We have not yet reached a place where making our moʻolelo available through translation to our people and those who would stand with us is no longer needed, but as we have seen throughout this book, the ea and mana of our lāhui require different approaches and responses from translators and translations, as our own needs and the political and cultural contexts change. In chapter 5, we shall see how aloha ʻāina are crafting their own responses to translation to meet those changing needs.

Chapter 5

"I Don't Want to Translate"
The Mana of Refusal

A sunburned man in the gallery yawned. None of those gathered in the worn red seats surrounding the House floor really wanted to hear about protecting lifeguards from liability, but that was part of the business of government. It was a staid session, with none of the tense arguments that had accompanied the passage of HB1, the Hawai'i Marriage Equality Act, the previous year, or the hushed tones of ethics violations discussions. It was just another unremarkable Tuesday in March, maybe a little cooler than normal, but not by much.

Representative Sharon Har, from the Kapolei district, a suburb outside of Honolulu, gave her testimony. All was going smoothly until John Mizuno, the House Speaker, called on Faye Hanohano, the representative from Puna, a district on the island of Hawai'i known for its connections to our volcano akua and a fierce Hawaiian pride.

With her fuzzy blue sweater with white sequined embroidery around the edge, and a flower over her right ear, the sixty-one-year-old former prison guard looked like any other aunty out for the day. She took a breath, and said:

"Mahalo, luna hoʻomalu ʻōlelo. Kākoʻo loa. Makemake au i ka haʻi ʻōlelo o ka luna makaʻāinana mai Kapolei mai e komo i loko o ka puke hale luna makaʻāinana."

An irritated but patient Mizuno responded, "Rep. Hanohano, could you please translate for the members?"

Hanohano replied, "ʻAʻole au e makemake e unuhi. I don't want to translate. Mahalo."

Clearly annoyed, Mizuno called for a recess, banging his gavel and tossing it down. When he returned, he announced indignantly that "rule 60.1 provides members should conduct themselves in a respectful *manner."* But an outspoken critic of Hanohano's jumped to her defense, reminding the Speaker that Hawai'i has two official languages, and that the representative from Puna was well within her rights to speak Hawaiian on the House floor. Mizuno responded that it was not the Hawaiian that was disrespectful, but that she refused to translate.

Faye Hanohano: "I Don't Want to Translate"

All of the upset in the House and the subsequent sensational coverage resulted from Hanohano's saying—and to be honest, not even in especially strong Hawaiian—what any other representative might have said: thanking the Speaker, expressing her support of the bill and appreciation for the speech, and asking that it go into the legislative register. But in Hawaiian. And she had already been under fire for how she interacted with staff at the Department of Land and Natural Resources (DLNR), and for allegedly using racial slurs about haole and Asians in her comments about the need for more Hawaiian artists in the public art program, so there was a relatively large public outcry after this story broke. News outlets more sympathetic to Hawaiian causes said there should be Hawaiian-language interpreters available at the legislature. Others called that a waste of time and money. None of the articles suggested that the other legislators should learn Hawaiian themselves.

As we have seen in chapters 3 and 4, after the overthrow of the Hawaiian Kingdom, the Hawaiian language was increasingly deinstitutionalized. However, 'Ōlelo Hawai'i has been an official language of the state for four decades now, dating back to the Constitutional Convention of 1978, though this has resulted in little more than being able to (sometimes) write checks in Hawaiian. Neither the lawmakers nor state institutions have adopted 'ōlelo Hawai'i in any meaningful way, but this inaction is hardly surprising when we look at some of the comments made in the aftermath of Hanohano's decision not to translate.

While the online comments section of any news outlet is often a den of hate and vitriol, the remarks from folks who are not obvious trolls can sometimes shed light on opinions held by people in the community. Debates around language use in areas (mistakenly) considered part of the United States catch afire very quickly, and often reveal powerful anger directed toward those who speak a language other than English. In a political climate still redolent of Trump, even in places known to be more familiar with and accepting of multilingualism, speaking languages considered to be immigrant or minority tongues can provoke verbal and sometimes physical attack. Numerous online videos and accounts display angry monolingualists lashing out at someone merely for speaking a language other than their own (Fermoso 2018; Little 2018). As earlier chapters have shown, language engenders and reflects identity in ways that few other qualities seem to do. The life and death of a person or culture are contained within their language, and encountering a different tongue means entering another world, where you are uncertain of the terrain, or the depth of the seas. Without such knowledge, it is hard to know your place in that world, and when someone is used to a particular place in the social hierarchy, that lack of knowledge grates.

Writing at length, a commenter named jusanopinion101 angrily denounced Hanohano:

> General practice when speaking to a group of people is to utilize the more common language the majority understands. This B S of acting out like a little child isn't in the best interest of "We the People" she is supposed to be representing. It is considered rude to "refuse" a translation, especially when it would be translated to a language the majority would understand.... Simple case of MANNERS. Not childish behavior instead of being an effective politician. Any place else in the world it's called, "MANNERS." ... Not all the people speak Hawaiian. They are the minority. It's called representing the people and making sure the hawaiian voice is heard and making sure the English voice is heard. Not just hawaiian. Do you really pay her to do less than half a job? or are you paying her to do 100% of a job? (jusanopinion101 2014)

That Hanohano in one instance refuses to translate one sentence somehow means that all of a sudden, only the "Hawaiian voice" is heard—as if she has marginalized those who speak English. Infantilizing Hanohano for her refusal, in the rest of their comment, jusanopinion101 types "MANNERS" in capital letters four more times, clearly outraged by the incivility they see in Hanohano's refusal to translate. This focus also suggests that jusanopinion101 considers the larger monolingual American culture to be the "host," even though we are in Hawai'i, and finds Hanohano's lack of manners disrespectful. Hanohano is not abiding by the House rules.

Though she used slightly fewer capital letters, commenter Louise Raitano Smith was even more offended: "So Rep Hanohano is saying ... f-you if you don't understand me. This is not a way a representative of Hawaii should express ones' [sic] self no matter what her feelings are. Go to Zippys and talk story in Hawaiian if you wish ... but when it comes to THE HOUSE Floor you owe all people of Hawaii a translation no matter what language you're speaking. 'Playground' bullying is how I see it. I thought we had standards for that in our classrooms" (2014). Again, in a realm featuring English 99.9999 percent of the time, the person who speaks the endangered language that was near collapse only a handful of decades ago is somehow the one bullying everyone else. Because people in positions of relative power seldom like to be confronted with their own ignorance, this brief moment of not knowing becomes amplified into being under siege by an entire power structure implicit in a marginalized language wielded by a bully. It is also telling that the restaurant Zippy's, a popular local plate-lunch chain, and "talking story" are the only things that 'ōlelo Hawai'i is good for, which adds both a racial and a class element to the argument.

Calling Hanohano childish and a playground bully not only relegates 'ōlelo Hawai'i to a child's realm, but also reinvokes those teleological models of development so popular with the missionaries and their descendants. In the 1901 legislature, the first of the territory era, the haole politicians and the executive branch not only placed Hawaiian legislators lower on the teleological/evolutionary scale for insisting on speaking 'ōlelo Hawai'i, but also characterized them as less than human. Governor Dole insisted that the Organic Act clearly required the use of English during official government business, and the haole press depicted the Hawaiian legislators as a group of monkeys swinging through the trees, complete with a caption from a Rudyard Kipling poem: "Jabber it quickly and all together! Excellent! Wonderful! Once Again! Now we are talking just like men" (Williams 2015, 26, 27).

Opinions about Hawaiians speaking their language in public have apparently not changed much over the past hundred years. Still other commenters on the Hanohano incident remarked, "America last time I looked. Translate" (Holman 2014), called Hawaiian a "dead language" (Campbell 2014), and suggested that "you're better off speaking simlish [the pseudo-language used in the video game *The Sims*] at that point, because at least then other people can chime in" (Tabag 2014). This is why it is important that Hanohano, and Kahoʻokahi Kanuha and Kaleikoa Kāʻeo, two Hawaiians we will discuss later, take the stands they do. By refusing to translate, they make themselves and us legible as Hawaiians. Too many people in Hawaiʻi have bought into the idea that this is "America last time I looked." But it really isn't America, and they haven't really looked. In their Hawaiian fantasy, our ʻōlelo is dead, and video game gibberish is more relevant than the language of the ʻāina.

This chapter will focus on another iteration of mana unuhi and how, in certain situations, refusing to translate is an affirmative insistence on legibility *as* Hawaiians, an embodied performance fighting against assimilation into a settler colonial system predicated on removing kānaka from ʻāina—what Patrick Wolfe has termed "elimination" (2008, 102) and what Kēhaulani Kauanui has characterized as "the elimination of the Native as *Native*" (2018, 9). It is vital that we refuse to treat translation as an innocuous or mechanical act. The truth is that translation, and the withholding of translation, make legible the terrain where some of our lāhui's most important battles are taking place. Paying attention to mana unuhi reveals what is at stake, particularly when the ones refusing translation are doing it in such an embodied way. The insufficiency of identity when wrapped up in the monolingual cogs of the settler colonial machine, and the willful ignorance and fear of the unknown that ʻōlelo Hawaiʻi and Hawaiians more generally provoke, stand in stark relief when you focus on the stutters and starts of the translational flow. As we have already seen and will continue to see throughout this chapter, language is an especially volatile issue for the larger public in Hawaiʻi. When that quality is strategically wielded to fight against elimination, particularly through the withholding of translation, so many possibilities for different kinds of engagement open up between the cogs in the machine. So much light shines through. Whether they want to be or not, bringing people to consciousness about ʻōlelo Hawaiʻi necessarily raises all the related issues swirling around language.

Like many other Indigenous communities, we see the beautiful things that our people are doing: restoring the productivity of our ʻāina, spreading our ʻōlelo in places where it hasn't been heard for over a hundred years, creating beautiful music and poetry, carrying our culture into new media, and standing against reckless development. We also see the problems of health, domestic violence, economics, incarceration, and houselessness in our community, and part of our cultural revitalization is looking for Hawaiian solutions to these problems. But once outside of our own community, we must often confront how mainstream Hawai'i sees us: violent, ignorant, ungrateful, anti-intellectual, inauthentic, whiny impediments to progress, trapped in the past and trying to pull everyone down with us, and, perhaps most attractively to their narrative of the world, still disappearing—in short, all those qualities encountered repeatedly in the first four chapters, and which other Indigenous folks will immediately recognize as components of their own reputation in their own places as natives.

Though often seen as reactionary by the mainstream, saying no to translation is paradoxically affirmative. Speaking of Indigenous communities on Turtle Island, the renowned Michi Saagiig Nishnaabeg scholar, writer, and artist Leanne Betasamosake Simpson writes that "we need to not just figure out who we are: we need to re-establish the processes by which we live who we are within the current context we find ourselves" (2011, 17), and it is through the refusal to give mana to certain acts of translation that we put ourselves on track to reestablish some of those processes that Simpson mentions. According to language scholar Mary Louise Pratt, "languages disappear only through being displaced by more powerful languages, which by one means or another (mainly by schooling) succeed in interrupting the steady passing down of languages from older to younger speakers" (2016, 246). It is really this interruption that is being refused. It is a refusal to believe that English has more mana than 'ōlelo Hawai'i, that it gives us more ea. Pratt also observes that "all languages belong to their speakers in a way they do not belong to everyone else" (246). This is true. But as the acts of refusal we will discuss in this chapter also make clear, 'ōlelo Hawai'i belongs to this land in a reciprocal relationship, each caring for the other. Those who feel connected to this 'āina are well served to feel connected to this language, this 'ōlelo, as well.

What became very clear after the Hanohano incident, when even the most supportive media outlets were calling at most for interpreters at the legislature, was that a good portion of the public continues to believe that Hawaiian exists solely to be translated. To them the mana of our language only exists in unuhi. The commenters' and commentators' general agreement that 'ōlelo Hawai'i has no social relevance unless translated and made legible to them amounts to a demand as always that the minority must make concessions so that the majority can remain as they are, their knowledge of their place in the world as seen through English unchallenged. This demand takes the assumptions underpinning the discourse of sufficiency and extractive modes of translation to their extreme but logical conclusion. Not just the original text, but the original language is no longer seen as necessary.

I often encountered this attitude when talking about my work on a project digitizing the Hawaiian-language nūpepa into a searchable database. Even though the result will grant profoundly improved access to arguably the most important Hawaiian-language repository, and even though sustained research in this archive has already transformed Hawaiian scholarship, the first question was almost always "When are you going to translate them all?" And when I replied that the goal was making the nūpepa available *in Hawaiian,* my respondent would usually offer a disinterested "cool, cool," before changing the subject. Given the unprecedented access to instant knowledge via the internet, making the newspaper database available only to those who have put in years and even decades of work learning 'ōlelo Hawai'i without some twinned effort to make everything in the newspapers accessible to the general public is unthinkable. But the current fights over translation make very clear that while Hawaiians are trying to nourish and sustain (in Leanne Simpson's words) "the processes by which we live *who we are* within the current context we find ourselves" (emphasis added), the tenets of settler colonialism and contemporary media access at the other end of the spectrum demand that everything Hawaiian, including 'āina, be available to all for unrestrained consumption. Refusing to translate therefore implicitly insists that *who we are* is different from who you *say* we are.

Translation theorist Mona Baker writes that "undermining existing patterns of domination cannot be achieved with concrete forms of activism alone (such as demonstrations, sit-ins, and civil disobedience) but must involve a direct challenge to the stories that sustain these patterns. As language mediators, translators and interpreters are uniquely placed to initiate this type of discursive intervention at a global level" (2010, 30). In the cases I am examining here, however, what challenges the dominant narratives is the *refusal* to mediate. This results in the twining of translation (or its refusal) with the concrete, embodied forms of activism Baker is talking about. Rejecting who *you* say we are is rejecting the certain kind of "recognition" offered by settler colonialism that, through enclosing Hawaiians into the box of being just another ethnic group in Hawaiʻi, brings us ever nearer to elimination, though as we shall see later, elimination looks a little different here in Hawaiʻi. There are times that the ideas of resistance and refusal themselves have been critiqued in our community for being too reactionary, too much of a response rather than a proactive step. But Leanne Simpson, one of the engines behind Canada's Idle No More movement, argues that "movement building is a productive or generative politics of refusal when we are building and reinvigorating and embodying and amplifying our instance of acting as peoples who belong to specific Indigenous nations. We are creating the alternative on the ground and in real time" (2015).

Here in Hawaiʻi, those refusing to translate engage in "movement building" in Simpson's sense by connecting their actions to those generative acts of refusal occurring in the kingdom and what followed it at the nineteenth century's turbulent end. In the wake of the overthrow in 1893, the great statesman and newspaper author and editor Joseph Nāwahī helped to found the Hui Aloha ʻĀina, a group committed to preventing annexation and restoring the Queen to her throne, and with his wife, Emma, he also started and ran the newspaper *Ke Aloha Aina*. His most celebrated speech, delivered to seven thousand people, makaʻāinana and aliʻi alike, at Palace Square a year after the overthrow, was a stunning call for refusal:

> He mea hauoli noʻu koʻu ike ana aku ia oukou e oʻu hoa makaainana ua hooko mai oukou i ka leo kahea a ko oukou mau alakai, no ko oukou akoakoa ana mai i keia ahiahi. Oiai hoi, no kakou ka Hale (Aupuni) e like me ka na Kamehameha i kukulu ai; aka, i ka la 17 o Ianuari, 1893, ua kipaku ia ae kakou e ka poe i aea hele mai, a komo iloko o ko kakou hale; a ke olelo mai nei ia kakou e komo aku a e noho iloko o ka hale kaulei a lakou i manao ai e kukulu iho a onou aku ia kakou a pau e komo aku. O kaʻu hoi e olelo aku nei ia oukou, e oʻu hoa makaainana, *mai noho kakou a ae iki.*
>
> [It gladdens my heart to see all of you, my beloved fellow citizens. You have answered the call of your leaders, gathering us all

together this evening. This house of government belongs to us, just as those of the Kamehameha lineage intended; yet on January 17, 1893, we were kicked out by wandering trespassers who entered our house, and they are telling us to go and live in the lei stand[1] that they thought to build and shove us into. But what I have to say to you, my beloved people, *we must not dare to assent in the slightest!*] ("Haehae ka Manu" 1894; emphasis added)

Reminding his Hawaiian audience of their history, he calls on them to refuse to be a part of the present the foreigners are thrusting upon them. But what Nāwahī is calling for, *mai noho kākou a 'ae iki,* does not forbid action, but rather demands that Hawaiians live the alternative, creating it on the ground in real time, and continuing to bring a Hawaiian future into being. A lei stand is not the place for our beloved people; the house that the Kamehameha lineage built definitely is.

Another event, a few years after Nāwahī's speech, resonates with those who in our time have recently refused to translate. Both the Hui Aloha 'Āina and the Hui Aloha 'Āina o nā Wāhine, the latter run by the formidable Kuaihelani Campbell and Emma Nāwahī, participated in arguably the most unified act of refusal in Hawaiian history. Lili'uokalani called Campbell and Nāwahī's hui one of the "societies much dreaded by the oligarchy now ruling Hawaii" (1991, 304). The haole-led provisional government responsible for the overthrow and the eventual Republic of Hawai'i had their eyes fixed on annexation to the United States. In 1897, Emma Nāwahī suggested to Kuaihelani Campbell that both Hui Aloha 'Āina draft a petition, in Hawaiian with an English translation, rejecting the annexation being proposed to the U.S. government (N. Silva 2004, 304). Hui Aloha 'Āina members hustled throughout the pae 'āina, acquiring the signatures of men, women, keiki, kūpuna—anyone against the overthrow and annexation. Large and small community meetings were held, and organizers headed out across the islands, urging the lāhui to sign. And sign they did.

The best-documented meeting took place at the Salvation Army Hall in Hilo, because Miriam Michelson, a writer for the *San Francisco Call,* found herself in a hall that held three hundred, with an even larger crowd gathered outside. In her article "Strangling Hands upon a Nation's Throat," Michelson vividly describes what took place—all of it relayed through an interpreter. "This land is ours—our Hawaii," Emma

Nāwahī, said to those gathered. "Say, shall we lose our nationality? Shall we be annexed to the United States?" The crowd shouted out its refusal: "'A'ole loa! 'A'ole loa!" (Never! Never!) Kuaihelani Campbell then inspired those listening, and also ended her remarks with a question: "Stand firm, my friends. Love of country means more to you and to me than anything else. Be brave; be strong. Have courage and patience. Our time will come. Sign this petition—those of you who love Hawaii. How many—how many will sign?" As she spoke, she raised a gloved hand, showing that her signature would stand as a refusal of the United States. Then, when she asked how many would join her, "in a moment the palms of hundreds of hands were turned toward her." The people of Hilo spoke with their words as well as their upraised hands, one man crying out from the back: "I speak for those behind me. They cannot come in—they cannot speak. They tell me to say, 'No annexation. Never.'"

"There are 100,000 people on the islands," Michelson wrote. "Of these not 3 per cent have declared for annexation. To the natives the loss of nationality is hateful, abhorrent." The petition made this abhorrence clear: twenty-one thousand men and women out of a population of forty thousand signaled their refusal on the Hui Aloha 'Āina petitions (N. Silva 2004, 150).[2] In Washington, DC, representatives of the Hui Aloha 'Āina formally presented the petitions to members of Congress. The treaty failed to pass (N. Silva 1998). The following year, the United States dropped all pretense of a treaty and "annexed" Hawai'i through the Newlands Resolution, a joint resolution of Congress that skipped a plebiscite and required only a simple majority vote to pass, something illegal even by the United States' own laws regarding annexation. But the massive act of refusal now known as the "Kū'ē Petitions" reverberates through our history and into the current day, inspiring those who would refuse translation and the United States' dominion alike.

In June of 2014, the Department of Interior (DOI), somewhat out of the blue and on very short notice, issued an advance notice of proposed rulemaking to hear from the public "whether and how the Department of the Interior should facilitate the reestablishment of a government-to-government relationship with the Native Hawaiian community" (Office of Native Hawaiian Relations 2015). As Noelani Goodyear-Ka'ōpua explains: "It was the first time the U.S. government held any public hearings in Hawaiʻi on federal recognition in well over a decade. At the fifteen DOI-led sessions held on six islands that summer, Kānaka packed auditoriums and school cafeterias in standing-room-only crowds. Speakers were limited to just three minutes of testimony each, and voices poured out like rain on a thin metal rooftop, even though advance notice on the proposed rulemaking had been issued only days earlier" (Goodyear-Kaʻōpua and Kuwada 2018, 4). More than a century after the Hilo meeting, the vast majority of those voices, including those of the two kānaka to be discussed shortly, responded to the DOI's questions in the same way: " ʻAʻole loa! ʻAʻole loa!" (Never! Never!)

A common critique of the ideas of resistance and refusal in our community comes in response to the often-heard cry to "kūʻē!" (resist/protest/oppose/stand apart) with "kūʻē i ke aha?" meaning, to "kūʻē against what?" Implicit in the question is a judgment that resistance and refusal are too amorphous, not directed enough, essentially just us Hawaiians being disagreeable. The thing that those who ask "kūʻē i ke aha" are missing out on, however, is that even if Hawaiians were taking the stance of kūʻē just to be disagreeable, just to act out, just to scream and shout, those acts of defiance would still be grounded in refusing the erasure that comes from existing within colonial structures.

Linguistically, there is overlap in the meanings of kūʻē and kūʻokoʻa, the word we looked at in chapter 3 related to ideas of independence and wholeness. Both begin with "kū," in the sense of standing or in a state of being, and " ʻē" and " ʻokoʻa" refer to being different, separate, or apart, though " ʻē" does not include the sense of wholeness that " ʻokoʻa" can. Perhaps unsurprisingly, " ʻē" was used in the Bible to refer to heathens. These acts of kūʻē and refusal are generative because, as Mohawk scholar Audra Simpson argues, "refusal comes with the requirement of having one's political sovereignty acknowledged and upheld, and raises the question of legitimacy for those who are usually in the position of recognizing: What is their authority to do so? Where does it come from? Who are they to do so?" (2014, 11).

To recall Anna Brickhouse's formulation brought up in chapter 4, this sort of refusal works toward the project of unsettlement. Colonial forces have their narratives and positions of authority unsettled through being confronted by the kinds of questions Audra Simpson brings up. These acts of refusal then have effects on the everyday existence of kānaka. Hanohano's refusal to translate—and, as we will see, those of Kahoʻokahi Kanuha and Kaleikoa Kāʻeo, both of whom were arrested on separate occasions for standing up for ʻāina—makes the lāhui Hawaiʻi legible as a sovereign entity by questioning the legitimacy of "those who are usually in the position of recognizing." Even though these issues seem to be exclusively about language, by forcing questions about the State of Hawaiʻi's authority and its source, they are inevitably forcing the discussion back to ea Hawaiʻi, what gets translated as Hawaiian sovereignty.

Pua Aiu of the State of Hawaiʻi's DLNR, a major participant in the events that led to the arrests of Kāʻeo and Kanuha, wrote in 2010 about the power at work when refusing to translate from ʻōlelo Hawaiʻi: "Ultimately, however, the choice not to translate strengthens the position of the Hawaiian language. Since you cannot understand Hawaiian without understanding the Hawaiian worldview, perceptions about land and culture are forced to change. When this happens, how we think and speak—ʻike and ʻōlelo—also change to accommodate the worldview that goes with the Hawaiian language. While this change is slow, over time there is a definite shift. Like the movement of a tsunami or a phalanx of soldiers, changes in worldview are subtle, patient, and inevitable" (2010, 105). Although "subtle" and "patient" aren't the first words I associate with "tsunami," Aiu's belief that incorporating a Hawaiian worldview will change perceptions and language is strong. Unfortunately, for this desired change to occur, those being refused translation must decide to go deeper and find out more. And as many of the online comments related to the Hanohano incident suggest, some people—and after twenty years in Hawaiian language revitalization efforts, I have concluded that "many people" would be more accurate—believe that ʻōlelo Hawaiʻi is something best kept at Zippy's, or in the mouths of children on the playground. That means it is entirely possible that untranslated ʻōlelo Hawaiʻi would just be skipped over and ignored as something unimportant, beneath notice. That is why it is so important that these refusals to translate are embodied in particular ways and take place within the legislature, the body responsible for passing and amending laws, and—in the upcoming examples of Kanuha and Kāʻeo—within the purview of the court system, the settler colonial state's body for enforcing those laws, and therefore the elimination enforcement arm.

These public refusals to translate, and the potential stakes for those refusing, have forced people to think about something that they have probably never had an opinion about before. Many who have lived in Hawai'i for years, and even decades, feel they "know" this place, "know" Hawaiians, and "know" *the* culture. Whether they ever engage with Hawaiians meaningfully or not, their time spent here makes them feel entitled to that knowledge. Tourists even feel they "know" Hawai'i after a few years in a timeshare, two weeks at a time. As for Hawaiians, they are "known" as musicians and dancers, and more recently, perhaps as scholars and protestors. It is therefore unsettling when Hawaiians refuse to allow themselves to be known, to be accessed, and the sputtering knee-jerk reactions, unfounded fear, and anger found in online comments indicate that something important is happening when a refusal to translate cuts off access to supposed understanding.

I would suggest that such refusals threaten to cut off untroubled participation in the settler colonial world that the online commenters and much of the general public have come to "know." Since settler colonialism plays a central role in my analysis of mana unuhi, translation, and refusal, we should examine briefly to what degree its theoretical application fits the specific case of Hawai'i. As Tuck and Yang state in their well-known article "Decolonization Is Not a Metaphor": "Settler colonialism is different from other forms of colonialism in that settlers come with the intention of making a new home on the land, a home-making that insists on settler sovereignty over all things in their new domain" (2012, 5). Appropriation and possession are constants: "Within settler colonialism, the most important concern is land/water/air/subterranean earth (land, for shorthand, in this article). Land is what is most valuable, contested, required. This is both because the settlers make Indigenous land their new home and source of capital, and also because the disruption of Indigenous relationships to land represents a profound epistemic, ontological, cosmological violence. This violence is not temporally contained in the arrival of the settler but is reasserted each day of occupation" (2012, 5). In the Hawaiian Kingdom era, these aspects of settler colonialism and the logic of elimination are not so clear. The massive influx of American citizens and plantation labor did not really accelerate until the last decade of the monarchy, and the earlier arrivals did not exactly fit the settler profile. (Chinese plantation workers, for instance, intermarried heavily with

Hawaiians, and the population of those with Chinese ancestry hovered between twenty thousand and thirty thousand for several decades [Schmitt 1968, 121].) It was during the territorial era that the key element of "settlers coming with the intention of making a new home on the land" really fell into place. One statistic tells much of the story. The number of Hawai'i residents born in the United States rose from 4,294 in 1900 to 128,952 in 1960 (Schmitt 1968, 121).

These demographics, and the fact that a Hawaiian ruler was on the throne until 1893, could lead to the conclusion that the tumultuous 1890s turned an Indigenous nation into an occupied settler colonial state. However, if the operations of settler colonialism "are not dependent on the presence or absence of formal state institutions or functionaries," as Patrick Wolfe suggests (2008, 108), and if Kēhaulani Kauanui is correct in saying that "the logic of elimination of the Native is also about the elimination of the Native as *Native*" (2018, 9), then perhaps some aspects of settler colonialism were at play in the kingdom. This is a fine line to walk. None of the Hawaiian governmental structures were dedicated to the physical elimination of Hawaiians, and we have to beware of taking away agency from our ancestors in the kingdom. But when we follow Kauanui and look at assimilative biocultural structures, things become more complicated.

What really helps to expose the complications of settler colonialism in Hawai'i is the understanding of mana unuhi developed over the previous chapters. Paying attention to its workings over time not only offers insight into the mechanics of settler colonialism, but also suggests strategies for constructing especially powerful modes of resistance and decolonization. Translation has been variously described as assimilating and domesticating or as alienating and "foreignizing." Many of the political, cultural, educational, social, legal structures of the kingdom operated on a parallel spectrum: some disciplining Hawaiians to become more like Westerners; others enabling or even requiring Hawaiians to remain, or even to become, more "foreign" to Western values by retaining a certain nativeness. But just as the domesticating/foreignizing spectrum is only a rough guide for conceiving of translation, the same holds for its usefulness in understanding the kingdom institutions in their interactions with colonialism, settler or not. As already noted, the lāhui Hawai'i appropriated Western technologies for their own purposes. Alphabetic print literacy, for example, became a weapon to resist the encroachments of U.S. imperialism and a tool for transmitting and preserving traditional Hawaiian thought and values inhering in mele, moʻolelo, and other modes of expression.

A comprehensive study of how settler colonialism, with its logic of elimination, infiltrated the Hawaiian Kingdom is not possible here. But any serious look at the historical sequence starting from the Bayonet Constitution, then passing through the overthrow, provisional government, republic, and into the territory, will detect the operations of "settler sovereignty," as the "settlers become the law, supplanting Indigenous laws and epistemologies" (Tuck and Yang 2012, 6), with the eventual illegal annexation the clearest possible example of the logic of elimination at play. Joseph Nāwahī's exhortation to *mai noho kākou a ʻae iki* and the Kūʻē petitions are conscious and vehement refusals of a future in which Hawaiians would no longer be legible *as Hawaiians*.

But the logic of elimination is complicated in the case of Hawaiʻi. The settler state undeniably took deliberate steps to eliminate native autonomy by attempting to sell off lands appropriated from the kingdom, by directing its educational efforts toward Americanizing Hawaiians in manner and language, and by the other expected colonial moves that commonly take place in an occupied nation. But for other compelling reasons, the survival, and even high visibility, of Hawaiians was of the utmost importance—most obviously within the developing tourist industry. As Jennifer Lynn Kelly says in her study of representations of Palestine, "tourism often facilitates and disappears past and present colonial violence" (2016, 726), so it should not be surprising that in 1903, three years after the Organic Act made Hawaiʻi a U.S. territory, and the last year of Sanford B. Dole's term as its first governor, the Hawaii Promotion Committee, which became the Hawaii Tourism Authority in 1915, began marketing Hawaiʻi as a visitor destination (Teves 2015a, 714). Right alongside the golden era of extractive translations described in chapter 4.

Hawaiians then became a crucial ingredient that would sell the image of Hawaiʻi as an idyllic paradise where available brown women and men cater to colonial and touristic desires. As Stephanie Nohelani Teves explains in her analysis of the deployment of a particular kind of aloha to further state interests, "with tourism as Hawaiʻi's primary economic base and aloha as its so-called gift to the world, the performing bodies of Kānaka Maoli (Hawaiian)—or whoever can pass as

'Hawaiian'—became necessary" (2015a, 713). What was unnecessary to this image, however, were Hawaiians on their own land or in positions of power. Teves also discusses how translation played a crucial factor in the state and tourist industry's deployment of aloha as an seductive opiate for the visiting masses. She foregrounds the missionary translation of aloha as synonymous with the love of God, accomplished through a "commingling between the 'ancient traditional' meaning of aloha, a Polynesian concept, and its Christian translation" (Teves 2015a, 707). I, however, would suggest that just as with the way the mission purposefully reduced aikāne to "friend," this push for translation also arose from a strong desire to tame the power of aloha ʻāina that drove Hawaiians to fight literally and figuratively for the lāhui prior to the territory, a desire that leads to translating "aloha" as something closer to "no make trouble" and "turn the other cheek."

Hawaiians are thus granted a special but limited status as the originators of the aloha spirit and therefore what makes Hawaiʻi unique, but the logic of elimination operates as the boundary of what is considered "the aloha spirit" in the touristic sense, meaning what tourists can be convinced is authentically Hawaiian, or in the political sense of Hawaiʻi as "the aloha state." When the "performing bodies" of Hawaiians do however step outside of their roles as happy-go-lucky locals or ambassadors of aloha for lobster-red tourists, the logic of elimination silences them by stripping their access to needed financial or natural resources, and then shaming them into reassuming their prescribed roles. In fact, the tourist industry will proactively try to hide Hawaiians who aren't displaying the proper aloha spirit. When ten thousand Hawaiians marched down Kalākaua Avenue in Waikīkī in 2015, peacefully protesting the planned construction of the Thirty Meter Telescope (TMT) on Maunakea (Terrell 2015), many tourists reported that the staff at their hotels told them to avoid the area completely.

Though it may be hard to pinpoint when the settler version of colonialism became dominant in Hawaiʻi (which is technically under belligerent military occupation), its power was fully on display during the Hawaiian Renaissance of the 1960s and '70s, when we were reclaiming our identities *as Hawaiians* in the struggles over Kalama Valley, the Chinatown evictions, Sand Island/Mokauea, and Waiāhole. Reclaiming the narrative of Hawaiian-ness from the tourist industry and the state also meant reviving and reclaiming mana unuhi, especially in how we understood and translated aloha. The greatest spur to this embrace of "aloha 'āina" as practiced by our kūpuna during the kingdom era was the movement to stop the bombing of Kahoʻolawe. We were reminded of how adding " 'āina" to "aloha" created something much fiercer, something that resisted the bounds of translation placed on "aloha" by the settler colonial tourist industry. Even the voyage of *Hōkūleʻa* was at its core about how we understood the Hawaiian relationship to land. And refusing to be eliminated, Kanuha and Kāʻeo both ended up in court over issues arising from their restored translation of aloha as intimately connected to ʻāina.

The framework of settler colonialism also provokes a critique of how all aspects of the state enact or support the further alienation of kānaka from ʻāina. As Turtle Mountain Ojibwe scholar Heidi Kiiwetinepinesiik Stark explains, "settler colonialism doesn't just try to eliminate but in its place, seeks to actively produce something new. In their attempts to 'eliminate,' or at least significantly diminish Indigenous political authority, the United States and Canada also sought to produce their own legality by reframing their criminal activities as lawful" (2016). That framing of the United States as "lawful" here in Hawaiʻi enables them and their local proxy, the State of Hawaiʻi, to act as the source of law. Even though Hawaiian traditional and customary rights are said to be an accepted part of state law, the State of Hawaiʻi is the translator of those rights and customs, being the final determinant of their scope and applicability, taking upon itself the ability to dictate things like whether Hawaiian-built structures are historically important and thus worthy of preservation or even how Hawaiian is defined. As for the "lawful" carceral arm of the State of Hawaiʻi, its court and prison system is arguably the institution that most blatantly enacts "the multifarious procedures whereby settler-colonial societies have sought to eliminate the problem of indigenous heteronomy through the biocultural assimilation of Indigenous peoples" (Wolfe 2008, 102). Indeed, political scientist Robert Nichols argues that these agents of state violence should be seen "as *constitutive* of territorialized sovereignty in a colonial context rather than extraneous and novel" (2014, 447; emphasis in original).

At its base, the way the prison system connects to dispossession is geographic and thus connected to ʻāina. As Ruth Wilson Gilmore notes, "incapacitation [in prison] doesn't pretend to change anything about people except where they are" (2007, 14), and Nichols explains that "this apparatus of capture operates as one armature of territorialized colonial sovereignty, a continuous process of dispossession that (always imperfectly) undermines indigenous practices of self-government by severing peoples from their historical relationship to the land" (2014, 452). The carceral arm of the state thus tries to empty the signification of aloha ʻāina as a fierce and powerful connection that drives Hawaiians to action and replace it with one in which aloha is translated as unconditional giving by the "host culture." For those who refuse that retranslation vehemently enough, incarceration echoes those past geographical relocations that many Indigenous peoples suffered when outsiders with the force of law behind them began clearing their ancestral lands for settlement. As Hawaiian scholar David Uahikea Maile puts it, "policing Kānaka ʻŌiwi is a precarious performance of U.S. settler sovereignty in Hawaiʻi—a spectacle attempting to piece together jurisdictional authority and territorial control" (2018). Quite conveniently, the carceral state apparatus takes Indigenous people not only away from their land and human connections, but also, in the cases of Standing Rock, the Unistʼotʼen Camp, and others in the past few years, away from the frontlines of land protests. The ever-accelerating militarization of the police is also at times linked to Indigenous resistance and processes of unsettlement, which becomes "the rationale and justification for the development and application of greater colonial control over Indigenous bodies and lands" (Stark 2016).

Kahoʻokahi Kanuha and Kaleikoa Kāʻeo have both been arrested multiple times at sites of land struggles—sometimes even the same site. But the two examples discussed in this chapter stem from their arrests at two different but related land struggles that led to their rejection of the state's attempts to translate aloha ʻāina as a passive part of the settler colonial narrative. To these kānaka we now turn.

Embodying Unsettlement
Kahoʻokahi Kanuha: "The Translator Is for You"

To tell the moʻolelo of Kahoʻokahi Kanuha's arrest, like most moʻolelo our kūpuna told, you have to start with a genealogy. This genealogy is one of struggle. In 2015, one of the most intense land confrontations in Hawaiʻi came to a head[3] when Hawaiians and other allies physically blocked the construction of the Thirty Meter Telescope atop the 13,796-foot-tall Maunakea. One of the most important and powerful ʻāina in Hawaiʻi, Maunakea is filled with mana and celebrated in mele and moʻolelo. Using the mauna for astronomy has been controversial from the moment University of Hawaiʻi (UH) acquired its sixty-five-year general lease in 1968 (*OHA v. State of Hawaiʻi* 2017, 10), with public concern growing steadily over UH's fifty-year tenure as manager of the mauna. In 1975, the Audubon Society stalled construction of the United Kingdom's submillimeter antenna (Mauna Kea Astronomy Outreach Committee n.d.). Three state audits were conducted; the first was a scathing indictment of both UH's and the state's (via the DLNR) mismanagement ("Timeline" 2016; *OHA v. State of Hawaiʻi* 2017, 12–16). In 2005, a court-ordered environmental impact statement concluded that thirty years of astronomy activity had caused "significant, substantial, and adverse" harm ("Timeline" 2016). And for years, a small but dedicated group of community members has been quietly fighting UH and organizations such as NASA in court to ensure the protection of Maunakea.

In October of 2014, the attention and tension became much greater. The Thirty Meter Telescope, an eighteen-story building that would stretch over five acres of conservation district when complete, scheduled a groundbreaking ceremony. This was disrupted and eventually stopped by folks who came to be known as kiaʻi mauna, or mauna protectors. Kahoʻokahi Kanuha, a young immersion school teacher, was among their number. Things were quiet for the next several months, but when the work was to begin again, kiaʻi mauna camped at an altitude of 9,200 feet, holding vigil across from the Visitor Information Center. Their numbers were initially small but soon really grew. On April 2, 2015, over three hundred kiaʻi blocked the roads accessing the proposed TMT site; thirty-one peaceful demonstrators including Kanuha were arrested (Inefuku 2015).

The kiaʻi had enjoyed a good amount of support to this point, but when footage of the arrests started appearing on social media, things really blew up, as images and videos of the struggles on the mauna were shared across the world.[4] The availability and savvy use of Facebook, Twitter, and Instagram for mass mobilization, sharing practical information, and spreading editorials, petitions, photos, and videos sympathetic to the movement distinguished Maunakea from previous land struggles in Hawaiʻi, and a cohesive and highly effective kiaʻi-led media strategy would become a hallmark of the 2019 stand as well. By the end of April 2015, for instance, an online petition with fifty-two thousand signatures opposing the TMT's construction was delivered to Hawaiʻi's governor.[5] The growing reach of the kiaʻi mauna could easily be measured from the number of engagements their posts would get. In March, as the action was ramping up and people were reporting from the encampment on the mauna, their posts would get eighty to ninety likes. As the movement built over the next few weeks, kiaʻi posts would routinely attract over a thousand likes (a large number at the time, though dwarfed by the social media response garnered in 2019). Though questions remain about how effective social media is at mobilizing people in general, without it, the Maunakea struggle would never have received so much attention.

On April 7, 2015, the governor called for a temporary halt to construction. When it was supposed to resume in June, over 750 kiaʻi blocked TMT crews from reaching the summit, and 12 more people were arrested, again including Kanuha ("Timeline" 2016). Seven arrests occurred on July 31, ironically a kingdom holiday celebrating the return of Hawaiian sovereignty after a six-month British takeover, and eight more on September 9, including seven women in the midst of prayer. Marches, banner drops, rallies, and sign wavings took place across the islands and wherever Hawaiians could gather, including in Las Vegas and California. The largest march took place in August, when an estimated ten thousand to eleven thousand people stretched over a mile and a half through the middle of Waikīkī (Terrell 2015).

In December of 2015, the Hawaiʻi Supreme Court vacated the Conservation District Use Permit for the TMT, sending it back to the Board of Land and Natural Resources to be reconsidered ("Timeline" 2016). After a contested case hearing, Judge Riki Amano recommended that the Thirty Meter Telescope be allowed to move forward ("Judge: Thirty Meter Telescope" 2018). On October 30, 2018, a 4–1 ruling from the State of Hawaiʻi's Supreme Court upheld the permit that the DLNR had granted the TMT corporation to build in the conservation district ("State Supreme Court" 2018). In his dissenting opinion, Justice Michael D. Wilson characterized the majority opinion as espousing the illogical "degradation principle," the idea that the summit of Maunakea had been so damaged by previous astronomy activity and construction, to a degree termed a "substantial adverse impact," that the building of the TMT could not have a further substantial adverse impact (2018, 1). When the TMT corporation tried to resume construction again, the kiaʻi created a basecamp, what they called a puʻuhonua (traditionally a consecrated area of refuge) at Puʻuhuluhulu, across from the base of the Maunakea Access Road, which housed thousands of protectors at any one time. From there, the kiaʻi blockaded the road, which resulted in the arrest of almost three dozen elders who had arrayed themselves across the roadway and kept construction from beginning. It was not until the worldwide COVID-19 pandemic that the majority of the kiaʻi came off the mountain. But since the attempted groundbreaking in 2014, no construction has taken place on the Mauna.

Though many wāhine, kāne, and māhū have stood staunchly as kiaʻi, and some like Kū Ching and Pua Case have been serving for years, Kahoʻokahi Kanuha has been one of the most visible leaders. All the kiaʻi mauna, from the veterans who have taken off time from work and taught themselves about legal procedures for their court cases, to those organizing events in support, to those placing themselves in front of the construction vehicles, deserve to be recognized for their aloha ʻāina, but Kanuha's specific relation to translation in the wake of the 2015 stand makes him our focus here. He was arrested in both April and June 2015. Those kiaʻi arrested in July and September 2015 were released because the circuit court threw out the DLNR's hastily implemented emergency rules banning camping on the mauna. Prosecutors also dropped charges against ten of the thirty-one arrested in April 2015 ("Some TMT Protesters' Charges" 2015), but Kanuha's case continued to trial in 2016.

He decided to defend himself and only spoke ʻōlelo Hawaiʻi in the courtroom. His rationale was as follows: "Hawaiian is ultimately my strongest language. It's my language of preference. It has been the primary language of my education since preschool—and I mean that all the way from preschool through elementary to middle school through high school and in through college. And so what I'm trying to do is I'm trying to—I'm trying to show that the language is alive. And it's about time that Hawaiian be truly recognized, at the very least, as an equal language to English" (quoted in Martin 2015). Kanuha's account of his schooling raises a major issue for those revitalizing and renormalizing ʻōlelo Hawaiʻi, and especially educators. Students in immersion schools like Kanuha know that outside the circles of their family and friends, not many people speak Hawaiian. While that pushes some to become even more staunch in their language use and try to shift things, many students find it more convenient to accommodate the person who doesn't speak Hawaiian, and switch to English, but the result is that the spaces where ʻōlelo Hawaiʻi can serve as the language of daily interaction shrink and shrink, until they mainly exist only at school. And while mele and hula are vitally important, our ʻōlelo should not be relegated to those "expected" realms where mainstream Hawaiʻi society "allows" ʻōlelo Hawaiʻi to be acceptable. Because Hawaiian needs to be more than a classroom or performance language, to show that it can exist in contemporary contexts, some speakers insist on using it when and wherever possible, even if it causes confusion and friction.

Kanuha's refusal to translate himself in court or to live in translation at the very least makes legible the fact that ʻōlelo Hawaiʻi is supple and modern. It also made visible the ramifications of insisting on speaking Hawaiian outside of the classroom. Unsurprisingly, Kanuha's stance of insisting on ʻōlelo Hawaiʻi outside of those acceptable areas ignited the ire of commenters in the same way that Hanohano's stance did. Or perhaps even more. The comments responding to Hanohano often infantilized Hawaiians, but Kanuha pushed commenter mikethenovice a step further: "Waste of money litigating a dog barking." Marauders_1959 scoffed: "Speaking 'Hawaiian' in a US court? Give Me a Break ! Was he also wearing native Hawaiian attire and appeared barefoot ?" We can't determine whether the quotation marks around ʻōlelo Hawaiʻi are commenting on the authenticity of Kanuha's language use, or yet another example of the extraneous or misused punctuation common in online comments. But the claim that Hawaiian does not belong in a U.S. court is *exactly* what Kanuha is rejecting. Using ʻōlelo Hawaiʻi there not only asserts that Hawaiian belongs everywhere, but also expresses the ea (life/breath/sovereignty/rising) of the Hawaiian nation: "I—as a Hawaiian standing up for my Hawaiian heritage, for my Hawaiian nationality, for my Hawaiian identity—can defend myself in my Hawaiian language" (Kanuha quoted in Martin 2015).

A large part of what makes mana unuhi and the refusals to translate discussed in this chapter so polarizingly powerful is that they are embodied performances. Not performance in the sense that it is inauthentic or artificial, but in the sense that there was a physical action taken that was seen by an audience of sorts. Elin Diamond boils it down to the following: "performance is always a doing and a thing done. On the one hand, performance describes certain embodied acts, in specific sites, witnessed by others (and/or the watching self). On the other hand, it is the thing done, the completed event framed in time and space and remembered, misremembered, interpreted, and passionately revisited across a pre-existing discursive field" (1996, 1). Thus this idea of performance does not just refer to our mele and our hula, but is much more encompassing. As Diana Taylor states, "civic disobedience, resistance, citizenship, gender, ethnicity, and sexual identity, for example, are rehearsed and performed daily in the public sphere" (2007, 3). What makes the performances discussed in this chapter different from, say, the highly effective written resistance of the aloha 'āina newspaper editors discussed in chapter 4 is that performances "are, in a sense, always in situ: intelligible in the framework of the immediate environment and issues surrounding them" (Taylor 2007, 3). It is the very place where the performance takes place that makes it relevant, "the framework of the immediate environment"; had these translational refusals taken place at Zippy's as the earlier online commenters would have preferred, they would have carried no real weight. They would likely not even have been considered a performance, merely a momentary choice during the everyday act of communication. But the fact that both Kanuha's and Kā'eo's acts of refusal took place in the court system gave them a powerful import, especially as vessels of embodied memory, echoing the experiences of our kūpuna in the legal system that, through their embodied performances, are "felt affectively and viscerally in the present" (Taylor 2007, 165).

Equal footing for Hawaiians in the courts and legal system was a big concern throughout the kingdom era and into the territory, though the power dynamic was very different in terms of ea and mana. Besides the struggles over legal translation outlined in chapter 2, Hawaiians with the means educated themselves in the law, and fought to preserve Hawaiian standing in the legal system. J. Kauwahi's guide to deeds and other legal contracts was the first book published by Hawaiians, and aloha 'āina were lawyers, including F. J. Testa, Joseph Nāwahī, and especially Joseph Poepoe, who wrote many series on law, and later translated and published the decisions of the Supreme Court (N. Silva

2018, 110; Forbes 1998d, 407). During the first decades of the territory, Hawaiians fought to preserve the right to express themselves as Hawaiians in courts of law. One of the bills in the first territorial legislature, introduced by H. M. Kaniho, representing Kaua'i and Ni'ihau, called for 'ōlelo Hawai'i to remain as an option for use in all territorial courts (Williams 2015, 32). In 1920, Z. P. K. Kawaikaumaiikamakaokaopua, also known as Kalokuokamaile, one of the wise kūpuna of Nāpo'opo'o, reported that Representative Kupihea repeatedly tried to pass that bill—but always unsuccessfully (Kawaikaumaiikamakaokaopua 1920, 3).

Indigenous theorist Audra Simpson offers a persuasive explanation for the waning ea of the lāhui Hawai'i and our 'ōlelo within settler state institutions during those times: "In situations in which sovereignties are nested and embedded, one proliferates at the other's expense; the United States and Canada can only come into political being because of Indigenous dispossession. Under these conditions there cannot be two perfectly equal, robust sovereignties. Built into 'sovereignty' is a jurisdictional dominion over territory, a notion of singular law, and singular authority (the king, the state, the band council, tribal council, and even the notion of the People)" (2014, 12). When Kanuha refuses translation and through 'ōlelo Hawai'i asserts ea Hawai'i in the courtroom after its long period of suppression, he is chipping away at the dominion of the United States as "the singular law" and "singular authority."

And whether they realize it or not, what provokes the irate online commenters is this chipping away. The monolingual U.S. settler confronted by another language fears the unfamiliar and, above all, the unknown. One way to illustrate this is through the distinction that Diana Taylor draws between the archive and the repertoire. In her formulation, the archive is the generalized repository of knowledge coming from "documents, literary texts, letters, archaeological remains, bones, videos, films, CDs, all those items supposedly resistant to change" (2007, 19). On the other hand, the repertoire "enacts embodied memory: performances, gestures, orality, movement, dance, singing" (20). The court system in this case is emblematic of the archive with its reliance on court transcripts, written statutes, precedents, and decisions, particularly in the way that it encloses Kānaka and other Indigenous peoples in legal language, the meaning of which is often dictated by colonial powers. Sam Raditlhalo, speaking of South Africa's Truth and Reconciliation Committee, makes the point that "stories...have been de-formed, stained, and made sterile by 'the dialect of record'" (2009, 93), and it is this de-forming, staining, and sterilizing that Kanuha is combatting by refusing translation, and thus refusing legibility to the archive.

As Diana Taylor points out, "performance...has a history of untranslatability" (2007, 6) and that "embodied memory, because it is live, exceeds the archive's ability to capture it"[6] (20–21). It is this untranslatability and uncapturability that makes Kanuha's embodied performance so threatening to the established colonial order. Settler colonialism names, orders, and encloses the world so that it is legible and beneficial to settlers. Hawai'i is a state, 'āina is real estate, Hawaiians are an ethnic group. Yet embodied performances such as Kanuha's are all about the project of unsettlement, which involves "concrete attempt[s] to annihilate or otherwise put an end to a European colony, or to forestall or eliminate a future colonial project" (Brickhouse 2015, 2). This unsettlement signals both the "contingency and noninevitability" (2) of this assumed colonial order. For Hawaiians and allies who witness this performance, they see a Hawaiian standing proudly on a foundation of ancestral knowledge and language, unconstrained by the imposed structures of the state's power; those who do not support Hawaiians see something else completely. Exposure to the language of this place, which orders their world differently, particularly through the orality of performance, not only suggests how tenuous settler power over this 'āina actually is, but also confronts settlers with their complete ignorance of how different Hawai'i might be from what they believe. So seeing 'ōlelo Hawai'i, this language they feel they do not need to know and has no real mana in their ordered society, not only being recognized but claiming authority in settler state institutions rather than being assimilated confronts them with the possibility that change is coming. And because they cannot, or refuse to, prepare for such change, they react violently when such personal indignities multiply until their comfortable understanding of how the world should be seems threatened by this alien language world. As Teves says, "remember, traditions are made and unmade through performances" (2015b, 262), and this is exactly what they fear, that these embodied performances of refusal and the memory and knowledge that they bring with them will stick around and be made into tradition.

An example of how the uncapturability of Kanuha's embodied performance disrupted the normal colonial order came through an especially savvy context shift that he made. After a Hawaiian-language interpreter was assigned for the case, he told the judge that the translator was not for him: "The translator is for *you*." As Kanuha explained in an interview for Hawai'i Public Radio, "the issue is when I speak to her she wasn't able to comprehend that.... And so my demand to her was, it's on you, it's your kuleana, it's your responsibility to find an interpreter for yourself so that you as a judge can competently make a ruling in this case, in this trial" (quoted in Hiraishi 2018). The logic is impeccable. Since Kanuha understands both Hawaiian and English, but is choosing to speak only in Hawaiian, and since Judge Barbara Takase only understands English, she needs an interpreter to do her job properly. Kanuha was therefore calling on a settler colonial institution to rectify its own shortcomings at the request of someone who did not recognize the court's authority. A daring strategy, but after some initial resistance, the judge gave in and got an interpreter for herself. This was an inspiring reversal of mana. Speakers of 'ōlelo Hawai'i are accustomed to having our efforts to use our language outside of the classroom treated as a request for concessions, but here was a staunch aloha 'āina dictating the terms of engagement, arguing that the court was the party that needed to catch up.

Despite the fact that "embodied and performed acts generate, record, and transmit knowledge" (Taylor 2007, 21), as the online commenters who denounced Faye Hanohano as childish or bullying confirm, Kanuha's refusal to translate can all too easily be seen as a refusal to communicate. Because the Latin word "translatus" means "carried across," translation is often described as a bridge that lets meaning flow across linguistic gaps. Refusing to translate can therefore seem like a desire not to communicate, a rejection of the offer to cross the bridge. For this reason, many online commenters claim that a refusal to translate shows poor "MANNERS" by rudely declaring "f-you if you don't understand me." What such online critics do not realize, or care to understand, is that these refusals to translate are actually offering a bridge that the critics are more than welcome to cross, and that will carry them to something we consider beautiful and hold dear in the very core of our being. It is not, however, a bridge between Hawaiian and English, but one to a world where the language of this ʻāina is spoken everywhere. This world once existed, when Hawaiians, Chinese, British, Americans, Greeks, other Pacific Islanders—all who lived here, in fact—spoke Hawaiian. We know about this world because we know our moʻolelo. As I have mentioned, one of our most repeated sayings is "I ka ʻōlelo nō ke ola, i ka ʻōlelo nō ka make" (In ʻōlelo there is life, and in ʻōlelo there is death). The bridge we are offering is to the entirety of that life and death, but to take the first steps, you must listen to what people are saying when they don't translate.

Kaleikoa Kāʻeo: "Eia nō au ke kū nei ma mua ou"

Like Kahoʻokahi Kanuha, Kaleikoa Kāʻeo is a Hawaiian-language educator, teaching at the college level for more than twenty-five years (Hiraishi 2018). He was also arrested in the Maunakea protests, but this chapter will focus on his arrest when protesting the Daniel K. Inouye Solar Telescope at Haleakalā, on his home island of Maui. Like the Maunakea kiaʻi, aloha ʻāina on Maui have been challenging the Inouye telescope in court, in this case for almost a decade (I. Loomis 2017). Though its footprint would be much smaller than the TMT, it would still be the world's largest solar telescope, standing fourteen stories high (I. Loomis 2017). Many of the Haleakalā protesters had either been on Maunakea, or were inspired by what happened there, and on July 31, 2015, over two hundred people blocked the base yard where a convoy was preparing to take equipment to the summit (Gutierrez 2015). Twenty were arrested, including Kāʻeo, but the convoy was stopped (Gutierrez 2015). Three weeks later, eight more were arrested for attempting to block construction ("6 Arrested" 2017). Two years later, construction was attempted again, and kiaʻi blocked the convoy, using crosswalks strategically, and a chain of kiaʻi with PVC pipe over their arms locked themselves together then lay down on the road. Kāʻeo was arrested again (I. Loomis 2017).

These arrests on Haleakalā differed strikingly from those on Maunakea because the police were far more militarized and physically aggressive. One of the kiaʻi was forced into unconsciousness and sent to the hospital during his arrest (I. Loomis 2017). The differences were so stark that sources familiar with the planning for the State of Hawaiʻi's response to expected protests over the TMT after the October 2018 Supreme Court decision said, "They don't want another fiasco where DOCARE officers are shedding tears and embracing protesters. They want this to be like Haleakala, where they were all over 'em" (Dayton 2018). Robert Nichols describes the nature of such a militarized police force: "Policing is thought to be militarized either when (1) it begins to employ certain technologies of intense violence normally not deployed against civilian citizenry (e.g., the use of armed personnel carriers, drones, aerial surveillance, etc.) or (2) when it begins to serve overtly political aims, exceeding its traditional mandate to 'serve and protect' the citizenry" (2014, 445). The Maui Police Department confronted the peaceful protests in tactical riot gear and body armor, but as Nichols explains, when "viewed from the vantage point of settler colonialism and indigenous critique," we can recognize that "there is nothing new" about "the nakedly fluid boundary between military and policing operations today." Within Anglo-American settler colonialism, "the extension of criminal jurisdiction has long been central to the subjugation and displacement of indigenous polities" (Nichols 2014, 446). When police carry out the political will of the settler/occupying state against Indigenous members of the occupied nation, the line between policing and military action becomes thin indeed, as "criminal control bleeds into war" (445).

It was in this militarized milieu that Kaleikoa Kāʻeo was arrested for his part in the last unsuccessful attempt to blockade the convoy from delivering the telescope's mirror to the summit. He had lain down in the road, directly in the path of one of the trucks. He was charged with disorderly conduct, refusing to comply with an officer's order, and obstructing a highway, though later news outlets reported that the second charge was actually obstructing a sidewalk ("Charges Dismissed" 2018). Kāʻeo's staunch aloha ʻāina had frequently put him in court for petty misdemeanors, often in front of the same judge, Blaine Kobayashi, and more than a dozen times he had been granted an interpreter so he could speak Hawaiian during his trial (Nabarro 2018a). This time, however, Kobayashi denied Kāʻeo's request, and that is when things got *interesting*.

A few different media outlets released footage of the courtroom proceedings, and the following is a transcript cobbled together from those sources documenting the bizarrely theatrical interaction that took place. Since Kāʻeo did not explicitly request not to be translated in the transcript, I have included English approximations of what he said:

Kobayashi: "State your name for the record."
Kaleikoa: "Ua hiki mai nei kēia kanaka 'o Kaleikoa" [This person named Kaleikoa is here].
Kobayashi: "Samuel Kā'eo?"
Kaleikoa: "Ua hiki mai nei kēia kanaka 'o Kaleikoa e kū nei i mua ou, e ka lunakānāwai" [This person named Kaleikoa is standing here before you, judge].
Kobayashi: "I know you understand English, Mr. Kā'eo, so I'm going to have to have you please identify in fact that your name is Samuel Kā'eo."
Kaleikoa: "Eia nō au ke kū nei ma mua ou" [Here I am standing right in front of you].
Kobayashi: "I don't know what that means, Mr. Kā'eo, what you just said."
Kaleikoa [slower]: "E kala mai, e ka luna kānāwai, 'o au nei ke kanaka e kū nei ma mua ou i hiki mai i kēia lā" [My apologies, judge, I am indeed here, the person standing in front of you on this day].
Kobayashi: "I'm going to give you another opportunity, Mr. Kā'eo, to just identify yourself, just so the record is clear. I'm going to ask you one more time, is your name Samuel Kā'eo?" (Maui Now 2018a)
Kaleikoa: "Eia au, ke kū nei i mua ou, 'o ia ke kanaka āu i kāhea mai nei, e kū nei i mua ou, e ka luna kānāwai. Aloha" [Here I am, standing right here, the person that you have just called out for stands here before you, judge. Aloha].
Kobayashi: "The court is unable to get a definitive determination for the record that the defendant seated in the court is Mr. Samuel Kā'eo. Bailiff, make three calls for the defendant."

[Bailiff calls out in the courtroom and then walks out into the hallway to call again before returning.]

Bailiff: "Three calls made, Your Honor. No response."
Kobayashi: "Okay, three calls having been made. No individual identifying himself as the defendant for today's proceedings, for *State of Hawai'i v. Samuel Kā'eo*.

A bench warrant [to] be issued in the amount, Ms. Skye?"

Prosecutor: "Your Honor, the state is requesting a bench warrant in the amount of $250 per count."

Kobayashi: "So ordered." (KITV 2018)

The stunning, almost fable-like theatricality transforms this encounter into an allegory for the Hawaiian experience with settler colonialism. It would be hard to think of a better example of the lengths the settler state is prepared to go when seeking to contain Hawaiians. A $750 bench warrant was issued for Kāʻeo due to his "failure to appear," even though he was standing right in front of the judge, who kept addressing him as "Mr. Kāʻeo"! The judge also insisted on referring to him as "Samuel," even though the court case lists him as Samuel Kaleikoa Kāʻeo, and Kāʻeo insisted on identifying himself as Kaleikoa. Could there be a clearer case of how the court, as a vehicle for enacting the logic of elimination, tried to erase Kāʻeo's identity as a Hawaiian?

The public outcry was immediate and massive. Some politicians saw the court as the problem. Running in 2018 for governor, Representative Andria Tupola in a video posted on Facebook blasted the entire judicial staff: "The judge pretended that he couldn't hear and then the clerks played along and then the prosecutors played along. We don't go to the courts to put on a show, it's not for theatrics, it is for justice" (quoted in Nabarro 2018a). In his own video response, Kaniela Ing promised to push for strong legislation that would mandate a Hawaiian-language interpreter in court (Nabarro 2018a). Other online comments ran along familiar infantilizing lines. "BRAT I see this person behaving like a Brat, 'it's my ball so we will play my way' also attempting to use the 'race' card, behaving like two year old," wrote P minz, and myauthorizedopinion goes on at still greater length: "Boy was in contempt of court. . . . Judge should have called it and locked bright boy up. Just call it a 'reality check.' . . . Boys [*sic*] lucky, he got off easy. Judge chose not to ' luc for contempt.' Boy needed a reality check and ended up getting coddled instead. Poor thing." I could go on at equal length about this comment, but by now, I don't think readers need me to speculate on what kind of person calls a fifty-one-year-old Hawaiian man "boy."

Opinions such as these notwithstanding, the following day, Judge

Kobayashi put out this notice: "The Court hereby recalls the bench warrant (D211844171) issued on January 24, 2018, in the above-captioned matter. Case No. 2DCW-17–0002038 is hereby rescheduled for status, trial setting, and further hearing on the issue of an interpreter on February 21, 2018, at 10:00 a.m. in Courtroom 3D." Swiftly recalling the warrant and revisiting the interpreter "issue" suggests that Kobayashi had not really thought through the performance that he, and the bailiff, and the prosecutor had put on in his courtroom, nor had he realized how many eyes were on what was taking place there. By insisting on 'ōlelo Hawai'i as a required engagement on the part of the court system, Kā'eo's and Kanuha's actions reverberate out into other arenas. By gumming up the works of the carceral machine of the settler state through their refusal to translate, they are effectively setting the stage for similar situations outside of the carceral system as well, when Hawaiians who were inspired by their refusals, their reiterating of Nāwahī's call to *mai noho kākou a 'ae iki,* take their own stands, in whatever contexts their aloha 'āina directs them to make it happen.

The Invisible Man
Kaleikoa Kā'eo had figured out something that all little kids who love superheroes are dying to know: how to become invisible. It turned out that all you had to do was speak Hawaiian. "Living as 'Ōiwi is a continual process of becoming," Noe Goodyear-Ka'ōpua writes. "Like breathing, resurgence and ea must be continuous to sustain a healthy life" (2015, 13). What Kā'eo's, Kanuha's, and Hanohano's refusals to translate did was make them visible, make them *legible,* not just as minorities within the legislative or justice system, but as *Kānaka Maoli* within the grip of the representative and carceral arms of the settler state. Pua Aiu acknowledges that "colonized people often feel they must self-translate or they will not be heard. Certainly when Hawaiians refuse to translate, they often in fact are not heard" (2010, 98). And certainly in Kā'eo's case, when he did not translate, the judge not only refused to hear him, but even refused to *see* him.

Though the ensemble cast of judge, bailiff, and prosecutor put on what can only be considered a farcical and absurdist bit of theater, Kā'eo, like Kanuha before him, was putting on an embodied performance of his own. In regards to the testimonies and narratives she had heard as a member of South Africa's Truth and Reconciliation

Committee, Pumla Gobodo-Madikizela asked, "What function does a traumatic narrative serve if it creates a gulf between language and experience?" (quoted in Raditlhalo 2009, 93), and that is one of the key differences between the archive and the repertoire. The logocentric narratives of the archive are indeed powerful, but at times cannot sufficiently convey experience, whereas Kāʻeo in his embodied performance, while using language to speak to a particular audience, used the performance of his own body to help cross that gulf between language and experience.

As Diana Taylor points out, "the repertoire requires presence: people participate in the production and reproduction of knowledge by 'being there,' being a part of the transmission" (2007, 20). It also "transmits live, embodied actions. As such traditions are stored in the body, through various mnemonic methods, and transmitted 'live' in the here and now to a live audience. Forms handed down from the past are experienced as present"[7] (24). In that way, though not everyone could understand what Kāʻeo was saying in ʻōlelo Hawaiʻi, they could bridge that gulf between language and experience by witnessing and receiving Kāʻeo's experience as a Hawaiian man made invisible by the structures of power. And the fact that tradition is stored in the body, as Taylor says, made them see and feel the echoes of how this happened to our ancestors as well, with Taylor pointing out further that "bearing witness is a live process, a doing, an event that takes place in real time, in the presence of a listener who 'comes to be a participant and a co-owner of the traumatic event' " (167).

Stephanie Nohelani Teves is instructional here when she says, "When I analyze performances, I look at the possible contributions performances make to new traditions, considering the messages they convey, the commentary performances produce, how performances build on old traditions, and how performances reference the continued presence of Hawaiian culture" (2015b, 264). Taylor also points to this power when she says that performances "reconstitute themselves, transmitting communal memories, histories, and values from one group/generation to the next" (2007, 21). In that sense it is likely that despite where these refusals to translate took place, the primary audiences for these embodied performances were not the court or legislature, or even the general public, but the lāhui Hawaiʻi itself. Kāʻeo and Kanuha are both educators who, like growing numbers of us, support independence from the United States. By making themselves visible in the courtroom, they are making their values visible/legible to the Hawaiian community as well. Though they refuse to translate, they still use mana unuhi to give mana to a particular story. One in which they present themselves as aloha 'āina—rooted in the land, connected to their language, and dedicated to living as part of an independent Hawai'i. The bridge in Kā'eo's case goes to a Hawai'i where Hawaiians are seen as human beings with the right to exercise our ea. As he said at a speech the day after the warrant was recalled:

> See, the idea of us being invisible is nothing new. What we witnessed in the courtroom on Wednesday is nothing new. It's not about the judge.... Yes, we can point the finger at Judge Kobayashi. But even if we change Judge Kobayashi, it does not change the system of racism and settlerism that exists in Hawai'i. It's a systematic problem in which they silence our voices. They treat us as if we're not human beings, and we don't know what's best for our people. That somehow five thousand miles away, they know better what is sacred and what is important for us. (maui808films 2018)

It is nothing new. What happened to him so visibly has happened to so many before invisibly. By refusing to translate for those who are literally and metaphorically five thousand miles away, Kā'eo's message becomes clearer for the lāhui Hawai'i.

As his quote reveals, and as many of the irate commenters liked to point out during Kā'eo's trial, Kaleikoa Kā'eo can speak English; he is in fact one of our most eloquent and stirring orators in either language. When long ago Representative Kaniho introduced the bill calling for more 'ōlelo Hawai'i in the court system, he really did have a hard time understanding English. Kā'eo has no such problems, and employs both languages strategically, selecting each time the one that will resonate most with his current audience as he insists on the primacy and power of 'ōlelo Hawai'i. Nor is he alone. The championing of 'ōlelo Hawai'i is being led by those of us who are bilingual, and this is why paying attention to translation, and refusals to translate, can yield such powerful insights. Becoming visible to Judge Kobayashi is not the goal, but rather, becoming increasingly legible as a lāhui, with our own values and systems of governance is. Growing our sense of Indigeneity, of

Hawaiian-ness, of ea as we navigate our everyday worlds is far more important than increasing the presence of 'ōlelo Hawai'i in settler institutions, though the former can benefit from the latter.

The Michi Saagiig Nishnaabeg intellectual and poet Leanne Betasamosake Simpson speaks to this idea with regard to her own context in settler Canada:

> When my Indigeneity grows I fall more in unconditional love with my homeland, my family, my culture, my language, more in line with the idea that resurgence is my original instruction, more in line with the thousands of stories that demonstrate how to live a meaningful life and I have more emotional capital to fight and protect what is meaningful to me. I am a bigger threat to the Canadian state and its plans to build pipelines across my body, clear cut my forests, contaminate my lakes with toxic cottages and chemicals and make my body a site of continual sexualized violence. (2015)

The more Hawaiians feel the strength of this unconditional love and pilina for homeland, family, culture, and language, the less they will accept their enclosure within the settler state. The less they will give their mana to its structures. It is no accident that these state institutions were chosen as the sites of these translational refusals. Audra Simpson spells out why: "The bureaucratized state is one frame in which visibility is produced, creating the conditions under which difference becomes apparent; political aspirations are articulated; and culture, authenticity, and tradition (Verdery 1993, 42) become politically expedient resources. The state, in framing what is official, creates the conditions of affiliation or distance. These disaffiliations arise from the state's project of homogenizing heterogeneity" (2014, 18). By taking back the idea of what is official—Kanuha's assertion that "the translator is for you," for instance—the refusal to translate calls into question the state's authority to set the conditions of affiliation or distance. By insisting on Hawaiian difference, these refusals also reveal *why* the case of Hawaiians should be different, why Hawaiians should stand apart.

Just as with her people, the Mohawks of Kahnawà:ke, Audra Simpson recognizes the trick of becoming visible in these settler contexts: "The desires and attendant practices of settlers get rerouted, or displaced, in liberal argumentation through the trick of toleration, of 'recognition'... an impossible and also tricky beneficence that actually may extend forms of settlement through the language and practices of, at times, nearly impossible but seemingly democratic inclusion (Wolfe 2011, 32). This inclusion, or juridical form of recognition, is only performed, however, if the problem of cultural difference and alterity does not pose too appalling a challenge to norms of the settler society" (2014, 20). In Hawaiʻi, the "trick of toleration, of 'recognition' " extends not only to formal forms such as federal recognition from the U.S. Department of the Interior, but also to recognition within state institutions, because that sort of recognition, particularly here in Hawaiʻi, leads to a flattening of sorts, with Hawaiians "recognized" as just another ethnic group in the stew, salad, hot pot, saimin, or whatever food metaphor is chosen to represent Hawaiʻi's multiracial mix. Rather than validating the amorphous blob of the American melting pot, all such metaphors acknowledge the distinctiveness of individual ethnicities. But none of them acknowledge Indigenous connections to ʻāina. They ahistorically recognize the diversity of Hawaiʻi, generally connecting Local identity back to the Massie case and the shared struggle of the sugar plantations and later land disputes, but no further (Rosa 2014, 5–6; Fujikane 2008, 25–29). None of them even recognize the multiethnic makeup of the Hawaiian Kingdom and that more than just Hawaiians lost their nation during the overthrow.

Though Local identity is an outgrowth of class solidarity and taking a collective stand against white supremacy, it developed after the overthrow of the kingdom and is generally invested in gaining power for Local people in the U.S. system. Its rootedness in pushing for agency in the settler state means that it is built upon a foundation of forgetting non-Hawaiian allegiance to the kingdom. Local identity is predicated on remembering and valorizing plantation solidarity: the three main trials after the 1889 counter-revolt to overturn the Bayonet Constitution were of famed Hawaiian patriot Robert Kalanihiapo Wilcox; of Albert Loomens, a Belgian soldier who joined the rebellion; and of Ho Fon, a young Chinese newspaperman accused of acting as the liaison between the rebels and the Chinese merchants who supported them (Chapin 1996b, 86). Immediately after the overthrow, Japanese laborers pledged their support to the Queen, and provoked the provisional government by letting out three cheers for her whenever they passed ʻIolani Palace (Palmer 1895, 13). And the roster of the more than three hundred people arrested for the 1895 counter-revolt includes such "foreign" names as Lycurgus, Juen, Moon Kin, de Rega, Muller, Matsumoto, and more, right next to Hakuole, Ahia, and Kekipi (Spencer 1895, 133–135).

It is undeniably more difficult to recognize Hawaiian historically as both a nationality—and therefore including individuals from different ethnic backgrounds—*and* as a marker of Indigeneity, indicating not only cultural identity and practices, but also particular claims to land, including, though extending well beyond, lands seized from the kingdom. Understandings of Local identity and solidarity expressed through assimilative food metaphors obscure the rich history of solidarity across ethnic lines in the Hawaiian Kingdom, and contribute to the elimination of the native *as native*. Recognizing this fact, and this history, is more liberatory for all involved, though it demands that we do the additional difficult work necessary to retain these nuances.

A Place in the Sun or a Place in the Courtroom

Tied to recognition through democratic inclusion within the settler state was a policy change in response to Kāʻeo's Hawaiian-language disappearing act that many viewed as a victory. Judge Kobayashi initially refused to grant Kāʻeo an interpreter because it was impractical and an unnecessary expense. There were precedents for the judge's refusal. In a 1993 federal case, the presiding judge found that if a person denied an interpreter could speak English, their due process rights were still protected (Hiraishi 2018), and Debi Tulang-De Silva, program director for the State Judiciary's Office of Equality and Access to the Courts, initially said: "Basically there's no legal requirement to provide language interpreters to court participants who speak English" (Hiraishi 2018). This opinion was, however, almost immediately overruled:

> The Judiciary today announced the following policy regarding Hawaiian language interpreters during courtroom proceedings:
>
> The Judiciary will provide or permit qualified Hawaiian language interpreters to the extent reasonably possible when parties in courtroom proceedings choose to express themselves through the Hawaiian language.
>
> The Judiciary will develop implementation procedures for this policy, and welcomes input from the community. ("Judiciary Announces" 2018)

Many in the community had been calling for this very thing. Since Hawaiian had been an official state language since 1978, many Hawaiians and non-Hawaiians felt such a policy was fair, just, and equitable. "We pay taxes just like everybody else," said Tiare Lawrence, an aloha ʻāina who herself had been arrested over Haleakalā. "If a Hawaiian comes into a courtroom and wants an interpreter, then they should be allowed that service" (quoted in Nabarro 2018b). At a January hearing for an amended bill that would require interpreter services if any party to a court proceeding requests that it be conducted in Hawaiian, testimony was said to be "emotional and teary" at times, as supporters of the bill stressed the importance of ʻōlelo Hawaiʻi (Wang 2018).

Kanuha's and Kāʻeo's canny refusals to translate laid the groundwork for greater access to Hawaiian-language interpretation services within the judicial system. This is undeniably an important victory for Hawaiian-language revitalization and renormalization efforts. We should be able to speak ʻōlelo Hawaiʻi wherever we go, and we should not wait until after achieving independence to make that happen. I wish that I could believe the judiciary's quick policy change was motivated by a sincere understanding that ʻōlelo Hawaiʻi is the language of this land, and not simply a scramble to re-enfold Hawaiians within the settler colonial system. Refusing to translate makes legible Hawaiian difference and questions the authority of the State of Hawaiʻi. Having your day in court with a Hawaiian interpreter graciously provided by the state does not.

I am not denying the importance of ʻōlelo Hawaiʻi being everywhere, but rather acknowledging the accuracy of Patrick Wolfe's observation that "settler societies characteristically devise a number of often coexistent strategies to eliminate the threat posed by the survival in their midst of irregularly dispossessed social groups who were constituted prior to and independently of the normative basis on which settler society is established. These strategies include expulsion and other forms of geographical sequestration, *as well as programs of incorporation* that seek to efface the distinguishing criteria—biology, culture, mode of production, religion, etc.—whereby native difference is constructed in settler discourse" (2008, 103; emphasis added). Incorporating Hawaiian language into the judiciary's Office of Equality and Access to the Courts is just such an effacement of Hawaiian difference, whereby rather than speaking ʻōlelo Hawaiʻi as part of our liberation and decolonization/deoccupation, Hawaiians become recipients of a service in the name of equality. Just another ethnic group.

As Tuck and Yang suggest, "this kind of inclusion is a form of enclosure, dangerous in how it domesticates decolonization" (2012, 3) because "the attainment of equal legal and cultural entitlements... is actually an investment in settler colonialism" (18). This is a hard line to walk in an occupied nation though. How do we fight to exist as Hawaiians against a system dedicated to our erasure without entrenching ourselves even further through the promise, or even the granting, of more rights? Or as Hawaiian intellectual, activist, and musician Jonathan Kay Kamakawiwoʻole Osorio puts it, "Do we conform our responses to the framework of the American political system, hoping that we might bring new benefits to our children thereby, or do we insist on clinging to every tradition that we can recover, insisting on our separateness, our distinctness, from a society that seemingly regards such distinction as anachronistic and dangerous?" (2001, 373). Writing in 2001, he points to a difficult yet necessary answer: "Yet when we consider the first option, we realize that American law is no more reliable a friend to the Native Hawaiian at the dawn of this century than it was at the turn of the last" (373).

After the bench warrant was issued for Kāʻeo's arrest, Hawaiian academic and legal scholar Kekailoa Perry remarked that

> the judge knew Kalei[koa], the prosecutor knew Kalei, everybody knows Kalei, but they put the blinders on and they said, "we're going to use the process to ignore you," to ignore not him, but all of us as Hawaiians.... It was a message that's being sent... to all of us: be careful because we have the power to suppress you, we have the power to shut you up.... And yet somehow we let ourselves get trapped into the thinking that somewhere along the line this government, this judge, this legal system going come out and protect us. Today is a message for all of us. There is no protection in the law. There is no protection in the US system. We're on our own. And you know what? Maika'i. [Good.] Because when we're on our own together, there is nothing that can stop us. (Dukelow 2018)

The thing is, we as Hawaiians know this. If any Hawaiian has paid attention to anything that has happened in the last century and a half or so, they will know that American law has never really been a friend to us. And yet. There are many Hawaiians who fight for federal recognition, many who say that if it weren't the United States who took us over, it would have been Japan or Russia, so we should be grateful for our freedom.

That is not to say that we should abandon all recourse to the law, or shut down Ka Huli Ao Center for Excellence in Native Hawaiian Law, or minimize the importance of Hawaiian victories in the courts, or stop filing suits, or requesting injunctions, or fighting for more protections within the system. But as Tuck and Yang remind us, "decolonization in a settler context is fraught because empire, settlement, and internal colony have no spatial separation" (2012, 7). In Hawai'i certainly, everything is jumbled together, often making what is what hard to see. The only option for us to really find our way out from here is to remind ourselves continually, sometimes by using our very own bodies, how settler colonialism works, and especially, to be alert to what Tuck and Yang have termed "settler moves to innocence": "those strategies or positionings that attempt to relieve the settler of feelings of guilt or responsibility without giving up land or power or privilege, without having to change much at all" (2012, 10). Greater availability of Hawaiian-language interpreters in court is indeed a victory, but it also represents a settler move to innocence. For a relatively small amount of money, the state has "helped" Hawaiians, contained the potentially disruptive power of refusing to translate, and kept Hawaiians safely ensconced in the idea of equality for all citizens.

Ka 'Ōlelo o ka 'Āina: "Sacred" Words

When speaking about their strategy of choosing to speak only in Hawaiian during their trials, both Kanuha and Kā'eo made connections between 'ōlelo Hawai'i and 'āina. Kanuha wanted "to highlight that the movement to revitalize the Hawaiian language is connected to the fight to protect Maunakea from desecration" ("Telescope Protestor" 2016). And according to Kā'eo, "there are things you can say in Hawaiian that you know really express through our cultural view of why it's important for us to defend our sacred sites" (quoted in Hiraishi 2018). While not all who support the revitalization and renormalization of 'ōlelo Hawai'i have the same opinions about these struggles over sacred sites, all would agree that our land and language are tied together and connected by ea. "Ea" is the word we use to talk about sovereignty; it is also our word for breath and for rising. We cannot speak our language without breath, without ea, and the more we speak, the more our ea grows. Kāʻeo explicitly connects ea and ʻāina: "What's important here is the Hawaiian concept: ua mau ke ea o ka ʻāina. Ke ea o ka ʻāina, the life of the land, the sovereignty of the land is that very place. Hawaiians don't see that their sovereignty comes from a particular king. Our sovereignty does not come from a constitution. The sovereignty doesn't come from the gun. The sovereignty doesn't come from arms. But in fact the sovereignty comes from the land. So even according to our own cultural understandings, the land itself is our sovereignty" (Bauknight 2009). Without these connections between ea and ʻāina, it is unlikely that Kāʻeo or Kanuha would have refused to translate in the courtroom.

But without this struggle over our ʻāina and our breath, would the push for our ʻōlelo have the same resonance? Would our naʻau reverberate the way they do when we hear our language spoken with skill and aloha? Rhetorical questions, perhaps. My sense is that the answer is no. Our ʻōlelo connects us to the place-names of our land, the names of the wind and the rain. ʻĀina is the backbone of our traditional moʻolelo and our mele. And as Hawaiian scholar Jamaica Heolimeleikalani Osorio explains, "this pilina to ʻāina is the standard by which we understand our pilina with each other. Our relationship to our ʻāina is our kumu, and every intimacy we practice thereafter echoes the intimacies learned from our beautiful home" (2018, 147–148). Everything that we learn in and about our language ties us more and more closely to ʻāina.

After the bench warrant was issued, Kāʻeo stood outside the courtroom and spoke about this connection between our ʻōlelo and our ʻāina. He reminded us that the Second Circuit Court was initially an institution of the Hawaiian Kingdom, and that systemic change was what was necessary: "Unfortunately, even having a translator is still not good enough, but at least I would be able to speak in my language, you see.... I refuse. I refuse that anybody should tell a Hawaiian when they should speak Hawaiian. Especially in the defense of our sacred lands. This whole case is about being Hawaiian" (Maui Now 2018c). Kanuha too echoed some of these thoughts when he talked about the testimony that he gave in Hawaiian during his trial, describing it as follows: "I was there to prevent desecration and it's a traditional and customary practice...I recited my genealogy...showing that I do have a genealogical connection to these people and that place. My ancestors recognized and revered this place as someplace sacred" ("Telescope Protestor" 2016). Just as Kāʻeo made clear in his testimony, Kanuha needed to speak about our relationship to ʻāina in the language most suited to expressing it.

These are the things that resist easy translation. Both use the word "sacred" to describe the reverence they feel for ʻāina; for both, the summits of Maunakea and Haleakalā are sacred, and the kiaʻi are trying to protect them from further desecration. But a problem arises when a single word, "sacred," is chosen to translate two completely different "original texts"—one drawn from a Hawaiian understanding and the other from a Western/American mainstream understanding. As readers and speakers, we are familiar with the word "sacred," so we think we know what Kanuha and Kāʻeo mean by "sacred" land. But does the word fully invoke for us the Hawaiian familial connection to ʻāina, which means "that which feeds," and the reciprocal relationship of care between land as elder sibling and person as younger sibling, just for starters? In American society, willingness to die for family members is an admired and understood virtue. Yet when Kāʻeo and other kiaʻi risk death to lay themselves in the path of semitrucks carrying equipment up the mountain, they are labeled "crazy Hawaiians" (I. Loomis 2017).

What is at issue is *not* that Hawaiian values and understandings of aloha ʻāina are completely incommensurate and illegible to Western society, but that as Hawaiians we must live and speak in translation whenever we challenge the apparatuses of settler colonialism and all those who wish to separate kānaka from ʻāina. "Living in translation" is not a metaphor. The concepts developed from living in connection with the ʻāina have come down from our ancestors rooted in ʻōlelo Hawaiʻi. That is where they gained their meaning, and where many of us have learned about and embraced them. But when we speak of such things to those who often have power over our bodies and our ʻāina, we must use English words to describe them, fitting for their benefit our understanding into little English-shaped slots. Acoma poet Simon Ortiz talks about the stakes of this kind of living: "Using the English language is a dilemma and pretty scary sometimes, because it means letting one's mind go willfully—although with soul and heart and shaky hands, literally—into the Western cultural and intellectual context, a condition and circumstance that one usually avoids at all costs on most occasions.... years later I admit I felt uneasy and even disloyal moments when I found myself to be more verbally articulate in the English language than in my own native Acoma language" (1997, xvi). Because each language has its own values and history—the "cultural and intellectual context" Ortiz mentions—articulating Hawaiian things with an English tongue inevitably leads to misunderstandings. Our two most prominent land struggles hinge on the word "sacred," and as Hawaiians, we know that we use that English word as a stand-in for mana, kapu, aloha ʻāina, ʻeʻehia, laʻa, moʻokūʻauhau, pilina, kulāiwi, ʻohana, ʻai, ea—for so many of those concepts that make up our identity. But when people in the general public hear "sacred," many think "really really special"—someplace you would take a picture of for Instagram, someplace on your bucket list you want to visit, someplace super pretty, beautiful even—a place you have a good feeling about. For others, it could mean even less. People who don't want to answer work emails on Saturday and Sunday might say, "Sorry, my weekends are sacred." And while many astronomers would agree that "sacred" means "really really special," they also hear "really really superstitious," or even "we are the Catholic Church from four hundred years ago coming to persecute you." Kealoha Pisciotta, a former telescope operator who is now one of the leaders of the fight against the TMT, had the perfect response: "We're not the church. You're not Galileo" (quoted in Overbye 2016).

This narrowing of Hawaiians' deep connection to ʻāina into a single English word with much less cultural weight—or weight and history in the wrong places, perhaps—has contributed greatly to reducing these struggles to the false dichotomies of science versus culture, or superstition versus progress. For Hawaiians, what Westerners distinguish as science and culture cannot be separated. We therefore had to invent a word for science, *not* because we could not comprehend the concept before Westerners arrived, but because our word ʻike enfolded what Westerners call science within our connections to land, our ancestors, the seen and unseen around us—everything of the world.

As Tuck and Yang explain, at the heart of all these false dichotomies lies the biggest, most violent binary of them all: "Everything within a settler colonial society strains to destroy or assimilate the Native in order to disappear them from the land—this is how a society can have multiple simultaneous and conflicting messages about Indigenous peoples" (2012, 9). Because the opponents of the kiaʻi quite literally wanted to "disappear them from the land" so they would stop blocking construction, the struggle was cast as between science and culture—and since Hawaiians were defending "culture," they were therefore "anti-science"—even though many Hawaiian scientists were among the kiaʻi. Yet in the same breath—not ea—the TMT proponents would point to decontextualized bits of our history, and triumphantly say, "Look, your ancestors were practicing science! Shouldn't you support our scientific efforts if you care so much about your ancestors?"

As Samuel Kamakau once said, "Aole na ka malihini e ao iaʻu i ka mooolelo o koʻu lahui, naʻu e ao aku i ka moolelo i ka malihini" (It is not the foreigner/outsider/neophyte who shall teach me the history of my people/nation; I am the one who shall teach it to them) (1865, 1). Few things are less welcome than being offered paltry knowledge of our people and language to teach us about our own kūpuna. In this case, celestial navigation is the topic. Predictably, astronomers and TMT supporters were quick to point to our voyagers both ancestral and contemporary as scientists. They were apparently unaware that this only became generally accepted as "scientific" knowledge a handful of decades ago, and that *Hōkūleʻa,* the reason they know anything about Hawaiian/Polynesian navigation at all, initially sailed because the scientists' own scientific ancestors did not consider such navigation as a rigorously tested system of knowledge, choosing instead to believe that our kūpuna settled Polynesia by being blown off course while fishing—though apparently with a wide array of plants and livestock on board, as well as strategically chosen groups of people with various skill sets that would enable entire civilizations to thrive.

Language and cultural revitalization are crucially important because when ʻōlelo Hawaiʻi and ʻike Hawaiʻi are more widespread within our communities, and the rest of Hawaiʻi as well, less living in translation will need to happen. Then, when we speak of Hawaiian things, or refer to traditional moʻolelo, or try to impress upon people the importance of ʻike kupuna, we will be standing on a shared foundation. But until that time, the mana unuhi of refusing to translate, refusing to live in translation, embodying ancestral memory and tradition within ourselves will all be essential. It reminds people, kanaka and non-kanaka alike, that Hawaiians are different, with a different story in play than what you are "getting" in English. It calls into question the authority of those we are refusing. And it communicates clearly that we are not interested in being another ethnic group within what is offered as equality. ʻO ke ea a me ka mana o ka ʻāina kā kākou e ʻimi nei, a ʻo ke ala i hiki aku ai i laila, ʻo ia nō ka ʻōlelo, ka nohona, a me ka ʻāina. Hōʻole nō kākou i ke ala a ʻoukou e kīpapa nei. A pehea, makemake ʻoe iaʻu e unuhi? Tsā, mai noho au a ʻae iki.

Epilogue

*He Mau Hua ma ka Umauma:
Words for the Future*

I have trouble taking on titles for myself sometimes. Though I have published both poetry and stories, I hesitate to call myself a poet or a fiction writer. I have had my photographs in magazines and galleries, and I hesitate to call myself a photographer. But since I have been translating from 'ōlelo Hawai'i to English for almost two decades, I think it is accurate to say that I am a translator.

For many reasons, some appearing in the preceding chapters, I am, however, a rather ambivalent translator. I haven't participated in a large translation project for several years now because of that ambivalence, and I am not sure if I ever will again. Nowadays I am more excited by the idea of creating and telling new mo'olelo, some in 'ōlelo Hawai'i and some not, and pushing my students to do the same. I want to see new mo'olelo of our akua interacting with today's world, so it does not seem like they all disappeared in the late nineteenth and early twentieth centuries, when all of the mo'olelo we are translating were published. I want to see more mo'olelo of kānaka in space (I was so excited when the participants of the Telling Mo'olelo through Video Games workshop I helped to put on chose that very thing for their game). I want to see us getting back to the cultural confidence that we had as a people at the height of the nūpepa era. Having explored in detail how translation out of Hawaiian and into English has created problems through translatorial intrusion, editorial obfuscation, and presentational delusion, at times I think that translating in that direction should be left by the wayside, never allowed to darken the doorways of our mo'olelo again.

This might seem to be the safest route to take. Learning ʻōlelo Hawaiʻi well enough to read our moʻolelo in their original language still speaks to a certain political and cultural commitment that is more likely to prevent cultural appropriation or misunderstanding. We will not agree on every issue—Maunakea, Hawaiian independence, demilitarization—but those willing to learn our language in this political and cultural climate are more likely to side with those of us pushing for the ea and mana of the lāhui. There are no guarantees, of course. Even within the last decade, scholars, creative folks, and internet influencers who have learned just enough ʻōlelo to enter the most basic levels of our moʻolelo and writings have immediately gone on to publish academic articles, create content, or make art out of what little they could glean.

But as this book has shown, we cannot afford to ignore translation. As postcolonial and translation theorist S. Shankar insists, "now, more than ever" we need to start building "a vigorous culture of translation—a widely disseminated and rich understanding of translation. Important as actual acts of translation are, it is also necessary to popularize a general understanding of translation that foregrounds interpretation rather than fidelity" (2012, 141). In a culture of translation, whether or not to translate, as I asked in one of the first articles I published as a young translator and MA student (Kuwada 2009), really is not the point anymore. What that culture really looks like at its core is just paying attention to mana unuhi on a lāhui-wide scale. There are some pretty concrete things that can be done to focus on mana unuhi and create a culture of translation, but setting the foundation for that takes a less-than-concrete step. To get to the mana unuhi starting line, we need to have a cultural certainty, the confidence I mentioned above that our kūpuna had during the nūpepa era when they were running rhetorical circles around those who were trying to oppress them. Due in large part to the damaging narratives in chapter 4 that have received mana after mana, a lot of us still think that we are disappearing, that so much of our culture is gone. And there is no question that we have indeed lost much. The massive population collapse we went through, the military occupation we are facing now, the constant attacks on our culture and our ʻāina. Almost all of the mānaleo, the native speakers of ʻōlelo Hawaiʻi, that I knew when I began to learn our language have passed away. But when we really take a look at our people and our 'āina and how we have risen, that is when we start to realize that there is also so much that we have not lost, and things begin to shift.

There is an abundance and a richness to what we have as a people, what our kūpuna have passed down to us through the newspapers and family stories and our cultural practices, and even what we have grown anew for ourselves. The number of speakers of 'ōlelo Hawai'i is on the rise. The 'āina has changed but it is still our elder sibling waiting for us to rediscover its stories and populate its landscape with new ones. Zealously hiding our culture away and guarding it from change is how we protect a treasure but also how we cut off its pilina, stifle its growth.

When we loosen that grip, we become open to the abundant possibilities for pilina both within our community and without. One of my favorite quotes that my poor students have to hear over and over comes from Scott Richard Lyons (Ojibwe/Dakota), who said, "The pursuit of sovereignty is an attempt to revive not our pasts but our possibilities" (2000, 450). The many mana of the narratives from chapter 4 tell us that we have only one path: disappearance. But when we realize how much possibility exists around us, we become comfortable and confident enough that everything coming in from the outside does not seem like a threat anymore (though some of it still will be). When we understand translation as no longer just "the central act of European colonization and imperialism" (Cheyfitz 1997, xii) and it becomes something by which our kūpuna made fun of Captain Cook and brought stories into our epistemologies and frames of reference and helped use the life and death within language for our own purposes, then we can begin to realize the mana of mana unuhi. Granted, this kind of cultural confidence is something that would benefit so many other aspects of our lāhui, and I want it for our people no matter what, but having this kind of space to breathe is necessary in order to reframe something that we have seen only as damaging for so long. It gives us more room for multilingualism, being open to the languages of 'āina and all the living beings upon it, and allows us to bring more things into our worldview.

Then, once enough people think this way, a culture of translation really just means asking the right questions. Those of us who feel we have the kuleana to tell our mo'olelo—literary practitioners, writers, translators, performers, filmmakers, even those scholars, influencers, and artists I mentioned above—always need to ask ourselves: "Who is this for? Who and what are we giving mana to?" We must pay attention to who is gaining access to this ʻike, who stands to benefit from this moʻolelo being made available to the world. In the case of the extractive translations described in chapter 4, for instance, Hawaiians were seldom if ever the ones intended to reap these benefits. But the translations we talked about in chapter 3 gave mana to the whole lāhui and aided in our fight for ea. A culture of translation that really pays attention to mana unuhi takes us past the point where we talk about translation only as an act of violence, past the point where we worry about translation sabotaging our efforts at language renormalization (it is clearly not). But it also takes us past the point where we do translation work just because there is a demand. Who are we giving mana to if we translate for scientists who do not care about us just so they can fulfill the requirements of the diversity clauses in their grants? What are we giving mana to if we do translations only for our academic work and do not think about how our work contributes to the community?

This is one of the main contributions I am trying to make: to ensure that we realize how important it is to pay attention to mana and translation. We do not actually have to practice translation. But members of the general public, and as the ones most affected by these translations, the Hawaiian community especially, need to know how unuhi operates and has operated here, and need to be able to debate the effects of translation in useful and incisive ways. As academic treatises and online comments both confirm, if you are not a practicing translator or have not done formal translations, it is all too easy to take very dogmatic stances about translation, or to ignore its effects completely. Or both. That is why we, as readers/translators/speakers/nonspeakers, must together build these understandings of translation and mana unuhi.

I personally think that it is no longer responsible to do scholarly work on Hawaiʻi, particularly anything before the end of the nūpepa, without using ʻōlelo Hawaiʻi sources. Not everyone is a scholar who has access to our ʻōlelo though. And for them, I think mana unuhi can be used to help identify and then navigate problematic translations. For the Kamakau translations, for example, if you have your list of caveats in hand that you discovered from tracing what was given mana in the translation (created under the aegis of those who helped overthrow the kingdom, dedicated to keeping us in the past figuratively and literally, translated by a committee of unevenly talented translators, reorganized to fit Western understandings, etc.), you can still pull useful information from the text, whether you then check it with people who do ʻōlelo Hawaiʻi or just make clear how provisional your conclusion is.

A culture of translation, then, would mean that we collectively understand the benefits and drawbacks of translation in specific contexts, and if we do translate, that we realize it is only one tool among many for telling and retelling our moʻolelo. As it was for the nūpepa, the reason for translating must always be to increase our ea and mana. This does not mean the indiscriminate translation of everything in ʻōlelo Hawaiʻi. It doesn't even necessarily mean countering the translation canon. It does however mean recognizing that we need our own foundation of moʻolelo, in whatever language serves our people best, in every genre and form possible—fiction, nonfiction, biography, sci-fi, fantasy, young adult, romance, poetry, movie, anime, documentary, whatever. Carried out and received with a fuller understanding of everything that comes with it, unuhi can contribute greatly to that effort.

Most translations are produced for audiences other than those the text was originally intended for. Films in English get translated into Cantonese, Portuguese novels into German. In Hawaiʻi, however, we most commonly translate these texts for ourselves, and in most Indigenous contexts, where each translation is a politically charged and potentially activist act, the expectations and responsibilities for translators must be radically different. Translation scholar Brian Swann points to the finesse and difficulty around translation that has a kuleana to Indigenous peoples:

> The art of translation [is] a discipline that is as much a matter of translating the spaces and silence between and around words as it is of translating the words themselves, of snagging the emotional and cultural associations words trail and of breathing the atmosphere they both make and live on. The skill in translating the Native world consists of making something inaccessible into accessible enough,

without making it totally accessible; to make something available without making it assimilable; to make it similar and different at the same time, while taking it seriously all the time; to keep it simultaneously intriguing and challenging; to create beauty, respect, and admiration with the desire to share and participate without the need to appropriate. (2011, 6)

Part of this quote was presented earlier, in chapter 4, but having it in full here shows the added complexity necessary for translating in Indigenous contexts. It takes into account the possibility of appropriation that comes from translation, but it is also convinced that translation can be done in a way to mitigate those possibilities. A powerful example of how translation that keeps these oft-contradictory goals in mind can be part of a multipronged effort to serve a particular community is "He Moʻolelo no ʻUmi: Kekahi Aliʻi Kaulana o Ko Hawaiʻi Nei Pae ʻĀina," carried out by Noʻeau Peralto in collaboration with the artist Haley Kailiehu and their organization Hui Mālama i ke Ala ʻŪlili (HuiMAU). A nonprofit based in the community of East Hāmākua, through ʻāina-centric projects and educational initiatives, HuiMAU focuses on community health in a broad sense. And while ʻUmi is a powerful story for the lāhui Hawaiʻi, for the people of Hāmākua, no moʻolelo could be more fitting.

Peralto followed a strategy reminiscent of how the moʻolelo initially appeared in the nūpepa. His new translation arrived in serial installments on the HuiMAU website and in the *Hamakua Times,* Hāmākua's community newspaper. He addresses his community readers in the intimate and familiar way nineteenth-century kākau moʻolelo did, but he also adopts the Loeb Classical Library facing-page format discussed in chapter 4, though for very different reasons. In 1932, Martha Beckwith challenged readers to check her facing-page translations of Kepelino's account of Hawaiian history against the original: "If anyone familiar with the Hawaiian language can propose a better reading for any passage, the text is here to test his judgment" (1932, 3). Peralto's motivation for providing the original is to show respect for and accountability to the moʻolelo, and to give readers easy access to an important ʻōlelo Hawaiʻi text. He therefore makes the moʻolelo available to the widest and most diverse audience possible, encompassing those who would prefer to read the 'ōlelo Hawai'i, those preferring the English, and those with reasons for wanting both. Hawaiian-language speakers can read the original text, but the translation is right there to help with any problems in understanding. As for English-only readers, the constant presence of the Hawaiian text, and Peralto's editorial discussion, remind them that they are reading a translation and there are limitations to what they are reading.

What makes this translation even more powerful is that it is part of a suite of moʻolelo that come in different genres and media that engender even more community interaction. Besides being available in the newspaper and online, the moʻolelo of ʻUmi has been presented informally at public workdays on ʻāina associated with ʻUmi, and more formally, through a community mural project at Paʻauilo Elementary and Intermediate School headed by Haley Kailiehu (Hui Mālama i ke Ala ʻŪlili, "ʻUmi-a-Līloa" n.d.), and through a hula drama featuring keiki aged five–fourteen as part of HuiMAU's HoAMa afterschool mentorship program (Hui Mālama i ke Ala ʻŪlili, "Ka Moʻolelo o ʻUmi" n.d.).

This wide-ranging and deeply rooted project shows us a radically different way of approaching translation. The starting point in the process is no longer the text, but the community and its needs. With regard to translation and social interactivity, André Lefevere states: "Potential translators therefore need to learn to proceed from the top down, that is, from the culture to the text to the structure of that text to paragraphs, lines, phrases and words or, if you prefer, from the macro to the micro level. On the micro level translators can use all the linguistic and hermeneutic techniques that they learned, but the finality of their endeavor is the text as part of the culture, not the much vaunted struggle with the word, the sentence, or the line" (1992, 13). If I consider carrying out a translation and do not start at the macro level—of community, of ʻāina, of lāhui—but act only for academic reasons—for instance, what will get me the most attention as a scholar or what will get my name out in front of the most people—I will have already failed. "To say that translation is resistant, engaged, or activist does not suffice to conclude that it is ethical or responsible," Maria Tymoczko writes (2010b, 251); only the community can tell me that.

The moʻolelo suite containing Peralto's translation and HuiMAU's dedication to the community of Hāmākua reminds those of us who choose to act as translators that we cannot afford to view ourselves as somehow outside of the fray, in the neutral third space between languages, between communities, and that therefore we are not responsible for that life and death. We need to embed ourselves in our Hawaiian language and Hawaiian community, making our allegiances clear to all involved, planting ourselves in the community, being nourished by the community, but also and always feeding the community.

To return to the question "Who is this for?," we can therefore answer by slightly tweaking Paulo Freire's classic formulation. If as members of the lāhui and the Hawai'i community we decide translation is a necessary route for a mo'olelo, we must translate not *about* our people, and not only *for* our people, but *with* our people. As they were for the nūpepa, Hawaiians need to be the primary audience and interlocutors, even if that means addressing a single community, as Peralto has. But Hawaiians also need to be the translators, just as they were in the nūpepa, and the editors, and the publishers, and so on. This challenge can be met by focusing more closely on the material practice of translation, and by ensuring that translators do not believe that their work is transparent—that they have no ideological effect on the text. As Hawaiian scholar Jamaica Osorio observes, "translation often recreates and reinforces such structures as patriarchy, heterosexism, and white supremacy," but "in turn our mo'olelo can assist us in deconstructing these imposed forces" (2018, 80). A more widespread culture of translation would allow the structures too often sustained by translations to be questioned, and would strengthen our abilities as translators to deconstruct those structures.

The forces out of which the canonical translations grew (colonialism, language loss, English-only education, heteropatriarchy, population decline) also have made it necessary for Hawaiians to turn to these captured translations to relearn about our own history and mo'olelo. Though many more of us are using the nūpepa, handwritten manuscripts, and other archival materials ma ka 'ōlelo Hawai'i nowadays, the effects of our long reliance on the extractive translation canon still echo throughout the way we speak about ourselves today. Try searching any local news site for how many times "ancient" comes up before the word "Hawaiian." Everything from hula to fishponds is routinely designated as "ancient," even though hula has never stopped being practiced, and some of the "ancient" fishponds remained in operation throughout the twentieth century up through the present. As for our moʻolelo, if you actually look at them, you will discover a powerful tradition of innovation. But because all good things Hawaiian are described as part of antiquity, so much of what we think we know has been powerfully shaped by the canon of translated texts designed to portray us as of the past. How differently would we see ourselves if the texts translated from Hawaiian had included *Kaua Kuloko 1895: Ka Hoao ana e Hookahuli i ke Aupuni i Lokahi ole ia, ka Repubalika o Hawaii* [1895 civil war: The attempt to overthrow the undesirable government, the Republic of Hawaiʻi], edited by Tamaki Spencer? Or Kahikina Kelekona's literary experiments, which combine his acute knowledge of Hawaiian moʻolelo and his masterful use of ʻōlelo Hawaiʻi with the dark influences of Edgar Allan Poe?

As the critical mass of folks whose ʻōlelo Hawaiʻi is advanced enough to read such texts expands, the texts in turn become more accessible, entering the public discourse as reminders of the evolving mana and ea of our lāhui. And yet, while the latest numbers from Ka Haka ʻUla o Keʻelikōlani, the Hawaiian Language College at UH-Hilo, indicate that we now have over twenty-six thousand speakers, that is still less than 2 percent of the population (Ka Haka ʻUla o Keʻelikōlani 2018). So while the growing number of speakers suggests there might be an expiration date for needing a lot of translation from Hawaiian, a culture to question and understand translation and mana unuhi still needs to be created and sustained to inform how we look at our history.

I believe that translators are uniquely qualified to influence and speak back to the operations of dominant narratives—to those texts in the translation canon certainly, but also those that continue to oppress people here in Hawaiʻi, and throughout the world. Learning about unuhi in the kingdom era could grant us some of the ʻike necessary to transform translation, as Tejaswini Niranjana has suggested, "from being a 'containing' force...into a disruptive, disseminating one" (1992, 186)—a force that can challenge the stories told about us for too long, and a force that can aid us in regaining and sharing our own moʻolelo.

By now, this book should have made clear that unuhi is immensely powerful, with effects that can be devastating or uplifting. Our moʻolelo have the mana to give us the strength necessary for creating a foundation from which we can grow. But when translated without care for our kānaka, our kaiaulu, or our lāhui, those same moʻolelo can wound us for generations. Kānaka are refinding our voices and speaking out, and we are exerting the power of our language and culture in arenas that would have been unthinkable a decade or two ago. But that is why we must be wary and ensure that we develop a culture of translation. Translation has something to offer us as a liberatory praxis, and I think that there is mana down that path. But just as importantly, translation has so powerfully influenced our history and culture, and shaped our very understandings of that history and culture, that we *must* pay attention to how mana unuhi operates so we are aware of the effects it has had and continues to have to this very day—whether another word of our ʻōlelo is ever translated or not.

Notes

Introduction

1. It is likely that there were encounters with people from other island groups, and there are moʻolelo about Spaniards shipwrecking in Hawaiʻi, though none of the interchanges between Hawaiians and these other folks seem to have been recorded in the written archive.

2. Current scholarship makes the point that Hawaiʻi is an independent nation under military occupation, having never been a colony of another nation (Sai 2008; Beamer 2014), but as might be expected, the forces of colonialism and settler colonialism still come into play, whether Hawaiʻi was officially a colony or not.

Chapter 1. In the Beginning Was Translation

1. For an in-depth analysis of the way that ʻŌpūkahaʻia's life was narrativized to serve the aims of the American Board of Commissioners for Foreign Missions (ABCFM), see chapter 3 of David Chang's *The World and All the Things upon It* (2016).

2. It should be remembered, however, that the United States was made up of fewer than twenty states at this point, with the majority of them along the East Coast.

3. John Ridge and Elias Boudinot, who played such prominent roles in the forced removal of the Cherokee Nation and the Trail of Tears, were also students at Cornwall.

4. The 1833 mission report explicitly addresses the idea of transforming Hawaiʻi into an American colony. The mission's stance was that it should provide as much information as possible about soil quality and general climate to assist people who want to come to Hawaiʻi to civilize it. The mission also felt that, if asked, they would advise the chiefs about the kinds of people who would make desirable immigrants.

5. The nineteenth-century Hawaiian historian Samuel Mānaiakalani Kamakau lists a fifth Hawaiian who sailed with the first missionaries, a Pāʻulaliʻiliʻi.

6. Liholiho would later become quite enamored of the palapala and objected to the missionaries teaching it to the makaʻāinana before he himself had mastered it (Arista 2018, 123).

7. As he would come to take charge of the English-medium Chiefs' Children's School only two years later, we can hope that this indifference lessened at some point because he and his wife were educating and caring for the aliʻi children who became the leaders of the Hawaiian Kingdom, including six who served as king or queen. As for Cooke's language abilities, Hiram Bingham was still rejecting his translations of religious tracts in 1839 (Cooke 1839–1840, November 6, 1839).

Liliʻuokalani, the last reigning monarch of the Hawaiian Islands, had this to say about her school experience:

> Our instructors were especially particular to teach us the proper use of the English language; but when I recall the instances in which we were sent hungry to bed, it seems to me that they failed to remember that we were growing children. A thick slice of bread covered with molasses was usually the sole article of our supper, and we were sometimes ingenious, if not over honest, in our search for food: if we could beg something of the cook it was the easier way; but if not, anything eatable left within our reach was surely confiscated. As a last resort, we were not above searching the gardens for any esculent root or leaf, which (having inherited the art of igniting a fire from the friction of sticks), we could cook and consume without the knowledge of our preceptors. (1898, 5)

While this passage shows the ingenuity of the chiefly children in procuring food, it is also mind-boggling that the future leaders of the Hawaiian nation would be treated in this fashion, forced to beg for meals or root in the garden for things to eat. This is a clear example of the mindset that went into the education of generations of Hawaiians; soon after the Royal School was opened, a law was enacted in 1840 that established a government-funded national system of common schools (Kuykendall 1938, 112).

8. The mission printer Elisha Loomis printed the first eight pages of the book in January, and the second eight pages in February, with an initial run of five hundred copies (Judd, Bell, and Murdoch 1978, 3).

9. So exclusively and relentlessly religious were these publications that in a letter dated October 6, 1833, even missionary Alonzo Chapin, who pro-

duced maps and woodcuts for some of these publications, wrote to Rufus Anderson, corresponding secretary at the ABCFM, that "we need something to interest, something that will be a greater variety or we cannot keep up the schools. I think more would be accomplished for the present good of the people by preparing a good school book than by translating the Scriptures."

10. Some sources such as Lyons (2017, 117) give 1826 as the start date; this likely refers to when the more formal and organized process of translating the Bible began.

11. Though the story of this work often operates at the personal level, describing the missionary hammering away at the text only when his sermons and serving the people could be laid aside, these efforts were also part of a massive industry that involved trans-oceanic shipping and large outlays of cash.

An 1861 article from the Hawaiian-language newspaper *Ka Hoku Loa* describes the funding received from the American Bible Society:

O ka Ahahui Baibala ma Amerika ka i kokua nui i ka hoolaha ana o ka Baibala ma Hawaii nei. He mau $10,000 i haawi ia mai e kela Ahahui no ka pai ana, a no ka hoolaha ana i na Baibala Hawaii. Nolaila ke kumu kuai haahaa o na Baibala maanei. (A1)

[The American Bible Society was greatly responsible for disseminating the Bible here in Hawai'i. The Society gave tens of thousands of dollars for the printing and dissemination of the Hawaiian Bibles, and that is the reason that Bibles are so affordable here.]

Artemas Bishop puts the sum at $50,000 (1844, 75); more generally, the American Bible Society grew from issuing 24,004 Bibles in their first two years of existence (American Bible Society, *Annual Reports* 55) to distributing over a million Bibles per year by the golden jubilee of the Baibala, with an annual income of $700,000 (A. Judd 1889, 58).

12. These descriptions of the language as lacking are repeated so frequently that contemporary scholars will still sometimes take them up uncritically. In Kapali Lyon's excellent study, he states that "words and concepts taken for granted in Massachusetts were simply not available in Hawaiian. Traditional Hawaiian understanding of sexuality, social structures, and especially religious attitudes and expectations had far more in common with the Greco-Roman society vilified in the book of Revelation than it did with nascent Christianity, Hellenistic Judaism, or, especially, New England Puritanism" (2017, 117).

While he makes an interesting point about Hawaiian society's resemblances to other cultures, it remains a mistake to say that ʻōlelo Hawaiʻi was not supple enough to translate foreign concepts. Even if a culture does not recognize or value a certain practice, it will almost certainly be able to describe it in its language. Thus, while it might be true that ʻōlelo Hawaiʻi likely did not have word-for-word or phrase-for-phrase substitutions available, it is untrue that these concepts could not be expressed in Hawaiian.

Chapter 2. Mai ke Kānāwai a i ka Law

1. For a wide-ranging and simultaneously in-depth analysis of the moʻolelo of Pele and her youngest sister Hiʻiakaikapoliopele, see kuʻualoha hoʻomanawanui's 2014 book *Voices of Fire: Reweaving the Literary Lei of Pele and Hiʻiaka*. Also see Jamaica Heolimeleikalani Osorio's 2021 book *Remembering Our Intimacies: Moʻolelo Aloha ʻĀina, and Ea* for a discussion of the intimate pilina found within the moʻolelo and the power that comes from their recovery.

2. For an incisive analysis of the ramifications of this kind of domesticating legibility for both nineteenth-century Hawaiians and contemporary Hawaiians in the sovereignty movement (and a brief discussion of translation and the seventh commandment), see Kēhaulani Kauanui's 2018 *Paradoxes of Hawaiian Sovereignty*, particularly chapter 3, "Gender, Marriage, and Coverture: A New Proprietary Relationship," and chapter 4, "ʻSavage' Sexualities."

3. "Moe kolohe" is a humorous example of translation as well, because the missionaries were pearl-clutchingly horrified when "it was found that [Hawaiians] had about twenty ways of committing adultery & of course as many specific names" (Charlot 2005, 218), and if the missionaries chose any of those specific names to stand in for what they considered "adultery" as a whole, it would forbid only that one specific act and give tacit permission for all the other acts. So they came up with "moe kolohe" or "sleeping mischievously" to refer to adultery as a whole.

4. These are, of course, Western terms and cateogories that describe aspects of Hawaiian culture, though Hawaiians did not have separate terms for a lot of these ideas as they were too common to be commented on.

5. Though the context generally implies a more medical translation, as provided here, it is possible that Kamakau is playing with double entendre as well, since "maʻi" is also the word for genitalia and "ʻike hāhā" can also be read as an understanding of how to touch/feel something.

6. Both Kuykendall (1938, 168) and Thurston attribute the translation of the constitution of 1840 to William Richards, though David Forbes

(1998b, 318–319) says that this is a mistake and that Gerrit P. Judd was the translator.

Chapter 3. Translation in the Wild

1. Historian Ron Williams Jr. tracks this trend in relation to the Hawaiian Evangelical Association and the struggle over/through Native Christianity in his 2013 dissertation "Claiming Christianity: The Struggle over God and Nation in Hawai'i: 1880–1900."

2. For a discussion of JW's translation of "Snow White," see Niklaus Schweizer's 1988 "Kahaunani: 'Snow White' in Hawaiian: A Study in Acculturation."

3. Orthographic note: I was taught that Ho'ohokukalani made the heavens hoku, fertile, rather than placed the stars, hōkū, in the heavens.

4. It is possible that even though the article says that the mo'olelo was translated from French that the version that Kanuha translated from may have been English. There is precedent for Hawaiians stating the language that the text originated in a particular language, such as Arabic, even though the specific work being translated into Hawaiian was itself a translation into English or French.

5. Tiffany Ing's 2019 book, *Reclaiming Kalākaua: Nineteenth-Century Perspectives on a Hawaiian Sovereign,* presents a very detailed look at how aloha 'āina and Missionary Party supporters alike critiqued Kalākaua, but pointing out important differences in their approaches and motives.

6. There had been a spate of libel lawsuits against newspapermen since the 1880s, including against John Bush, Robert Wilcox, and the Chinese newspaper owner and journalist Ho Fon (Chapin 1996b, 87).

Chapter 4. Entombed in Translation

1. These are all kāne in the list, and I am not familiar with any wahine who had significant bodies of historical writing in the nūpepa, but that is a shortcoming of my own knowledge and an indicator of the creeping introduction of heteropatriarchy and who had publication opportunities. Emma Nāwahī was a founder and editor of *Ke Aloha Aina,* so likely contributed a lot of the editorials and opinions in the newspaper, but I am unsure of the extent of her writings in terms of length and topic.

Chapter 5. "I Don't Want to Translate"

1. This can also be translated as "unstable," but popular understandings of this tend to lean toward "lei stand."

2. Another group, the Hui Kālaiʻāina, also gathered seventeen thousand signatures on their own petitions.

3. This would happen again on a much larger scale in 2019, as the kiaʻi, or protectors, of Maunakea set up a puʻuhonua/refuge/encampment at the foot of the Maunakea access road and successfully blocked a subsequent attempt to begin construction of the Thirty Meter Telescope.

4. The same would happen during the 2019 stand when footage of nearly three dozen kūpuna, or elders, being arrested for blocking access to the mountain went viral, gaining the movement exposure and support from people such as Bernie Sanders, Alexandria Ocasio-Cortez, Jason Momoa, the Rock, and others.

5. As an indicator of the way that the kiaʻi social media presence has grown, the petition created for the 2019 stand currently has over 490,000 signatures (https://www.change.org/p/gordon-and-betty-moore-foundation-the-immediate-halt-to-the-construction-of-the-tmt-on-mauna-kea).

6. Oftentimes oral "performances" of ʻōlelo Hawaiʻi in official circumstances are quite literally uncapturable in the archive as those transcribing or captioning the proceedings will merely write something along the lines of "speaking in Hawaiian" or, more egregiously, "speaking a foreign language" rather than writing what was actually said. Some of this is due to the individual transcribers' or reporters' lack of ʻōlelo Hawaiʻi ability, but the larger problem is that the institutions responsible for the hearings being transcribed see no value in including ʻōlelo Hawaiʻi in the archive.

7. Though many people saw Kāʻeo's embodied performance in the courtroom through video of the event, Diana Taylor makes the point that "performance can never be captured or transmitted through the archive. A video of a performance is not a performance, though it often comes to replace the performance as a thing in itself (the video is part of the archive; what it represents is part of the repertoire" (2007, 20).

References

"6 Arrested in Protests over Construction of Telescope atop Haleakala." 2017. *Hawaii News Now*, August 2. http://www.hawaiinewsnow.com/story/36022915/officials-gear-up-for-potential-protests-ahead-of-telescope-construction-atop-haleakala.

Adamski, Mary. 2006. "New Hawaiian Bible Is Online." *Honolulu Star Bulletin*, October 14. http://archives.starbulletin.com/2006/10/14/features/adamski.html.

"Advertise." 1862. *The Polynesian*. July 19, 1.

Aiu, Pua'alaokalani D. 2010. "Ne'e Papa i ke Ō Mau: Language as an Indicator of Hawaiian Resistance and Power." In *Translation, Resistance, Activism*, edited by Maria Tymoczko, 89–107. Amherst: University of Massachusetts Press.

Alexander, W. D. 1894. *Kalakaua's Reign: A Sketch of Hawaiian History*. Honolulu: Hawaiian Gazette.

———. 1896. *History of Later Years of the Hawaiian Monarchy and the Revolution of 1893*. Honolulu: Hawaiian Gazette.

The Alphabet. 1822. Honolulu: Mission Press.

American Bible Society. 1838. *Annual Reports of the American Bible Society*. New York: Daniel Fanshaw.

American Board of Commissioners for Foreign Missions (ABCFM). 1816. *A Narrative of Five Youth from the Sandwich Islands, Now Receiving an Education in This Country*. New York: J. Seymour.

———. 1817. *Annual Report for 1816*. Boston: T. R. Marvin.

———. 1818. *Annual Report for 1817*. Boston: T. R. Marvin.

———. 1819a. *Annual Report for 1818*. Boston: T. R. Marvin.

———. 1819b. *Instructions from the Prudential Committee of the ABCFM to Members of the Mission to the Sandwich Islands*. Boston: Samuel T. Armstrong.

———. 1821. *Annual Report for 1820*. Boston: T. R. Marvin.

———. 1824. *Annual Report for 1823*. Boston: T. R. Marvin.

———. 1826. *Annual Report for 1825*. Boston: T. R. Marvin.

———. 1827. *Annual Report for 1826*. Boston: T. R. Marvin.

———. 1828. *Annual Report for 1827*. Boston: T. R. Marvin.

———. 1832. *Extracts from the Minutes of the General Meeting of the Sandwich Islands Mission, 1831*. Honolulu: Mission Press.

———. 1835. *Extracts from the Minutes of the General Meeting of the Sandwich Islands Mission*. Honolulu: Mission Press, 1834.

Andrews, Lorrin. 1832. "An Essay on the Best Practical Method of Conducting Native Schools. Read before the Hawaiian Association." June 13. Hawaiian Mission Houses, Honolulu.

———. 1837. "Remarks on the Hawaiian Dialect of the Polynesian Language; Prepared for the Repository." *Chinese Repository* 5: 12–21.

Arista, Noelani. 2010. "Navigating Uncharted Oceans of Meaning: *Kaona* as Historical and Interpretive Method." *PMLA* 125, no. 3: 663–669.

———. 2018. *The Kingdom and the Republic: Sovereign Hawai'i and the Early United States*. Philadelphia: University of Pennsylvania Press.

———. 2020. "Ka Waiwai Palapala Mānaleo: Research in a Time of Plenty. Colonialism and the Hawaiian-Language Archives." In *Indigenous Textual Cultures: Reading and Writing in the Age of Global Empire*, edited by Tony Ballantyne, Lachy Paterson, and Angela Wanhalla, 31–59. Durham, NC: Duke University Press.

Asensio, Rubén Fernández. 2010. "Language Policy in the Kingdom of Hawai'i: A Worldly English Approach." *Second Language Studies* 28, no. 2: 1–48.

Ashton, Rosemary. 2008. "From the SDUK to the Passmore Edwards Settlement: Widening Access to Education in Bloomsbury." *Bloomsbury Project*, Wellcome Trust Centre for the History of Medicine at UCL, June 26. Unpublished Conference Paper. University College of London, Bloomsbury.

Bacchilega, Cristina. 2007. *Legendary Hawai'i and the Politics of Place: Tradition, Translation, and Tourism*. Philadelphia: University of Pennsylvania Press.

Bacchilega, Cristina, and Noelani Arista. 2007. "The *Arabian Nights* in the *Kuokoa*, a Nineteenth-Century Hawaiian Newspaper: Reflections on the Politics of Translation." In *The Arabian Nights in Transnational Perspective*, edited by Ulrich Marzolph, 157–182. Detroit, MI: Wayne State University Press.

Baker, Mona. 2010. "Translation and Activism: Emerging Patterns of Narrative Community." In *Translation, Resistance, Activism*, edited by Maria Tymoczko, 23–41. Amherst: University of Massachusetts Press.
Ballou, Howard M., and George R. Carter. 1908. "The History of the Hawaiian Mission Press, with a Bibliography of the Earlier Publications." *Papers of the Hawaiian Historical Society* 14: 9–44.
Barrère, Dorothy. 1964. "Preface." In Samuel Mānaiakalani Kamakau, *Ka Poʻe Kahiko: The People of Old*. Honolulu: Bishop Museum Press.
———. 1989. "A Tahitian in the History of Hawaiʻi: The Journal of Kahikona." *Hawaiian Journal of History* 23: 75–107.
Barrère, Dorothy, and Marshall Sahlins. 1979. "Tahitians in the Early History of Hawaiian Christianity: The Journal of Toketa." *Hawaiian Journal of History* 13: 19–35.
Bauknight, Catherine, dir. 2009. *Hawaiʻi: A Voice for Sovereignty*. Othila Media.
Beamer, Kamanamaikalani. 2014. *No Mākou Ka Mana: Liberating the Nation*. Honolulu: Kamehameha Publishing.
Beckwith, Martha. 1932. "Foreword." In *Kepelino's Traditions of Hawaii*. Honolulu: Bernice P. Bishop Museum.
Benedetto, Robert. 1982. *The Hawaii Journals of the New England Missionaries 1813–1894: A Guide to the Holdings of the Hawaiian Mission Children's Society Library*. Honolulu: Hawaiian Mission Children's Society.
Bermann, Sandra. 2005. "Introduction." In *Nation, Language, and the Ethics of Translation*, edited by Sandra Bermann and Michael Wood, 1–14. Princeton, NJ: Princeton University Press.
Beyer, Kalani. 2014. "Comparing Native Hawaiian Education with Native American and African American Education during the Nineteenth Century." *American Educational History Journal* 41, no. 1: 59–75.
Binamu, H. 1834. "Helu 1. He Olelo Hoomoakaka i ka Paulo Palapala i ko Roma." *Ke Kumu Hawaii*, November 12, 2–3.
———. 1839. "Ka Unuhi ana i ka Baibala." *Ke Kumu Hawaii*, April 10, 91.
Bingham, Hiram. 1847. *A Residence of Twenty-One Years in the Sandwich Islands*. Hartford, CT: Hezekiah Huntington.
Bishop, Artemas. 1844. "Address: A Brief History of the Holy Scriptures into the Hawaiian Language." *The Friend*, August 1, 74–75.
Bishop Museum. 1914–1918. *Occasional Papers of Bernice P. Bishop Museum*. Vol. 6. Honolulu: Bishop Museum Press.

Board of Education, Kingdom of Hawaiʻi. 1880. *Biennial Report of the President of the Board of Education.* By Charles Reed Bishop.
Board of Education, Republic of Hawaiʻi. 1895. *Biennial Report of the President of the Board of Education.* By William DeWitt Alexander.
Brickhouse, Anna. 2015. *The Unsettlement of America: Translation, Interpretation, and the Story of Don Luis de Velasco, 1560–1945.* Oxford: Oxford University Press.
Brooks, Lisa. 2018. *Our Beloved Kin: A New History of King Philip's War.* London: Yale University Press.
Buchanan, Shirley E. 2011. "Indigenous Destinies: Native Hawaiian and Native American Crossroads." Master's thesis, California State, Northridge.
Calvin, John. 1816. *Institutes of the Christian Religion.* Vol. 1. Translated by John Allen. New Haven, CT: Hezekiah Howe.
Campbell, Scott. 2014. Comment on "Rep Hanohano Prevails in Language Flap." *KITV 4,* March 4. http://www.kitv.com/news/hawaii/rep-hanohano-prevails-in-language-flap/.
Casanova, Pascale. 2010. "Consecration and Accumulation of Literary Capital: Translation as Unequal Exchange." In *Critical Readings in Translation Studies,* edited by Mona Baker, 285–303. New York: Routledge.
Chamberlain, Levi. 1826. "Journal Volume 0006 and Insert 1826.06.21–1826.11.27." Hawaiian Mission Houses Digital Archive. https://hmha.missionhouses.org/items/show/36.
Chang, David A. 2016. *The World and All the Things upon It: Native Hawaiian Geographies of Exploration.* Minneapolis: University of Minnesota Press.
———. 2018. "The Good Written Word of Life: The Native Hawaiian Appropriation of Textuality." *William and Mary Quarterly* 75, no. 2: 237–258.
Chapin, Helen. 1996a. *Guide to Newspapers of Hawaiʻi: 1834–2000.* Honolulu: Hawaiian Historical Society.
———. 1996b. *Shaping History: The Role of Newspapers in Hawaiʻi.* Honolulu: University of Hawaiʻi Press.
"Charges Dismissed against Telescope Protestor Who Insisted on Speaking Hawaiian in Court." 2018. *Honolulu Star-Advertiser,* July 13. www.honolulustaradvertiser.com/2018/07/13/breaking-news/charges-dismissed-against-telescope-protestor-who-insisted-on-speaking-hawaiian-in-court.

Charlot, John. 2005. *Classical Hawaiian Education: Generations of Hawaiian Culture*. Pacific Institute. Lāʻie: Brigham Young University–Hawaiʻi.

Cheyfitz, Eric. 1997. *The Poetics of Imperialism: Translation and Colonization from the Tempest to Tarzan*. Philadelphia: University of Pennsylvania Press.

Cook, James. 1906. *Captain Cook's Voyages of Discovery*. New York: E. P. Dutton.

Cook, Kealani. 2018. *Return to Kahiki: Native Hawaiians in Oceania*. Cambridge: Cambridge University Press.

Cooke, Amos Starr. 1836–1838. "Journal 1836–1838." Hawaiian Mission Houses Digital Archive. https://hmha.missionhouses.org/items/show/65.

———. 1839–1840. "Journal 1839–1840." Hawaiian Mission Houses Digital Archive. https://hmha.missionhouses.org/items/show/66.

Correspondence between the Government of the Republic of Hawaii and Her Britannic Majesty's Government in Relation to the Claims of Certain British Subjects Arrested for Complicity in the Insurrection of 1895 in the Hawaiian Islands. 1899. Honolulu: Hawaiian Gazette.

Creutz, Edward C. 1978. "The Role of the Bishop Museum in the Pacific." In *Captain Cook and the Pacific Islands*, edited by Jane N. Hurd and Michiko Kodama, 13–23. Honolulu: Pacific Island Studies Program, University of Hawaiʻi.

Cunningham, Robert Hays, ed. 1889. *Amusing Prose Chap-Books, Chiefly of the Last Century*. London: Hamilton, Adams.

Dana, Richard Henry. 1969. *Two Years before the Mast: A Personal Narrative of Life at Sea*. New York: P. F. Collier.

Day, A. Grove, and Albertine Loomis. 1973. *Ka Paʻi Palapala: Early Printing in Hawaii*. Honolulu: Printing Industries of Hawaii.

Dayton, Kevin. 2018. "Chin Leads State Planning to Address TMT Protests." *Honolulu Star-Advertiser*, October 31. http://www.staradvertiser.com/2018/10/31/hawaii-news/chin-leads-state-planning-to-address-any-protests/.

Deloria, Philip J. 2004. *Indians in Unexpected Places*. Lawrence: University Press of Kansas.

Department of Public Instruction, Kingdom of Hawaiʻi. 1895. *Biennial Report of the President of the Board of Education*. By W. D. Alexander. Honolulu.

Diamond, Elin. 1996. *Performance and Cultural Politics*. New York: Routledge.

Dibble, Sheldon. 1839. *History and General Views of the Sandwich Islands' Mission.* New York: Taylor & Dodd.

———. 2005. *Ka Mooolelo Hawaii: The History of Hawaii.* Honolulu: Hawaiian Historical Society.

"Dorothy Barrére, 96." 2009. *Montana Standard,* November 10. https://mtstandard.com/news/local/obituaries/dorothy-barr-re/article_9bfbe1fb-e63b-5fcf-8f4f-5e5e844790f8.html.

Dukelow, Kahele. 2018. Video: "THE JUDGE REFUSED TO RECOGNIZE KALEIKOA UNLESS HE SPOKE ENGLISH. RACISM IS ALIVE AND WELL IN HAWAIʻI. Post trial analysis." Facebook, January 24, 2:54 p.m. https://www.facebook.com/kahele.dukelow/videos/10213894130645645/.

Dunn, Barbara. 2004. "William Little Lee and Catherine Lee, Letters from Hawaiʻi 1848–1855." *Hawaiian Journal of History* 38: 59–88.

Dwight, Edwin. 1819. *Memoirs of Henry Obookiah, a Native of Owhyhee, and a Member of the Foreign Mission School, Who Died at Cornwall, Conn. Feb. 17, 1818, Aged 26 Years.* New Haven, CT: N. Whiting.

"Ecclesiastical Thunder." 1862. *The Polynesian,* November 1, 2.

Elbert, Samuel H. 1953. "The Hawaiian Dictionaries, Past and Future." *Sixty-Second Annual Report of the Hawaiian Historical Society,* 5–18.

Emory, Kenneth. 1959. "Foreword." In John Papa ʻĪʻī, *Fragments of Hawaiian History,* translated by Mary Kawena Pukui, ix–x. Honolulu: Bishop Museum Press.

"F. J. Testa, (Hoke)." 1895. *Ka Makaainana,* April 15, 3.

Farnham, April. 2021. "Leaving 'Hewa Hawaiʻi': Native Hawaiian Immigrants and American Missionary Paternalism in Gold Rush California (1848–1868)." *Sonoma State History Journal* 25, no. 1.

Fermoso, Jose. 2018. "Why Speaking Spanish Is Becoming Dangerous in America." *Guardian,* May 22. https://www.theguardian.com/us-news/2018/may/22/speaking-spanish-dangerous-america-aaron-schlossberg-ice.

Forbes, David. 1998a. *Hawaiian National Bibliography, 1780–1900.* Vol. 1, *1780–1830.* Honolulu: University of Hawaiʻi Press.

———. 1998b. *Hawaiian National Bibliography, 1780–1900.* Vol. 2, *1831–1850.* Honolulu: University of Hawaiʻi Press.

———. 1998c. *Hawaiian National Bibliography, 1780–1900.* Vol. 3, *1851–1880.* Honolulu: University of Hawaiʻi Press.

———. 1998d. *Hawaiian National Bibliography, 1780–1900.* Vol. 4, *1881–1900.* Honolulu: University of Hawaiʻi Press.

Fornander, Abraham. 1878. *An Account of the Polynesian Race: Its Origins and Migrations, and the Ancient History of the Hawaiian People to the Times of Kamehameha I*. London: Trubner.

———. 1916–1917. *Fornander Collection of Hawaiian Antiquities and Folk-Lore*. Vol 4. Honolulu: Bishop Museum.

Frazier, Frances N. 2001. "Introduction." In *The True Story of Kaluaikoolau*. Translated by Frances Frazier. Honolulu: University of Hawai'i Press.

Frean, Nicola. 1997. "Māori Newspapers." *Book and Print in New Zealand: A Guide to Print Culture in Aotearoa*. Wellington: Victoria University Press. https://nzetc.victoria.ac.nz/tm/scholarly/tei-GriBook-_div3-N11F9E.html.

Frear, Walter F. 1906. "Hawaiian Statute Law." *Annual Report of the Hawaiian Historical Society* 13, no. 1: 15–61.

Fujikane, Candace. 2008. "Asian Settler Colonialism in the U.S. Colony of Hawai'i." In *Asian Settler Colonialism: From Local Governance to the Habits of Everyday Life in Hawai'i*, edited by Jonathan Y. Okamura and Candace Fujikane, 1–42. Honolulu: University of Hawai'i Press.

Gilmore, Ruth Wilson. 2007. *Golden Gulag: Prisons, Surplus, Crisis, and Opposition in Globalizing California*. Berkeley: University of California Press.

Goodyear-Ka'ōpua, Noelani. 2015. "Reproducing the Ropes of Resistance: Hawaiian Studies Methodologies." In *Kanaka 'Ōiwi Methodologies: Mo'olelo and Metaphor*, edited by Katrina-Ann R. Kapā'anaokalāokeola Nākoa Oliveira and Erin Kahunawaika'ala Wright, 1–29. Honolulu: University of Hawai'i Press.

Goodyear-Ka'ōpua, Noelani, and Bryan Kamaoli Kuwada. 2018. "Making 'Aha: Independent Hawaiian Pasts, Presents and Futures." *Daedalus: Journal of the American Academy of Arts and Sciences* 147, no. 2: 49–59.

Gregory, Herbert E. 1923. *Report of the Director for 1922*. Honolulu: Bishop Museum.

Gutierrez, Ben. 2015. "At Least 20 Arrested in Attempt to Block Work on Daniel K. Inouye Solar Telescope on Maui." *Hawaii News Now*, July 31. http://www.hawaiinewsnow.com/story/29677494/protestors-block-work-on-daniel-k-inouye-telescope-on-haleakala.

"Haehae ka Manu, Ke Ale nei i ka Wai." 1894. *Ka Leo o ka Lahui*, July 3, 2.

"Halawai ma Kaumakapili." 1862. *Ka Nupepa Kuokoa*, April 12, 1.

Hale Naua. 1890. *Constitution and By-Laws of the Hale Naua or Temple of Science: Ancient Secret Society of the Order of Nauas, or Order of the Temple of Science*. Honolulu: Hale Naua.

Hale Naua Society, 1886–1891: Translation of Documents at the Hawai'i State Archives and Hawaiian Mission Children's Society Library. 1999. Hawaiian Mission Society.

Handy, E. S. Craighill, and Mary Kawena Pukui. 1950. *The Polynesian Family System in Ka'ū.* Honolulu: Mutual Publishing.

Hawaii Supreme Court. 1857. *Reports of Some of the Judgments and Decisions of the Courts of Record of the Hawaiian Islands.* Vol. 1. Honolulu: Robert Grieve.

———. 1866. *Reports of a Portion of the Decisions Rendered by the Supreme Court of the Hawaiian Islands in Law, Equity, Admiralty and Probate.* Vol. 2. Honolulu: Government Press.

Hawaiian Mission Children's Society. 1969. *Missionary Album: Portraits and Biographical Sketches of the American Protestant Missionaries to the Hawaiian Islands.* Honolulu: Hawaiian Mission Children's Society.

"He Eehia, he Welina Aloha no G W Kanuha." 1876. *Ka Nupepa Kuokoa,* June 24, 2.

"He Iwakalua Tausani Legue Malalo o ke Kai." 1875–1878. *Ka Nupepa Kuokoa,* December 18, 1875–March 30, 1878.

"He Kaao Hou no na Mea Kupanaha o ka Moana." 1875. *Ka Nupepa Kuokoa,* September 18, 2.

"He Mahalo ia Uilama Hoonaueueihe." 1867. *Ka Nupepa Kuokoa,* January 19, 2.

"He Mau Elemakule." 1834. *Ka Lama Hawaii,* April 4, 2.

"He Olelo no ka Hoonoho i ka Hoohalikeolelo a i Kakauolelo hoi no ke Aupuni." 1842. *Ka Nonanona,* June 21, 6.

Hengel, Martin. 2004. *Septuagint as Christian Scripture: Its Prehistory and the Problem of Its Canon.* London: T & T Clark International.

Hiraishi, Ku'uwehi. 2018. "Maui Telescope Protestor Battles over Hawaiian Language Use in Court." *Hawai'i Public Radio,* January 24. http://www.hawaiipublicradio.org/post/maui-telescope-protestor-battles-over-hawaiian-language-use-court.

"History of the Cherokee Phoenix." 2015. *Cherokee Phoenix,* January 13. http://www.cherokeephoenix.org/Article/index/9955.

Hoapili, Robert. 1876. "He Moolelo no Tamaki Ionakana Iakekona." *Ka Lahui Hawaii,* July 30, 4.

Holman, Janet Susan. 2014. Comment on "Rep Hanohano Prevails in Language Flap." *KITV 4,* March 4. http://www.kitv.com/news/hawaii/rep-hanohano-prevails-in-language-flap/.

"Holo ana Mai Maui i Oahu." 1837. *Ke Kumu Hawaii,* November 22, 49.
hoʻomanawanui, kuʻualoha. 2014. *Voices of Fire: Reweaving the Literary Lei of Pele and Hiʻiaka.* Minneapolis: University of Minnesota Press.
"Hoopaapaa Nupepa." 1860. *Ka Hae Hawaii,* May 16, 2.
Hoʻoulumāhiehie. 1905–1906a. "Ka Moolelo o Hiʻiakaikapoliopele." *Ka Naʻi Aupuni.*
———. 1905–1906b. "Ka Moolelo o Kamehameha I." *Ka Naʻi Aupuni.*
———. 2007a. *The Epic Tale of Hiʻiakaikapoliopele.* Translated by Puakea Nogelmeier, Sahoa Fukushima, and Bryan Kamaoli Kuwada. Honolulu: Awaiāulu Press.
———. 2007b. *Ka Moʻolelo o Hiʻiakaikapoliopele.* Honolulu: Awaiāulu Press.
Hori, Joan. 2001. "Background and Historical Significance of Ka Nupepa Kuokoa." http://libweb.hawaii.edu/digicoll/nupepa_kuokoa/kuokoa_htm/kuokoa.html.
Horsley, G. H. R. 2011. "One Hundred Years of the Loeb Classical Library." *Buried History* 47: 35–58.
Hui Mālama i ke Ala ʻŪlili. n.d. "Ka Moʻolelo o ʻUmi: A Hula Drama, Depicting the Moʻolelo of ʻUmi-a-Līloa." http://www.alaulili.com/umi-a-liloa-mural.html. Accessed February 14, 2024.
———. n.d. " ʻUmi-a-Līloa Mural Project: Paʻauilo Elementary & Intermediate School." n.d. http://www.alaulili.com/umi-a-liloa-mural.html. Accessed February 14, 2024.
ʻĪʻī, John Papa. 1869. "Hunahuna Moolelo Hawaii." *Ka Nupepa Kuokoa,* August 14, 1.
Inefuku, Terri. 2015. "Protesters Arrested for Allegedly Blocking Access to Mauna Kea Summit." *KHON2 News,* April 2. https://www.khon2.com/news/local-news/protesters-arrested-for-allegedly-blocking-access-to-mauna-kea-summit_20180309113623175/1025595582.
Ing, Tiffany. 2015. "Ka Hoʻomālamalama ʻana o nā Hōʻailona o ka Mōʻī Kalākaua a me Kona Noho Aliʻi ʻana: Illuminating the American, International, and Hawaiʻi Representations of David Kalākaua and His Reign, 1874–1891." PhD diss., University of Hawaiʻi.
———. 2019. *Reclaiming Kalākaua: Nineteenth-Century Perspectives on a Hawaiian Sovereign.* Honolulu: University of Hawaiʻi Press.
Johnson, Rubellite. 1976. *Kukini ʻAhaʻilono: Carry on the News.* Honolulu: Topgallant.
Judd, A. F. 1889. "Translation of the Address of Hon. A. F. Judd on the Jubilee of the Hawaiian Bible." *Annual Report of the Hawaiian Evangelical Society* 27: 52–59.

Judd, Bernice, Janet E. Bell, and Clare G. Murdoch, eds. 1978. *Hawaiian Language Imprints, 1822–1899*. Honolulu: University of Hawai'i Press.

Judd, Laura Fish. 1880. *Honolulu: Sketches of Life, Social, Political, and Religious, in the Hawaiian Islands from 1828 to 1861*. New York: A. D. F. Randolph.

"Judge Blaine J. Kobayashi." n.d. *Hawaii State Judiciary*. http://www.courts.state.hi.us/courts/district/judges/judge_blaine_kobayashi.

"Judge: Thirty Meter Telescope Should Be Given OK to Move Forward." 2018. *Hawaii News Now*, July 27. http://www.hawaiinewsnow.com/story/35981511/judge-in-tmt-contested-case-hearing-recommends-project-move-forward.

"Judiciary Announces Hawaiian Language Interpreter Policy." 2018. *Hawaii State Judiciary*, January 26. http://www.courts.state.hi.us/news_and_reports/press_releases/2018/01/judiciary-announces-hawaiian-language-interpreter-policy.

jusanopinion101. 2014. Comment on "Rep Hanohano Prevails in Language Flap." *KITV 4*, March 6. http://www.kitv.com/news/hawaii/rep-hanohano-prevails-in-language-flap/.

"Ka Baibala Hawaii." 1861. *Ka Hoku Loa*, July, 1.

Ka Haka 'Ula o Ke'elikōlani, University of Hawai'i-Hilo. 2018. "Through, of and about Hawaiian." Infographic.

"Ka Hoku o ka Pakipika." 1861. *Ka Hoku o ka Pakipika*, September 26, 4.

"Ka Mahele Olelo o ke Aupuni." 1867. *Ka Nupepa Kuokoa*, January 19, 2.

"Ka Make ana o ka mea Hanohano G. M. Robikana." 1867. *Ka Nupepa Kuokoa*, March 16, 2.

"Ka Olelo Makuahine a ka Lahui Hawaii." 1912. *Hawaii Holomua*.

"Ka Wa ia Kaomi." 1861. *Ka Hae Hawaii*, September 11.

Kam, Ralph Thomas. 2006. "Language and Loyalty: Americanism and the Regulation of Foreign Language Schools in Hawai'i." *Hawaiian Journal of History* 40: 131–147.

Kamakau, Samuel M. 1865. "Hooheihei ka Nukahalale, ka Nukahalale, Ouou ka Leo o ka Pohu o Opuku." *Ke Au Okoa*, October 16, 1.

———. 1964. *Ka Po'e Kahiko: The People of Old*. Honolulu: Bishop Museum Press.

———. 1976. *The Works of the People of Old: Na Hana a Ka Po'e Kahiko*. Honolulu: Bishop Museum Press.

———. 1992. *Ruling Chiefs of Hawai'i*. Honolulu: Kamehameha Schools Press.

———. 1996. *Ke Kumu Aupuni*. Honolulu: ʻAhahui ʻŌlelo Hawaiʻi.
———. 2001. *Ke Aupuni Mōʻī*. Honolulu: Kamehameha Schools Press.
Kānepuʻu, J. H. 1862. "Ka Mokupuni a Lopikana Kuluko i Noho ai." *Ka Hoku o ka Pakipika*, January 2, 3.
———. 1878. "Ahe! He Nupepa Hou Ka!!" *Ko Hawaii Pae Aina*, February 2, 1.
"Kanuha Found Not Guilty of Obstruction on Mauna Kea." 2016. *Big Island Video News*, January 8. http://www.bigislandvideonews.com/2016/01/08/kanuha-found-not-guilty-of-obstruction-on-mauna-kea/.
Kauanui, J. Kēhaulani. 2018. *Paradoxes of Hawaiian Sovereignty: Land, Sex, and the Colonial Politics of State Nationalism*. Durham, NC: Duke University Press.
Kauwahi, J. G. 1857. *He Kuhikuhi o na Kanaka Hawaii*. Honolulu: H. M. Wini.
Kauwahi, J. W. K. 1861. "No ka Hoku o ka Pakipika." *Ka Hoku o ka Pakipika*, September 26, 3.
Kawaikaumaiikamakaokaopua, Z. P. K. 1920. "Ka Olelo Hawaii." *Ka Nupepa Kuokoa*, June 17, 3.
"Ke Akamai o na Elepani." 1834. *Ke Kumu Hawaii*, December 10, 19.
"Ke Kumu o ka Naaupo." 1834. *Ka Lama Hawaii*, February 14, 1.
Kelekona, Kahikina. 1996. *Ka Puke Moʻolelo o Hon. Iosepa K. Nāwahī*. Hilo: Hale Kuamoʻo.
Kelly, Jennifer Lynn. 2016. "Asymmetrical Itineraries: Militarism, Tourism, and Solidarity in Occupied Palestine." *American Quarterly* 63, no. 3: 723–741.
Kimura, Larry. 1983. *Native Hawaiian Study Commission Minority Report*. Vol. 1, 173–203, 214–223. U.S. Department of the Interior.
Kingdom of Hawaiʻi. 1839. *He Kumukanawai a me ke Kanawai Hooponopono Waiwai no ko Hawaii Nei Pae Aina*.
———. 1841. *Ke Kumu Kanawai a me na Kanawai o ko Hawaii Pae Aina*.
———. 1842. *Translation of the Constitution and Laws of the Hawaiian Islands, Established in the Reign of Kamehameha III*.
———. 1845–1846. *Minutes of the Privy Council*.
———. 1848–1849. *Minutes of the Privy Council*.
———. 1850. *Penal Code of the Hawaiian Islands, Passed by the House of Nobles and Representatives on the 21st of June, A. D. 1850; To Which Are Appended the Other Acts Passed by the House of Nobles and Representatives during Their General Session for 1850*.

———. 1851–1853. *Journal of the House of Representatives.*

———. 1859. *The Civil Code of the Hawaiian Islands, Passed in the Year of Our Lord 1859: To Which Is Added an Appendix, Containing Laws Not Expressly Repealed by the Civil Code; the Session Laws of 1858–9.*

Kirch, Adam. 2011. "The Other Socrates." *Barnes and Noble Book Blog,* September 7. https://www.barnesandnoble.com/review/the-other-socrates.

Kirtley, Bacil F., and Esther T. Mookini. 1977. "Kepelino's 'Hawaiian Collection': His 'Hooiliili Havaii,' Pepa I, 1858." *Journal of Hawaiian History* 11: 39–68.

KITV. 2018. "Haleakala Protestor Speaks Hawaiian in Court." Facebook, January 24, 3:45 p.m. https://www.facebook.com/KITV4/videos/10155042274251861/.

Krug, Kalehua. 2016. "He Ha'awina ka Mo'olelo, he Mo'olelo ka Ha'awina." *Hūlili: Multidisciplinary Research on Hawaiian Wellbeing* 10, no. 1: 101–123.

"Kula Kaikamahine, Wailuku, Maui." 1842. *Ka Nonanona,* December 20, 73.

Kuwada, Bryan Kamaoli. 2009. "To Translate or Not to Translate: Revising the Translating of Hawaiian Language Texts." *Biography: An Interdisciplinary Quarterly* 32, no. 1: 64–65.

Kuykendall, Ralph S. 1938. *The Hawaiian Kingdom.* Vol. 1, *1778–1854: Foundation and Transformation.* Honolulu: University of Hawai'i Press.

———. 1953. *The Hawaiian Kingdom.* Vol. 2, *1854–1874: Twenty Critical Years.* Honolulu: University of Hawai'i Press.

"The Late Hon. G. W. Pilipo." 1887. *Hawaiian Gazette,* March 29, 1.

Lefevere, André. 1992. *Translating Literature: Practice and Theory in a Comparative Literature Context.* New York: Modern Language Association.

Leow, Rachel. 2018. *Taming Babel: Language in the Making of Malaysia.* Cambridge: Cambridge University Press.

"The Lightning Detective." 1887. *Pacific Commercial Advertiser,* May 3, 3.

Lili'uokalani, trans. 1897. *The Kumulipo: An Account of the Creation of the World according to Hawaiian Tradition.* Boston: Lee and Shepard.

———. 1898. "Ka Buke Moolelo Hawaii i Hakuia e Ka Moiwahine Liliuokalani, ma Wasinetona." *Ke Aloha Aina,* April 2, 3.

———. 1991. *Hawaii's Story by Hawaii's Queen.* Honolulu: Mutual Publishing.

Little, Simon. 2018. " 'Go Back to Your Country': Video Captures Angry Exchange on Vancouver Bus." GlobalNews.ca, June 24. https://globalnews

.ca/news/4294198/go-back-to-your-country-video-captures-angry-exchange-on-vancouver-bus/.
"Loeb Classical Library, 2021." 2021. Harvard University Press. https://issuu.com/harvard-university-press/docs/hup-brochure-2021-loeb-classical-library.
Loomis, Elisha. 1824–1826. "Journal 1824–1826." *Hawaiian Mission Houses Digital Archive*. https://hmha.missionhouses.org/items/show/82.
Loomis, Ilima. 2017. "How the World's Largest Solar Telescope Rose on Maui While Nearby Protests Derailed a Larger Scope." *Science*, August 1. http://www.sciencemag.org/news/2017/08/how-world-s-largest-solar-telescope-rose-maui-while-nearby-protests-derailed-larger.
Lucas, Paul F. Nahoa. 2000. "E Ola Mau Kākou I Ka ʻŌlelo Makuahine: Hawaiian Language Policy and the Courts." *Hawaiian Journal of History* 34: 1–28.
Luomala, Katherine. 1966. Review of *Ka Poʻe Kahiko. The People of Old. Journal of American Folklore* 79, no. 313: 501–502.
Lydecker, Robert C. 1918. *Roster Legislatures of Hawaii, 1841–1918: Constitutions of Monarchy and Republic, Speeches of Sovereign and President*. Honolulu: Hawaiian Gazette.
Lydgate, J. M. 1917. "The Early Missionaries and Primitive Education." *The Friend*, April, 84–85.
Lyon, Jeffrey Kapali. 2017. "No ka Baibala Hemolele: The Making of the Hawaiian Bible." *Ka Palapala: A Journal for Hawaiian Language and Literature* 1, no. 1: 113–151.
Lyons, Curtis J. 1893. "The Song of Kualii of Hawaii, Sandwich Islands." *Journal of the Polynesian Society* 2, no. 3: 160–178.
Lyons, Scott Richard. 2000. "Rhetorical Sovereignty: What Do American Indians Want from Writing?" *College Composition and Communication* 51, no. 3: 447–468.
Maile, David Uahikeaikaleiʻohu. 2018. "Precarious Performances: The Thirty Meter Telescope and Settler State Policing of Kānaka Maoli." *Abolition Journal*, September 9. https://abolitionjournal.org/precarious-performances/.
Malo, David. 1951. *Hawaiian Antiquities*. Translated and edited by Nathaniel Emerson. Honolulu: Bishop Museum Press.
———. 1987. *Ka Moʻolelo Hawaiʻi*. Edited by Malcolm Naea Chun. Honolulu: Folk Press.
"Maloo na Iwi i ka La." 1895. *Ka Makaainana*, December 16, 5.
Marauders_1959. 2016. Comment on "Telescope Protestor Found Not Guilty

after Trial in Hawaiian." *Honolulu Star-Advertiser,* January 9, 11:57 a.m. http://www.staradvertiser.com/2016/01/08/breaking-news/telescope-protester-found-not-guilty-after-trial-in-hawaiian/.

Martin, Rachel. 2015. "Even without Interpreter, Hawaiian Judge Brings a Message." *National Public Radio,* November 29. https://www.npr.org/2015/11/29/457756725/even-without-interpreter-hawaiian-judge-brings-a-message.

Massoud, Mark Fathi. 2013. *Law's Fragile State: Colonial, Authoritarian, and Humanitarian Legacies in Sudan.* Cambridge: Cambridge University Press.

Maude, H. E. 1973. "The Raiatean Chief Auna and the Conversion of Hawaii." *Journal of Pacific History* 8: 188–91.

Maui Now. 2018a. "kaleikoa project part 2b." YouTube, January 24. https://www.youtube.com/watch?v=UuYXG04W8YA&t.

———. 2018b. "kaleikoa project part 3." YouTube, January 24. https://www.youtube.com/watch?v=UuYXG04W8YA&t.

———. 2018c. "kaleikoa project part 4." YouTube, January 24. https://www.youtube.com/watch?v=UuYXG04W8YA&t.

maui808films. 2018. "Kaleikoa Kaʻeo Speech 01/26/18." YouTube, January 27. https://www.youtube.com/watch?v=9ie0bPpT7io.

Mauna Kea Astronomy Outreach Committee. n.d. "History." http://www.mkaoc.org/history. Accessed February 14, 2024.

McKean, Frederick, Jr. 1929. "British Statutes in American Jurisdictions." *University of Pennsylvania Law Review and American Law Register* 78, no. 2: 195–230.

Medicine, Beatrice. 2001. *Learning to Be an Anthropologist and Remaining "Native": Selected Writings.* Champaign: University of Illinois Press.

Merry, Sally Engle. 2004. "Law and Identity in an American Colony." In *Law and Empire in the Pacific: Fiji and Hawaiʻi,* edited by Sally Engle Merry and Donald Lawrence Brenneis, 123–152. Santa Fe, NM: SAR Press.

Metzger, Bruce M. 1993. "Important Early Translations of the Bible." *Bibliotheca Sacra* 150, January–March: 35–49.

Michelson, Miriam. 1897. "Strangling Hands upon a Nation's Throat." *San Francisco Call,* September 30, 1.

mikethenovice. 2016. Comment on "Telescope Protestor Found Not Guilty after Trial in Hawaiian." *Honolulu Star-Advertiser,* January 8, 3:58 p.m. http://www.staradvertiser.com/2016/01/08/breaking-news/telescope-protester-found-not-guilty-after-trial-in-hawaiian/.

Mookini, Esther. 1974. *The Hawaiian Newspapers*. Honolulu: Topgallant.
Morris, Robert J. 2008. "Translators, Traitors, and Traducers: Perjuring Hawaiian Same-Sex Texts through Deliberate Mistranslation." *Journal of Homosexuality* 51, no. 3: 225–247.
myauthorizedopinion. 2018a. Comment on "Rallies across the State Call Attention to Hawaiian Language." *KITV4 Island News*, January 26, 8:08 p.m. http://www.kitv.com/story/37361814/rallies-across-the-state-call-attention-to-hawaiian-language.
———. 2018b. Comment on "Rallies across the State Call Attention to Hawaiian Language." *KITV4 Island News*, January 28, 12:24 p.m. http://www.kitv.com/story/37361814/rallies-across-the-state-call-attention-to-hawaiian-language.
"Na Mea Hou o Hawaii Nei." 1862. *Ka Nupepa Kuokoa*, October 18, 2.
Nabarro, Moanikeʻala. 2018a. "Arrest Warrant Recalled for Man Who Refused to Address Maui Judge in English." *KITV4 Island News*, January 25. http://www.kitv.com/story/37344220/arrest-warrant-issued-for-man-who-refused-to-address-maui-judge-in-english.
Nailiili, John. L. 1861. "Kue ia ka Hoku o ka Pakipika." *Ka Hoku o ka Pakipika*, October 3, 2.
Nākoa, Sarah. 1993. *Lei Momi o ʻEwa*. Honolulu: Ke Kumu Lama.
Nāwahī, Joseph. 1895. "Ka Mana o ka Mageneti." *Ke Aloha Aina*, November 1, 7.
"The New Native Newspaper." 1861. *The Polynesian*, October 19, 2.
Nichols, Robert. 2014. "The Colonialism of Incarceration." *Radical Philosophy Review* 17, no. 2: 435–455.
Niranjana, Tejaswini. 1992. *Siting Translation: History, Post-Structuralism, and the Colonial Context*. Berkeley: University of California Press.
"No ka Elepani." 1834. *Ka Lama Hawaii*, February 14, 3.
"No ka Hoku o ka Pakipika." 1861. *Ka Hoku o ka Pakipika*, October 3, 2.
"No ka Holo a me ka Hikiwawe o na Oihana Ao a na Misionari." 1868. *Ka Nupepa Kuokoa*, January 18.
"No ka Olelo." 1834. *Ka Lama Hawaii*, September 12, 2.
"No ka unuhi ana i ka Palapala Hemolele iloko o ka Olelo Hawaii." 1857. *Ka Hae Hawaii*, July 8, 57–58.
"No Loko ae o ka Hae Hawaii." 1861. *Ka Hoku o ka Pakipika*, September 26, 2.
"No na Kanaka o Polenesia." 1834. *Ke Kumu Hawaii*, December 10, 21.

Nogelmeier, Puakea. 2010. *Mai Paʻa i ka Leo: Historical Voice in Hawaiian Primary Materials, Looking Forward and Listening Back.* Honolulu: Bishop Museum Press.

Office of Native Hawaiian Relations, United States Department of Interior. 2015. *Advance Notice of Proposed Rulemaking*, October. https://www.doi.gov/hawaiian/reorg.

OHA v. State of Hawaiʻi. 2017. 17-1-1823-11JPC, First Circuit Court of Hawaiʻi.

Oliveira, Katrina-Ann R. Kapāʻanaokalāokeola Nākoa. 2014. "E Ola Mau ka ʻŌlelo Hawaiʻi: The Hawaiian Language Revitalization Movement." In *A Nation Rising: Hawaiian Movements for Life, Land, and Sovereignty*, edited by Noelani Goodyear-Kaʻōpua, Erin Kahunawai Wright, and Ikaika Hussey, 78–85. Durham, NC: Duke University Press.

Ortega y Gasset, Jose. 2000. "The Misery and the Splendor of Translation." In *The Translation Studies Reader*, edited by Lawrence Venuti, 49–64. New York: Routledge.

Ortiz, Simon J., ed. 1997. *Speaking for the Generations: Native Writers on Writing.* Tucson: University of Arizona Press.

Osorio, Jamaica Heolimeleikalani. 2018. "(Re)membering ʻUpena of Intimacies: A Kanaka Maoli Moʻolelo beyond Queer Theory." PhD diss., University of Hawaiʻi.

———. 2021. *Remembering Our Intimacies: Moʻolelo, Aloha ʻĀina, and Ea.* Minneapolis: University of Minnesota Press.

Osorio, Jonathan Kamakawiwoʻole. 2001. "ʻWhat Kine Hawaiian Are You?': A Moʻolelo about Nationhood, Race, History, and the Contemporary Sovereignty Movement in Hawaiʻi." *Contemporary Pacific* 13, no. 2: 359–379.

———. 2002. *Dismembering Lāhui: A History of the Hawaiian Nation to 1887.* Honolulu: University of Hawaiʻi Press.

Overbye, Dennis. 2016. "Under Hawaii's Starriest Skies, a Fight over Sacred Ground." *New York Times*, October 3. https://www.nytimes.com/2016/10/04/science/hawaii-thirty-meter-telescope-mauna-kea.html.

Owens, Pamela Jean. 2006. "Bible Translation and Language Preservation: The Politics of the Nineteenth Century Cherokee Bible Translation Projects." *Bible Translator* 57, no. 1: 1–10.

P minz. 2018. Comment on "Rallies across the State Call Attention to Hawaiian Language." *KITV4 Island News*, January 27, 10:55 a.m. http://www.kitv.com/story/37361814/rallies-across-the-state-call-attention-to-hawaiian-language.

Palmer, Julius A. 1895. *Again in Hawaii*. Boston: Lee and Shepard Publishers.
Perkins, ʻUmi. 2015. "On Constitutionalism." *The Umiverse*, September 22. https://theumiverse.wordpress.com/2015/09/22/on-constitutionalism/.
———. 2016. "The 1840 Hawaiian Kingdom Constitution—One of the World's First Modern Constitutions." *The Umiverse*, November 26. https://theumiverse.wordpress.com/2016/11/22/the-1840-hawaiian-kingdom-constitution-one-of-the-worlds-first-modern-constitutions/.
Perschon, Mike. 2009. "Finding Nemo: Verne's Antihero as Original Steampunk." *Steampunk Scholar*, May 15. http://steampunkscholar.blogspot.com/2009/05/finding-nemo-vernes-antihero-as.html.
Pho, Diana. 2009. "#2: The Great Nemo Debate." *Beyond Victoriana*, November 1. https://beyondvictoriana.com/2009/11/01/beyond-victoriana-2-the-great-nemo-debate/.
Pickering, John. 1820. *An Essay on a Uniform Orthography for the Indian Languages of North America*. Cambridge: Cambridge University Press.
Piliole, W. 1862. "Ia G. M. Koha." *Ka Nupepa Kuokoa*, May 3, 3.
"Poe Haku Manao no ke Kuokoa." 1867. *Ka Nupepa Kuokoa*, January 12, 2.
Poepoe, Joseph. 1908. "Ka Moolelo Kaao o Hiiakaikapoliopele." *Kuokoa Home Rula*, January 10, 1.
Pratt, Mary Louise. 2016. "Lessons for Losing." *CR: The New Centennial Review* 16, no. 1: 245–251.
Pukui, Mary Kawena. n.d. "How Legends Were Taught." In *Hawaiian Ethnological Notes*. Vol. 1, 1602–1606. Honolulu: Bishop Museum.
Pukui, Mary Kawena, and Samuel H. Elbert. 1986. *Hawaiian Dictionary: Revised and Enlarged Edition*. Honolulu: University of Hawaiʻi Press.
Punimaemae. 1861. "E ka Hae Hawaii." *Ka Hae Hawaii*, September 25, 102–103.
Raditlhalo, Sam. 2009. "Truth in Translation: The TRC and the Translation of the Translators." *Biography* 32, no. 1: 89–101.
Raitano Smith, Louise. 2014. Comment on "Rep Hanohano Prevails in Language Flap." *KITV 4*, March 4. http://www.kitv.com.com/news/hawaii/rep-hanohano-prevails-in-language-flap/.
Reichardt, A. Zuercher. 2018. "Translation." *Early American Studies: An Interdisciplinary Journal* 16, no. 4: 801–811.
Reynolds, Stephen W. 1989. *Journal of Stephen Reynolds*. Edited by Pauline King. Honolulu: Kū Paʻa Inc.
Richards, William. 1943. "Report to the Sandwich Islands Mission on His First Year in Government Service, 1838–1839." *Report of the Hawaiian Historical Society* 51: 65–70.

Rosa, John. 2014. *Local Story: The Massie-Kahahawai Case and the Culture of History*. Honolulu: University of Hawai'i Press.

Round, Philip H. 2010. *Removable Type: Histories of the Book in Indian Country, 1663–1880*. Chapel Hill: University of North Carolina Press.

Ruggles, Samuel, and Nancy Ruggles. 1819–1820. "Journal 1819–1820." *Hawaiian Mission Houses Digital Archive*. https://hmha.missionhouses.org/items/show/85.

Sahlins, Marshall. 1996. *How "Natives" Think: About Captain Cook, for Example*. Chicago: University of Chicago Press.

Sai, Keanu. 2008. "The American Occupation of the Hawaiian Kingdom: Beginning the Transition from Occupied to Restored State." PhD diss., University of Hawai'i.

Schiff, Judith Ann. 2004. "Aloha Blue." *Yale Alumni Magazine*, July/August. http://archives.yalealumnimagazine.com/issues/2004_07/old_yale.html.

Schmitt, Robert C. 1968. *Demographic Statistics of Hawaii 1778–1965*. Honolulu: University of Hawai'i Press.

Schütz, Albert J. 1994. *The Voices of Eden: A History of Hawaiian Language Studies*. Honolulu: University of Hawai'i Press.

———. 2017. "Reading between the Lines: A Closer Look at the First Hawaiian Primer (1822)." *Palapala: A Journal for Hawaiian Language and Literature* 1, no. 1: 1–29.

———. 2020. *Hawaiian Language: Past, Present, Future*. Honolulu: University of Hawai'i Press.

Schweizer, Niklaus R. 1988. "Kahaunani: 'Snow White' in Hawaiian: A Study in Acculturation." In *East Meets West: Homage to Edgar C. Knowlton, Jr.*, edited by Roger L. Hadlich and J. D. Ellsworth, 283–289. Honolulu: University of Hawai'i Press.

Shankar, S. 2012. *Flesh and Fish Blood: Postcolonialism, Translation, and the Vernacular*. Berkeley: University of California Press.

Shenk, Wilbert R. 2004. "Introduction." In *North American Foreign Missions, 1810–1914: Theology, Theory, and Policy*. Grand Rapids, MI: W. B. Eerdmans.

Siddal, John William. 1921. *Men of Hawaii: A Biographical Reference Library, Complete and Authentic, of the Men of Note and Substantial Achievement in the Hawaiian Islands*. Honolulu: Honolulu Star-Bulletin.

Silva, Kalena. 1997. "The Adoption of Christian Prayer in Native Hawaiian Pule." *Pacific Studies* 20, no. 1: 89–99.

Silva, Noenoe. 1998. "The 1897 Petitions Protesting Annexation." In *The*

Annexation of Hawaii: A Collection of Documents. libweb.hawaii.edu/digicoll/annexation/petition/pet-intro.

———. 2004. *Aloha Betrayed: Native Hawaiian Resistance to American Colonialism.* Durham, NC: Duke University Press.

———. 2016. "Mana Hawai'i: An Examination of Political Uses of the Word Mana in Hawaiian." In *New Mana: Transformations of a Classic Concept in Pacific Languages and Cultures,* edited by Matt Tomlinson and Ty P. Kāwika Tengan, 37–54. Acton: Australia National University Press.

———. 2018. *The Power of the Steel-Tipped Pen: Reconstructing Native Hawaiian Intellectual History.* Durham, NC: Duke University Press.

Silverman, Jane L. 1982. "Imposition of a Western Judicial System in the Hawaiian Monarchy." *Hawaiian Journal of History* 16: 48–64.

Simpson, Audra. 2014. *Mohawk Interruptus: Political Life across the Borders of Settler States.* Durham, NC: Duke University Press.

Simpson, Leanne Betasamosake. 2011. *Dancing on Our Turtle's Back: Stories of Nishnaabeg Re-Creation, Resurgence, and a New Emergence.* Winnipeg: ARP Books.

———. 2015. "The Misery of Settler Colonialism: Roundtable on Glen Coulthard's Red Skin, White Masks and Audra Simpson's Mohawk Interruptus American Studies Association Annual Meeting." October 8. https://www.leannesimpson.ca/writings/the-misery-of-settler-colonialism-roundtable-on-glen-coulthards-red-skin-white-masks-and-audra-simpsons-mohawk-interruptus.

SKK. 1861. "Ka Hoku o ka Pakipika." *Ka Hoku o ka Pakipika,* September 26, 4.

"Some TMT Protesters' Charges to Be Dropped." 2015. *Hawaii Tribune Herald,* May 29. https://www.hawaiitribune-herald.com/2015/05/29/hawaii-news/some-tmt-protesters-charges-to-be-dropped/.

Spencer, Thomas P. 1895. *Kaua Kuloko ma Honolulu.* Honolulu: Papapai Mahu Press.

Spivak, Gayatri. 2005. "Translating into English." In *Nation, Language, and the Ethics of Translation,* edited by Sandra Bermann and Michael Wood, 93–110. Princeton, NJ: Princeton University Press.

Stark, Heidi Kiiwetinepinesiik Stark. 2016. "Criminal Empire: The Making of the Savage in a Lawless Land." *Theory and Event* 19, no. 4.

State of Hawaii v. Samuel Kaleikoa Kaeo. 2018. Order Recalling Bench Warrant, District Court of the Second Circuit, Wailuku Division, State of Hawaii, January 25.

"State Supreme Court Rules in Favor of Thirty Meter Telescope's Construction." 2018. *Hawaii News Now,* October 30. https://www.hawaiinewsnow.com/2018/10/30/state-supreme-court-rules-favor-thirty-meter-telescopes-construction/.

Stewart, Charles Samuel. 1830. *Journal of a Residence in the Sandwich Islands.* London: H. Fisher, Son & P. Jackson.

Stockton, Betsey. 1825. "Betsey Stockton's Journal." *Christian Advocate,* January, 36–41.

Swann, Brian. 2011. "Introduction." In *Born in the Blood.* Lincoln: University of Nebraska Press, 1–16.

Tabag, Joshua Ka'mea'lanakila [*sic*]. 2014. Comment on "Rep Hanohano Prevails in Language Flap." *KITV 4,* March 4. http://www.kitv.com.com/news/hawaii/rep-hanohano-prevails-in-language-flap/.

TallBear, Kim. 2013. "Genomic Articulations of Indigeneity." "Indigenous Body Parts and Postcolonial Technoscience." Special issue, *Social Studies of Science* 43, no. 4: 509–533.

Tatar, Maria. 2004. *Secrets beyond the Door: The Story of Bluebeard and His Wives.* Princeton, NJ: Princeton University Press.

———. 2019. *The Hard Facts of the Grimms' Fairy Tales.* Princeton, NJ: Princeton University Press.

Taylor, Diana. 2007. *The Archive and the Repertoire: Performing Cultural Memory in the Americas.* Durham, NC: Duke University Press.

"Telescope Protestor Found Not Guilty after Trial in Hawaiian." 2016. *Honolulu Star-Advertiser,* January 9. http://www.staradvertiser.com/2016/01/08/breaking-news /telescope-protester-found-not-guilty-after-trial-in-hawaiian/.

Terrell, Jessica. 2015. "Thousands Turn Out for Aloha Aina Unity March." *Civil Beat,* August 9. https://www.civilbeat.org/2015/08/thousands-turn-out-for-aloha-aina-unity-march/.

Teves, Stephanie Nohelani. 2015a. "Aloha State Apparatuses." *American Quarterly* 67, no. 3: 705–726.

———. 2015b. "Tradition and Performance." In *Native Studies Keywords,* edited by Stephanie Nohelani Teves, Andrea Smith, and Michelle Raheja, 257–269. Tucson: University of Arizona Press.

Thurston, Lorrin A., ed. 1904. *The Fundamental Law of Hawai'i.* Honolulu: Hawaiian Gazette.

"Timeline of Mauna Kea Legal Actions since 2011." 2016. *Kāhea: The Hawaiian Environmental Alliance,* September 10. http://kahea.org/issues/sacred-summits/timeline-of-events.

Tipene, Jillian. 2014. "Te Tuhirau i Rehu i Ringa: Translating Sacred and Sensitive Texts: An Indigenous Perspective." PhD diss., University of Waikato.

Tomlinson, Matt, and Ty P. Kāwika Tengan, eds. 2016. *New Mana: Transformations of a Classic Concept in Pacific Languages and Cultures.* Acton: Australian National University Press.

Townsend, Henry Schuler. 1897. *Biennial Report of the President of the Board of Education.* Honolulu.

Tuck, Eve, and K. Wayne Yang. 2012. "Decolonization Is Not a Metaphor." *Decolonization: Indigeneity, Education and Society* 1, no. 1: 1–40.

Tymoczko, Maria. 2010a. "Translation, Resistance, Activism: An Overview." In *Translation, Resistance, Activism*, edited by Maria Tymoczko, 1–22. Boston: University of Massachusetts Press.

———. 2010b. "The Space and Time of Activist Translation." In *Translation, Resistance, Activism*, edited by Maria Tymoczko, 227–254. Boston: University of Massachusetts Press.

"Unuhi Olelo Paewaewa." 1862. *Ka Hoku o ka Pakipika,* February 20, 2.

Van Dyke, Jon M. 2007. *Who Owns the Crown Lands of Hawai'i?* Honolulu: University of Hawai'i Press.

Venuti, Lawrence. 1995. *The Translator's Invisibility: A History of Translation.* New York: Routledge.

Verne, Jules. 2004. *The Mysterious Island.* Translated by Jordan Stump. New York: Modern Library.

Visson, Lynn. 2005. "Simultaneous Interpretation: Language and Cultural Difference." In *Nation, Language, and the Ethics of Translation*, edited by Sandra Bermann and Michael Wood, 51–64. Princeton, NJ: Princeton University Press.

Walch, David B. 1967. "The Historical Development of the Hawaiian Alphabet." *Journal of the Polynesian Society* 76, no. 3: 353–366.

Wang, Frances Kai-Hwa. 2018. "Hawaiian Language Finds New Prominence in Hawaii's Courts Decades after Near Disappearance." *NBC News,* February 28. https://www.nbcnews.com/news/asian-america/hawaiian-language-finds-new-prominence-hawaii-s-courts-decades-after-n851536.

Westervelt, W. D. 1911. "The First Twenty Years of Education in the Hawaiian Islands." In *Nineteenth Annual Report of the Hawaiian Historical Society,* 16–26. Honolulu: Paradise of the Pacific Print.

Wiener, Joel H. 1971. "The Press and the Working Class, 1815–1840." *Victorian Periodicals Newsletter* 11, no. 1: 1–4.

Williams, Ronald C., Jr. 2013. "Claiming Christianity: The Struggle over God and Nation in Hawai'i: 1880–1900." PhD diss., University of Hawai'i.

———. 2015. "Race, Power, and the Dilemma of Democracy: Hawai'i's First Territorial Legislature, 1901." *Hawaiian Journal of History* 49: 1–45.
Wilson, Michael D. 2018. "Amended Dissenting Opinion." *In the Matter of Contested Case Hearing Re Conservation District Use Application (Cdua) Ha-3568 for the Thirty Meter Telescope at the Mauna Kea Science Reserve, Ka'ohe Mauka, Hāmākua, Hawai'i, Tmk (3) 404015:009 Scot-17-0000777, Scot-17-0000811, And Scot-17-0000812: Appeal from the Board of Land and Natural Resources*, November 30. www.courts.state.hi.us/wp-content/uploads/2018/11/SCOT-17-0000777disam.pdf.
"Woahoo Journal." 1823. *Missionary Herald* 19, no. 2: 38–44.
Wolfe, Patrick. 2008. "Structure and Event: Settler Colonialism, Time, and the Question of Genocide." In *Empire, Colony, Genocide: Conquest, Occupation, and Subaltern Resistance in World History*, edited by A. Dirk Moses, 102–132. New York: Berghahn Books.
Wood, Houston. 1999. *Displacing Natives*. New York: Rowman & Littlefield.
Wyss, Hilary E. 2012. *English Letters and Indian Literacies: Reading, Writing, and New England Missionary Schools*. Philadelphia: University of Pennsylvania Press.

Index

20,000 Legue ma lalo o ke Kai/20,000 Leagues under the Sea, 91, 125–131

abundance, 129, 219
Act 57, 141, 146, 149
"A hīkapalalē, hīkapalalē, hīnolue, ʻoalaki, walawalakī, waiki poha," 1
aikāne, 65, 122–123; John Young as, 20, 122; Kamehameha had many, 122; meaning of, xxii–xxiii, 65; Moe as, 66; translation as "friend," xxiii, 66, 67, 122–123, 188. *See also* Kaomi. *See also under* pilina; sex
ʻāina, 52, 216; relationship between aliʻi and, 76, 88; relationship between kānaka and, 14, 76, 88, 126, 140, 177, 207; relationship to kānaka dictated by law, 57, 59–60, 88; relationship to ʻōlelo Hawaiʻi, 2, 121, 177, 199, 209, 211–215; source of ea, xx, 212; struggles over, 188, 190, 218; translation versus Hawaiian understanding, xxi, 127, 129, 162. *See also* aloha ʻāina
Aiu, Pua, 184, 203
Alexander, W. D., 146, 160, 168
aliʻi, 1; ambivalence toward Christianity and missionaries, 20, 21–22, 65; children, 28; connection to Christianity, 30; and governance, 70; and kānaka, 76, 88; and kapu, 57; land as, xxi; language learning, 26; and law, 57, 71, 72; and mele, 212; prosperity comes from pono of, 19; relationship to palapala, 22, 98
aloha ʻāina, 80, 141, 200, 231n5; as explained by Joseph Nāwahī, 3–4; attempt to tame through translation, 188; fierce, 189–190; of kiaʻi mauna, 193; and the law, 193, 195–196, 199, 211; magnetic draw, 3–4; meaning of, xxi–xxii, 123–124, 126; relation to ea, xxii; relation to rigorous paraphrase, xxiv. *See also* Hui Aloha ʻĀina; Nemo. *See also under* Counter-Revolt of 1895; newspapers
American Board of Commissioners for Foreign Missions (ABCFM), 18–19, 44, 46, 47; alphabetic literacy and, 25, 97; as agents of American colonialism, 18, 19, 36; ambivalence toward, 20, 22, 105; background of, 18; church membership, 64; expense of printing press, 23; grammar and alphabet, 29; hopes for ʻŌpūkahaʻia, 17; horror at sight of Hawaiians, 39; influence on law, 62; inseparability of literacy and Christianity, 23, 229n9; lack of translators, 24, 27; language teaching or learning, 23–24, 26; missionaries sent to, 18; shipping presses into Indian Country, 93; threatened by Indigenous literacy, 106; views on language and

255

translation, 26, 34, 48. *See also* Foreign Mission School; salvation. *See also under* Cherokee; education
Andrews, Lorrin, 27, 31, 48, 79–80, 81, 84, 100, 102–103, 112
Arch, John, 46, 47
Arista, Noelani, 19–20, 22, 59, 92, 95, 99, 105, 151
Armstrong, Richard, 107
arrests: of kiaʻi mauna, 191–193, 199, 209, 232n4; of koa aloha ʻāina, 208; of newspaper editors, 136–138, 141, 168. *See also under* Kāʻeo, Kaleikoa; Kanuha, Kahoʻokahi; mana unuhi; Nāwahī, Joseph
Asensio, Rubén Fernández, 82, 84
Auna, 44, 66

Bacchilega, Cristina, 99, 105, 156, 160
Barrère, Dorothy, 45, 159, 163
Beamer, Kamana, 63, 64–65
Bible, 19; Baibala.org, 53; Cherokee, 46, 94; first printing in North America, 17, 93; funding, 229n11; Hawaiian translation of, 6, 16, 27, 30, 31, 47, 51, 60, 78, 86, 89, 93, 98, 122; *Ka Baibala Hemolele*, 36, 52, 53; King James, 33; list of missionary translators, 31; necessity of translation for dissemination of, 18, 23, 25; perfection in translation, 36, 52; problems translating into Hawaiian, 47–48; as provider of law, 61–62, 64, 68; as sign of "civilization" and "salvation," 42, 52; strategy for translating into Hawaiian, 31–33, 35; Tahitian, 32, 33, 44, 45; Tsalagi, 34; translatability, 34; Vulgate, 33; Wôpanâak, 34, 92, 93. *See also under* mana unuhi; translators (general understanding of)
Bihopa. *See* Bishop, Artemas
Binamu. *See* Bingham, Hiram
Bingham, Hiram, 20–21, 25, 27, 31, 32, 34–35, 39, 42, 43, 50–51, 65–66, 100, 112, 228n7

Bishop, Artemas, 18, 31, 32, 36, 43, 47, 48, 50–51, 112, 229n11
Bishop, Charles Reed, 73, 145, 168
Bishop Museum, 168–169, 171; first Pacific Islander head of, 21; problematic Board of Trustees, 168, 171
"Bluebeard," 119, 121–124, 131
Boudinot, Elias, 16, 39, 46, 227n3; as face of the Foreign Mission School, 17
Brickhouse, Anna, 8, 136, 139, 183
Brown, David, 16, 46, 47; as face of the Foreign Mission School, 17
Buck, Peter. *See* Te Rangi Hīroa
Bush, John E., 132, 137, 144, 231n6; coming of age during a time of literacy, 113

Campbell, Kuaihelani, 181–182
Chamberlain, Levi, 22, 27
Chang, David, 21, 227n1.1
Chapin, Helen, 100–101, 103, 108, 117, 136
Cherokee: language, 48; mission, 94; nation, 16, 24, 26, 94; people, 16–17, 39, 46, 94, 227n3; removal, 94, 227n3; syllabary, 26, 93, 94. *See also under* Bible; literacy; press; translators (general understanding of)
Cherokee Phoenix, 94–95
Cheyfitz, Eric, 37–40, 49, 156
Chinese: citizenship in kingdom, xxii; intermarriage with Hawaiians, 185–186; language, 146–147, 150; speakers of ʻōlelo Hawaiʻi, 87; trial of Ho Fon and others who supported counter-revolt, 207
Choctaw: language, 48, 97; nation, 16, 24, 26
Choctaw Intelligencer, 97
"civilization," 16, 23–25, 39, 57, 121; law as sign of, 62–63; not enough, 113. *See also under* Bible
colonialism, 145, 149, 186, 224; American, 18; inevitability of, 8, 136, 139, 211; missionaries as

Index

agents of, 36. *See also* settler colonialism
constitution: 1840 (Lua'ehu Constitution), 69, 70–71, 74, 75, 77, 104; 1852, 71, 73; 1864, 105; 1895, 135, 137, 139; Bayonet, 132–133, 137, 187, 207; British, 73, 89; convention, 174; and international recognition, 74; Lili'uokalani and, 133, 134; and monarchical government, 57, 61, 70; outlawed slavery in the kingdom, 71; quick development of, 70–71, 89, 113; U.S., 70. *See also under* translators (general understanding of)
Cooke, Amos Starr, 28, 50, 112, 228n7
Cook, James, 1–2, 6, 21, 100, 219
Cornwall, Connecticut. *See* Foreign Mission School
Counter-Revolt of 1889: trials, 207
Counter-Revolt of 1895, 137, 139, 141, 225; multiethnic koa aloha 'āina, 137, 208
cultural confidence, 5, 11, 118, 218–219. *See also under* translation (as an entity)

Daniel K. Inouye Solar Telescope, 199
Declaration of Rights, 70, 104
degradation principle, 192–193
Dibble, Sheldon, 31, 48–49, 50, 104
Dole, Sanford B., 113, 168, 176

ea, 8, 47–48, 52, 121, 126, 131, 212, 215, 216; assertion of, 68, 178, 194, 206; meaning of, xx, 46; undermined by legal language, 60. *See also* Lā Ho'iho'i Ea. *See also under* aloha 'āina; literacy; sovereignty; translation
education: ABCFM-led, 15–18, 22–25, 28, 29, 54, 100, 228n7; formalized Western-style, 26, 67, 96, 102, 104, 113, 126, 148, 168, 224; Hawaiian or Indigenous-led, 22, 67, 93, 142, 149–150, 172; immersion, 191, 193–194; language of instruction, 141, 145–147, 172 oppressive, 7, 147, 187, 224, 228n7; school statistics, 54, 145, 147. *See also* Act 57
elimination, 177, 180, 184–188, 202
embodied: activism, 180; memory, 195, 196, 197, 215; performance, 184, 194–198, 204, 232n7; tradition, 204

figuration (in language), 37–42, 48–49, 57, 59–60, 106, 156, 178; rejections of, 65–66, 68, 88. *See also under* law
Foreign Mission School, 16, 24, 26, 39, 45, 46, 227n3; faces of, 17; student origins, 16
Fornander, Abraham, 106, 110, 154, 167

genealogical axiom, 82, 84, 88, 89, 114
Goodyear-Ka'ōpua, Noelani, 182–183, 203
Greek: citizenship in kingdom, xxii; language in the Bible, 23, 32, 33, 45, 118; language spoken in the kingdom, 2; speakers of 'ōlelo Hawai'i, 87

Haalelea v. Montgomery, 83, 88
Haleakalā, 199–200, 209, 213
Hale Nauā, 129–130
Hale'ole, S. N., 167, 168
Hāmākua, 222–223
Hanohano, Faye, 173–177, 178, 184, 198, 203
Hardy v. Ruggles, 78–79, 85
Hawaiian Chiefs' Children's School, 28
Hawaiian Renaissance, 172, 188
Hawaii Holomua, 132, 134, 139–140, 148
heteropatriarchy, 53, 66, 75, 122, 224, 231n4.1
Hi'iakaikapoliopele, xx, 58, 124, 156–157, 160, 230n1; calmed by aikāne Wahine'ōma'o, xxiii
hīkapalalē. *See* "A hīkapalalē, hīkapalalē, hīnolue, 'oalaki, walawalakī, waiki poha"

Hoapili, 43, 45, 47
Ho Fon, 207, 231n6
Honoliʻi, John, 16, 39
Hoʻohokukalani, 124, 231n3
hoʻomanawanui, kuʻualoha, 5, 22, 92, 144, 230n1
Hopu, Thomas, 16, 24, 26, 39
Hui Aloha ʻĀina, 134–135, 141, 180, 182
Hui Aloha ʻĀina o nā Wāhine, 181
Hui Kālaiʻāina, 141, 232n2
hula, 67, 151, 195, 223, 224; as "expected" realm of language, 194; kaona in, xxiii; outlawed, 64

ʻĪʻī, Daniel, 71
ʻĪʻī, John Papa, 21, 43, 45, 47, 71, 73, 100, 116; his written works, 117, 153, 159, 167, 168, 170
"I ka ʻōlelo nō ke ola, i ka ʻōlelo nō ka make," 5, 28, 50, 59–60, 77, 175, 199, 219, 223
independence (Hawaiian), xx, 80, 117, 128, 183, 205, 209, 218, 227
infantilization. *See* paternalism
Ing, Tiffany, 132, 231n5
interpreter, 69, 140, 179, 181, 200, 202–203, 208–209; importance of, 75
ʻIolani Palace, 99, 129, 151, 208

Japanese: citizenship in kingdom, xxii; language schools, 150; vocal support for Liliʻuokalani, 208
Judd, Albert Francis, 52, 75, 168
Judd, Gerritt P., 54, 82, 105, 231n6
judiciary, 72, 208–209; largely made up of foreigners, 74, 89, 114

Kaʻahumanu, 20, 44, 65, 66, 67, 124; proclaiming laws, 62–63
Kaʻaumoku, 45
Kāʻeo, Kaleikoa, 177, 189, 203, 208; arrest, 184, 190, 199–200, 210; bench warrant, 202–203, 205, 210, 212; trial, 200–203, 205, 212, 232n7
Ka Hae Hawaii, 31, 107, 115, 147

Kahaulelio, Daniel, 171
Kahikona, 45
Ka Hoku Loa, 229n11
Ka Hoku o ka Pakipika, 104, 106, 107–114, 115, 116, 118; evils of subscribing to, 116; founding members, 107; progenitor of nationalist newspapers, 131–134
Kailiehu, Haley, 222–223
Ka Lahui Hawaii, 119, 132
Kalākaua, 98, 125, 129, 132–133, 231n5; "editor King," 107. See also under *Nautilo/Nautilus*
Ka Lama Hawaii, 54, 100, 102, 103, 116
Ka Leo o ka Lahui, 132, 133, 134
Kalokuokamaile, 168, 196
Kaluaikoʻolau, 125, 158
Ka Makaainana, 130, 132
Kamakau, Kēlou, 31, 43, 45, 47, 167
Kamakau, Samuel Mānaiakalani, 67, 69–70, 215, 227n5, 230n5; his written works, 117, 152, 153, 154, 160, 161, 163, 167–171, 220
Kamehameha I, 19–20, 58, 68. *See also under* aikāne
Ka Naʻi Aupuni, 148
kānāwai, 61; time of many, 63 traditional meaning of, 58; transition out of, 59, 64
Kānepuʻu, Joseph, 107, 109, 115, 117, 131–132
Kanuha, G. W., 125, 127, 129, 131, 231n4; celebrated as a translator, 125–126
Kanuha, Kahoʻokahi, 177, 184, 189, 190, 203, 211; arrest, 184, 190–193; as leader in Maunakea movement, 193; educator, 191, 204; trial, 193–199, 206, 209, 212, 213
Kanui, William, 16, 39
Ka Nupepa Elele, 133
Ka Nupepa Kuokoa, 114–117, 118, 125, 126, 131, 149; editors of, 117
Ka Oiaio, 133
Kaomi, 65, 68; abrogation of Western laws during Ka Wā iā Kaomi, 67–68, 72; background and

parentage of, 66–67; captured, 68; fell out of favor, 69; worries over foreign influence, 80
kaona, xxiii, 140–141
kapu, 57–59, 61, 68; as oral law, 59; system, 57; transition out of, 59, 64
Kapuāiwa, Lot, 105
Kauanui, Kēhaulani, 59, 64, 65, 177, 186, 230n2
Kauikeaouli, 45, 65–66, 68, 122–123; giver of first constitution, 69, 74; "he aupuni palapala koʻu," 69; and law, 71–72
Kaumualiʻi, George, 16, 26, 39
Kauwahi, J., 107, 111–112, 195
Ka Wā iā Kaomi. *See* Kaomi
Kawelo, Gabby, 171
Ke Aloha Aina, 132, 141, 180, 231n4.1
Ke Au Okoa, 132
Keʻelikōlani, Ruta, 25
Ke Kumu Hawaii, 34, 103, 115
Kelekona, Kahikina, 117, 132, 134, 136, 138–139, 144, 168; and literary experimentation, 145, 225
Kendall, Thomas, 29, 44
Kenyon, George Carson, 136, 138
Kepelino, 153, 157, 167, 168, 222
Kimura, Larry, 120–121, 147
kingdom, 30; care of given to Liholiho, 19; centrality of translation in, 21, 61; inevitability of colonial victory, 8; language primacy, 8; languages spoken in, 2; multiethnic makeup of, xxii, 207; progressive, 70; roles within dictated by translation, 60; shifts in governmental structure, 57. *See also under* overthrow
Ko Hawaii Ponoi, 132
Korean (language), 2
Kuakini, 31, 43, 45, 47
kūʻauhau. *See* moʻokūʻauhau
kūʻē: in relation to kūʻokoʻa, 183
Kuokoa Home Rula, 156

Lāhainaluna, 56, 71, 102, 103
Lā Hoʻihoʻi Ea, 46, 133–134, 192
lāhui: meaning of, xxii. *See also under* mana; mana unuhi; newspapers

language: Acoma, 214; Algonquin, 37, 76; California Indian, 93; cultural value of, 5; disappearing knowledge of, 152–153; Indigenous writing systems as threat, 26; lack of missionary knowledge of, 27, 45; Latin, 32–33, 45, 84, 118, 163–165, 198; Māori, 29, 93; Nez Perce, 92; power of bilinguality, 54, 75, 110, 132–133, 135, 205; power of legal, 59–60; primacy of, 2, 8, 26, 59, 69, 74, 82–83, 88, 89, 145–148, 154, 193; rabid monolingualism, 175, 196; "reducing" Indigenous languages to writing, 93; sign, 93; simlish, 177; spoken in the kingdom, 2, 199; syllabary, 93; "Talk American" campaign, 150; teaching, 26; Wôpanâak, 17, 34. *See also* ʻōlelo Hawaiʻi. *See also under* Cherokee; Chinese; Greek; Liholiho, Alexander
law, 149–150, 210; as agent of figuration, 57, 88, 196; brought by missionaries, 71; civil law, 73, 77, 88–89; common law, 72, 73, 77, 81, 82, 89, 90; dual system of laws, 61, 74–75, 77; enforcement, 58, 184, 190, 199–200; Hawaiian authorship of, 71–72, 113; language used for law, 73, 77–79, 88, 196; penal code, 73; penal colonies, 64; reasons for, 63; strategic adoption of, 63, 114; transition to Western, 59. *See also under* aliʻi; "civilization"; Kaomi; settler colonialism
Lee, William Little, 73, 81, 83, 85, 88; author of 1852 Constitution, 73; decision regarding legal language, 78–80
Lefevere, André, 33, 166, 223
libel, 102, 135–138, 144, 231n6
Liholiho, 19–21, 22, 44, 228n6; death of, 62; suspicions toward Christianity, 20, 65
Liholiho, Alexander, 105; polyglot, 104–105

Liliʻuokalani, 114, 133, 134, 137, 138, 141, 180, 181, 207, 228n7; coming of age during a time of literacy, 113. *See also under* constitution; translator(s)
literacy (alphabetic), 66, 97; and American nationalism, 94; as driver of beneficial and detrimental change, 18; as tool for ea, 55, 92, 94, 186–187; Cherokee, 94–95; connections between Christianity, "civilization," and, 15–17, 21–24, 29; general teaching and learning of, 28; Hawaiian enthusiasm for, 25, 54, 89, 96–97; Hawaiian literary aesthetic, 96, 97; Hawaiian literary practitioners, 92, 96–97, 113, 142, 145, 219; "he aupuni palapala koʻu," 69; Indigenous, 16, 94; lack in the United States, 25; near universal, 54, 92, 113, 157; qualifications, 105; spawned an industry, 104; taken for granted by new generation, 113; taught by Tahitians, 44
Local (identity), 207–208
Loeb Classical Library, 163–165, 168, 222
London Missionary Society (LMS), 29, 44
Loomis, Elisha, 93, 100, 228n8
Lyon, Kapali, 47, 229n10, 229n12
Lyons, Scott Richard, 219

Mahune, Boaz, 56, 71
"mai noho kākou a ʻae iki," 180–181, 187, 203, 215
makaʻāinana: and kapu, 57; and literacy, 98; petitions, 80; rejection of salvation, 68; traditional role as, 60, 88, 162. *See also under* translation of terms
Makani, John, 93
Malo, David, 43, 44, 56, 71, 153, 159–160, 168
mana, 8, 48, 50, 121, 122, 155–156, 191, 216, 220, 226; assertion of, 68, 89; at stake in Bible translation, 46; connection to pilina, xxi, 3–4; given to colonial structures and narratives, 53, 165, 206, 218; and kapu, 57; of the lāhui, 8, 47–48, 60, 126, 131, 195, 218, 221, 225; and law, 57, 71, 82; meaning of, xx–xxi, 3–5, 99; in missionary discourse, 40; missionary mana in Bible translation, 33; in print, 92–93, 125; reversal of, 198; undermined by legal language, 60; wahine, 124. *See also* mana unuhi. *See also under* pilina
mana unuhi: available to all, 98; claimed for one language but denied for another, 79, 85, 178; flowing back and forth, 55, 61, 120; on a lāhui-wide scale, 218–219; meaning and importance of, 3–7, 99, 226; and models of resistance, 186; in relation to Bible translation, 43, 45, 50, 52; in relation to extractive translation, 151, 153, 170–171; in relation to law, 59, 72, 75, 89; in relation to newspapers, 104, 110, 136; reclamation of, 65, 67, 189; and refusal, 177, 178, 194, 205, 215; to avoid arrest and imprisonment, 138–141, 142; to empower Hawaiian voices, 90, 111, 117–118, 121, 125, 131, 134; to navigate problematic translations, 220–221; use in examining power dynamics, 6, 37, 61, 186, 205, 226
Manu, Moses, 168
Massie case, xxii, 125, 151, 207
Maunakea, 188, 199, 211, 213, 218, 232n3; background of struggle over, 191–193. *See also under* mele
mele, 48, 67, 107, 129, 152–153, 167, 171, 195; archived through print, 55, 95, 99, 117; as "expected" realm of language usage, 194; disputes over, 108–110, 165; and Maunakea, 191; outlawed, 64; supposed lack of knowledge regarding, 153

Metcalf v. Kahai, 77
Michelson, Miriam, 181–182
Montezuma, Carlos, 113
moʻokūʻauhau, 129–130, 167, 170, 214; relation to rigorous paraphrase, xxiv. *See also* Papa Kūʻauhau
moʻolelo, 167, 190, 199, 225; as blockbusters, 124; as foundation, 114, 215, 221, 222, 225; importance of interesting telling, 96, 124; importance of telling new, 217, 219, 223; meaning of, xxiii–xxiv; and nūpepa, 98, 119; parity of, 99; relation to rigorous paraphrase, xxiv

Nautilo/Nautilus, 91, 127–128, 129, 144; Kalākaua's model, 130
Nāwahī, Emma, 141, 180, 181–182, 231n4.1
Nāwahī, Joseph, 141, 180–181, 195, 203; arrested for libel, 136–137, 141; coming of age during time of literacy, 113; description of aloha ʻāina, 3–4; "Ka Mana o ka Mageneti," 3–4; and Reciprocity Treaty, 127–128, 130–131. *See also* "mai noho kākou a ʻae iki"
Nemo/Nimo, 126–131; staunch anti-colonialist, 127
newspapers, 52, 82; as contested realm, 90, 98, 105–106; boom in Indigenous-language newspapers, 97; British, 102, 133; circuit, 135; development of in Hawaiʻi, 99–104, 157; didactic, 96; editorials, 55, 142, 148–150; English-language in Hawaiʻi, 104, 106, 110, 114, 115, 116, 147–148, 181; "establishment newspapers," 103–104, 117; Hawaiian power and excellence in, 95, 96, 98, 101–102, 110, 111, 132, 145; and Hawaiian worldview, 95; importance of literary aesthetics in, 96; kūpuna reading aloud, 91, 97; massive archive of Hawaiian-language writing, 92; mission-related, 54; nūpepa aloha ʻāina, 102, 133–141, 195, 221; and preservation/dissemination of traditional forms of expression, 55, 95, 101, 148, 187; revolutionary power of, 138–139; suppression of Hawaiian voice in, 95, 135–136, 144; U.S., 102; usage of lāhui in, xxii. *See also* press. *See also under* translation (material practice of)
New Zealand Grammar and Vocabulary, 29, 44
Norrie, Edmund, 136, 137, 138

Obookiah. *See* ʻŌpūkahaʻia, Heneri
Occom, Samson, 92
occupation, 18, 185, 188, 218, 227n1
ʻōlelo Hawaiʻi, 120, 194, 203, 225; animal language, 176; as threat, 175, 177; "dead" language, 152, 163–164, 176–177; eroding legal authority of, 81; and invisibility, 203–204, 205, 208; large archive of, 92, 95; legal knowledge valued over, 81; mānaleo, 218; necessity of ʻōlelo Hawaiʻi sources, 220, 224; official state language, 174, 209; only for translation out of, 86–87, 176, 178–179; political commitment of learning, 218; renormalization of, 153, 170, 193, 209, 212, 220, 219; seen as deficient, 34, 36, 48–49, 51–52, 79, 84–85, 229–230n12; spoken by all ethnicities in kingdom, 87, 118; structural similarity to Hebrew, 16; transformation of, 53; uncapturable, 232n6; waning usage, 144, 152. *See also under* ʻāina
Oni v. Meek, 87–88
online comments, 174–177, 194, 195, 198, 202, 220
ʻŌpūkahaʻia, Heneri, 14–15, 19, 26, 227n1.1; death of, 17; impetus for Christian mission, 15, 18–19; translator, 15. *See also under* salvation

oral tradition: Hawaiians only as vessels of, 97, 166–167
Ortiz, Simon, 213–214
Osorio, Jamaica Heolimeleikalani, 122–123, 126, 212, 224, 230n1; rigorous paraphrase, xxiv, 66
Osorio, Jonathan Kay Kamakawiwoʻole, 25, 59, 60, 80, 87, 132, 210
overthrow of the Hawaiian Kingdom, 75, 117, 133–135, 141, 146, 168, 174, 187, 220; loss of multiethnic kingdom, xxii, 207; Hawaiian response to, 114, 135, 139, 142, 180–181

palapala, 17, 21, 22, 69, 112, 228n6; derision toward "kanaka palapala," 22–23. *See also under* aliʻi; Kauikeaouli
pale lauʻī, 19, 68
Papa Kūʻauhau, 129–130
paternalism, 112–113, 175–176, 184, 198
Pāʻulaliʻiliʻi, 227n5
Pele, xxiii, 58, 122, 160, 165, 230n1
Peleioholani, Solomon, 168
Peralto, Noʻeau, 222–223
Perry, Kekailoa, 210
Pickering, John, 92, 94
pilina, 15, 212, 219, 230n1; and aikāne, xxiii, 66, 122–123; and ʻāina, 123–124, 206, 212; and aloha, xxi; and family, 124; and kaona, xxiii; and mana, xxi, 3–4, 40, 41, 120, 150, 152
Pilipo, George, 166
Poepoe, Joseph, 117, 132, 148, 156–157, 195
political economy, 69–70, 71
Poopohee. *See* Pupuhi, Stephen
press: boom in Hawaiian-language, 97; Cherokee press destroyed, 94–95; circuit of, 92–93, 100; confiscation, 144; cost of Sandwich Island Mission, 23; freedom of, 135–136; government, 115; Hawaiian control of, 95, 108; Hawaiians learn mechanics of, 100; Indigenous demand for, 93; Indigenous erasure, 93; Lapwai Mission, 92; mission, 96, 101, 103–104, 115, 116
proper (as figured in language), 37–40, 60
publish salvation, 17, 19, 103
Pukui, Mary Kawena, 95–96, 97, 159, 170–172
Pupuhi, Stephen, 16, 45

Readerly Indians, 106
Reciprocity Treaty, 127–128, 130–131, 132
recognition, 46, 180, 183–184, 193, 197, 198, 207–208; federal, 183, 206–208, 211; in legal system, 63, 76, 87; international, 63, 74
refusal, 180–183, 185, 187, 189, 195, 197, 203. *See also* "mai noho kākou a ʻae iki." *See also under* translation (as an entity)
Richards, William, 31, 32, 43; kingdom interpreter and translator, 69, 72, 230n6
Ricord, John, 72–73, 81
Ridge, John, 16, 227n3; as face of the Foreign Mission School, 17
rigorous paraphrase, xxiv
Rikeke. *See* Richards, William
Robertson, George, 77, 82–89; lack of legal qualifications, 81
Round, Philip, 93, 94–95

sacred: as a term, 211–214; person, 68; stories, 95; writer, 32, 36, 47, 52
salvable people, 16, 42, 48, 51, 52, 57, 88; rejection of being, 65–66, 68
salvation, 24, 42, 52; ʻŌpūkahaʻia as embodiment of, 17, 39, 40–41; rejection of, 68; translation important to, 17, 25, 45–46, 50; worthy of, 39–41, 45. *See also under* Bible
Schütz, Albert, 21
settler colonialism, 58, 168, 177, 179, 180, 185, 197, 198, 209, 213, 227n2; and carceral structures,

200, 202–203, 205; and determination of "lawfulness," 189; difference in Hawai'i, 185–189; and inclusion/incorporation, 209–211, 215; and militarized police, 199–200; and removal from land, 189, 190, 215. *See also* law: enforcement

sex: adulterous and group, 67–68; metaphoric references to, xxiii, 140, 230n5; moe kolohe, 66, 230n3; not a big deal, xxiii, 65; regarding aikāne relationships, xxiii

science versus culture, 214–215

Shankar, S., 6, 37, 218

Sheldon, John. *See* Kelekona, Kahikina

Silva, Noenoe, 104, 105, 106

Simpson, Audra, 183, 196, 206

Simpson, Leanne Betasamosake, 178, 179, 180, 206

Siwinowe Kesibwi (*Shawnee Sun*), 97

social media, 191–192, 202, 232nn4,5

sovereignty: connection to aloha 'āina, 3, 141; connection to ea, xx, 46, 145, 183–184, 194, 212; inherent, 60; movement, 230n2; nested, 196; related to law, 63, 89; settler, 185, 187, 190; territorialized, 189–190; translation/writing as a tool of, 8, 106; waning, 150. *See also* ea

Spencer, Thomas (Tamaki), 132–133, 137, 225

State of Hawai'i v. Samuel Kaleikoa Kā'eo, 201

Stockton, Betsey, 40

Supreme Court (kingdom), 73; justices, 73, 75, 77, 78, 81, 83, 196

Supreme Court (state), 192

surfing, 130

Swann, Brian, 155, 159, 221

Tahitian: alphabet, 29, 93; citizenship in kingdom, xxii; and 'ōlelo Hawai'i, 6, 44, 87; first manuscript in 'ōlelo Hawai'i written by, 45; influence in Hawai'i, 44, 93; language, 2, 29. *See also under* Bible; translator(s)

Tarzan, 119, 124, 142, 150

Tatina. *See* Thurston, Lorrin

Tau'a, 44, 45

Tau'awahine, 45

Taylor, Diana, 195–198, 204, 232n7

Te Karere o Niu Tireni, 97

teleological model of development, 42, 153, 162, 176

Te Rangi Hīroa, 21

Testa, F. J., 132, 137, 195

Teves, Stephanie Nohelani, 187–188, 197, 204

Thirty Meter Telescope (TMT), 188, 191–193, 199, 214–215, 232n3

Thurston, Lorrin, 31, 43, 113, 230n6

Toketa, 44

tourism, 151, 185, 187–189

toxic monogamy, 66

translation (as an entity): ABCFM perspectives of, 24; as consecration, 99, 155; as domesticating force, 59; as provider of scientific value, 151, 169; as sign of cultural confidence, 98–99, 118, 144; as tool for ea, 92, 95, 117, 134; canon of literature, 153–155; and colonialism, 8, 37, 42; contested and complex process of, 5, 8; culture of, 218–221, 224–225; and daily life, 57; embedded, 223–224; fixing Hawaiians in the past, 165, 224; for Hawaiians and Hawaiian purposes, 99, 113, 118, 120; invisibility/transparency of, 6, 21, 48; lazy metaphor, 7; and liberation, 225; little academic attention given to, 6, 21; living in, 213–214, 215; misunderstandings of, 79, 82, 86; motivated mistranslation, 139–141; more than about loss and violence, 6, 119–124, 220; necessary for print culture, 118–119; popular understandings of, 7, 33; redefining relationships, 60; refusal of, 176–181, 184–185, 190, 194–199, 203–206, 209, 211–212, 216; rejection of easy translation, 7, 61. *See also* unsettlement; unuhi. *See also under* aloha ʻāina; Bible; colonialism; kingdom; salvation

translation (material practice of): as interpretation, 35, 155; consigning Hawaiians to the realm of the natural, 166–167; editorial effects on, 159–162; and equivalence, 34–35, 36, 75, 78–79, 83, 86; and erasure of difference, 42, 161–162; extractive, 142, 150–154, 157, 159, 162, 187, 224; Hawaiian skill in, 96; legal translation, 74, 78–79, 98; "literal"/mechanical translation, 7, 8, 152, 155, 158–159, 177; literary translation, 78; miscommunication through, 21; multidirectional flow, 61; in newspapers, 98; right and wrong, 33, 36, 47, 78, 158

translation of terms: "aloha," 162, 188–189; "aupuni," 128, 130; "hoaʻāina," 87; "kanaka," 75–76, 77; "kūʻokoʻa," 128–129, 130; "makaʻāinana," 86, 87; "moe kolohe," 230n3; "mōʻī," 38, 76; "*weroance*," 37–38, 76. *See also under* aikāne; ʻāina

translators (general understanding of), xix, 82, 148, 219–220, 224, 225; of 1840 Constitution, 71–72, 77; ABCFM's lack of, 24, 27; as gateways to salvation, 25; biases of, 35, 157; of Cherokee Bibles, 46; divinely inspired, 33; ethics in Indigenous contexts, 4–5, 155, 221, 223; feminist, 8; Hawaiian Bible, 31, 43, 48; hinge of legal system, 74, 75; insufficient, 212; invisibility of, 6, 21, 159; in kingdom employ, 69; missionary incompetence as, 25, 34, 43, 45, 47, 48, 50–51, 81; power of, xxiv, 179–180; Tahitian, 44; understandings of Hawaiian Bible translation, 36, 43; of Wôpanâak Bible, 93

translators (specific individuals): Alexander Liholiho as, 105; author's experience as, xx, xxiv, 168, 172, 216, 218; C. J. Lyons as, 151; David Brown as, 46; Frances Frazier as, 158; G. W. Mila as, 107; John Arch as, 46; John Wise as, 159, 171; JW as, 121–123, 231n2; Liliʻuokalani as, 151; Martha Beckwith as, 152, 159, 222; Nathaniel B. Emerson as, 159–160, 165; Samuel Worcester as, 46; Thomas Hopu as, 24; Thomas Thrum as, 151, 153, 159, 167; Tupaia as, 21; Wawaus, Cockenoe, Job Nesuton, Joel Iacoomes, and Caleb Cheeshateaumuck as, 93; William Luther Wilcox as, 140–141. *See also* Boudinot, Elias; Kanuha, G. W.; ʻŌpūkahaʻia, Heneri; Pukui, Mary Kawena

Tuck, Eve, 185, 210–211, 214–215

Tupaia, 21

Tute, 45

unsettlement, 8, 139–141, 183, 185, 190, 197

unuhi: assumption of success and transparency, 6, 21; in contrast to translation, 7; Hawaiian understanding of, 33, 35, 36, 99, 131, 220, 225; marking earliest foreign interactions, 2; missionary lack of skill in, 31–33; misunderstandings of, 83; possibilities for Indigenous people with, 92–93; power in relation to law, 60, 64; relation to language dynamics, 2, 8, 28; in relation to law, 61, 78, 88. *See also* mana unuhi; translation (multiple entries)

Venuti, Lawrence, 5–6

Verne, Jules, 125, 127, 129

Wahineʻōmaʻo: aikāne of Hiʻiakaikapoliopele, xxiii

Wawaus, 93

white supremacy, 207, 224
Whitney, Henry, 114–115, 116–117, 119, 124
Wilcox, Robert, 132, 137, 207, 231n6
Wolfe, Patrick, 177, 186, 209
Writerly Indians, 106, 107, 110–111
Wyss, Hilary, 46, 106

Yamashiro, Aiko, xiii
Yamashiro, Kalihilihiaʻiaʻipuahoʻomohala Jeong, xv
Yang, K. Wayne, 185, 210–211, 214–215

Zitkála-Šá, 113

About the Author

BRYAN KAMAOLI KUWADA is a writer, poet, and photographer. A professor at the Kamakakūokalani Center for Hawaiian Studies at the University of Hawaiʻi Mānoa, he uses Hawaiian traditional knowledge and stories to navigate and imagine Hawaiian futures. Kamaoli has published in ʻōlelo Hawaiʻi and in English. His poetry appears in *The Offing, Bettering American Poetry*, vol. 2, and *Yellow Medicine Review*, and his fiction in *Black Marks on the White Page, Pacific Monsters, The Dark Magazine*, and *the Hawaiʻi Review of Books*. He coedited a special issue of *Biography: An Interdisciplinary Quarterly* entitled "Aloha ʻĀina Narratives of Protest, Protection, and Place," with curated interviews, poetry, photography, and academic reflections about the struggle over Maunakea. Kuwada's portrait work has appeared in the Ori Gallery (Portland, Oregon) and Yerba Buena Center for the Arts (San Francisco, California), as well as the *Honolulu Star-Advertiser*. His surf photography (@waterbearfoto), which tries to reintroduce Hawaiian traditions and understandings of the ocean into the surf world, can be found in *Pacific Longboarder Magazine*.